DATE DUE			

A WESTVIEW ENCORE EDITION

THE ORIGINS OF
TOTALITARIAN
DEMOCRACY

J. L. Talmon

Westview Press / Boulder and London

321.9
T/40
145324
oct. 1988

Copyright © 1985 by J. L. Talmon

Published in 1985 in the United States of America by Westview Press, Inc., 5500 Central Avenue, Boulder, Colorado 80301; Frederick A. Praeger, Publisher

First published in 1952 by Martin Secker and Warburg Ltd.

Library of Congress Catalog Card Number: 85-40394
ISBN: 0-8133-0165-3

Printed and bound in the United States of America
6   5   4   3   2   1

To G.

Je pense donc que l'espèce d'oppression dont les peuples démocratiques sont menacés ne ressemblera à rien de ce qui l'a précédée dans le monde ; nos contemporains ne sauraient en trouver l'image dans leurs souvenirs. Je cherche en vain moi-même une expression qui reproduise exactement l'idée que je m'en forme et la renferme ; les anciens mots de despotisme et de tyrannie ne conviennent point. La chose est nouvelle ; il faut donc tâcher de la définir, puisque je ne peux la nommer.

ALEXIS DE TOCQUEVILLE

PREFACE

THIS book owes much to a number of people. The first to be mentioned is the late Professor Harold Laski, who befriended the author with that kindness for which he was so noted. Professor R. H. Tawney has given me the privilege of his friendship, the inspiration of his ripe wisdom and the stimulus of acute criticism. Professor E. H. Carr and Dr. Alfred Cobban followed the progress of this work at every stage and contributed much to the clarification of many of its ideas. Professor Martin Buber of my own University read the manuscript and made some useful criticism in a friendly spirit.

I could hardly exaggerate the debt I owe to my former teacher and present colleague at the Hebrew University of Jerusalem, Professor R. Koebner, from whom I received my earliest training, and with whom I have been engaged in fruitful debate these many years.

I have had the opportunity of discussing the subject of this book with Professors Georges Lefebvre and C. E. Labrousse of the Sorbonne, Mr. Isaiah Berlin at Oxford, Mr. Ralph Miliband of the London School of Economics, and Signor A. Galante Garrone at Turin (unfortunately after the book had gone to the printers). I wish to thank them all for their stimulating suggestions. The one man whose help has been quite indispensable and without whom this book might have never been completed is my dear friend Mr. T. E. Utley. No words could express my sense of gratitude for the untiring interest, the detailed and brilliant criticism, and the painstaking effort to correct the style of the book—the English language being a comparatively recent acquisition of the author—which have been forthcoming from Mr. Utley. No less a debt of gratitude is owed by me to Mr. Gerald M. FitzGerald of Cambridge, who offered me wonderful hospitality when I arrived in England as a war refugee, and initiated me into what is best in English life and English thought.

I wish to thank Dr. Renée Winegarten for her generous and patient help in revising the English, as well as Mrs. Daphne Gordon for reading the proofs and verifying the references, a service of vital importance, in view of the fact that I had to do the proof reading without the help of the British Museum, where this book was written, or indeed of any adequate University Library, as my University is unfortunately—owing to war circumstances—cut off from its Library on Mount Scopus.

I have been enabled to write this study by generous financial assistance from the Israel Zangwill Fund and the British Council. I wish to thank them publicly.

This present study on the Origins of Totalitarian Democracy will be continued in two further volumes. The one will be devoted to the vicissitudes of the totalitarian-democratic trend in nineteenth-century Western Europe ; the other will deal with the history of totalitarian democracy in Eastern Europe, Russia and the " people's democracies " from about 1860 till our own days, and will also touch on contemporary events in the Far East.

Finally a word of warm appreciation is due to the staff of the British Museum.

I hardly need add that no one but the author is responsible for the views expressed in this work.

J. L. TALMON

THE HEBREW UNIVERSITY,
JERUSALEM,
 Spring 1951.

CONTENTS

CONTENTS

CONTENTS

INTRODUCTION

THIS study is an attempt to show that concurrently with the liberal type of democracy there emerged from the same premises in the eighteenth century a trend towards what we propose to call the totalitarian type of democracy. These two currents have existed side by side ever since the eighteenth century. The tension between them has constituted an important chapter in modern history, and has now become the most vital issue of our time.

It would of course be an exaggeration to suggest that the whole of the period can be summed up in terms of this conflict. Nevertheless it was always present, although usually confused and obscured by other issues, which may have seemed clearer to contemporaries, but viewed from the standpoint of the present day seem incidental and even trivial. Indeed, from the vantage point of the mid-twentieth century the history of the last hundred and fifty years looks like a systematic preparation for the headlong collision between empirical and liberal democracy on the one hand, and totalitarian Messianic democracy on the other, in which the world crisis of to-day consists.

(1) THE TWO TYPES OF DEMOCRACY, LIBERAL AND TOTALITARIAN

The essential difference between the two schools of democratic thought as they have evolved is not, as is often alleged, in the affirmation of the value of liberty by one, and its denial by the other. It is in their different attitudes to politics. The liberal approach assumes politics to be a matter of trial and error, and regards political systems as pragmatic contrivances of human ingenuity and spontaneity. It also recognizes a variety of levels of personal and collective endeavour, which are altogether outside the sphere of politics.

The totalitarian democratic school, on the other hand, is based upon the assumption of a sole and exclusive truth in politics. It

I

may be called political Messianism in the sense that it postulates a preordained, harmonious and perfect scheme of things, to which men are irresistibly driven, and at which they are bound to arrive. It recognizes ultimately only one plane of existence, the political. It widens the scope of politics to embrace the whole of human existence. It treats all human thought and action as having social significance, and therefore as falling within the orbit of political action. Its political ideas are not a set of pragmatic precepts or a body of devices applicable to a special branch of human endeavour. They are an integral part of an all-embracing and coherent philosophy. Politics is defined as the art of applying this philosophy to the organization of society, and the final purpose of politics is only achieved when this philosophy reigns supreme over all fields of life.

Both schools affirm the supreme value of liberty. But whereas one finds the essence of freedom in spontaneity and the absence of coercion, the other believes it to be realized only in the pursuit and attainment of an absolute collective purpose. It is outside our scope to decide whether liberal democracy has the faith that totalitarian democracy claims to have in final aims. What is beyond dispute is that the final aims of liberal democracy have not the same concrete character. They are conceived in rather negative terms, and the use of force for their realization is considered as an evil. Liberal democrats believe that in the absence of coercion men and society may one day reach through a process of trial and error a state of ideal harmony. In the case of totalitarian democracy, this state is precisely defined, and is treated as a matter of immediate urgency, a challenge for direct action, an imminent event.

The problem that arises for totalitarian democracy, and which is one of the main subjects of this study, may be called the paradox of freedom. Is human freedom compatible with an exclusive pattern of social existence, even if this pattern aims at the maximum of social justice and security? The paradox of totalitarian democracy is in its insistence that they are compatible. The purpose it proclaims is never presented as an absolute idea, external and prior to man. It is thought to be immanent in man's reason and will, to constitute the fullest satisfaction of his true interest, and to be the guarantee of his freedom. This is the reason why the extreme forms of popular sovereignty became the essential concomitant of this absolute purpose. From the difficulty of reconciling freedom with the idea of an absolute purpose spring all the particular problems and antinomies of totalitarian democracy. This difficulty could only be resolved by thinking not in terms of men as they are, but as they were meant to be, and would be, given the proper conditions. In so far as they are at variance with the absolute ideal they can be ignored, coerced or intimidated into conforming, without any real violation of the democratic principle being involved. In the proper conditions, it is held, the conflict between spontaneity and duty would disappear, and with it the need for coercion. The practical question is, of course, whether constraint will disappear because all have learned to act in harmony, or because all opponents have been eliminated.

(2) THE EIGHTEENTH-CENTURY ORIGINS OF POLITICAL MESSIANISM ; THE SCHISM

Enough has been said already to indicate that totalitarian democracy will be treated in these pages as an integral part of the Western tradition. It is vital to add that much of the totalitarian democratic attitude was contained in the original and general eighteenth-century pattern of thought. The branching out of the two types of democracy from the common stem took place only after the common beliefs had been tested in the ordeal of the French Revolution.

From the point of view of this study the most important change that occurred in the eighteenth century was the peculiar state of mind which achieved dominance in the second part of the century. Men were gripped by the idea that the conditions, a product of faith, time and custom, in which they and their forefathers had been living, were unnatural and had all to be replaced by deliberately planned uniform patterns, which would be natural and rational.

This was the result of the decline of the traditional order in Europe : religion lost its intellectual as well as its emotional hold ; hierarchical feudalism disintegrated under the impact of social and economic factors ; and the older conception of society based on status came to be replaced by the idea of the abstract, individual man.

The rationalist idea substituted social utility for tradition as the main criterion of social institutions and values. It also suggested a form of social determinism, to which men are irresistibly driven, and which they are bound to accept one day. It thus postulated a single valid system, which would come into existence when everything not accounted for by reason and utility had been removed. This idea was, of course, bound to clash with the inveterate irrationality of man's ways, his likings and attachments.

The decline of religious authority implied the liberation of man's conscience, but it also implied something else. Religious ethics had to be speedily replaced by secular, social morality. With the rejection of the Church, and of transcendental justice, the State remained the sole source and sanction of morality. This was a matter of great importance, at a time when politics were considered indistinguishable from ethics.

The decline of the. idea of status consequent on the rise of individualism spelt the doom of privilege, but also contained totalitarian potentialities. If, as will be argued in this essay, empiricism is the ally of freedom, and the doctrinaire spirit is the friend of totalitarianism, the idea of man as an abstraction, independent of the historic groups to which he belongs, is likely to become a powerful vehicle of totalitarianism.

These three currents merged into the idea of a homogeneous society, in which men live upon one exclusive plane of existence. There were no longer to be different levels of social life, such as the temporal and the transcendental, or membership of a class and citizenship. The only recognized standard of judgment was to be social utility, as expressed in the idea of the general good, which was spoken of as if it were a visible and tangible objective. The whole of virtue was summed up as conformity to the rationalist, natural pattern. In the past it was possible for the State to regard many things as matters for God and the Church alone. The new State could recognize no such limitations. Formerly, men lived in groups. A man had to belong to some group, and could belong to several at the same time. Now there was to be only one framework for all activity : the nation. The eighteenth century never distinguished clearly between the sphere of personal self-expression and that of social action. The privacy of creative experience and feeling, which is the salt of freedom, was in due course to be swamped by the pressure of the permanently assembled people, vibrating with one collective emotion. The fact that eighteenth-century thinkers were ardent prophets of liberty and the rights of man is so much taken for granted that it scarcely needs to be mentioned. But what must be emphasized is the intense preoccupation of the eighteenth century with the idea of virtue, which was nothing if not conformity to the hoped-for pattern of social harmony. They refused to envisage the conflict between liberty and virtue as inevitable. On the contrary, the inevitable equation of liberty with virtue and reason was the most cherished article of their faith. When the eighteenth-century secular religion came face to face with this conflict, the result was the great schism. Liberal democracy flinched from the spectre of force, and fell back upon the trial-and-error philosophy. Totalitarian Messianism hardened into an exclusive doctrine represented by a vanguard of the enlightened, who justified themselves in the use of coercion against those who refused to be free and virtuous.

The other cause for this fissure, certainly no less important, was the question of property. The original impulse of political Messianism was not economic, but ethical and political. However radical in their theoretical premises, most eighteenth-century thinkers shrunk from applying the principle of total renovation to the sphere of economics and property. It was however extremely difficult to theorize about a rational harmonious social order, with contradictions resolved, anti-social impulses checked, and man's desire for happiness satisfied, while leaving the field of economic endeavour to be dominated by established facts and interests, man's acquisitive spirit and chance. Eighteenth-century thinkers became thus involved in grave inconsistencies, which they attempted to cover with all kinds of devices. The most remarkable of these certainly was the Physiocratic combination of absolutism in politics with the laissez-faire theory in economics, which claimed that the free, unhampered economic pursuits of men would set themselves into a harmonious pattern, in accordance with the laws of demand and supply. But before the eighteenth century had come to an end, the inner logic of political Messianism, precipitated by the Revolutionary upheaval, its hopes, its lessons and its disappointments, converted the secular religion of the eighteenth century from a mainly ethical into a social and economic doctrine, based on ethical premises. The postulate of salvation, implied in the idea of the natural order, came to signify to the masses stirred by the Revolution a message of social salvation before all. And so the objective ideal of social harmony gave place to the yearnings and strivings of a class ; the principle of virtuous liberty to the passion for security. The possessing classes, surprised and frightened by the social

dynamism of the idea of the natural order, hastened to shake off
the philosophy which they had earlier so eagerly embraced as a
weapon in their struggle against feudal privilege. The Fourth
Estate seized it from their hands, and filled it with new meaning.
And so the ideology of the rising bourgeoisie was transformed into
that of the proletariat.

The object of this book is to examine the stages through which
the social ideals of the eighteenth century were transformed—on
one side—into totalitarian democracy. These stages are taken to
be three : the eighteenth-century postulate, the Jacobin improvisation, and the Babouvist crystallization ; all leading up to the
emergence of economic communism on the one hand, and to the
synthesis of popular sovereignty and single-party dictatorship on
the other. The three stages constitute the three parts into which
this study is divided. The evolution of the liberal type of democracy is outside its scope.

Modern totalitarian democracy is a dictatorship resting on
popular enthusiasm, and is thus completely different from absolute
power wielded by a divine-right King, or by a usurping tyrant.
In so far as it is a dictatorship based on ideology and the enthusiasm
of the masses, it is the outcome, as will be shown, of the synthesis
between the eighteenth-century idea of the natural order and the
Rousseauist idea of popular fulfilment and self-expression. By
means of this synthesis rationalism was made into a passionate faith.
Rousseau's " general will ", an ambiguous concept, sometimes conceived as valid *a priori*, sometimes as immanent in the will of man,
exclusive and implying unanimity, became the driving force of
totalitarian democracy, and the source of all its contradictions and
antinomies. These are to be examined in detail.

(3) TOTALITARIANISM OF THE RIGHT AND
TOTALITARIANISM OF THE LEFT

The emphasis of this theory is always upon Man. And here
is the distinguishing mark between totalitarianism of the Left, with
which this study is concerned, and totalitarianism of the Right.
While the starting-point of totalitarianism of the Left has been and
ultimately still is man, his reason and salvation, that of the Right
totalitarian schools has been the collective entity, the State, the

nation, or the race. The former trend remains essentially individualist, atomistic and rationalist even when it raises the class or party to the level of absolute ends. These are, after all, only mechanically formed groups. Totalitarians of the Right operate solely with historic, racial and organic entities, concepts altogether alien to individualism and rationalism. That is why totalitarian ideologies of the Left always are inclined to assume the character of a universal creed, a tendency which totalitarianism of the Right altogether lacks. For reason is a unifying force, presupposing mankind to be the sum total of individual reasoning beings. Totalitarianism of the Right implies the negation of such a unity as well as a denial of the universality of human values. It represents a special form of pragmatism. Without raising the question of the absolute significance of the professed tenets, it aspires to a mode of existence, in which the faculties of man may—in a deliberately limited circumference of space, time and numbers—be stirred, asserted and realized so as to enable him to have what is nowadays called a wholly satisfying experience in a collective *élan*, quickened by mass emotion and the impact of impressive exploits ; in brief, the myth.

The second vital difference between the two types of totalitarianism is to be found in their divergent conceptions of human nature. The Left proclaims the essential goodness and perfectibility of human nature. The Right declares man to be weak and corrupt. Both may preach the necessity of coercion. The Right teaches the necessity of force as a permanent way of maintaining order among poor and unruly creatures, and training them to act in a manner alien to their mediocre nature. Totalitarianism of the Left, when resorting to force, does so in the conviction that force is used only in order to quicken the pace of man's progress to perfection and social harmony. It is thus legitimate to use the term democracy in reference to totalitarianism of the Left. The term could not be applied to totalitarianism of the Right.

It may be said that these are distinctions that make little difference, especially where results are concerned. It may further be maintained that whatever their original premises were, totalitarian parties and régimes of the Left have invariably tended to degenerate into soulless power machines, whose lip service to the original tenets is mere hypocrisy. Now, this is a question not only of academic interest, but of much practical importance. Even if we accept this diagnosis of the nature of Left totalitarianism when triumphant, are we to attribute its degeneration to the inevitable process of corrosion which an idea undergoes when power falls into the hands of its adherents ? Or should we seek the reason for it deeper, namely in the very essence of the contradiction between ideological absolutism and individualism, inherent in modern political Messianism ? When the deeds of men in power belie their words, are they to be called hypocrites and cynics or are they victims of an intellectual delusion ?

Here is one of the questions to be investigated. This essay is not concerned with the problem of power as such, only with that of power in relation to consciousness. The objective forces favouring the concentration of power and the subordination of the individual to a power machine, such as modern methods of production and the *arcana imperii* offered by modern technical developments, are outside the scope of this work. The political tactics of totalitarian parties and systems, or the blueprints of social positivist philosophies for the human hive, will be considered not for their own sake, but in their bearing on man's awareness and beliefs. What is vital for the present investigation is the human element : the thrill of fulfilment experienced by the believers in a modern Messianic movement, which makes them experience submission as deliverance ; the process that goes on in the minds of the leaders, whether in soliloquy or in public discussion, when faced with the question of whether their acts are the self-expression of the Cause or their own wilful deeds ; the stubborn faith that as a result of proper social arrangements and education, the conflict between spontaneity and the objective pattern will ultimately be resolved by the acceptance of the latter, without any sense of coercion.

(4) SECULAR AND RELIGIOUS MESSIANISM

The modern secular religion of totalitarian democracy has had unbroken continuity as a sociological force for over a hundred and fifty years. Both aspects, its continuity and its character as a sociological force, need stressing. These two essential features permit us to ignore the isolated literary ventures into Utopia in the earlier centuries, without denying the influence of Plato, Thomas More or Campanella upon men like Rousseau, Diderot, Mably, or

Saint-Just and Buonarroti. If one were in search of antecedents, one would also have to turn to the various outbursts of chiliasm in the Middle Ages and in the Reformation, especially to the extreme wing of the Puritan Revolution in seventeenth-century England. The coexistence of liberal democracy and revolutionary Messianism in modern times could legitimately be compared to the relationship between the official Church and the eschatological revolutionary current in Christianity during the ages of faith. Always flowing beneath the surface of official society, the Christian revolutionary current burst forth from time to time in the form of movements of evangelical poverty, heretical sects, and social-religious revolts. Like the two major trends of the modern era, the Church and the rebels against it derived their ideas from the same source. The heterodox groups were, however, too ardent in their literal interpretation of God's word. They refused to come to terms with the flesh and the kingdom of this world, and were unwilling to confine the ideal of a society of saints to the exclusively transcendental plane.

There were, however, vital differences between the chiliastic movements of the earlier centuries and modern political Messianism. The former were only sporadic occurrences, although the tension from which they sprang was always latent. A flame burst forth and was soon totally extinguished, or rendered harmless to society at large. The crisis might leave behind a sect. The myth might survive and perhaps rekindle a spark in some remote place and at some later date. Society as a whole went on much as before, although not quite free from the fear and mental discomfort left by the conflagration, and not wholly immune to the influence of the new sect.

There was however a fundamental principle in pre-eighteenth-century chiliasm that made it impossible for it to play the part of modern political Messianism. It was its religious essence. This explains why the Messianic movements or spasms of the earlier type invariably ended by breaking away from society, and forming sects based upon voluntary adherence and community of experience. Modern Messianism has always aimed at a revolution in society as a whole. The driving power of the sects was the Word of God, and the hope of achieving salvation by facing God alone and directly, without the aid of intermediary powers or submission to them, whether spiritual or temporal, and yet as part of a society of equal saints. This ideal is not unlike the modern expectation of a society of men absolutely free and equal, and yet acting in spontaneous and perfect accord. In spite of this superficial similarity, the differences between the two attitudes are fundamental. Although the Christian revolutionaries fought for the individual's freedom to interpret God's word, their sovereign was not man, but God. They aimed at personal salvation and an egalitarian society based on the Law of Nature, because they had it from God that there lies salvation, and believed that obedience to God is the condition of human freedom. The point of reference of modern Messianism, on the other hand, is man's reason and will, and its aim happiness on earth, achieved by a social transformation. The point of reference is temporal, but the claims are absolute. It is thus a remarkable fact that the Christian revolutionaries, with few exceptions, notably Calvin's Geneva and Anabaptist Münster, shrunk from the use of force to impose their own pattern, in spite of their belief in its divine source and authority, while secular Messianism, starting with a point of reference in time, has developed a fanatical resolve to make its doctrine rule absolutely and everywhere. The reasons are not far to seek.

Even if the Monistic principle of religious Messianism had succeeded in dominating and reshaping society the result would still have been fundamentally different from the situation created by modern political "absolutism". Society might have been forbidden the compromises which are made possible by the Orthodox distinction between the kingdom of God and the earthly State, and as a consequence social and political arrangements might have lost much of their flexibility. The sweep towards the enforcement of an exclusive pattern would nevertheless have been hampered, if not by the thought of the fallibility of man, at least by the consciousness that life on earth is not a closed circle, but has its continuation and conclusion in eternity. Secular Messianic Monism is subject to no such restraints. It demands that the whole account be settled here and now.

The extreme wing of English Puritanism at the time of the Cromwellian Revolution still bore the full imprint of religious eschatology. It had already acquired modern features however. It combined extreme individualism with social radicalism and a totalitarian temperament. Nevertheless this movement, far from initiating the continuous current of modern political Messianism, remained from the European point of view an isolated episode. It was apparently quite unknown to the early representatives of the movement under discussion. While eighteenth-century French thinkers and revolutionary leaders were alive to the political lessons of the "official" Cromwellian Revolution as a deterrent against military dictatorship, and a writer like Harrington was respected as a master, it is doubtful whether the more radical aspects of the English Revolution were much known or exercised any influence in France before the nineteenth century. The strongest influence on the fathers of totalitarian democracy was that of antiquity, interpreted in their own way. Their myth of antiquity was the image of liberty equated with virtue. The citizen of Sparta or Rome was proudly free, yet a marvel of ascetic discipline. He was an equal member of the sovereign nation, and at the same time had no life or interests outside the collective tissue.

(5) QUESTIONS OF METHOD

Objections may be urged against the view that political Messianism as a postulate preceded the compact set of social and economic ideas with which it has come to be associated. It may be said that it is wrong to treat Messianism as a substance that can be divorced from its attributes ; to consider it altogether apart from the events which produced it, the instruments which have been used to promote it, and the concrete aims and policies of the men who represented it at any given moment. Such a procedure, it may be said, presupposes an almost mystical agency active in history. It is important to answer this objection not less for its philosophical significance than for the question of method it raises.

What this study is concerned with is a state of mind, a way of feeling, a disposition, a pattern of mental, emotional and behaviouristic elements, best compared to the set of attitudes engendered by a religion. Whatever may be said about the significance of the economic or other factors in the shaping of beliefs, it can hardly be denied that the all-embracing attitudes of this kind, once crystallized, are the real substance of history. The concrete elements of history, the acts of politicians, the aspirations of people, the ideas, values, preferences and prejudices of an age, are the outward manifestations of its religion in the widest sense.

The problem under discussion could not be dealt with on the plane of systematic, discursive reasoning alone. For as in religion, although the partial theological framework may be a marvel of logic, with syllogism following syllogism, the first premises, the axioms or the postulates must remain a matter of faith.. They can be neither proved nor disproved. And it is they that really matter. They determine the ideas and acts, and resolve contradictions into some higher identity or harmony.

The postulate of some ultimate, logical, exclusively valid social order is a matter of faith, and it is not much use trying to defeat it by argument. But its significance to the believer, and the power it has to move men and mountains, can hardly be exaggerated. Now, in Europe and elsewhere, for the last century and a half, there have always been men and movements animated by such a faith, preparing for the Day, referring all their ideas and acts to some all-embracing system, sure of some pre-ordained and final dénouement of the historic drama with all its conflicts into an absolute harmony. Jacobins may have differed from the Babouvists, the Blanquists from many of the secret societies in the first half of the nineteenth century, the Communists from the Socialists, the Anarchists from all others, yet they all belong to one religion. This religion emerged in the second part of the eighteenth century and its rise will be traced in these pages. The most difficult problem of the secular religion was to be the antinomy of freedom and the exclusive Messianic pattern.

Complex, intricate and at times magnificent as the theories evolved by the various Messianic trends in the later days were, the original phase, which is the subject of this study, reveals the first elements and threads in a crude, naïve and simple form. This fact should help towards understanding the historic phenomenon as a whole. For some of the basic ideas of the late and highly developed Messianic secular religion, especially, as it will be shown, those relating to human nature, ethics and philosophical principles, have remained the same as they were in the eighteenth century.

It is in the nature of doctrines postulating universal abstract patterns to be schematic and grey. They lack the warmth, limpidity and richness which is to be found in living human and national tissues. They do not convey the tensions which arise between unique personalities, in conflict with each other and their surroundings. They fail to offer the absorbing interest of the

unpredictable situation and the pragmatic approach to it.   But all
these, absent in the doctrine, emerge in the vicissitudes of the
doctrine as a sociological force.

This study is neither purely a treatise on political theory, nor a
recital of events. Justice would not be done to the subject by
treating it in terms of the individual psychology of a few leaders.
Nor would the point be made clear by an analysis in terms of mass
psychology. Religion is created and lived by men, yet it is a
framework in which men live. The problem analysed here is only
partly one of behaviour. The modern secular religion must first
be treated as an objective reality. Only when this has been done
will it be possible to consider the intellectual and historical patterns
created by the interplay between the secular religion and particular
men and situations. This interplay becomes particularly interesting,
when it results in contradictions between, on the one side, the
impersonal pattern and, on the other, the demands of the particular
situation and the uniqueness of personality.

PART I

THE EIGHTEENTH-CENTURY ORIGINS
OF POLITICAL MESSIANISM

. . . à l'époque où l'influence de ces progrès sur l'opinion, de l'opinion sur les nations ou sur leurs chefs, cessant tout à coup d'être lente et insensible, a produit dans la masse entière de quelques peuples, une révolution, gage certain de celle qui doit embrasser la généralité de l'espèce humaine. Après de longues erreurs, après s'être égarés dans des théories incomplètes ou vagues, les publicistes sont parvenus à connaître enfin les véritables droits de l'homme, à les déduire de cette seule vérité qu'il est un être sensible, capable de former des raisonnements et d'acquèrir des idées morales.

CONDORCET

Rousseau, den ihr noch einmal über das andere einen Träumer nennt, indes seine Träume unter euren Augen in Erfüllung gehen, verfuhr viel zu schonend mit euch, ihr Empiriker ; das war sein Fehler.

JOHANN GOTTLIEB FICHTE

Dieses merkt euch, ihr stolzen Männer der That. Ihr seid Nichts als unbewusste Handlungen der Gedankenmänner, die oft in demüthigster Stille euch all euer Thun aufs bestimmteste vorgezeichnet haben. Maximilien Robespierre war Nichts als die Hand von Jean Jacques Rousseau, die blutige Hand, die aus dem Schosse der Zeit den Leib hervorzog, dessen Seele Rousseau geschaffen.

HEINE

Chapter One

NATURAL ORDER : THE POSTULATE

(a) THE SINGLE PRINCIPLE

IN 1755 Morelly in the *Code de la Nature* set out to " lift the veil "
so that all should be able to behold " with horror, the source and
origin of all evils and all crimes ", and learn " the simplest and
most beautiful lessons of nature perpetually contradicted by vulgar
morality and vulgar politics ". He placed on the one side the
science of natural morality, which was meant to be the same for all
nations, and was as simple and as self-evident in its axioms and
consequences " que les mathématiques elles-mêmes " ; and on the
other side the chaos of errors, absurdities, false starts and loose
ends, presented by the whole of human history. Morelly's aim
was to find a situation where it would be " almost impossible for
man to be depraved and vicious ", and in which man would be
as happy as possible. Chance, " cette prétendue fatalité ", would
be exorcised from the world.

Morelly thought in terms of deliberate planning, but at the
same time claimed to be only discovering an objective pattern of
things. This pattern is conceived by him as a social mechanism,
a " marvellous automatic machine ". It is described as " tout
intelligent qui s'arrangeât lui-même par un mécanisme aussi simple
que merveilleux ; ses parties étaient préparées et pour ainsi dire
taillées pour former le plus bel assemblage ". Like any being in
nature, mankind has " un point fixe d'intégrité ", to which it is
ascending by degrees. The natural order is this ultimate fulfilment
of mankind.

Morelly's *Code de la Nature* is the earliest in the series of writings
with which this study is concerned. It was the first book in modern
times to put fully-fledged communism on the agenda as a practical
programme, and not merely as a Utopia. It became Babeuf's
Bible, although he happened to attribute the work to Diderot. A
soulless, badly written book, very crude in its premises and argu-

ment, not very influential in the pre-Thermidorian period of the Revolution, it expresses nevertheless in an exaggerated form the common tenets of eighteenth-century thought.

All the eminent French political writers of the second part of the century were engaged in a search for a new unitary principle of social existence. Vague as to the concrete nature of the principle, they all met on common ground as far as the postulate of such a principle was concerned. The formulæ differed only in emphasis, and some of these differences deserve to be illustrated.

Helvetius, laying all the emphasis on utilitarianism, of which he was, in his *De l'Esprit* (1758), the first teacher, and Holbach, writing in the seventies, and preaching materialist determinism, both postulated a kind of cosmic pragmatism, of which the social order was only a replica. The structure of the world- is such that if society were properly balanced, all that is true would also be socially useful, and all that is useful would also be virtuous. None therefore would be vicious except fools, and none unhappy but the ignorant and wicked, in other words, those who presume to kick against the necessary, natural order of things.

Mably, who like Morelly was in the last resort a Communist, and therefore had a fixed image of the desired natural pattern, in contrast to the vagueness of the utilitarian postulate, strove for scientific certainty in social and human affairs. He believed that politics could develop from the most conjectural into a most exact science, once the recesses of the human heart and passions had been explored, and a scientific system of ethics defined.

Condorcet, writing at the height of the Revolution in 1793, when he was in hiding and about to die the victim of the triumph of his ideas, summed up in a most moving manner the achievement of his age by claiming that it had come into the possession of a universal instrument equally applicable to all fields of human endeavour. The same instrument was capable of discovering those general principles which form the necessary and immutable laws of justice, of probing men's motives, of "ascertaining the truth of natural philosophy, of testing the effects of history and of formulating laws for taste". Once this instrument had been applied to morals and politics, a degree of certainty was given to those sciences little inferior to that which obtained in the natural sciences. This latest effort, Condorcet claimed, had placed an everlasting barrier between the human race and the " old mistakes of its infancy that

will forever preserve us from a relapse into former ignorance ".
The analogy with the claims of dialectical materialism in the next
century is evident.

Placed in this context Rousseau occupies a position all his own.
He starts from the same point as the others.   He wants to investigate
the nature of things, right, reason and justice in themselves, and the
principle of legitimacy.   Events and facts have no claim to be taken
for granted, and to be considered natural, if they do not conform to
one universally valid pattern, no matter whether such a pattern
has ever existed.   And yet, Rousseau makes no attempt to link up
his ideal social order with the universal system and its all-embracing
principle.   A mighty fiat conjures up the social entity whatever its
name, the State, the social contract, the Sovereign or the general
will.   The entity is autonomous, without as it were antecedents
or an external point of reference.   It is self-sufficient.   It is the
source and maker of all moral and social values, and yet it has an
absolute significance and purpose.   A vital shift of emphasis from
cognition to the categorical imperative takes place.   The sole, all-
explaining and all-determining principle of the *philosophes*, from
which all ideas may be deduced, is transformed into the Sovereign,
who cannot by definition err or hurt any of its citizens.   Man has
no other standards than those laid down by the social contract.
He receives his personality and all his ideas from it.   The State
takes the place of the absolute point of reference embodied in the
universal principle.   The implications of this shift of emphasis will
be examined later.

Eighteenth-century thought, which prepared the ground for the
French Revolution, should be considered on three different levels :
first, criticism of the *ancien régime*, its abuses and absurdities ;
second, the positive ideas about a more rational and freer system of
administration, such as, for instance, ideas on the separation of
powers, the place of the judiciary, and a sound system of taxation ;
and lastly, the vague Messianic expectation attached to the idea of
the natural order.   It is due to this last aspect that social and political
criticism in eighteenth-century writings always seems to point to
things far beyond the concrete and immediate grievances and
demands.   So little is said directly about, for instance, feudal abuses
or particular wrongs, and so much, however vaguely, about eternal
principles, the first laws of society, and the cleavage of mankind
into ruling and exploiting classes, into haves and have-nots, that

has come into existence in contradiction to the dictates of nature. An incalculable dynamism was immanent in the idea of the natural order. When the Revolution came to test the eighteenth-century teachings, the sense of an imminent and total renovation was almost universal. But while to most the idea of the natural order preached by the *philosophes* appeared as a guiding idea and a point of reference, only to be approximated and never really attained, to the more ardent elements it became charged with a driving power that could never be halted till it had run out its full and inexorable course. And that course appeared to expand into boundlessness.

It is easy to imagine the horror of Robespierre's listeners at the Convention when, desperately anxious to know where all the purges and all the terror were leading, after all possible Republican and popular measures had already been taken, and the sternest reprisals against counter-revolutionaries applied, they heard the Incorruptible say that his aim was to establish at last the natural order and to realize the promises of philosophy. There was something strikingly reminiscent of the medieval evangelical revolutionaries quoting the Sermon on the Mount to the dignitaries of the Church in Babeuf's pleading before the Court at Vendôme. He read extract after extract from Rousseau, Mably, Morelly and others, and asked his judges, haunted by the memory of Robespierre's reign of virtue, why he should be tried for having taken the teachings of the fathers of the Revolution seriously. Had they not taught that the natural order would result in universal happiness ? And if the Revolution had failed to realize this promise, could one claim that it had come to an end ? The survivors of the Gironde restored to power after the downfall of Robespierre, who in 1792 were still using the same vocabulary as Robespierre and keeping up a constant appeal to nature and its laws, had learned their frightful lesson in year II of the Republic. Writers like Benjamin Constant and Mme de Staël were soon to develop their brand of liberal empiricism in answer to 1793. It was out of that inner certainty of the existence of a natural and wholly rational and just order that scientific socialism and the idea of an integral Revolution grew.

Already, however, by the end of 1792 a Girondist " liberal " grew alarmed. Thus Salle wrote to Dubois-Crancé :

" The principles, in their metaphysical abstractness and in the form in which they are being constantly analysed in this society—

no government can be founded on them ; a principle cannot be rigorously applied to political association, for the simple reason that a principle admits of no imperfection ; and, whatever you may do, men are imperfect. I say more : I make bold to say, and indeed, in the spirit of Rousseau himself, that the social state is a continuous violation of the will of the nation as conceived in its abstract relationships. What may not be the results of these imprudent declamations which take this will as a safe basis ; which, under the pretext of full and complete sovereignty of the people, will suffer no legal restriction ; which present man always in the image of an angel ; which, desirous of discovering what befits him, ignore what he really is ; which, in an endeavour to persuade the people that they are wise enough, give them dispensation from the effort to be that ! . . . I would gladly, if you like, applaud the chimera of perfection that they are after. But tell me, in divesting in this way man of what is human in him, are they not most likely to turn him into a ferocious beast ? "

(b) THE SECULAR RELIGION

Eighteenth-century *philosophes* were never in doubt that they were preaching a new religion. They faced a mighty challenge. The Church claimed to offer an absolute point of reference to man and society. It also claimed to embody an ultimate and all-embracing unity of human existence across the various levels of human and social life. The Church accused secular philosophy of destroying these two most essential conditions of private and public morality, and thereby undermining the very basis of ethics, and indeed society itself. If there is no God, and no transcendental sanction, why should men act virtuously ? Eighteenth-century philosophy not only accepted the challenge, but turned the accusation against the Church itself. The *philosophes* felt the challenge so keenly that, as Diderot put it, they regarded it their sacred duty to show not only that their morality was just as good as religious ethics, but much better. Holbach was at pains to prove that the materialistic principle was a much stronger basis for ethics than the principle of the " spirituality of the soul " could ever claim to be. A great deal of eighteenth-century thought would assume a different complexion, if it was constantly remembered that though a philosophy of protest, revolt and spontaneity, eighteenth-century philosophy, as already hinted, was intensely aware of the challenge to redefine the guarantees of social cohesion and morality. The *philosophes* were most anxious to show that not they, but their opponents, were the anarchists from the point of view of the natural order.

The philosophical line of attack on the Church was that apart from the historic untruth of the revealed religion, it also stood condemned as a sociological force. It introduced "imaginary" and heterogeneous criteria into the life of man and society. The commandments of the Church were incompatible with the requirements of society. The contradiction was harmful to both, and altogether demoralizing. One preached ascetic unworldliness, the other looked for social virtues and vigour. Man was being taught to work for the salvation of his soul, but his nature kept him earthbound. Religion taught him one thing, science another. Religious ethics were quite ineffective, where they were not a source of evil. The promise of eternal reward and the threat of everlasting punishment were too remote to have any real influence on actual human conduct. This sanction at best engendered hypocrisy. Where the teachings of religion were successful, they resulted in human waste, like monasticism and asceticism, or in cruel intolerance and wars of religion. Moreover, the "imaginary" teachings and standards of the Church offered support and justification to tyrannical vested interests harmful to society as a whole. Rousseau, Morelly, Helvetius, Holbach, Diderot, Condorcet, not to mention of course Voltaire, were unanimous in their insistence on the homogeneous nature of morality. Some, the Voltairians and atheists, speak in terms of a deliberate plot against society, when attacking the claims of religious ethics. Others, like Rousseau, lay all the emphasis on matters of principle, above all the principle of social unity : you cannot be a citizen and Christian at the same time, for the loyalties clash.

"It is from the legislative body only," wrote Helvetius, "that we can expect a beneficent religion . . . let sagacious ministers be clothed with temporal and spiritual powers, and all contradiction between religious and patriotic precepts will disappear . . . the religious system shall coincide with the national prosperity . . . religions, the habitual instruments of sacerdotal ambition, shall become the felicity of the public."

Holbach taught the same, and although Rousseau and Mably quarrelled bitterly with the two atheistic materialists, there was hardly a fundamental disagreement between them. For even to them the vital consideration was not really the existence of a Divine Being, but guarantees for social ethics. Rousseau, the master of Robespierre, and Mably, whose religious ideas made such a deep impression upon Saint-Just, were nearer Hebrew Biblical and classical pagan conceptions than Christian ideas. Robespierre's Jewish idea of Providence hovering over the Revolution was a conclusion from the eighteenth-century view that the moral drama is played out under the judgment of Nature exclusively within the framework of social relations. No eighteenth-century thinker recognized any distinction between membership of a kingdom of God and citizenship of an earthly state, in the Christian sense. Whether, as the eighteenth century as a whole, in the spirit of the Old Testament, believed, that reward and punishment for the deeds of one generation are distributed to posterity, or whether, as Rousseau and Mably thought, it was the individual who comes to judgment to be rewarded or punished as an individual soul, the only virtues or sins recognized were those of social significance.

The only difference between Helvetius and Holbach, on the one hand, and Rousseau and Mably, on the other, was that according to the materialists social legislation and arrangements alone were sufficient to ensure moral conduct, while Rousseau and Mably feared that man may elude the law. It was vital that man should always remember that even if he eludes the magistrate, the account would still have to be settled elsewhere and before a higher tribunal. It was not less important that the unhappy and the injured should not despair of justice in society, even if it fails to come to their succour on earth. Rousseau, transcending the limits of mechanical materialist rationalism, harked back to antiquity. He felt compelled by the ancient sense of awe at the idea of a Divinity hovering over the city-state, and imbuing every act of its life with a solemn significance. He was fascinated by the pomp and thrill of collective patriotic worship in the national religious fêtes, games and public displays, while Mably was convinced that no religion was possible without external forms, institutions and fixed rites.

The articles of Rousseau's civil religion, other than those concerning the existence of Divinity and the immortality of the soul, do not materially differ from " the principles that are eternal and invariable, that are drawn from the nature of men and things, and like the propositions of geometry are capable of the most rigorous demonstration ", upon which Helvetius believed a universal religion should be founded.   They refer to the laws of the State and articles of the Social Contract.   It was not only theism that caused Rousseau to make the belief in Divinity a social necessity.   It was also the fact that his and Mably's approach differed from that of the rationalists on the fundamental point, already made.   The social harmonious pattern of Helvetius, Morelly and Holbach was a matter of cognition.   It was there to be discerned and applied.   In the case of Rousseau and Mably it was a categorical imperative, a matter of will.   The materialist determinists felt confident that knowledge would be translated into action.   Not so Rousseau and Mably, with their different attitude to human nature, and their deep sense of sin.   Hence Rousseau felt driven to demand the death penalty for one who disbelieved in the civil religion, while Mably wished to ban all atheists and even deists, who claim that a religion of the heart was all that was wanted.   Man had to be made to fear God, and made to experience the sense of fear constantly and vividly.

Too much has been made of the contradiction between the chapter on the Civil Religion in the *Social Contract* and the *Profession de Foi du Vicaire Savoyard*.   The latter may well have been a shock to the materialists in so far as the purely philosophical problem of the existence of a personal deity was concerned.   The direct and intensive relationship between man and God of the Vicar of Savoy need not, however, necessarily be taken as a refutation of the self-sufficiency of the religion of society.   It would be so if the State or society were to be considered as purely human contrivances. If the State or Society are, as in the case of Robespierre, regarded as existing under the personal Providence of God, like the pre-exilic Hebrew society, and if the relationship between God and man, unlike that presented by the Old Testament, does not entail a hierarchical organization and a system of laws and duties outside the framework of social institutions and laws, then the purely religious sense of awe and patriotic piety not only need not clash, but are likely to become fused into the Robespierre type of mysticism.   There are no other priests than the magistrates, religious and patriotic ceremonial are the same, and to serve your country is to serve God.

(c) APRIORISM AND EMPIRICISM

The faith in a natural order and the immutable, universal principles deduced from it was the cause of the almost universal opposition in the second part of the eighteenth century to Montesquieu's central idea, in spite of the high esteem in which the father of the idea of republican virtue was held.

The lack of understanding for the pragmatic evolution of social forms was so great that Morelly took the *Esprit des Lois* to be a didactic tract designed to show the vagaries and follies of mankind, once they had deviated from and abandoned the state of nature.

Politics, according to Sieyès, was an art, and not a descriptive science like physics. Its object was to plan, to create reality and to do so in obedience to a permanent pattern. It was, Sieyès maintained, natural law that was old, and the errors of existing societies were new. Diderot did not think that a knowledge of history must precede that of morality. It seemed to him more useful and expedient to gain an idea of the just and unjust " before possessing a knowledge of the actions and the men to whom one ought to apply it ".

The emphasis upon " ought " instead of " why " was Rousseau's answer to Montesquieu. In the much quoted passage in *Émile* Rousseau says that Montesquieu was the only man capable of creating the " great and useless " science of politics, or rather political right, but unfortunately contented himself with dealing with the positive laws of the established governments, " et rien au monde n'est plus différent que ces deux études ". Rousseau's own references to relativism conditioned by different geographical circumstances do not affect his general approach. They appear to be the necessary tribute he feels obliged to pay to political geography, and they usually occur when the subject is economics.

Condorcet, like Rousseau, thought that Montesquieu would have done better had he been less occupied with finding " the reasons for that which is there than with seeking that which ought to be ".

More interesting and less noticed was eighteenth-century criticism of Montesquieu which implied that his relativism was due to his having given preference to geographical and other factors over the human factor. The underlying assumption of this criticism—a point to be developed later—was the idea that while

objective conditions make for variety, it was human nature that
called for uniformity. Even Montesquieu himself, never quite a
" Montesquieu'ist "—as Marx not a Marxist—believed in natural
laws derived from man's inner being as a constant and immutable
quality. Helvetius and Mably maintained that Montesquieu's
thesis was vitiated by his failure to recognize that human psychology
was the only vital factor in shaping political systems. To Helvetius
it was the desire for power and the ways of obtaining it. Mably
recognized human passions, and not climatic differences or the
particular configuration of a territory, as the decisive factor in
politics. He believed that human psychology was the same in
every climate. Hence, knowledge of psychology was the safest
way to scientific politics.

Condorcet and others put the main emphasis on the rights of
man as the condition of an exclusive social system. His criticism
should be read together with his comparison between the French
Revolution and the political systems of antiquity and the United
States of America. The case between rationalist politics and political
empiricism has nowhere been made clearer on the side of eighteenth-
century French philosophy. Condorcet objects to the empiricism
of the ancient Greek political philosophy. It was a science of facts,
but not a true theory founded upon general, universal principles,
nature and reason. The Greek thinkers aimed less at extirpating
the causes of evil than at destroying their effects by opposing their
causes one to another. In brief, instead of applying a systematic
and radical cure, they tried to play up to prejudices and vices, and
play them off against each other so as to cancel their effects. No
effort to disperse and suppress them was made. The result was
that these policies deformed, misled, brutalized and inflamed men,
instead of refining and purifying them. Condorcet seems at one
time to come very near Morelly's condemnation of what to-day
would be called reformism : the perennial effort, in the words of
the *Code de la Nature*, to perfect the imperfect. This procedure
—claimed Morelly—only complicates the chain of evils, misleads
the people and kills the energy for a radical reform.

Like all his eighteenth-century predecessors, Condorcet based
his idea of a radical reform on the immutable necessities of human
nature, or rather the rights of man derived from them. He thought
that the Greeks had a consciousness of rights, but failed to compre-
hend their coherent structure, their depth, extent and real nature.

They saw in them, as it were, a heritage, a set of inherited rights, and not a coherent, objective framework.

Even the American Revolution had not yet achieved the full consciousness of these principles. The Americans had not yet acquired principles sufficiently invariable not to fear that legislators might introduce into the political institutions their particular prejudices and passions. Their object could not as yet therefore be to build on the firm, permanent basis of nature and universal maxims a society of men equal and free ; they had to be content with establishing " laws to hereditary members ", that is to say, within the context of the given realities and expediency. The American system therefore offered an example of a search for a mean between the oligarchy of the rich and the fickleness of the poor, inviting tyranny. The French Revolution marked the absolute turning point. " We arrived at the period when philosophy . . . obtained an influence on the thinking class of men, and these on the people and their governments that ceasing any longer to be gradual produced a revolution in the entire mass of certain nations, and gave thereby a secure pledge of the general revolution one day to follow that shall embrace the whole human species . . . after ages of error, after wandering in all the mazes of vague and defective theories, writers . . . at length arrived at the knowledge of the true rights of man . . . deducted from the same principle . . . a being endowed with sensation, capable of reasoning . . . laws deduced from the nature of our own feeling . . . our moral constitution."

The French Revolution compared with the American Revolution had been an event on quite a different plane. It had been a total revolution in the sense that it had left no sphere and no aspect of human existence untouched, whereas the American Revolution had been a purely political change-over. Furthermore, while the French Revolution had enthroned equality and effected a political transformation based upon the identity of the natural rights of man, the American Revolution had been content to achieve a balance of social powers based on inequality and compromise.

It was this human hubris and impious presumption that frail man is capable of producing a scheme of things of absolute and final significance that, on the one hand, provoked some of Burke's most eloquent passages and, on the other, led Joseph de Maistre, Bonald and their school to proclaim the idea of theocratic absolutism.

Chapter Two

THE SOCIAL PATTERN AND FREEDOM
(HELVETIUS AND HOLBACH)

(a) IDENTITY OF REASON

WE now reach the core of our problem, the paradox of freedom. The fighting argument of the teachers of the natural system was that the powers that be and their theoretical defenders deliberately or ignorantly took no heed of human nature. All the evils, vices and miseries were due to the fact that man had not consulted his true nature, or had been prevented from doing so by ignorance, which was spread and maintained by vested interests. Had man probed his true nature, he would have discovered a replica of the universal order. By obeying the postulates of his own nature he would have acted in accordance with the laws of Nature as a whole, and thus avoided all the entanglements and contradictions in which history has involved him.

Now the paradox is that human nature, instead of being regarded as that stubborn, unmanageable and unpredictable Adam, is presented here as a vehicle of uniformity, and as its guarantee.

The paradox is based upon vital philosophical premises. There is a good deal of confusion as to the philosophical kinship of the eighteenth-century philosophers. It is made worse by the fact that the *philosophes* were not philosophers in the strict sense of the word. They were eclectics. They were as much the heirs of Plato and Descartes as pupils of Locke and Hume, of philosophical rationalism and empirical scepticism, of Leibnitz and Condillac's associationist theory. Not even a founder of utilitarianism like Helvetius, or one of the most important teachers of materialist determinism like Holbach, ever made their position unequivocally clear. But it is necessary to sum up what all the eighteenth-century thinkers had in common in their underlying premises as far as it affects the subject of this investigation. Following the footsteps of Descartes, the *philosophes* believed in truth that is objective and

28

stands on its own, and which can and would be recognized by man. To Holbach truth was the conformity of our ideas with the nature of things. Helvetius believed that all the most complicated metaphysical propositions could be reduced to questions of fact that white is white and black is black. Nature has so arranged that there should be a direct and unerring correlation between objects and our powers of cognition. Helvetius, Holbach and Morelly repeatedly say that error is an accident only. We all would see and judge rightly if it were not for the ignorance or the particular passions and interests that blind our judgment, these being the result of bad education or the influence of vested interests alien to man. Everyone is capable of discovering the truth, if it is presented to him in the right light. Every member of Rousseau's sovereign is bound to will the general will. For the general will is in the last resort a Cartesian truth.

Helvetius goes so far as to deny any inherent differences of ability and talent. These are nothing but the product of conditions and chance. Uniform education, the placing of all children in as similar conditions as possible, their subjection to exactly the same impressions and associations, would reduce the differences of talent and ability to a minimum. With what eagerness this theory was seized upon by the revolutionary egalitarians, especially Buonarroti! Genius can be reared, and you can multiply men of genius according to plan, taught Helvetius.

Rationalists and empiricists at the same time, eighteenth-century thinkers felt no incongruity when boasting that in contrast to their opponents they based their theories on experience alone. They never tired of urging people to observe and study man in order to learn how he behaves and what are his real needs. But this emphasis on empiricism was directed not against philosophical rationalism, but only against the authoritarian, revealed religion and the teachings of tradition. Their empiricism was vitiated by the rationalist premise of Man *per se*, human nature as such ultimately endowed with only one unifying attribute, reason, or at most two, reason and self-love.

If there is such a being as Man in himself, and if we all, when we throw off our accidental characteristics, partake of the same substance, then a universal system of morality, based on the fewest and simplest principles, becomes not only a distinct possibility, but a certainty. Such a system would be comparable in its precision to geometry, and the most cherished dream of philosophers since Locke would come true. Since this universal system of ethics is a matter of intellectual cognition, and since it is quite sure that Nature intended the moral order to be purposeful and conducive to happiness, it becomes quite clear that all the evils that exist, all chaos and misery, are due simply to error or ignorance.

Man, however, is a creature not only of reason but of individual and unpredictable passion. " Will the simplicity and uniformity of these principles agree with the different passions of men ? " Helvetius' answer to his own question is that however different the desires of men may be, their manner of regarding objects is essentially the same.

There is no need to accept the individual's actual refusal to submit his passionate nature to reason as a fact that must be taken for granted and will always be with us. And here eighteenth-century philosophy was immensely helped by the associationist psychology of Condillac, with its roots in Locke. The mind is at birth a *tabula rasa*, with no innate ideas, characteristics or vices. All are formed by education, environment and associations of ideas and impressions. Man is a malleable creature. He is by nature neither good nor bad, rather good in so far as he is accommodating to what Nature intended him to be. All his actual badness and viciousness is a result of evil institutions, and may be traced still further to the " first little chain " of evils, the original fatal error as Morelly and Holbach called it, the idea that man is bad. The institutions and laws erected on this premise were calculated to thwart man and his legitimate aspirations. They acted as an irritant and made man evil, which the powers that be took for a further justification of their oppressive methods.

Man is a product of education. Education in the widest sense of the word, including of course the laws, is capable of reconciling man with the universal moral order and objective truth. It can teach him to throw off the passions and urges which act against the harmonious pattern, and develop in him the passions useful to society. In a society from which the Church had been excluded and which treated social utility as the sole criterion of judgment, education like everything else was bound to be focused in the governmental system. It was a matter for the Government. Helvetius, Holbach, Mably, the Physiocrats and others, in the same way as Rousseau himself, believed that ultimately man was nothing but the product of the laws of the State, and that there was nothing that a government was incapable of doing in the art of forming man. How fascinated Helvetius was by the power and greatness of the founder of a monastic order, able as he was to deal with man in the raw, outside the maze of tradition and accumulated circumstances, and to lay down rules to shape man like clay. Rousseau's adored Legislator is nothing but the great Educator.

(b) SELF-INTEREST

The problem of man's self-interest is the central point of the eighteenth-century theory. *Prima facie*, man's self-love is calculated to be the rock upon which any harmonious social pattern might founder. Eighteenth-century thinkers declared it however to be the most important asset for social co-operation. They hailed it as the most precious gift of Nature. Without the desire for happiness and pleasure, man would sink into sloth and indifference and, as Helvetius, Rousseau, Morelly, Mably, Holbach and others all agreed, would have never attained his real self-fulfilment, which can be achieved only in organized society and in the relationships maintained by it.

Self-love is the only basis of morality, for it is the most real and most vital element in man and human relations. It therefore offers a simple and safe standard to judge how people would act and what could satisfy them. But the main value of the principle is in the fact that man's self-interest in the natural state, far from setting him irretrievably at variance with his fellow men and society, draws them together as nothing else, no transcendental commandments, could. Self-love, as Morelly defined it, is by nature indissolubly bound up with the instinct of benevolence, and thus plays in the sphere of social relations the same part as Newton's law of gravitation in the physical world. According to Helvetius and Holbach, nature has so arranged that man cannot be happy without the happiness of others, and without making others happy. Not only because he needs the sight of happiness in others to feel happy himself, but also because, owing to cosmic pragmatism, our courses and interests are so linked up in a higher unity that man working for his own welfare inevitably helps others and society. Holbach called the vicious man a bad calculator. Virtue is nothing but the wise choice of what is truly useful to himself and at the same time to others. Reason is the intellectual capacity for making the right choice, while liberty is the practical knowledge of what is conducive to happiness, and the ability to act on it. No sacrifice of self-interest is required. On the contrary, a legislator demanding it would, in the words of Mably, be insane. What the individual may be asked is to forgo immediate advantages for more solid and permanent gains in the future. He may properly be invited to lose his soul to win it back, to surrender some selfish interests to society so as to be able to increase the solid totality of good, embodied in the social good, from which his own particular interest inevitably flows. For ultimately, if group interests within society are eliminated, and replaced by a general interest, deduced from human nature, common to an equal degree to everyone, the general interest is nothing but one's individual interest writ large. Man's real interest is immanent in the general social good.

Selfishness and vice do not pay. In words reminiscent of Plato, Holbach speaks of a harmony of the soul that constitutes happiness, and comes into existence when man is at peace with himself and his environment. The man torn by passions, tormented by cupidity, worn out by frustration, tossed about by heterogeneous urges, has his harmony disturbed and becomes miserable. In brief, even from the strictly utilitarian point of view, virtue is its own reward. The virtuous man, as our writers never tire of repeating, cannot fail to be happy. The happiest is the man who realizes that his happiness lies in self-adjustment to the necessary order of things, that is to say, in the pursuit of happiness in harmony with others. All misery is the outcome of a vain attempt to kick against the natural order from which man can never depart without peril to himself. All misery and all vices come, as Rousseau put it, from the preference man gives to his *amour-propre* over his *amour de soi*, legitimate and natural self-love.

What is useful is virtuous and true. Not just in the sense of limited pragmatism that that is true which in a limited sphere produces results. It is so owing to what has been called here cosmic pragmatism. Things were meant to fit, and their appropriateness is demonstrated by results. Their appropriateness is also their truth, for the universe is simultaneously a system of truths and a wonderful machine designed to produce results.

The pattern of social harmony cannot be left to work itself

out by itself. The designs of nature to be realized require deliberate arrangements. The natural identity of interests must be reproduced by the artificial identification of interests.

It is the task of the Legislator to bring about social harmony, that is to say, reconcile the personal good with the general good. It is for the Legislator, as Helvetius put it, to discover means of placing men under the necessity of being virtuous. This can be achieved with the help of institutions, laws, education and a proper system of rewards and punishments. The Legislator, acting on man's instinct of self-love, is capable of forcing him to be just to others. He can direct man's passions in such a way that instead of being destructive they would come to bear good fruit. The object of the laws is to teach man his true interest, which is after all another name for virtue. This can be done if there is a clear and effective distribution of rewards and punishments. A proper system of education in the widest sense would fix firmly in the minds of men the association of virtue with reward, and of vice with punishment, these embracing of course also public approval and disapproval. " The whole art of this sublime architecture consists in making laws which are wise and learned enough to direct my self-love in such a way that I neglect, so to speak, my particular advantage, and to reward me liberally for the sacrifice," wrote Mably. It is a question of external arrangements and of education at the same time. The personal good may be made with the help of appropriate institutions and arrangements to flow back from the general good so that the citizen, having his legitimate needs satisfied, would have no incentive to be anti-social. He can be made fully conscious of this and made to behave accordingly.

Helvetius and Holbach taught that the temporal interest alone if handled cleverly was sufficient to form virtuous men. Good laws alone make virtuous men. This being so, vice in society is not the outcome of the corruption of human nature, but the fault of the Legislator. This statement is not invalidated even if it is admitted that man as he is would naturally always prefer his personal to the general good. For man is only a raw element in regard to the edifice of social harmony. A legislation is possible under which none would be unhappy but fools and people maimed by nature, and none vicious but the ignorant and stupid. That such a society has not yet come into existence is due not to man, but to the failure of governments to form man with the help of education and proper laws. For the restoration of the natural order would be effected only as a result of a total change in man's actual nature. And so the natural identity of interests is completely over-shadowed by the postulate of their artificial identification.

Until now education had been left to chance and made the prey of false maxims. It was now time to remember that all felicity was the outcome of education. "Men have in their own hands the instrument of their greatness and their felicity, and . . . to be happy and powerful nothing more is requisite than to perfect the science of education." Legislators, moralists and natural scientists should combine to form man on the basis of their teachings, the conclusions of which converge upon the same point. Governments have it in their power to rear genius, to raise or lower the standard of ability in a nation. This, as Helvetius and Holbach insist, has nothing to do with climate or geography. Since human thought is so important for man's disposition towards the general good and towards his fellow citizens, and the harmonious pattern in general, it is only natural and necessary that a government should take a deep interest in shaping the ideas of men and exercise a censorship of ideas.

(c) THE NATURAL ORDER, THE LEGISLATOR, AND THE INDIVIDUAL

These ideas on self-interest and the power of education have strong political and social implications. As justice only has meaning in reference to social utility, it is clear that a just action is one that is useful to the greater number. It could thus be said that morality consists in the interest of the greater number. The greater number embodies justice. "It is evident," says Helvetius, "that justice is in its own nature always armed with a power sufficient to suppress vice, and place men under necessity of being virtuous." Why have the few, representing a minority and therefore an immoral interest, for so long dominated the greater number? Because of ignorance and misleading influences. The existing powers are interested in maintaining ignorance and in preventing the growth of genius and virtue. It is therefore clear that a reform of education could not take place without a change of political constitution. The art of forming man, in other words education, depends ultimately on the form of government.

Self-love as applied to the political sphere means the love of power. Political wisdom consists not in thwarting this natural instinct, but in giving it an outlet. The satisfaction of this urge like the satisfaction of man's legitimate self-interest is conducive to virtue. From this point of view democracy appears as the best system, as it satisfies the love of power of all or of most.

The totalitarian potentialities of this philosophy are not quite obvious at first sight. But they are nevertheless grave. The very idea of a self-contained system from which all evil and unhappiness have been exorcised is totalitarian. The assumption that such a scheme of things is feasible and indeed inevitable is an invitation to a régime to proclaim that it embodies this perfection, to exact from its citizens recognition and submission and to brand opposition as vice or perversion.

The greatest danger is in the fact that far from denying freedom and rights to man, far from demanding sacrifice and surrender, this system solemnly re-affirms liberty, man's self-interest and rights. It claims to have no other aims than their realization. Such a system is likely to become the more totalitarian, precisely because it grants everything in advance, because it accepts all liberal premises *a priori*. For it claims to be able by definition to satisfy them by a positive enactment as it were, not by leaving them alone and watching over them from the distance. When a régime is by definition regarded as realizing rights and freedoms, the citizen becomes deprived of any right to complain that he is being deprived of his rights and liberties. The earliest practical demonstration of this was given by Jacobinism.

Thus in the case of Rousseau his sovereign can demand from the citizen the total alienation of all his rights, goods, powers, person and life, and yet claim that there is no real surrender. In the very idea of retaining certain rights and staking out a claim against the sovereign there is, according to Rousseau, an implication of being at variance with the general will. The proviso that the general will could not require or exact a greater surrender than is inherent in the relationship between it and the subject does not alter the case, since it is left to the sovereign to decide what must be surrendered and what must not. Rousseau's sovereign, like the natural order, can by definition do nothing except secure man's freedom. It can have no reason or cause to hurt the citizen. For it to do so would be as impossible as it would be for something in the world of things to happen without a cause.

There is no need to insist that neither Helvetius, Holbach nor any one of their school envisaged brute force and undisguised coercion as instruments for the realization of the natural system. Nothing could have been further from their minds. Locke's three liberties figure prominently in all their social catechisms. They could not conceive any clash between the natural social pattern and the liberties, the real liberties, of man. The greater the freedom, the nearer, they believed, was the realization of the natural order. In the natural system there would simply be no need to restrict free expression. Opposition to the natural order would be unthinkable, except from fools or perverted individuals. The Physiocrats, for instance, were second to none in their insistence on a natural order of society " simple, constant, invariable and susceptible of being demonstrated by evidence ". Mercier de la Rivière preached " despotism of evidence " in human affairs. The absolute monarch was the embodiment of the " force naturelle et irrésistible de l'évidence ", which rules out any arbitrary action on the part of the administration. The Physiocrats insisted at the same time on the freedom of the press and the " full enjoyment " of natural rights by the individual. A government conducted on the basis of scientific evidence could only encourage a free press and individual freedom !

Eighteenth-century believers in a natural system failed to perceive that once a positive pattern is laid down, the liberties which are supposed to be attached to this pattern become restricted within its framework, and lose their validity and meaning outside it. The area outside the framework becomes mere chaos, to which the idea of liberty simply does not apply, and so it is possible to go on re-affirming liberty while denying it. Robespierre was only the first of the European revolutionaries who, having been an extreme defender of the freedom of the press under the old dispensation, turned into the bitterest persecutor of the opposition press once he came into power. For, to quote the famous sophism launched during the later period of the Revolution against the freedom of the press, the very demand for a free press when the Revolution is triumphant is counter-revolutionary. It implies freedom to fight the Revolution, for in order to support the Revolution there is no need for special permission.   And there can be no freedom to fight the Revolution.

On closer examination the idea of the natural order reaches the antithesis of its original individualism.   Although *prima facie* the individual is the beginning and the end of everything, in fact the Legislator is decisive.   He is called upon to shape man in accordance to a definite image.   The aim is not to enable men as they are to express themselves as freely and as fully as possible, to assert their uniqueness.   It is to create the right objective conditions and to educate men so that they would fit into the pattern of the virtuous society.

Chapter Three

TOTALITARIAN DEMOCRACY (ROUSSEAU)

(a) THE PSYCHOLOGICAL BACKGROUND

ROUSSEAU often uses the words nature and the natural order in the same sense as his contemporaries to indicate the logical structure of the universe. He also uses nature, however, to describe the elemental as opposed to the effort and achievement of the spirit in overcoming and subduing the elemental. The historical state of nature before organized society was the reign of the elemental. The inauguration of the social state marked the triumph of the spirit.

It must be repeated that to the materialists the natural order is, so to speak, a ready-made machine to be discovered and set to work. To Rousseau, on the other hand, it is the State, when it has fulfilled its purpose. It is a categorical imperative. The materialists reached the problem of the individual versus the social order only late in their argument. Even then, supremely confident of the possibility of mutual adjustment, they failed to recognize the existence of the problem of coercion. To Rousseau the problem exists from the beginning. It is indeed the fundamental problem to him.

A motherless vagabond starved of warmth and affection, having his dream of intimacy constantly frustrated by human callousness, real or imaginary, Rousseau could never decide what he wanted, to release human nature or to moralize it by breaking it ; to be alone or a part of human company. He could never make up his mind whether man was made better or worse, happier or more miserable, by people. Rousseau was one of the most ill-adjusted and ego-centric natures who have left a record of their predicament. He was a bundle of contradictions, a recluse and anarchist, yearning to return to nature, given to reverie, in revolt against all social conventions, sentimental and lacrimose, abjectly self-conscious and at odds with his environment, on the one hand ; and the admirer of Sparta and Rome, the preacher of discipline and the submergence of the individual in the collective entity, on the other. The secret of this dual personality was that the disciplinarian was the envious dream of the tormented paranoiac. The *Social Contract* was the sublimation of the *Discourse on the Origins of Inequality*. Rousseau speaks of his own predicament, when describing in *Émile* and elsewhere the unhappiness of man, who, after he left the state of nature, fell prey to the conflict between impulse and the duties of civilized society ; always " wavering between his inclinations and his duties ", neither quite man nor quite citizen, " no good to himself, nor to others ", because never in accord with himself. The only salvation from this agony, if a return to the untroubled state of nature was impossible, was either a complete self-abandonment to the elemental impulses or to " denature (*dénaturer*) man " altogether. It was in the latter case necessary to substitute a relative for an absolute existence, social consciousness for self-consciousness. Man must be made to regard himself not as a " unité numérique, l'entier absolu, qui n'a de rapport qu'à lui-même ", but as a " unité fonctionnaire qui tient au dénominateur et dont la valeur est dans son rapport avec l'entier, qui est le corps social ". A fixed rigid and universal pattern of feeling and behaviour was to be imposed in order to create man of one piece, without contradictions, without centrifugal and anti-social urges. The task was to create citizens who would will only what the general will does, and thus be free, instead of every man being an entity in himself, torn by egotistic tensions and thus enslaved. Rousseau, the teacher of romantic spontaneity of feeling, was obsessed with the idea of man's cupidity as the root cause of moral degeneration and social evil. Hence his apotheosis of Spartan ascetic virtue and his condemnation of civilization in so far as civilization is the expression of the urge to conquer, the desire to shine and the release of human vitality, without reference to morality. He had that intense awareness of the reality of human rivalry peculiar to people who have experienced it in their souls. Either out of a sense of guilt or out of weariness, they long to be delivered from the need for external recognition and the challenge of rivalry.

Three other representatives of the totalitarian Messianic temperament to be analysed in these pages show a similar paranoiac streak. They are Robespierre, Saint-Just and Babeuf. In recent times we have had examples of the strange combination of psychological ill-adjustment and totalitarian ideology. In some cases, salvation from the impossibility of finding a balanced relationship with fellow-men is sought in the lonely superiority of dictatorial leadership. The leader identifies himself with the absolute doctrine and the refusal of others to submit comes to be regarded not as a normal difference of opinion, but as a crime. It is characteristic of the paranoiac leader that when thwarted he is quickly thrown off his precarious balance and falls victim to an orgy of self-pity, persecution mania and the suicidal urge. Leadership is the salvation of the few, but to many even mere membership of a totalitarian movement and submission to the exclusive doctrine may offer a release from ill-adjusted egotism. Periods of great stress, of mass psychosis, and intense struggle call forth marginal qualities which otherwise may have remained dormant, and bring to the top men of a peculiar neurotic mentality.

(b) THE GENERAL WILL AND THE INDIVIDUAL

It was of vital importance to Rousseau to save the ideal of liberty, while insisting on discipline. He was very proud and had a keen sense of the heroic. Rousseau's thinking is thus dominated by a highly fruitful but dangerous ambiguity. On the one hand, the individual is said to obey nothing but his own will ; on the other, he is urged to conform to some objective criterion. The contradiction is resolved by the claim that this external criterion is his better, higher, or real self, man's inner voice, as Rousseau calls it. Hence, even if constrained to obey the external standard, man cannot complain of being coerced, for in fact he is merely being made to obey his own true self. He is thus still free ; indeed freer than before. For freedom is the triumph of the spirit over natural, elemental instinct. It is the acceptance of moral obligation and the disciplining of irrational and selfish urges by reason and duty. The acceptance of the obligations laid down in the Social Contract marks the birth of man's personality and his initiation into freedom. Every exercise of the general will constitutes a reaffirmation of man's freedom.

The problem of the general will may be considered from two points of view, that of individual ethics and that of political legitimacy. Diderot in his articles in the Encyclopædia on the *Législateur* and *Droit naturel* was a forerunner of Rousseau in so far as personal ethics are concerned. He conceived the problem in the same way as Rousseau : as the dilemma of reconciling freedom with an external absolute standard. It seemed to Diderot inadmissible that the individual as he is should be the final judge of what is just and unjust, right and wrong. The particular will of the individual is always suspect. The general will is the sole judge. One must always address oneself for judgment to the general good and the general will. One who disagrees with the general will renounces his humanity and classifies himself as " dénaturé ". The general will is to enlighten man " to what extent he should be man, citizen, subject, father or child ", " et quand il lui convient de vivre ou de mourir ". The general will shall fix the nature and limits of all our duties. Like Rousseau, Diderot is anxious to make the reservation in regard to man's natural and most sacred right to all that is not contested by the " species as a whole ". He nevertheless hastens, again like Rousseau, to add that the general will shall guide us on the nature of our ideas and desires. Whatever we think and desire will be good, great and sublime, if it is in keeping with the general interest. Conformity to it alone qualifies us for membership of our species : " ne la perdez donc jamais de vue, sans quoi vous verrez les notions de la bonté, de la justice, de l'humanité, de la vertu, chanceler dans votre entendement ". Diderot gives two definitions of the general will. He declares it first to be contained in the principles of the written law of all civilized nations, in the social actions of the savage peoples, in the conventions of the enemies of mankind among themselves and even in the instinctive indignation of injured animals. He then calls the general will " dans chaque individu un acte pur de l'entendement qui raisonne dans le silence des passions sur ce que l'homme peut exiger de son semblable et sur ce que son semblable est en droit d'exiger de lui ". This is also Rousseau's definition of the general will in the first version of the *Social Contract.*

Ultimately the general will is to Rousseau something like a mathematical truth or a Platonic idea. It has an objective existence of its own, whether perceived or not. It has nevertheless to be discovered by the human mind. But having discovered it, the human mind simply cannot honestly refuse to accept it. In this way the general will is at the same time outside us and within us. Man is not invited to express his personal preferences. He is not asked for his approval. He is asked whether the given proposal is or is not in conformity with the general will. " If my particular opinion had carried the day, I should have achieved the opposite of what was my will ; and it is in that case that I should not have been free." For freedom is the capacity of ridding oneself of considerations, interests, preferences and prejudices, whether personal or collective, which obscure the objectively true and good, which, if I am true to my true nature, I am bound to will. What applies to the individual applies equally to the people. Man and people have to be brought to choose freedom, and if necessary to be forced to be free.

The general will becomes ultimately a question of enlightenment and morality. Although it should be the achievement of the general will to create harmony and unanimity, the whole aim of political life is really to educate and prepare men to will the general will without any sense of constraint. Human egotism must be rooted out, and human nature changed. " Each individual, who is by himself a complete and solitary whole, would have to be transformed into part of a greater whole from which he receives his life and being." Individualism will have to give place to collectivism, egoism to virtue, which is the conformity of the personal to the general will. The Legislator " must, in a word, take away from man his resources and give him instead new ones alien to him, and incapable of being made use of without the help of other men. The more completely these natural resources are annihilated, the greater and the more lasting are those which he acquires, and the more stable and perfect the new institutions, so that if each citizen is nothing and can do nothing without the rest, and the resources acquired by the whole are equal or superior to the aggregate of the resources of all individuals, it may be said that legislation is at the highest possible point of perfection." As in the case of the materialists, it is not the self-expression of the individual, the deployment of his particular faculties and the realization of his own and unique mode of existence, that is the final aim, but the loss of the individual in the collective entity by taking on its colour and principle of existence. The aim is to train men to " bear with docility the yoke of public happiness ", in fact to create a new type of man, a purely political creature, without any particular private or social loyalties, any partial interests, as Rousseau would call them.

(c) THE GENERAL WILL, POPULAR SOVEREIGNTY, AND DICTATORSHIP

Rousseau's sovereign is the externalized general will, and, as has been said before, stands for essentially the same as the natural harmonious order. In marrying this concept with the principle of popular sovereignty, and popular self-expression, Rousseau gave rise to totalitarian democracy. The mere introduction of this latter element, coupled with the fire of Rousseau's style, lifted the eighteenth-century postulate from the plane of intellectual speculation into that of a great collective experience. It marked the birth of the modern secular religion, not merely as a system of ideas, but as a passionate faith. Rousseau's synthesis is in itself the formulation of the paradox of freedom in totalitarian democracy in terms which reveal the dilemma in the most striking form, namely, in those of will. There is such a thing as an objective general will, whether willed or not willed by anybody. To become a reality it must be willed by the people. If the people does not will it, it must be made to will it, for the general will is latent in the people's will.

Democratic ideas and rationalist premises are Rousseau's means of resolving the dilemma. According to him the general will would be discerned only if the whole people, and not a part of it or a representative body, was to make the effort. The second condition is that individual men as purely political atoms, and not groups, parties or interests, should be called upon to will. Both conditions are based upon the premise that there is such a thing as a common substance of citizenship, of which all partake, once everyone is able to divest himself of his partial interests and group loyalties. In the same way men as rational beings may arrive at the same conclusions, once they rid themselves of their particular passions and interests and cease to depend on "imaginary" standards which obscure their judgment. Only when all are acting together as an assembled people, does man's nature as citizen come into active existence. It would not, if only a part of the nation were assembled to will the general will. They would express a partial will. Moreover, even the fact that all have willed something does not yet make it the expression of the general will, if the right disposition on the part of those who will it was not there. A

will does not become general because it is willed by all, only when
it is willed in conformity to the objective will.

Exercise of sovereignty is not conceived here as the interplay
of interests, the balancing of views, all equally deserving a hearing,
the weighing of various interests. It connotes the endorsement of
a truth, self-identification on the part of those who exercise sovereignty with some general interest which is presumed to be the
fountain of all identical individual interests. Political parties are
not considered as vehicles of the various currents of opinion, but
representatives of partial interests, at variance with the general
interest, which is regarded as almost tangible. It is of great importance to realize that what is to-day considered as an essential
concomitant of democracy, namely, diversity of views and interests,
was far from being regarded as essential by the eighteenth-century
fathers of democracy. Their original postulates were unity and
unanimity. The affirmation of the principle of diversity came
later, when the totalitarian implications of the principle of homogeneity had been demonstrated in Jacobin dictatorship.

This expectation of unanimity was only natural in an age which,
starting with the idea of the natural order, declared war on all
privileges and inequalities. The very eighteenth-century concept
of the nation as opposed to estates implied a homogeneous entity.
Naïve and inexperienced in the working of democracy, the theorists
on the eve of the Revolution were unable to regard the strains and
stresses, the conflicts and struggles of a parliamentary democratic
régime as ordinary things, which need not frighten anybody with
the spectre of immediate ruin and confusion. Even so moderate
and level-headed a thinker as Holbach was appalled by the " terrible " cleavages in English society. He considered England the
most miserable country of all, ostensibly free, but in fact more
unhappy than any of the Oriental despot-ridden kingdoms. Had
not England been brought to the verge of ruin by the struggle of
factions and contradictory interests ? Was not her system a hotch-
potch of irrational habits, obsolete customs, incongruous laws, with
no system, and no guiding principle ? The physiocrat Letronne
declared that " the situation of France is infinitely better than that
of England ; for here reforms, changing the whole state of the
country, can be accomplished in a moment, whereas in England
such reforms can always be blocked by the party system ".

It is worth while devoting a few words to the Physiocrats at

sovereignty taken to the extreme, and totalitarianism. The paradox calls for analysis. It is commonly held that dictatorship comes into existence and is maintained by the indifference of the people and the lack of democratic vigilance. There is nothing that Rousseau insists on more than the active and ceaseless participation of the people and of every citizen in the affairs of the State.

The State is near ruin, says Rousseau, when the citizen is too indifferent to attend a public meeting. Saturated with antiquity, Rousseau intuitively experiences the thrill of the people assembled to legislate and shape the common weal. The Republic is in a continuous state of being born. In the pre-democratic age Rousseau could not realize that the originally deliberate creation of men could become transformed into a Leviathan, which might crush its own makers. He was unaware that total and highly emotional absorption in the collective political endeavour is calculated to kill all privacy, that the excitement of the assembled crowd may exercise a most tyrannical pressure, and that the extension of the scope of politics to all spheres of human interest and endeavour, without leaving any room for the process of casual and empirical activity, was the shortest way to totalitarianism. Liberty is safer in countries where politics are not considered all-important and where there are numerous levels of non-political private and collective activity, although not so much direct popular democracy, than in countries where politics take everything in their stride, and the people sit in permanent assembly.

In the latter the truth really is that, although all seem to be engaged in shaping the national will, and are doing it with a sense of elation and fulfilment, they are in fact accepting and endorsing something which is presented to them as a sole truth, while believing that it is their free choice. This is actually implied in Rousseau's image of the people willing the general will. The collective sense of elation is subject to emotional weariness. It soon gives way to apathetic and mechanical behaviour.

Rousseau is most reluctant to recognize the will of the majority, or even the will of all, as the general will. Neither does he give any indication by what signs the general will could be recognized. Its being willed by the people does not make the thing willed the expression of the general will. The blind multitude does not know what it wants, and what is its real interest. "Left to themselves, the People always desire the good, but, left to themselves, they do

not always know where that good lies. The general will is alway;
right, but the judgment guiding it is not always well informed.
It must be made to see things as they are, sometimes as they ought
to appear to them."

(d) THE GENERAL WILL AS PURPOSE

The general will assumes thus the character of a purpose and as
such lends itself to definition in terms of social-political ideology,
a pre-ordained goal, towards which we are irresistibly driven ; a
solely true aim, which we will, or are bound to will, although we
may not will it yet, because of our backwardness, prejudices,
selfishness or ignorance.

In this case the idea of a people becomes naturally restricted to
those who identify themselves with the general will and the
general interest. Those outside are not really of the nation. They
are aliens. This conception of the nation (or people) was soon to
become a powerful political argument. Thus Sieyès claimed that
the Third Estate alone constituted the nation. The Jacobins restricted
the term still further, to the *sans-culottes*. To Babeuf the proletariat alone was the nation, and to Buonarroti only those who had
been formally admitted to the National Community.

The very idea of an assumed preordained will, which has not
yet become the actual will of the nation ; the view that the nation
is still therefore in its infancy, a " young nation ", in the nomenclature of the *Social Contract*, gives those who claim to know and
to represent the real and ultimate will of the nation—the party of
the vanguard—a blank cheque to act on behalf of the people, without reference to the people's actual will. And this, as we hope
later on to show it has, may express itself in two forms or rather
two stages : one—the act of revolution ; and the other—the effort
at enthroning the general will. Those who feel themselves to be
the real people rise against the system and the men in power, who
are not of the people. Moreover, the very act of their insurrection,
e.g. the establishment of a Revolutionary (or Insurrectionary)
Committee, abolishes *ipso facto* not only the parliamentary representative body, which is in any case, according to Rousseau, a
standing attempt on the sovereignty of the people, but indeed all
existing laws and institutions. For " the moment the people is

legitimately assembled as a sovereign body, the jurisdiction of the government wholly lapses, the executive power is suspended, and the person of the meanest citizen is as sacred and inviolable as that of the first magistrate ; for in the presence of the person represented, representatives no longer exist ".   The real people, or rather their leadership, once triumphant in their insurrection, become Rousseau's Legislator, who surveys clearly the whole panorama, without being swayed by partial interests and passions, and shapes the " young nation " with the help of laws derived from his superior wisdom.   He prepares it to will the general will.   First comes the elimination of men and influences not of the people and not identified with the general will embodied in the newly established Social Contract of the Revolution ; then the re-education of the young nation to will the general will.   The task of the Legislator is to create a new type of man, with a new mentality, new values, a new type of sensitiveness, free from old instincts, prejudices and bad habits.   It is not enough to change the machinery of government, or even reshuffle the classes.   You have to change human nature, or, in the terminology of the eighteenth century, to make man virtuous.

Rousseau represents the most articulate form of the *esprit révolutionnaire* in each of its facets.   In the *Discourse on Inequality* he expresses the burning sense of a society that has gone astray. In the *Social Contract* he postulates an exclusively legitimate social system as a challenge to human greatness.

Chapter Four

PROPERTY (MORELLY AND MABLY)

(*a*) PREMISES AND CONCLUSIONS—THE DISCREPANCY

THE idea of the natural social pattern as analysed in the foregoing pages must appear unsatisfactory. It is an abstract postulate, a shell without contents ; nothing but a form. The social and economic concreteness, which alone could give it a substance, has been missing from the analysis.

There has been much controversy on the amount of socialism in eighteenth-century thought. Some have found fully fledged socialism in it, others not a great deal of socialism, or no hint of socialism at all. The truly remarkable feature of eighteenth-century thinking is not the presence or absence of socialism, but the discrepancy between the boldness of the premises and the timidity of the practical conclusions, where the problem of property was concerned. The Marxist historian may well feel justified in pointing out that this discrepancy was due to the bourgeois background of the writers. They appealed to a sole principle of social existence, and to the equality inherent in natural rights, against the privileges of the feudal classes. They beat a retreat, when this political and philosophical postulate proved to carry with it a threat to property. When speaking of Man, it did not occur to some of our thinkers that the " canaille " was included in the term. Some even emphatically rejected the idea. Only the bourgeois was Man. Those beneath him were too ignorant, too brutalized, had too little share in maintaining society, to be counted at all.

And yet, the socialist dynamism in the idea of the natural system can hardly be denied. The very idea of a natural, rational order carried with it the implication of an orderly social pattern, unless it be held, as the Physiocrats did hold, that free economics are the very essence of the natural order, since they are bound in the end to result in perfect harmony. In the idea of the rights of Man, in the conception of the individual Man as the first and last

50

element of the social edifice, there was inherent the implication that all existing forms and interests may and should be upset and entirely reshaped, so as to give Man his due. On these principles property could not be regarded as a sacred natural right to be taken for granted. Everything could be remodelled at any time. The argument was not, as it used to be, that the poor and unfortunate citizen has a right to expect succour from the paternal royal Government, and in order to bring it the Government may override any interests. Man in the natural order does not ask for charity, he is the focus of the whole social and economic system.

The egalitarian idea condemned unequal classes and privileges as an evil that came into existence in contradiction to the teachings of Nature and the needs of Man. Some writers went so far as to brand the existing State and all its legislation as a weapon of exploitation and a ruse of the haves to hold down the have-nots. Furthermore, if virtue was conformity to the natural pattern, its greatest enemy was clearly the spirit of selfish avarice engendered by private property.

Not only avowed Communists like Morelly and Mably, but also Rousseau, Diderot and Helvetius were agreed that " all these evils are the first effect of property and of the array of evils inseparable from the inequality to which it gave birth ". Diderot contrasted the " esprit de propriété " with the " esprit de communauté ". He admonished the Legislator to combat the former and to foster the latter, if his aim were to make man's personal will identical with the general will. Rousseau's eloquent passage on the first man who enclosed a plot of land with a fence, deceived his neighbours into the belief in the legality of his act, and thus became the author of all the wars, rivalries, social evils and demoralization in the world, is not more radical than Morelly's and Mably's obsessive insistence that property is the root cause of all that has gone wrong in history.

Rousseau's condemnation of the laws as an instrument of the rich to make the poor accept exploitation and misery is a counterpart of Helvetius's statement that " the excessive luxury, which almost everywhere accompanies despotism, presupposes a nation already divided into oppressors and oppressed, into thieves and those robbed. But if the thieves form only a very small number, why do not they succumb "—Helvetius asks—" to the efforts of the greatest number ? To what do they owe their success ? To the

impossibility to make common causes (' se donner le mot ') in which
the robbed ones find themselves."

Helvetius was on common ground with most of his contemporaries, when he claimed that only a régime of State ownership, with
money banished, offered a possibility of a legislation, stable and
unalterable, calculated to preserve general happiness. He added his
own utilitarian gloss. If it be true that man is motivated by self-
interest alone, he will in a country of powerful private interests be
naturally attracted to serve those interests, instead of the national
interests. Where the nation is the sole distributor of rewards, a
person would have no need to serve any other interest than the
national. In Rousseauist theory " the State by the reason of the
Social Contract is the master of all its members' goods ", since
every citizen on entering the Social Contract has surrendered all his
property to the State. He received it back to hold it as trustee of
the Commonwealth, but his rights and powers are always subordinated to the overriding claim of the community. Rousseau
would actually have wished to see all property concentrated in the
hands of the State, and no individual admitted to any share of the
common stock " save in proportion to his services ". Rousseau
would have arranged that with the demise of the owner all his
property should escheat to the State. He proposes in the *Projet
de Constitution pour le Corse* the establishment of a large public
domain. The State would alienate holdings to private citizens
for a number of years on a trust. Government land would be
cultivated by a system of *corvées*.

All these ideas, however, were contradicted by the very writers
who put them forward. Rousseau, Helvetius and Mably con-
curred that private property had become the cement of the social
order, and the foundation stone of the Social Contract. Helvetius
called private property " le droit le plus sacré . . . dieu moral des
empires ". The inconsistency is the most flagrant in the case of
Mably, whose manner of wrestling with it is, in spite of his extremism,
representative of the school as a whole.

(b) MORELLY, THE COMMUNIST

The only consistent Communist among the eighteenth-century
thinkers was Morelly. According to him, avarice, " cette peste

universelle . . . cette fièvre lente ", would never have come into being, if there had been no private property. All trouble in the world is born either of cupidity or of insecurity. If all goods were in common, and nobody had anything in particular, there would be no irritant for cupidity, and no fear of insecurity. All would naturally have worked for the common good, obeying their natural desire for personal happiness, and inevitably contributing to the happiness of others. " Ôtez la propriété aveugle et l'impitoyable intérêt qui l'accompagne . . . plus de passions furieuses, plus d'actions féroces, plus de notions, plus d'idées de mal moral." Every moral, social and political evil is due to property, and no remedy short of the abolition of private property was possible. It is no use blaming accident or fate for the troubled conditions of states and empires. In the state of nature, where there is no private property, everything works with the regularity and precision of a clock.

Morelly regards Communism as a practical proposition. This gives a peculiar complexion to his approach to the question of compulsion to induce man to conform to the general good. He recognizes that a transitional régime of " some severity " may be necessary to restore the natural Communist order. There is, however, no violence involved, he claims, in an attempt to bring man back to nature, which means to his true nature. The argument that human nature, as it has come to be under the influence of civilization and evil circumstances, cannot be changed, is false. This deformed, distorted nature of man is not his real nature. Nature, like truth, is constant and invariable. It does not alter because man has turned his back on it. The truth is that Morelly confuses liberty with security. Liberty, furthermore, is achieved according to him not in privacy or nonconformity, but in co-operation and in fitting into the collective whole so that the machine as a whole functions smoothly. The author of *Code de la Nature* firmly upholds the creed of Theodicy. Providence could not have delivered humanity to eternal chaos and hazard. There must be a conclusion after a long period of trial and error. This Messianic conclusion will be the Communist state of nature.

Morelly is one of the very few Utopian Communists who were not ascetics. In a striking passage he rebuffed Rousseau, without mentioning him by name, for his condemnation of the arts and civilization as producing immorality. He called Rousseau a cynical sophist. The arts have ennobled our existence. If they had also contributed to our deterioration, this was due solely to their association with the "principe venimeux de toute corruption morale, qui infecte tout ce qu'il touche".

Morelly's Communist vision of the perfect society presupposes spiritual totalitarianism, in addition to perfect planning. The system of production and consumption would be based on public stores to which all produce would be brought, and from which it would be distributed according to needs. There would be an overall plan. Every city would fix the number of those who should take up a particular branch of science or art. No other moral philosophy would be taught than that which forms the basis of the laws. This social philosophy will have as its foundations the utility and wisdom of the laws, the "sweetness of the bonds of blood and friendship", the services and the mutual obligations which the citizens owe to each other, the love and usefulness of labour, and the rules of good order and concord. "Toute métaphysique se réduira à ce qui a été précédamment dit de la Divinité." Speculative and experimental sciences would be free, but moral philosophy "retranché". "There will be one kind of public code of all sciences, to which nothing will ever be added in what concerns metaphysics and ethics beyond the limits prescribed by the laws; added will be only physical, mathematical and mechanical discoveries confirmed by experience and reason." Laws would be engraved on obelisks, pyramids and public squares. They would be followed literally, without the slightest alteration being permitted.

(c) MABLY AND ASCETIC VIRTUE

Mably worked on the same premises and arrived at the same Communist conclusions as Morelly. But only in theory. While Morelly was a convinced optimist, Mably was a man of a morose pessimistic nature. His thinking was hampered and his position made most difficult by the hard core of his catholicism. The juxtaposition of catholicism and eighteenth-century categories of thought make Mably a singularly interesting case. His whole attitude was determined by a secularized idea of the fall of man and original sin. Hence his fundamental distinction between the ideally and solely true and just, and the half-truths, the semi-justice and the palliatives of the world in which, for our sins, we are destined to live. Like a medieval moralist he wrote : " si notre avarice, notre vanité et notre ambition sont des obstacles insurmontables à un bien parfait, subissons sans murmurer la peine que nous méritons." Mably was a Messianic type gone sour. If the element of original sin is left out, Mably easily qualifies as a prophet of Communist Messianism, and in fact he became the prophet of Babouvism.

For Mably there is always in the background the vision of an ideal social harmony of egalitarian Communism projected into the golden age of a remote past or into the realm of a natural and a solely valid scheme of things. It is never quite clear whether the sinful disposition of man destroyed the original harmony, or whether the destruction of this harmony by private property and inequality has ruined man's innocence. Mably not only does not consider the original natural community of goods a chimera, but claims never to have ceased to be surprised that men abandoned that state at all. He can see nothing in mankind's history since then but one everlasting Walpurgis of the passions, of greed and avarice above all. This is a constant theme in his writings and is elaborated *ad nauseam* on every occasion. Although admitting that without the driving power of passion, nothing positive would ever have been achieved, Mably only reluctantly considers the passions as releasing creative forces, and seldom acknowledges the mystery, or what Hegel was to call " die List der Vernunft ", that evil ingredients are inseparable from the process of achieving good things. As if foreshadowing psychoanalysis, and following Hume, Mably seeks all motives of human action in dark urges, aggressive impulses, irrational aversions and inhibitions. Reason is always the handmaid of the passions. Conscious ideas and alleged evidence are at bottom rationalizations of our irrational urges. " The passions are so eloquent, so lively and so active that they need no evidence to convince our reason, or to force reason to become their accomplice." " Elles bravent même l'évidence." The most imperious, indeed the common denominator, of all passions is self-love. A benevolent instinct in the state of nature, since the establishment of inequality and private property, self-love has erected a barrier between man and man, and when it seems to bring us together, it is only in order to arm one against the other.

This state of things would continue until a " community of goods and equality of conditions has imposed a silence upon them ". This is the only arrangement that can destroy those particular interests which will always triumph over the general interest. Equality alone, without a community of goods, would be ephemeral, giving place within two or three generations to the same glaring inequalities, misery on the one hand, and luxury and exploitation on the other. But as this " plus haut degré de perfection " can hardly be expected, there is need to fix a régime for mankind in the state of sin. The first condition of some order in this sinful state is respect for property. Mably emphatically disclaims any intention of raising a " sacrilegious hand " against private property, under the pretext of producing the " great good ". In the early days all that tended to loosen the natural community of goods, and directly or indirectly to introduce private property, was an unmitigated crime. Once private property had been established, however, any law is wise which deprives the passions of every means or pretext of hurting or endangering the rights of property in the slightest degree. In the state of sin attacks on property are no less an expression of cupidity than the love of property.

Mably thus becomes entangled in the gravest incongruities and contradictions. Property is the source of all evil, and yet he would protect it. In common with all eighteenth-century thinkers he takes human self-love for granted and man's desire for happiness as the basis for all social arrangements. He is at the same time deeply suspicious and contemptuous of human nature. Like his contemporaries he is a determinist, but at the same time overwhelmed by the anarchy and unpredictability of human passions. The outcome of these contradictions is the egalitarian Jacobin idea of ascetic virtue equated with happiness, and a thoroughly restrictive conception of economics. Man should be made happy. But happiness is not to Mably a release of vitality, but—a phrase destined to become a favourite with Robespierre, Saint-Just and Babeuf—" bonheur de médiocrité " ; " Nature has but one happiness in spite of the vagaries of societies ", and this it offers equally to all men. Resorting to psychological determinism, Mably declares that the fixing of an equal quantity of happiness is made possible by the essential likeness of human passions and similarity of their inevitable effects. He believes in " an art of government fixed, determinate and unchangeable, since the nature of man, whose happiness is the scope of policy, is connected with and depends on a fixed, determinate and unchangeable principle ". The safest road to happiness is the sentiment of equality, just as the sole criterion by which the laws should be judged is their contribution to the establishment of equality.

Men and nations are under the same law : every type of hubris, be it exaggerated ambition or an over-great success, must end in ruin. And so the greatest happiness is to Mably the tranquillity of the soul, with passions at rest ; the wisest policy—moderation and frugality ; and the greatest strength—mediocrity that goes without ambition and scheming.

In order to make man happy, the State must imbue him with the sentiment of virtuous equality. It must " regulate the movements of your heart ", to make you " contract honest habits, and defend your reason against the blows of your passions ". Legislation must keep our passions " under strict subjection, and by thus strengthening the sovereignty of reason, give a superior activity to the virtues ". All legislation must start with a reform of morals. The supreme task of government is to employ the sacred violence which tears us away from under the sway of the passions. Mably's moral asceticism leads him to a denial of the value of culture. " A community which maintains moral purity will never allow the invention of new arts." To Mably the progress of the arts is tantamount to the progress of vice, and the work of artists is pandering to the caprices and vices of the rich and ostentatious. In all artistic endeavour Mably can see nothing else than a colossal waste of skill, effort and genius—and all to arouse a dangerous admiration. Hardly another thinker in modern times preached the doctrine of the incompatibility of the good and the beautiful with the same vehemence as this morose Abbé. " When I think ", he writes, " how disastrous all the agreeable accomplishments had been to the Athenians, how much injustice, violence and tyranny were inflicted upon the Romans by the pictures, statues and vases of Greece, I ask myself what use we have for an Academy of Fine Arts. Let the Italians believe that their ' babioles ' are an honour to a nation. Let people come to seek models of laws, manners and happiness among us, and not of painting."

Rousseau and Mably agreed that there was nothing more dangerous than vice when brilliant. As could be expected, Mably's ideas on education are Spartan. The Republic should take away children from under the exclusive tutelage of their parents. Otherwise there is bound to arise a diversity of manners which would militate against equality. Mably thinks that as most people are

" condemned to the permanent infancy of their reason ", being moved by " an instinct a little less coarse than that of the animals ", it would be dangerous to allow a free press or full religious toleration, until men were mature enough for it. It is true that freedom of thought could not flourish under censorship. But it would only be safe to grant freedom of discussion to the learned, for their errors would be no danger to society, and would only stimulate discussion. It was an error on the part of the newly-established United States of America to grant freedom of political expression to its people, still so much imbued with the bad ideas and habits of the Old World. And yet Mably would not agree that he was advocating a system of oppression. He wrote in the best eighteenth-century fashion that the aim of society was nothing else than to preserve for all men the rights which they hold from " the generous hands of nature ". The Legislator had no other commission than to impose duties which it was essential for everyone to carry out. " You will easily perceive how important it is to study the natural law . . . the law of equality among men. Without such study, morality, without certain principles, would run the risk of erring at every step." Mably claimed to be a staunch upholder of the dignity of man, which should be " inviolably respected " in every human being. Similarly Rousseau, having laid down a blueprint of a totalitarian régime for Corsica, triumphantly concludes that the measures prescribed by him will secure to the Corsicans all possible freedom, since nothing would be demanded of them which is not postulated by nature.

(d) RESTRICTIONIST ECONOMICS

As applied to economics this philosophy of virtuous happiness means ascetic restrictionism. Here Mably found himself on common ground with other contemporaries. If you cannot abolish property, you must watch over it. " La propriété . . . ouvre la porte à cent vices et à cent abus," wrote Mably, " il est donc prudent que des lois rigides veillent à cette porte." Rousseau claimed for the State the right and power " to give it (property) a standard, a rule, a curb to restrain it, direct it, subdue it and keep it always subordinate to the public good ". He wished the individual to be as independent as possible of his neighbour, and as dependent as possible on the State. Precisely because the individual has the supreme right to a secure existence, the State must have both the means of securing it, and the power of putting a check on those who claim or attempt to have more than their due by robbing others. Rousseau supplied Babeuf with his main catchword, when he commanded the State to see to it that all have enough and nobody more than enough.

Hardly any of the thinkers with whom we are concerned thought of economics in terms of expansion and increase of wealth and comfort. Their primary consideration was egalitarian social harmony, and the defence of the poor. Derived from this was something like the medieval monk's fear of the *appetitus divitiarum infinitis*, the anti-social passion, which kills the virtuous love of the general good. This expressed itself in two ways, in the demand for restricting the size of property by legislation, and in the outspoken condemnation of the rising industrial and commercial civilization. Mably wanted large fortunes to be continually broken up by legislation. He wished to fix a maximum of property to be allowed to a citizen, and also preached the idea of an agrarian law : the redistribution of the land on an egalitarian basis. Rousseau taught that no citizen should be so rich as to be able to buy up another, and none so poor as to have to sell himself. He advocated a progressive income tax to check the growth of fortunes and, like Mably, was in favour of taxing luxury as heavily as possible. There is no more baffling feature in French eighteenth-century social philosophy than the almost total lack of presentiment or understanding of the new forces about to be released by the Industrial Revolution. Few saw in the expansion of trade and industry a promise of increased national prosperity. Most treated it as the excrescence of the acquisitive spirit on the part of a small, selfish and unscrupulous class ; not a possibility of improvement for the workers, but a new way of degrading and enslaving them. All were agreed in considering the people on the land as the backbone of the nation, indeed the nation itself. Rousseau thought that an agricultural society was the natural home of liberty, and Holbach believed that only those who owned land could be considered citizens. Rousseau wanted the " colon " to lay down the law for the industrial worker. In his famous speech on England Robespierre took it for granted that the English nation of merchants must be morally inferior to the agricultural French people.

All feared and despised commerce, big capital cities and urban civilization in general. Rousseau called industry " cette partie trop favorisée ". Holbach saw in commerce a social enemy. All the recent wars, he claimed, had been caused by the greed of commercial interests and had as their aim markets and the advantage of a small part of the nation. " The capitalists and big merchants have no fatherland ! " was the universal cry. They pay no heed to the national interest, their sole consideration is private, anti-social profit. " Négociants avides et qui n'ont d'autre patrie que leurs coffres." " La tranquilité, l'aisance, les intérêts les plus chers d'un état sont imprudemment sacrifiés à la passion d'enrichir un petit nombre d'individus." All this happens because the money that commerce brings in is regarded as an instrument of power and happiness. All forget the inflation caused by the surplus of money, and the people's hardships that ensue from it. National credit is one of the most pernicious inventions. " Rien n'est plus destructeur pour les mœurs d'un peuple que l'esprit de finance." The memory of the Law disaster and other financial and commercial scandals was still fresh. Far from desiring to extend man's personality by inspiring him with new aspirations and needs, far from seeing the value of civilization in diversity and variety, most eighteenth-century political writers —moralists in the first place—condemned industry and commerce for precisely provoking new and " imaginary needs ", and stirring up man's caprices : " désirs extravagants . . . fantaisies bizarres d'un tas de désœuvrés." Mably coupled in this condemnation also the arts and crafts. He saw " millions of artisans occupied with stirring up our passions ", and providing us with things which we would be only too happy not to have heard of. And here Mably, the fanatical egalitarian, and preacher of the sacred dignity of man, makes the astonishing suggestion that the whole class of artisans and workers should be excluded from the right to exercise national sovereignty, " espèces d'esclaves du public . . . qui sont sans fortune, et qui, ne subsistant que par leur industrie, n'appartiennent en quelque sorte à aucune société ". These classes are condemned to cater for the vices and caprices of the rich, they depend on the favours of their employers, and thus are too debased and too ignorant to partake in the formation of the national will. They lack the dignity, independence and freedom necessary for a Legislator, and have no interest in the maintenance of the social framework. Holbach wrote in almost precisely the same terms. Mably urged

the Legislator to deal with the " slaving " classes kindly, for otherwise they may easily become the enemies of society.

Mirabeau complained that all attention was being paid to the
large factories called " manufactures réunies ", where hundreds of
workers would work under a single director, and hardly any thought
to the so very numerous workers and artisans working on their own.
" C'est une très grande erreur, car les derniers font seuls un objet de
prospérité nationale vraiment important ". The "fabrique réunie "
may enrich one or two entrepreneurs, but the workers in it
will for ever remain wage earners neither concerned with nor
benefiting from the factory as such. In a " fabrique séparée " no
one will get rich, but many a worker will be comfortably off, and
a few industrious ones may manage to collect a little capital. Their
example will stimulate others to economy and effort, and thus help
them towards advancement. A slight rise in the wages of a factory
worker is of no consequence to the national economy : " elles ne
seront jamais un objet digne de l'intérêt des lois."

No one was so radical in his demand for State control and
interference with trade as Mably. He particularly advocated control
of the corn trade, and thus made an important contribution to the
discussion before and during the Revolution on this most vital
sector of the French economy. Like Rousseau, he loathed foreign
trade. Its sole motives were greed and luxury. It destroyed the
righteous spirit of the virtuous Republic set up by Calvin, for
Calvin's Geneva and Sparta were Mably's and Rousseau's inspiration. As moral and political considerations were to them at bottom
the same, they viewed economic, especially commercial, expansion
as a peril not only to morals, but also to liberty. Mably regarded
commerce as " essentiellement contraire à l'esprit de tout bon
gouvernement ". Encourage avarice and luxury under the pretext
of favouring commerce, and all laws that you make to strengthen
your liberty would not prevent you from becoming slaves.

Mably defiantly asserts that the effect of all his restrictions will
be to benumb and enfeeble (engourdir) men. " C'est ce que je
souhaite, si par cet engourdissement on entend l'habitude qu'ils
contracteront de ne rien désirer au-delà de ce que la Loi leur permet
de posséder." As to the objection that some people would rather
flee the country than submit to laws engendering torpor, Mably's
answer is that those whose passions are too strong to obey salutary
laws had better go soon, as they are enemies of the Republic, its

laws and its morals. " But nobody will flee ; the tyranny of a government and magistrates sometimes drive out people, but just laws, on the contrary, attach them to their country by dint of their austerity."

And so once more the theory has come full circle. The postulate of liberty should have suggested the release of spontaneity. Instead, we are faced with the idea of the State acting as the chief regulator, with the purpose of enforcing ascetic austerity. The initial and permanent aim was to satisfy man's self-interest, acclaimed as the main and laudable motive of action, and at the end a brake is imposed on all human initiative. Liberty has been overcome by equality and virtue ; spontaneity and the revolt against traditional restrictions, by the postulate of the natural social harmony. There is the same incongruity in eighteenth-century economic thinking as there is in its approach to political ethics. Eighteenth-century thinkers spoke the language of individualism, while their pre-occupation with the general interest, the general good and the natural system led to collectivism. They did not intend men to submit obediently to an external principle standing on its own, but so to mould man that he would freely come to think that principle his own. The same applies to the social-economic sphere. The writers in question certainly abhorred the idea of industrial concentration, and the vision of great multitudes of workers under the umbrella of a large State-owned or private concern. That meant slavery and the degradation of man's dignity. They wanted to see as many as possible, all if possible, become free and independent small farmers and artisans. Even Communists, like Morelly and Mably, considered economic organization in terms of contributions by individual producers to the public stores, and the distribution of the products to the individual consumers. Eighteenth-century thinkers wished somehow to combine étatism and individualism, with the State acting as a brake upon excesses of inequality, or as regulator and provider, or as the guarantor of social security to the poor and weak. They lived before the age of large-scale industry and industrial centralization. Few of them also had any feeling for the image of a nation engaged in a mighty productive effort. Man was primarily a moral being to them. Of the major Revolutionary figures Sieyès and Barnave were the first to think in terms of a collective productive effort. The industrial expansion under Napoleon and the Restoration alone gave a great impetus to this line of thought.

And yet, the eighteenth-century restrictionist attitude, essentially sterile and reactionary, is less interesting and less important for what it says than for what it fails to say. It fails to run out its course, it halts timidly in the middle. Impelled by a revolutionary impetus of total renovation, and by the idea of a society reconstructed deliberately with a view to a logical and final pattern, it nevertheless shrinks from throwing into the melting-pot the basis of social relations, property. Eighteenth-century thinkers did much to undermine the sanctity of property, and to make the State the chief arbiter in the economic life. They shrank from drawing the final conclusions and tried to be as conservative as possible. But the impetus of the idea was too strong. The French Revolution came with its Messianic call and its economic and social strains and stresses. The awakened masses, carried along by the idea of universal happiness, could not grasp why the Revolution should be only political and not social. They could not understand why the Legislator, so omnipotent in all other spheres, should not have the power to subdue the selfishness of the rich and to feed the poor, and in general should not be able to solve the social problem on the pattern of the natural scheme and in accordance with the "necessity of things". The very idea of democracy appeared to imply an ever closer approximation to economic equality. A purely formal political democracy, without social levelling, had no meaning in the eighteenth century, brought up as it was on the ideas of antiquity. It was a later product. Jacobin dictatorship was caught unprepared by these whirlwinds. It had to improvise a half-way house. Carried on by the Messianic urge and their vague vision, the Jacobins, like their eighteenth-century teachers, lacked the courage to make a frontal attack on the property system. This is why the "reign of virtue" postulated by them appears so unsatisfactory and so elusive an ideal as almost to be meaningless, and why the dictatorial social and economic policies which necessity imposed upon them were adopted by them with so much reluctance. Nobody realized better than Saint-Just that an irresistible dynamism was driving the Jacobins into a direction of which they had hardly dreamt in the beginning.

As we shall see, Babeuf and Buonarroti discovered that the

Jacobin half-way house was a heart-break house. It was necessary to go the whole way towards a State-owned and State-directed economy. The solution of the economic problem was the condition of the Jacobin Republic of Virtue. The Thermidorian reaction learned a similar lesson from Jacobin dictatorship, but drew the opposite conclusions : property must become the rock of the social edifice, and social welfare must be put outside the scope of state politics.

It may be said that the French Revolution followed stage by stage the teachings of Mably, but in a reverse order. Out of his despair of ever seeing the solely valid Communist system established, Mably developed a whole series of practical policies for the state of sin, which had a deep influence upon the course of the Revolution. Babouvism was a Mablyist conclusion derived from the failure of these policies, when tried, to solve the problems of society, and a vindication of Mably's original promise that all reforms would be ineffective without the abolition of property. Only, while Mably thought the latter a hopeless dream, Babeuf and his followers resolved that the Revolutionary changes had brought it into the realm of practical politics, and that the failure of the Revolutionary palliatives had indeed made it inescapable.

Mably's political thinking—a subject not within the scope of this work as such—could be presented as a series of layers, each of which corresponded to and inspired a particular phase of the Revolution. He laid down a prophetic blue-print of the initial stage of the Revolution. Accepting the division of society into estates and classes as an unavoidable evil as long as men could not " all be brothers ", he foretold that by reasserting their particular interests and liberties the various orders would isolate and weaken royal despotism. The Parliaments would become the " anchor of salvation ", and the crisis forced by them would compel the King to summon the Estates General. These would establish themselves as a National Assembly meeting at fixed periods.

The *Constituante* learnt from Mably the principle of the absolute supremacy of the Legislature over a weak, despised and always suspect royal executive ; and the sacredness of the principle of parliamentary representation, direct democracy having been rejected by Mably as a régime which gives rein to an anarchical, capricious and ignorant multitude. The Jacobins took from Mably, not less than from Rousseau, their idea of virtuous, egalitarian happiness.

On the very eve of Thermidor Saint-Just brings with him copies of Mably to the Committee of Public Safety, and distributes them among his colleagues, the other dictators of Revolutionary France, in order to win them over definitely for his plan of enthroning virtue, and thereby completing and insuring the regeneration of the French people, and the emergence of a new type of society. Finally, Babouvism adopted Mably's Communism, while the post-Thermidorian régime based the exclusion of the propertyless from political life also on Mably's precepts.

PART II
THE JACOBIN IMPROVISATION

Mais elle existe, je vous en atteste, âmes sensibles et pures ; elle existe, cette passion tendre, impérieuse, irrésistible, tourment et délices de cœurs magnanimes, cette horreur profonde de la tyrannie, ce zèle compatissant pour les opprimés, cet amour sacré de la patrie, cet amour plus sublime et plus saint de l'humanité, sans lequel une grande révolution n'est qu'un crime éclatant qui détruit un autre crime ; elle existe, cette ambition généreuse de fonder sur la terre la première République du monde ; cet égoïsme des hommes non dégradés, qui trouve une volupté céleste dans le calme d'une conscience pure et dans le spectacle ravissant du bonheur public. Vous le sentez, en ce moment, qui brûle dans vos âmes ; je le sens dans la mienne.

ROBESPIERRE

Chapter One

THE REVOLUTION OF 1789—SIEYÈS

(*a*) THE REVOLUTIONARY ATTITUDE

ON the threshold of the French Revolution the Revolutionary forces found their chief spokesman in Sieyès. The author of the most successful political pamphlet of all time—the Communist Manifesto, whatever its delayed influence, had little effect when it appeared—summed up eighteenth-century political philosophy with a view to immediate and practical application. For the first time in modern history, and perhaps in history altogether, a political pamphlet was consciously and enthusiastically seized upon by statesmen and politicians, indeed by public opinion in the widest sense of the word, as a complete guide to action ; not just as an analysis of reality by an acute mind, containing wise reflections and stimulating ideas, the way in which a political pamphlet would have been treated in the past. This in itself was an event of incalculable importance.

It was a signal of the new importance acquired by ideas as historic agents. In the past ideas mattered little as factors in political change. Deeply rooted respect for tradition and precedent worked for stability and continuity. Under a traditional monarchy the administration was recruited from the aristocracy, or civil service families. Government was a question of management by those to whom it was a traditional occupation. With the replacement of tradition by abstract reason, ideology and doctrine became all-important. The ideologists came to the fore.

Moreover, ideas had reached the masses. Statistics have been adduced to show that the works of the philosophers were neither widely distributed nor widely read in the years before the Revolution, and the influence of eighteenth-century ideas upon the Revolution has been seriously questioned. On becoming acquainted with the Revolutionary literature one is almost tempted to answer that statistics is no science. The prevalence of philosophical canon books in libraries or the number of their actual readers is in reality no index to their influence. How many people in our own days have actually read the *Capital* of Marx or the works of Freud ? Few however would deny that the ideas propagated in these books have entered contemporary thinking and experience to a degree that defies measurement. There is such a thing as a climate of ideas, as ideas in the air. Such ideas reach the half-literate and semi-articulate second, third or even fourth hand. They nevertheless create a general state of mind. Tocqueville found many references to the " rights of man " and the " natural order " in peasant *cahiers*.

From the point of view of this enquiry Sieyès's writings of 1788–9 deserve special attention in that they embody the Revolutionary eighteenth-century philosophy as a still undivided complex. There is no explicit suggestion of a fissure yet. The schism into two types of democracy was to develop soon. The question is whether Sieyès's pamphlets of that period suggest the possibility of a split, and whether one can discern in them a tension between incompatible elements. This is not an easy question to answer. It requires a good deal of detachment. Sieyès's ideas of the early period of the Revolution have become part and parcel of Western European consciousness and have entered into the woof of modern liberal-democratic thinking to an extent which makes it difficult to bring home how revolutionary they were at the time they appeared, and to realize the far-reaching totalitarian-democratic potentialities immanent in them.

Yet, these very ideas, which became a landmark in the growth of liberal democracy, were calculated to set the modern State on the path of totalitarianism. They helped to initiate that process of ever-growing centralization that leads to the totalitarianism of facts, towards which the modern State has been moving for the last century and a half. They also marked a decisive advance in the direction of the totalitarianism of ideas based on an exclusive creed.

Sieyès's postulate of a rational régime in place of the slavish acceptance of established and time-hallowed incoherences, and of arrangements long void of meaning ; his rejection of the old idea that government was the King's business, while that of the subjects was to give their loyalty and yield taxes ; his condemnation of privileges ; the demand that the Estates General, based on feudal class distinctions and convoked to help the King to solve the problem of the deficit, should give place to a National Assembly representing the sovereign nation, and called upon to apply its unlimited powers to the total reshaping of the body politic ; Sieyès's raising of the homogeneous nation—above orders and corporations—to the level of the only real and all-embracing collective entity—all these ideas now so widely accepted as axiomatic were of the utmost revolutionary significance at the time, and, moreover, released a dynamic force, which soon swept beyond the conscious objectives of those who set it in motion, and is to-day more powerful than ever. The absurdities, incongruities and abuses of the *ancien régime* were indefensible. Sieyès's impatience with, and contempt for, the old parchments, the cult for precedent, the "extase gothique" of "proof" hunters and timid slaves of "facts", cannot fail to win sympathy. But it must not be forgotten that this clash of attitudes, stripped of grotesqueness and stupid, selfish conservatism, on the one side, and of compelling verve, on the other, marked the beginning of the fundamental and fateful conflict between two vital attitudes, not in the sphere of abstract thought alone, but in the realm of practical politics as well. One stands for organic, slow, half-conscious growth, the other for doctrinaire deliberateness ; one for the trial-and-error procedure, the other for an enforced solely valid pattern. The Legislator, writes Sieyès, " doit se sentir pressé de sortir enfin de l'effroyable expérience des siècles . . . enfin penser des vrais principes ". There is no respect in this attitude for the wisdom of ages, the accumulated, half-conscious experience and instinctive ways of a nation. It shows no awareness of the fact that strictly rationalist criteria of truth and untruth do not apply to social phenomena, and that what exists is never a result of error, accident or vicious contrivance alone, but is a pragmatic product of conditions, slow, unconscious adjustment, and only partly of deliberate planning.

These are the principles, exclaims Sieyès, or we must renounce the idea of a social order altogether. When contrasting the character of an art peculiar to politics (the " social art ") with the descriptive nature of physics, Sieyès foreshadows Marx's famous dictum by saying of politics that it is " l'art plus hardi dans sa vol, se propose de plier et d'accommoder les faits à nos besoins et à nos jouissances, il demande ce qui doit être pour l'utilité des hommes. . . . Quelle doit être la véritable science, celle des faits ou celle des principes ? " This approach determines his judgment of the British Constitution. That so vaunted *chef-d'œuvre* would not stand an impartial examination by the principles of a " veritable political order ". A product of hazard and circumstances rather than of lights, " un monument de superstition gothique " (the House of Lords), in the past regarded as a marvel, it was in fact nothing but an " échafaudage prodigieux " of precautions against disorder, instead of being a positive scheme for a true social order.

This type of absolutist approach caused Sieyès to become the first exponent of what we propose to call the Revolutionary attitude. It is an answer to the question as to what attitude a Revolution, which claims to realize a solely valid system, should take to the representatives of the past scheme of things, and to opposition in general. From one angle, it is the problem of Revolutionary coercion. Sieyès was clear in his mind that a Revolution had the characteristics of a civil war, and was in its nature incompatible with compromise or any kind of give-and-take. The attacked old system and its representatives benefiting from so many vested interests could not be expected to dissolve of their own volition. However old and decrepit a man may be, Sieyès says, he will not willingly abandon his place to a young man. There must be a removal by force. The representatives of the two privileged estates, the nobility and clergy, will thus try to distract the attention of the Third Estate by small concessions such as, for instance, the offer to pay taxes equal to those paid by the latter. In order to stave off the attack on their privileges they will talk of the necessity of reconciliation between the classes. All these ruses, Sieyès insists, must not overshadow the fundamental fact of the life-and-death struggle between the two systems, which the new and old social forces represented. The two camps had no common ground, for there could be no common basis for oppressors and the oppressed. It was impossible to call a halt in 1789 : it was imperative to go either the whole way, or backward, abolish privileges altogether, or legalize them. It was impossible to bargain. No class willingly renounces its power and privileges, and no class can expect fairness or generosity from the other, or even conformity to some general objective standard. Thus in Sieyès's opinion the Third Estate could rely only on its own courage and inspiration. " Scission " was therefore the sole solution : a Revolutionary break and the total subordination of the few to the many. Furthermore, a Revolution has not accomplished its task even when it has abolished the powers that be which prevent the will of the people from being expressed and prevailing, and has enabled it with no delay or subterfuge of any kind to speak and to fix the mode of existence it desires. An equally and perhaps more important objective is to prevent the old system from coming back. The old forces are bound to try to worm their way back by all means. Sieyès therefore lays down that the Third Estate shall be barred from sending members of the two privileged orders as their representatives. Should not, the question may be asked, people be permitted to act foolishly, if they choose ? No, they must not, for the question of the National Assembly and the general good are involved. It would, Sieyès maintains, be like electing British Ministers of State to represent Frenchmen at the French National Assembly, at a time of war. The nobles are aliens, enemy aliens of the Third Estate, that is to say, of the French nation, to the same degree as members of the British Cabinet. The implication of Revolutionary dictatorship is clear. The provision, however necessary at the moment, may be regarded as a thin end of the wedge pierced into the framework of popular sovereignty, on the very eve of its triumph.

(b) POPULAR SOVEREIGNTY

This is the more remarkable, since the whole burden of Sieyès's case for a rational principle in politics and for the revolutionary replacement of one system by another is the theory of the unlimited sovereignty of the people. The " veritable political order " is realized by the will of the people becoming the sole source of law, in place of the power of the King and authority of tradition. When the nation enters upon its own, and assembles to speak its mind, all established laws and institutions are rendered null and void.

The situation in 1789 was that the King had summoned the Estates General for a particular purpose—to remedy the deficit ; and under certain conditions and rules—the three orders were according to custom to deliberate separately. Sieyès urged the Estates General, or at least the Third Estate, to declare themselves an extraordinary National Assembly and to act like men just emerging from the state of nature and coming together for the purpose of signing a Social Contract. He thus wanted the Estates (or Assembly) to act in a

Revolutionary way, as if there had been no laws and no regulations before then. The nation was the sovereign. Once assembled it could not be bound by any conditions or prescriptions. It would be alienating its very being, if it was. The nation expressed justice by the mere fact of its being and willing. " La volonté nationale . . . n'a besoin que de sa réalité." An extraordinary National Assembly, such as Sieyès wanted the Estates General to become, embodied this national will in the raw, being not just a representative body, but Rousseau's people in assembly really ; while an ordinary National Assembly laid down by the constitution created by the Extraordinary Assembly—an ordinary representative body—would be bound by the rules fixed in the Constitution. The Extraordinary Assembly may and would, of course, for convenience' sake declare most of the existing laws valid till their replacement by new ones, but this expedient in no way affected the principle.

Who is the nation ? Sieyès answers : all the individuals in the forty thousand parishes of France. These individuals, stripped of all their other attributes and affiliations, like membership of a class, profession, creed or locality, have the common attribute of citizenship and the same interest in the common general good. " Les volontés individuelles sont les seuls éléments de la volonté commune." Whoever claimed a position different from that assigned by common citizenship is the enemy of all other citizens and of the national good. The most dangerous enemy of the latter is *esprit de corps*, the sectional interests of groups, whether these groups were traditional privileged orders, social classes or corporations with a special status. The existence of groups implied partial selfish interests. The common national will was formed by the concurrence of individual wills alone, and was falsified and destroyed, indeed could not even be brought forth, where sectional interests were operative. Thus the Estates General in its old composition could not claim to be more than an " Assemblée clérico-nobili-judicielle ". It constituted a body where representatives of three separate nations met, and negotiated, but could not form one national representation, voicing one common national and one general interest. So far Sieyès is interpreting Rousseau. Now the Third Estate—and this is Sieyès's original contribution occasioned by the all-important controversy of the hour—comprised the crushing numerical majority of the nation, all those who had no pretensions to privilege or status different from that implied in common citizenship, all those, moreover, who by their skill and effort maintained the social fabric. They were therefore the nation. The privileged orders were aliens, an encumbrance, an idle limb. The nobles might as well go back to the Franconian swamps and forests, where they claim to have come from originally, and leave the freed old Roman stock alone. They would thus seal their claim to be a superior race.

Sieyès's egalitarian conception of a monolithic nation and unlimited popular sovereignty was an argument for the elimination of feudal privilege and regional incongruities. It was, however, calculated to open the way to that democratic centralization, under which the long unhampered arm of the central power resting on the idea of a single national interest, and carried by the energy of popular feeling, sweeps away all intermediate clusters of social activity whether functional, ideological, economic or local. The problem becomes more acute in the light of Sieyès's two reservations : first, that the people should not be allowed to act foolishly against its own interest, and second, that in order that the nation may become a monolithic entity, nonconforming groups should be eliminated. This would mean that unlimited popular sovereignty, although in theory resting with the totality of the nation alone, may come to be deposited in a part only of the nation, which claims to constitute the real monolithic people, and to embody the single national interest.

According to Sieyès, the basis of all social order is equality. The sense of equality is also the essence of happiness, because it silences pretentious pride as well as envy, vanity and servility. Equality is a postulate of reason as of justice. The cleavage of society into unequal parts, oppressors and oppressed, has come into existence in contradiction to the dictates of reason and fairness. Sieyès employs the famous simile of the law as the centre of an immense globe and the citizens placed, without exception, in the same distance on the circumference. But here comes the vital shift. The whole trend of thought becomes deflected by the question of property.

(c) PROPERTY

The aspects of Sieyès's thought emphasized till now, such as the absolutist doctrinaire temperament, Revolutionary coercion, egalitarian centralism, the conception of a homogeneous nation, contained totalitarian implications. The question of property pushes Sieyès's ideas back firmly on the path of liberalism. The law in the focus of his globe must not, he states, interfere with the citizen's use of his innate or acquired faculties and more or less favourable chances to increase his possessions. " . . . N'enfle sa propriété de tout ce que le sort prospère, ou un travail plus fécond pourra y ajouter, et ne puisse s'élever, dans sa place légale, le bonheur le plus conforme à ses goûts et le plus digne d'envie." From the point of view of the law, economic inequality had no more significance than inequality of height or looks, difference of sex or age. Moreover, in the tradition of Locke, private property is presented by Sieyès as the very essence of liberty, as only an extension of the property of one's person, and of man's freedom to employ his faculties and labour. " La propriété des objets extérieurs ou la propriété réelle, n'est pareillement qu'une suite et comme une extension de la propriété personnelle." The right of first occupation is, again in the spirit of Locke, only a specific personal right to the deployment of skill and effort. It gives the first occupant an exclusive right of ownership, from which others are shut out.

The outcome of this conception of property as a natural right is the liberal conception of the role of the State : to allow men to follow their economic pursuits, without hindrance, and to interfere only when an attempt on a man's property is made by his neighbour. The role of the State is to insure safety ; not to grant rights, but to protect them. " Tous ces individus (on the circumference of the globe with the law in its centre) correspondent entre eux, ils s'engagent, ils négocient, toujours sous la garantie commune de la loi ; si dans ce mouvement général quelqu'un veut dominer la personne de son voisin ou usurper sa propriété, la loi commune réprime cet attentat, et remet tout le monde à la même distance d'elle même."

Only once or twice does Sieyès seem to reflect uneasily on the advantage unequal property accords to its owners. On one occasion he remarks that most property was still with the privileged orders. He hastens, however, to reassure his readers that he has no intention of touching property. It is a natural right. Sieyès's conception of property leads him to the most flagrant violation of his egalitarian principles, even in the political sphere. So eloquent in the condemnation of privilege and group interests as an insult to human dignity and the immoral foe of the national interest, Sieyès is brought to make the distinction between two kinds of rights, natural and civil. Preservation and development of the natural rights is the purpose for which society has been formed ; while political rights are those by which society is maintained. Hence the distinction between active and passive citizens. The latter have only natural rights, the right to the protection of their persons, liberty and property. They have no part in the formation of the public powers. This is reserved to the active citizens alone. They alone contribute to the establishment and maintenance of the public weal. They alone are " les vrais actionnaires de la grande entreprise sociale ". The term is highly significant. Society is reinterpreted from a moral and political arrangement based on the natural rights of man into a joint stock company.

Sieyès's conception of property is more conservative than any so far encountered in this essay. The reason is not far to seek. The earlier thinkers, spinning their ideas in a vacuum, with little faith in putting them into practice, could be radical, although even they flinched from drawing the final conclusion. Sieyès was writing guides for immediate action. Sieyès, like so many architects of the Revolution, felt the urgency of reaffirming the sanctity of property while opening all the other floodgates of the Revolution.

Chapter Two

BALANCE OR REVOLUTIONARY PURPOSE—
UNDER THE CONSTITUTIONAL MONARCHY

(a) LEGALITY AND THE SUPREMACY OF THE REVOLUTIONARY PURPOSE

SIEYÈS was one of those who caused the initial absolutist impulse of the Revolution to spend itself in the abolition of the feudal Monarchy. The shock became so to say absorbed in a system of balance, established by the Constituent Assembly and consecrated by the Constitution of 1791. The new order was in a sense the negation of the basic ideas of a " veritable political order ", in the name of which the Revolution of 1789 had been accomplished : the sovereignty of the people and the rights of man. A hereditary Monarchy with the power of veto was retained, and the poorer strata of the nation were disfranchised. The idea of a solely valid social order, underlying Sieyès' attitude in 1788–9, gave way to the claim that the Revolution had accomplished its task in that it had released the social forces, till then suppressed, and created the conditions for those forces to reach a harmonious balance by them-selves. That a major force, namely the poor, the majority of the nation, had not been given a chance to enter the contest was con-veniently overlooked.

The whole subsequent development of the Revolution may be described as a struggle between two attitudes, one based on the idea of balance and the newly established legality, and the other emanating from the idea of the primacy of the Revolutionary purpose, and implying the legality of Revolutionary coercion and violence (Jacobinism).

Certain dates and events stand out as decisive in this struggle.

The bourgeois system of balance came to an end on August 10th, 1792, as a result of an armed coup by the disfranchised elements under the leadership of the insurrectionary Paris Com-mune. The coup was carried out in the name of the primacy of the Revolutionary purpose, against the established legal authorities, above all the Legislative Assembly, which had been elected on the basis of a property qualification. The Monarchy, which had never recovered from the shock it had received as a result of the King's flight a year earlier, was abolished. The distinction between active and passive citizens ceased to exist. The last remaining feudal dues, which the Constituent Assembly had retained on the grounds that they were derived from property relations and not from personal dependance, were soon finally annulled. The last conclusions were thus drawn from the original premises of the Revolution of 1789, which had been whittled down into the Constitutional Monarchical and bourgeois compromise : the undisputed supremacy of popular sovereignty, and the equal rights of man. It could thus be said that the Revolutionary purpose, which was enthroned by the unlawful events of August, 1792, the brief dictatorship of the Commune, the massacres of September, 1792, and the Ministry of Danton, was embodied in these two ideals.

The same could not be said about the Revolutionary purpose which, on June 2nd, 1793, led to the attack on the Convention, culminating in the expulsion of the Girondist deputies. The latter had been duly elected on a free ballot, and till a very short time earlier commanded the majority of the Convention. The Jacobin Revolutionary purpose in this case was the salvation of the Revolution. The Revolution meant to the Jacobins the Republic one and indivisible, and the defence of the welfare of the masses, menaced by tendencies running counter to their ideological and administrative centralization, and aiming at the preservation of established economic (bourgeois) interests. The dictatorship of the Committee of Public Safety and the declaration of the Revolutionary Government which followed the June coup implied the claim that at that stage the Revolutionary purpose had come to be embodied in a single party, Jacobinism, representing the true will and the real interest of the people, or rather the popular masses. The terrorist Jacobin political and economic dictatorship was an improvisation precipitated by war, economic emergency, internal treason and party strife. With the passing of the imminent military danger, and the destruction of the Enragés, Hébertists and Dantonists, the first two groups representing anarchical social violence, and the latter a wish for a return to legality and some form of balance, the dictatorial régime should have come to an end. The Revolutionary purpose, which was its justification, seemed realized with the defeat of its enemies. Robespierrist dictatorship and terror continued. The question of the Revolutionary purpose, involving the question of the purpose of the terror, assumed thus a new and vital significance. It could no longer be summed up as unrestricted popular sovereignty. Social policies alone and as an end in themselves did not exhaust it either. It thus came to signify the reign of virtue, the idea of an exclusive and final scheme of things. But this conception was not something new or improvised. It was there in Jacobinism from the start, as a postulate. It only reached self-awareness during the régime of terror, to clash at once with the ideas of liberty and popular self-expression, values with which it had for a long time been identified, to be soon defeated on Thermidor 9th by a reaction reasserting the idea of balance, and to re-emerge in a flicker of total self-awareness in the plot of Babeuf in 1796.

(b) JACOBINISM—MENTAL AND PSYCHOLOGICAL ELEMENTS

The driving power of Jacobinism, or as for the purposes of this study it would be more correct to say, Robespierrism, was the vague, mystical idea that the way to a natural rational and final order of things had been opened by the French Revolution. " Nous voulons, en un mot, remplir les vœux de la nature, accomplir les destins de l'humanité, tenir les promesses de la philosophie, absoudre la providence du long règne du crime et da la tyrannie." This Messianic attitude of Robespierre and his followers must be constantly borne in mind, otherwise the whole significance of Jacobinism will be lost. It was incompatible with the acceptance of the theory of balance, and implied an absolute, dynamic purpose, to be pursued in all circumstances, and imposed.

For the understanding of Jacobinism it is vital to remember that abstract, collective concepts were to them not abridgments, combinations of ideas, or guiding maxims, but almost tangible and visible things, truths that stand on their own and compel acceptance. " Eternal principles ", the " natural order ", " the reign of virtue " had an all-important meaning to Robespierre and Saint-Just, just as such concepts as " classless society ", " the leap from the realm of necessity to the realm of freedom " have to an orthodox Marxist. Hence disagreement could not be considered by them as mere difference of opinion, but appeared as crime and perversion, or at least error. It was usual for Robespierre to preface his statements with the explicit premise that as there could be only one morality and one human conscience, he felt sure that his opinion was that of the Assembly. In his famous clash with Guadet on the subject of Providence and Divinity Robespierre declared that believing, as he did, that all patriots had the same principles, it was impossible that they should not admit the eternal principles voiced by him. " Quand j'aurai terminé . . . je suis sûr que M. Guadet se rendra lui-même à mon opinion ; j'en atteste et son patriotisme et sa gloire, choses vaines et sans fondement, si elles ne s'appuyaient sur les vérités immuables que je viens de proposer." In the circumstances such words were, of course, tantamount to blackmail.

This mental attitude was interwoven with certain psychological peculiarities. Robespierre was quite incapable of separating the personal element from differences of opinion. That every polemical argument became in Robespierre's mouth a torrent of personal denunciation may be explained by his implicit conviction that as there is only one truth, he who disagreed with it was prompted by evil motives. But less explicable seems Robespierre's habit of declaring himself a victim of persecution, of embarking upon a dirge of self-pity and of invoking death as solace, every time he was opposed. Here we are faced with a paranoiac streak, a strange combination of a most intense and mystical sense of mission with a self-pity that expressed itself in an obsessive preoccupation with martyrdom, death and even suicide. It is the psychology of the neurotic egotist, who must impose his will—rationalized into divine truth—or wallow in an ecstasy of self-pity. The refusal of the world to submit becomes to such a nature a source of endless anguish, usually rationalized into a Weltschmerz.

At every setback or humiliation, the world grows instantly dark, deformed and contorted with pain. Its order begins to appear wrong beyond remedy, and all men banded together in an evil plot. A similar mentality is discernible in Saint-Just, Robespierre's junior colleague, the philosopher of Jacobin dictatorship, and one of its most formidable representatives. After the failure to get elected to the Legislative Assembly in 1792, because he had

not yet reached the prescribed age of twenty-five, Saint-Just wrote
this passionate, astounding letter :
" I have been impelled by a republican fever that devours and
eats me up.   You will find me great some day . . . I have a feeling that I can soar above the rest in this age.   Adieu !   I am above
misfortune.   I will bear everything, but I will tell the truth.   You
are all cowards, you have not appreciated me.   My palm will rise
nevertheless and perhaps obscure yours.   Infamous creatures that
you are.   I am a rogue, a rascal, because I have no money to give
you.   Tear out my heart and devour it ;   you will become what
you are not.   Great !   O God !   Must Brutus languish forgotten,
far from Rome !   My decision is made meanwhile.   If Brutus
does not kill the rest, he will kill himself."

At a later date, as one of the dictators of France, Saint-Just
wrote that on the day he would become convinced that it was
impossible to give the French people " mœurs douces, énergiques,
sensibles et inexorables pour la tyrannie et l'injustice ", he would
stab himself.   Few confessions could equal the one found in Saint-
Just's *Institutions Républicaines*.   A youth of barely twenty-six,
compelled to " isolate himself from the world ", he " throws his
anchor into the future, and presses posterity to his heart ".   God,
the protector of innocence and virtue, had sent him on the perilous
mission of unmasking perverse men surrounded by fame and fear.
He was destined to put crime into chains, and to make men practise
virtue and probity.   " J'ai laissé derrière moi toutes ces faiblesses,
je n'ai vu que la vérité dans l'univers, et je l'ai dite.   Les circumstances ne sont difficiles que pour ceux qui reculent devant le
tombeau.   Je t'implore, le tombeau, comme un bienfait de la
Providence, pour n'être pas témoin de l'impunité des forfaits ourdis
contre ma patrie et l'humanité.   Certes, c'est quitter peu de chose
qu'une vie malheureuse, dans laquelle on est condammé à végéter le
complice ou le témoin impuissant de crime . . . Je méprise la poussière qui me compose et qui vous parle ; on pourra la persécuter et
faire mourir cette poussière.   Mais je défie qu'on m'arrache cette vie
indépendante que je me suis donné dans les siècles et dans les cieux."

The breath-taking incongruity between the invocation to death
as solace and the role of executioner-in-chief of the author is only
equalled by another strange contrast, that between Saint-Just's
atrocious denunciations of opponents and his sentimental Rousseauist declamations.   The terrible indictment of Danton opens

with the uncanny enunciation : " il y a quelque chose de terrible dans l'amour sacré de la patrie, il est tellement exclusif, qu'il immole tout sans pitié, sans frayeur, sans respect humain, à l'intérêt public." In another speech the Republic is said never to be safe as long as a single opponent is left alive, and the sword is brandished against not only the opponents, but also the " indifferents ". But this does not prevent Saint-Just from weaving the blissful dream of a cottage on the banks of a river, from appealing to Frenchmen to love and respect each other, and from imploring the Government to let everyone find his own happiness.

This is a self-righteous mentality which is quite incapable of self-criticism, divides reality into watertight compartments and adopts contradictory attitudes to the same thing, making judgment wholly dependent on whether it is " me ", by definition represent-ing truth and right, or the opponent who is associated with it.

(c) THE DEFINITION OF THE GENERAL WILL

The Jacobin absolute purpose was not to be imposed externally. It was held to be immanent in man and sure to restore to man his rights and freedoms. It was realizable only in the collective ex-perience of active popular self-expression. Jacobinism was not satisfied with acquiescence. It insisted on active participation, and condemned neutrality or indifference as vicious egoism. Jacobinism did not ask for obedience, it wanted to exact living, active com-munion with the absolute purpose.

Robespierre declared it to be the duty of every man and citizen to contribute as much as was in his power to the success of the sublime undertaking of the Revolution : the re-establishment of the inalienable rights of man, which is the sole object of society, and the sole legitimate motive of revolutions. Man must sacrifice his personal interest to the general good. He must, so to say, bring to the common pool the part of public force and of the people's sovereignty which he holds, " ou bien il doit être exclu, par cela même, du pacte social ". Needless to add that whoever wants to retain unjust privileges and distinctions incompatible with the general good, and whoever wants to arrogate to himself new powers at the expense of public liberty, is the enemy of the nation and of humanity.

This was the central problem of Jacobinism : the dilemma of the single purpose and the will of men. It could be defined as the problem of freedom, conformity and coercion in a régime which claims to achieve two incompatible aims, Liberty, and an exclusive form of social existence. It is at bottom Rousseau's problem of the general will, with an equally strong emphasis placed on active and universal participation in willing the general will as on the exclusive nature of the general will.

Saint-Just came to grips with the issue in a striking passage at the end of his remarkably moderate, even complacent exposition of the Revolutionary ideals in his book of 1791, L'Esprit de la Revolution et de la Constitution (of 1791). He sets out there to answer a presumed challenge as to whether the new Constitution was the will of all. Saint-Just's answer is firmly negative. It would be impossible, he goes on to say, that the change of the Social Contract should not divide into two camps, the " fripons " or the egoists, who stand to lose by the change, and the unfortunates who were oppressed under the old compact. But it would be an inadmissible abuse of the letter of the law to consider the resistance of some criminals as a part of the national will, since such resistance could not claim to be a legitimate opposition. Saint-Just goes much further. As a general rule, he declares, every will, even the sovereign will, inclined to perversion, is nil. Rousseau had not said all, when he described the general will as incommunicable, inalienable, eternal. The general will, to be such, must also be reasonable. In this respect Saint-Just quite mistakenly " corrects " Rousseau. The author of the Social Contract did not intend to say anything different from what Saint-Just goes on to say, namely, that a will may be tyrannical, even if willed by all, and that it would be no less criminal for the sovereign to be " tyrannized by himself " than by others. For in this case, the laws flowing from an impure source, the people would be licentious, and each individual would be both a tyrant and a slave. " La liberté d'un peuple mauvais est une perfidie générale, qui n'attaquant plus le droit de tous ou la souveraineté morte, attaque la nature qu'elle représente." The objective content is equally essential for the concept of liberty. " Liberté ! Liberté sacrée ! "—exclaims Saint-Just—" tu serais peu de chose parmi les hommes, si tu ne les rendais qu'heureux, mais tu les rappelles à leur origine et les rends à la vertu." Liberty deserves to be loved only to the extent that it

leads " to simplicity through the power of virtue ". Otherwise
liberty is nothing but " the art of human pride ". Clearly, the
spontaneously expressed will of man or people cannot as such claim
to be taken for granted as the exercise of sovereignty. All depends
on its objective quality, on its conforming to the general good, the
reasonable general will, and virtue ; all three in fact meaning the
same thing, an objective standard. Who is to define it ? By what
is it to be recognized ? How rigid or how flexible a standard is it
likely to be ? These are the vital, but unanswered, questions.

At a later date in the debate on the Constitution of 1793, Saint-
Just enunciated a totally different definition of the general will and
one which shows an unmistakable awareness of the dangers inherent
in the earlier conception. Saint-Just seemed now to remove all
objective quality from the general will, reducing the question to
a matter of counting votes and interests, all of which are explicitly
recognized as valid. Moreover, the postulate of objectivity is
violently assailed. " La volonté générale, proprement dite, et dans
la langue de la liberté, se forme de la majorité des volontés particulières, individuellement recueillies sans une influence étrangère ;
la loi, ainsi formée, consacre . . . l'intérêt général, de la majorité
des volontés a dû résulter celle des intérêts." Saint-Just condemns
the substitution of what he calls " a speculative will " for the real
general will, of the philosophical view (" vues de l'esprit ") for
the interests of the *corps social*. " Les lois étaient l'expression du
goût plutôt que de la volonté générale." Thus if the actual,
expressed will of the people is not taken for the general will, and
some allegedly objective, external idea is proclaimed to constitute
the general will, the general will becomes depraved. Liberty no
longer belongs to the people. It becomes a law alien to public
prosperity. This is Athens voting at its twilight, without democracy,
the loss of its freedom. This idea of liberty, Saint-Just declares,
if it prevails, will banish freedom for ever. He goes on to make an
eloquent and terrible prophecy, which events vindicated to the letter.

" Cette liberté sortira du cœur et deviendra le goût mobile de
l'esprit ; la liberté sera conçue sous toutes les formes de gouvernement possibles ; car dans l'imagination, tout perd ses formes
naturelles et tout s'altère, et l'on y crée des libertés comme les yeux
créent des figures dans les nuages . . . Dans vingt ans le trône
soit rétabli par les fluctuations et les illusions offertes à la volonté
générale devenue speculative."

It took less than twenty years for Napoleon to make the claim that he embodied the general will of the French nation and to find theoretical support for it.

Where does Saint-Just after all take his stand ? Is the general will to him what is actually willed by the people in flesh, whatever its contents, " la volonté matérielle du peuple, sa volonté simultanée ", the aim of which, as he says, is to consecrate the active interest of the greater number, and not their passive interest ? Or does the general will need the attribute of objective truth to become the general will, in which case the actual count of votes takes a second place behind the objective doctrine embodied in the enlightened ?

Neither Robespierre nor Saint-Just ever stated their position quite unequivocally, but the latter attitude is implicit in their whole approach.   As will be shown, Saint-Just's definition of the general will, made in the course of the Constitutional debate in 1793, came not as an answer to the challenge of a " speculative " idea claiming to constitute the general will, but as an argument in a debate on the mode of organizing the expression of popular sovereignty. Robespierre's insistence on the exclusion of those who do not bring with them to the common pool and common effort their part of popular sovereignty, is a clear indication of his attitude.

It is proposed to examine in the coming pages the development of the Jacobin attitude on this point throughout the Revolution as illustrated by the thought of the two leading and most representative figures of Jacobin dictatorship, Robespierre and Saint-Just.

(d) THE IDEA OF BALANCE—SAINT-JUST

The evolution of Robespierre's thinking on this matter is more interesting and more elaborate than that of Saint-Just.   He wrestled with the problem for a much longer time than his younger friend, who, when he arrived on the central Revolutionary scene, found the dilemma largely resolved by circumstances.   Robespierre was active at the centre of affairs from the very earliest days of the Revolution.   Up to the period of the Convention Saint-Just was only an impatient onlooker of the great events from his native little town, and no more than a local Revolutionary activist.   This may explain why in the case of Robespierre the outline of his future intellectual development is discernible quite early, whereas in the case of Saint-Just the passage from complacency in his book of 1791 to Revolutionary dictatorial extremism in 1793 appears abrupt and almost unexpected. Saint-Just made the passage from obscurity to supreme power in one leap.

A fundamental difference between Robespierre and Saint-Just is revealed by a comparative analysis of their views in the pre-Convention period. In spite of the far-reaching totalitarian implications of Saint-Just's above quoted definition of the general will, contained in his book on the 1791 Constitution, the underlying attitude of the work is the orthodox view of the day that the Revolution had been accomplished in the sense that it had liberated the social forces and enabled them to set themselves freely into a harmonious pattern, the essence of which is balance. Robespierre was never prepared to adopt this approach. To him the aim of the Revolution had not been achieved by giving the social and political forces a free play to reach a balance. He was not prepared to be content with letting the forces out and watching them. His whole attitude is dominated by the idea of a dynamic purpose. The Revolution constitutes the unfolding of this purpose. There is no question of a balance of forces. The decisive fact is the deadly struggle between two forces, Revolution and counter-revolution, which between themselves sum up the whole of reality.

" The omission of what you could do would be a betrayal of trust . . . a crime of lèse-nation and lèse-humanity. More than that : if you do not do all for Liberty, you have not done a thing. There are no two ways of being free : either you are entirely free or return to be a slave. The slightest opening left to despotism will re-establish soon its power "—declared Robespierre in the debate in the *Constituante* on the franchise on August 11th, 1791, when hotly opposing the followers of the ideology of equilibrium, who adopted the *marc d'argent* as a qualification for eligibility to the Legislative Assembly.

It may be convenient to throw a glance at Saint-Just's ideas in 1791 first, before proceeding to Robespierre. The contrast between the idea of balance and of Revolutionary purpose will thus be brought into sharp relief.

Saint-Just speaks in glowing approval of the 1791 principles. France had produced a synthesis (*coalisé*) of democracy (*état civil*), aristocracy (the legislative power), and monarchy (executive). In the best tradition of Montesquieu, Saint-Just explains that a large country like France must have a monarchical régime, as a republic would not suit it. At all events, the new Constitution was the nearest possible approximation in the conditions of France to a popular régime, with a minimum of monarchy, notwithstanding the formal supremacy of the executive power, necessitated also incidentally by the people's love for the King.

The new régime appears to Saint-Just to be eminently safe because of the essential sanity of the French people : presumption, which characterizes the English people and prevents the establishment of democracy in England, is not the principle of French democracy ; violence is not the essence of French aristocracy ; and justice, not caprice, is the characteristic of the new French monarchy.

" Le chef d'œuvre de l'Assemblée Nationale est d'avoir tempéré cette démocratie." The golden balance, the right measure between a popular and despotic régime, has been achieved. The nation has been given the degree of liberty necessary to its sovereignty, legislation has become popular through equality, and the monarchy had retained only enough power to be a vehicle of justice. " The legislators of France have devised the wisest equilibrium."

Wisdom could not place too strong a barrier between the Legislative and Executive. But the deliberations of the Legislature should be submitted for royal acceptance so that the particular interests of the two powers should cancel each other out. An eye watching over the lawgiver himself, a power able to arrest his arm, is needed. This role can best be performed by an executive-head who does not change, and is the repository of laws and principles, which the instability of the legislators should not be allowed to upset. It would be absurd to consult the people in these deliberations, because of the slowness of the procedure, the people's lack of prudence, and its vulnerability to evil influences. " Where the feet think, the arm deliberates, the head marches." This is indeed out of tune with the plebiscitary tendencies of the 1793 Constitution. The judiciary, the best regulated and most passive organ of the State, should be vested with the supervision of the exercise of sovereignty.

Saint-Just's views on equality in 1791 are particularly significant. Complete equality like that established by Lycurgus—an equality suitable for the poverty of a republic—would produce a revolution or engender indolence in a country like France. The land would have to be divided and industry suppressed. A free industry was however the source of political rights, and inequality in fact has always given birth to an ambition that is " vertu " in itself. There is no social harmony with all men socially and economically equal. Natural equality would confuse society. There would be no authority, no obedience, and the people would flee to the desert. While abolishing abuses, the legislators have wisely respected interests. " Et l'on a bien fait ; la propriété rend l'homme soigneux : elle attache les cœurs ingrats à la patrie."

As to political equality—the only form of equality suitable for France, a country built on commerce—its essence lies not in equal strength, but in the individual's having an equal share in the sovereignty of the people. Unlike Robespierre, Saint-Just nevertheless fully approves the division into active and passive citizens. The completely indigent class who would be classified as passive citizens and deprived of franchise is not large and would not be condemned to sterility, and the Constitution would benefit by not becoming too popular and anarchical. Possessed of independence and a chance of emulation, the poor will enjoy the social rights of natural equality, security and justice. The legislators had taken a wise course in not humiliating the poor, while making opulence unnecessary. It did not occur to Saint-Just or to most of his contemporaries to enquire how many people were to be disfranchised under the scheme. He is content to observe that the inequality established by the division into active and passive citizens does not offend natural rights, but only social pretensions.

Saint-Just's analysis of the problem of the individual versus the State anticipates Benjamin Constant's distinction between the legislators of antiquity and the spirit of modern liberty. The ancients wished that the happiness of the individual should be derived from the well-being of the State, the moderns have an opposite attitude. The ancient State was based upon conquest, because it was small and surrounded by inimical neighbours, and the fate of the individuals thus depended on the fortunes of the republic. The vast modern State has no ambitions beyond self-preservation and the happiness of its individual citizens. Following Rousseau closely, Saint-Just declares that the severity of the laws should correspond inversely to the size of the territory. The Rights of Man would have proved the undoing of such small city-republics as Athens or Sparta. France, who has renounced conquests, is strengthened by the Rights of Man. " Ici la patrie s'oublie pour ses enfants."

The future prophet of the " swift sword " cannot forgive Rousseau his justification of the death penalty. " Quelque vénération que m'impose l'autorité de J. J. Rousseau, je ne te pardonne pas, ô grand homme, d'avoir justifié le droit de mort." For if the right of sovereignty cannot be transferred, no more can man's right over his own life. Before passing a death sentence, the Social Contract should be altered, because the crime on which sentence was given was the result of an alteration in the contract. A repressive force cannot be a social law. As soon as the Social Contract is perverted, it becomes null and void, and then the people must assemble and form a new Social Contract for its regeneration. The Social Contract is, according to Rousseau, made for the preservation of the partners ; indeed, but for their conservation by *vertu* and not by force, says Saint-Just. In the circumstances of 1791 Saint-Just had no perception that his theory of balance was in the long run hardly compatible with his idea of the predicated general will. At all events, he presupposed an extremely wide area of common agreement, and consequently the margin of illegitimate opposition was thought by him to be so narrow as not to deserve serious attention. As the common area, upon which the play of social forces could be allowed to move, grew narrower, the predicated general will became more rigidly defined, and the exclusions more numerous.

(e) ROBESPIERRE AND THE REVOLUTIONARY PURPOSE —THE IDEA OF THE PEOPLE

At first, the dynamic purpose of the Revolution was to Robespierre the unhalted advance towards the complete realization of the democratic ideal. Freedom of man and unrestricted popular sovereignty were supreme purposes. In the earlier phase of the Revolution, Robespierre was profoundly convinced that the people's will, if allowed free, genuine and complete expression, could not fail to prove identical with the true general will. " L'intérêt du peuple c'est le bien public . . . pour être bon, le peuple n'a besoin que de se préférer lui même à ce qui n'est pas lui." With this conviction of Robespierre's went the all-pervading consciousness of a deadly struggle between the popular Revolutionary purpose and the forces opposed to it, which could not be resolved by compromise, but only by total victory and subordination.

The liberation of man ; the dignity of the human person ; government of the people, by the people, and for the people—meant things very real to Robespierre. They were almost tangible, visible objects to him. There is a ring of genuine fervour in Robespierre's condemnation of the traditional distinction between rulers and subjects, ruling classes and oppressed classes, and in his impatient anger with snobbish pretensions, and with contempt for those beneath oneself. It is important to emphasize that, like Rousseau, Robespierre, when speaking of man's dignity and freedom, means the absence of personal dependence, in other words, equality. Rousseau had said that man should be as independent as possible of any other person, and as dependent as possible on the State. Human dignity and rights are degraded, when man has to acknowledge another man as his superior, but not in equal dependence of all on the collective entity, or the people, on ourselves in brief. Throughout the ages, Robespierre says, the art of government was employed for the exploitation and subjugation of the many by the few. Laws were designed to perfect these attempts into a system. All the legislators, instead of endeavouring to release the popular forces and satisfy their longing for freedom, dignity, happiness and self-government, have always thought in terms of governmental power. Uppermost in their minds were precautions against popular discontent and insurrection, convinced as they were that the people are by definition bad and mutinous. " L'ambition, la force et la perfidie ont été les législateurs . . . asservi raison." They proclaimed reason to be nothing but folly, equality to be anarchy. The vindication of natural rights became to them rebellion, and nature was ridiculed as a chimera. " C'est à vous maintenant de faire la vôtre, c'est à dire de rendre les hommes heureux et libres par vos lois." Robespierre denounced all references to the Roman tribunate. This ancient and so much vaunted institution implied the people's bondage. As if the people needed special advocates to plead on its behalf before some superior powers and a higher tribunal ! The people had no desire of going on strike on the Mountain, and wait there till its grievances had been answered. The people was the master in its own house, and not a client or supplicant. It intended to stay in Rome and expel the tyrants. And so we see Robespierre almost alone in the Constituent Assembly fighting for universal suffrage. There was no stronger advocate of the principle of popular election of all officers of State, administrative, judicial and other. He laid the greatest emphasis upon the spread of political consciousness in the masses, and encouraged its expression through the various channels—popular societies, the press, petitions, public discussions, demonstrations, and even extra-legal direct action by the people. Robespierre's determined stand against the death penalty and his fervent defence of the unrestricted freedom of the press were not only a struggle for values good in themselves, but a fight against the instruments of traditional governmental tyranny, and for means of popular self-expression.

It was in the very nature of a government " not of the people " never to be satiated with power. Every government " not of the people " was a vested interest against the people. The evils of society never come from the people, always from the government. " C'est dans la vertu et dans la souveraineté du peuple qu'il faut chercher un préservatif contre les vices et le despotisme du gouvernement." The first object of a Constitution is to protect the people from its own government and their abuses. Robespierre was of course out of tune with Montesquieu's idea of the separation of powers, reaffirmed by the Constituent Assembly. For whatever the Constitutional devices for subordinating the Executive to the Legislature adopted by the Assembly, there remained nevertheless in the 1791 Constitution the fact of a permanent head of the Executive, unelected, primeval, so to say, in the same way as the people was in regard to the Legislative power.

The British system appeared to Robespierre a fraud and a plot against the people. In the past, in the era of bondage, the idea may have been to temper tyranny by creating tension between the various governmental agencies and sowing discord among the various powers. But the aim of the Revolution was to extirpate tyranny altogether, and to let the people rule. Robespierre was at heart a Republican before he ever knew it.

Robespierre was filled with a constant anxiety not to allow the agencies of power to fall into the hands of the Executive. In those hands they were bound to become anti-popular counter-revolutionary forces. There could be little hesitation for him as to what attitude to take up on such questions as the royal veto and the royal sanction for Legislative decrees. In his determination to neutralize the Executive's power to do harm, Robespierre fought to deprive the King of every possible prerogative. This was consistently his line on every issue that came up in the great constitutional debates of 1789–91 on the reform of the French State. He was, for instance, against the royal command of the National Guards. He violently condemned the employment of the old *Maréchaussée* and its officers, recruited from the *Armée de ligne* under royal command, for police duties and functions of justice of the peace (regular judges of the peace were to be elected). Robespierre demanded that military courts be composed of an equal number of officers and men, for otherwise the courts martial, consisting of officers alone, would be punishing patriotic soldiers, under the guise of penalties for indiscipline. In all the incidents which occurred in the first two or three years of the Revolution between popular demonstrations and the police Robespierre invariably took the side of the former, accusing the authorities and the police of counter-revolutionary designs, provocation or ill-will. As if by definition any popular riot was the expression of the people's righteous anger, and every action of the authorities counter-revolutionary. The question as to who is the nation, and who is not " of the nation ", whether the nation is the sum total of persons born on French soil, a community of faith, or is equivalent to the people as a social category, is not yet decided. It was to unfold itself gradually. But already at the time Robespierre's conception of the nation had no room for corporate bodies. The nation, as Rousseau and Sieyès had taught, recognized no other components than individuals. The nation thus composed was a collective and yet monolithic personality, with one interest and one general will. Corporate bodies equated with partial wills were not " of the nation ". They were directly opposed to, or at least at variance with, the general good. Although not a militant anti-clerical, Robespierre would not thus allow the Church to continue as a separate corporation. He supported the idea of clerical marriage, and insisted that bishops should be elected not by the clergy alone, but, like any other public servants, by the people of the diocese, spiritual and lay. Robespierre demanded guarantees that the National Guards not only would not fall under the control of the administration, but would be prevented from forming an *esprit de corps*. Officers were to be changed every two years. External marks were not to be worn off duty. Robespierre demanded an elected jury for civil cases in the same way as for criminal cases, because he feared the *esprit de corps* which a professional body of judges was bound to develop. Robespierre made no protest against the ban on trade unions in the famous Loi Le Chapelier promulgated in defence of the homogeneity of the national will and the national interest.

It was only gradually that Robespierre came to brand a social class as being not " of the nation ". Sieyès had condemned the privileged orders for placing themselves outside the national community. After the abolition of feudal privileges, it became a sign of good Revolutionary sentiment to emphasize the unity of the French nation and to depreciate anything that might discriminate for or against any part of the community by assigning to it a special status. The French nation was composed of Frenchmen, and not of classes or castes. Even before this principle was finally violated by the disfranchisement of the poorer classes, Robespierre became acutely aware of the fact that national unity was giving way to a split into two warring social classes, the haves and the have-nots. He was at first desperately anxious to prevent it, not only by vehement opposition to the *marc d'argent*. He fought for the admission of the poor into the National Guard, insisted on the eligibility of the poor as members of jury, made a determined and successful stand against a ban on petitions by passive citizens. He repeatedly warned the Assembly that if the agencies of power were to be reserved to one class, they would inevitably become instruments of class domination and oppression. France would become divided into two separate nations, and the subjugated people would feel no obligation to their country. They would become aliens. He scoffed the defenders of the *marc d'argent*, attributing to them the idea that " human society should be composed exclusively of proprietors, to the exclusion of men ". Robespierre was to go through a fateful evolution in this respect. Having started with passionate opposition to the exclusion of the lower strata from the body of the sovereign and politically active nation, an opposition based on the idea of the sacred and equal rights of man, he finished by declaring the popular masses alone the nation, and by virtually outlawing the rich, if not the bourgeoisie as a whole. The " nation " came to be identified with the " people ", " this large and interesting class, hitherto called ' the people ' . . . the natural friend and the indispensable champion of liberty . . . neither corrupted by luxury, nor depraved by pride, nor carried away by ambition, nor troubled by those passions which are inimical to equality . . . generous, reasonable, magnanimous and moderate ".

Far from accepting the idea of equilibrium between the social forces, Robespierre labours under an acute awareness of a mortal struggle which is being waged with no respite. The counter-revolution is conceived by him as an actual, or latent, permanent conspiracy. It is lurking in the dark corners, scheming, plotting, waiting only for an opportunity, insidiously preparing its forces. Robespierre cannot help viewing every issue, even *prima facie* a neutral problem, from the same and sole angle of the opportunities it offers, and the perils it holds out, to either of the two combatants. Whatever widens the area of popular sovereignty and democracy is a gain for the Revolution, a position won on the road to victory, a defeat and loss to the counter-revolution. All the same, although Robespierre has a permanent dynamic objective, and not just a pragmatic party programme, he is also a tactician. In a war the objective is fixed, but the tactics may change. No tactical move should be judged in isolation and on its own ; the wider context is what determines the significance as well as the moral character of a particular move. And so Robespierre, the tactician, at times considers a slight retreat an improvement of the democratic position. He declared himself the defender of the Constitution of 1791, many provisions of which he had originally opposed bitterly. He frowned upon premature Republican propaganda. A believer in popular direct action, he is conscious of the ambushes and provocations that the counter-revolution is scheming, and warns the people not to expose itself, while the enemy is too strong, to the charge of anarchy, calling for suppression by police action.

Robespierre may be regarded as the father of the theory which operates with the basic distinction between a people's war and a counter-revolutionary war. Brissot and the Girondists wanted war, because they hoped that a national emergency, heightened by proselytizing enthusiasm, would sweep away all counter-revolutionary sentiment and plotting, unite the nation, and then carry the Revolution across Europe. True to his general line of thought, Robespierre judged the question of war from the angle of the irreconcilable conflict between Revolution and counter-revolution. It seemed to him clear that in the case of war, the armed forces, the concentration of wartime powers, the patriotic anxiety and pride engendered by a national emergency, were bound to be utilized by the counter-revolution as weapons to crush the Revolution, in alliance with foreign courts. Robespierre himself would have liked to turn the war into a people's war, that is, into an opportunity for the establishment of a popular régime based on Revolutionary stringency and military discipline. This could open the way to purges, and to a complete reshuffling of the officer corps and the administration, and perhaps sweep away the throne altogether. Robespierre never ceased to think and feel that " if we do not destroy them, they will annihilate us ". " They " were not necessarily men, individuals, although the tone of violent personal invective and denunciation is calculated to suggest this, but a criminal system as such, collective forces, of which the individual criminal was only a representative sample.

Thus after the flight of the King, Robespierre is less concerned with the King's actual offence than with the lesson of more general significance contained in the flight : the fact that Louis could not have made his escape, if there had been no powerful forces to encourage and help him. The existence and strength of these forces, just revealed, was what mattered most in Robespierre's opinion.

This attitude determined Robespierre's conception of justice as it found an expression in his speeches on the reform of the judicial system and above all on the trial of the King. The problem is of fundamental importance. Is there such a thing as objective, independent justice based upon a code that has nothing to do with the tug of war between contending social and political forces, and employs the sole criterion of strict evidence ? Or is justice to be considered in reference to the political struggle that is on, as a weapon of the victorious party ? Robespierre clearly inclined to the latter conception. It was not cynicism on his part, not a dis-belief in objective justice altogether. On the contrary. He was only convinced that all justice was, in the widest sense of the word, embodied in one party, and none in the other, by definition. The question of evidence was really secondary. Whether the actual crime was actually committed in the way envisaged in the criminal code was not all that mattered. What really mattered more was that it could, and in all certainty would, have taken place, given the opportunity. Man does not matter by himself either way, only as a part of a system. And the system as a whole is a crime and a standing conspiracy. " A King cannot rule innocently." Louis must die that the Republic should live. " Une mesure de salut public à prendre, un acte de providence nationale à exercer" (Robespierre). As early as October, 1790, Robespierre was instrumental in setting up a supreme court to deal with charges of lèse-nation. The Tribunal was to have the power to destroy all counter-revolutionary designs, and be composed of " friends of the Revolution ". Judges were to Robespierre magistrates of the Government ; in a free country, functionaries elected by the people. Their domain and the basis of their judgment was not a special science of jurisprudence, but the laws of the Constitution. " Indeed, the word jurisprudence ought to be struck out of the French vocabulary. In a state possessing a constitution and a legislature the courts need no jurisprudence but the text of the law." Thus the nation as the source of all laws was to be the sole interpreter of the Constitution and sole censor over the courts, and not some independent body. This line of thought was to lead to the precedence given under the system of terror to patriotic conscience and popular instinct over legal competence and legal proof. Furthermore, in this whole approach there is already implied the Terrorist concept of " suspect ", a person being considered guilty, before having been convicted on any particular charge, simply because of membership of a class of people, and because of past affiliations. On the eve of his death on the guillotine one of the architects of Jacobinism, Desmoulins, was to discover the enormity of this conception of justice. " Il n'y a point de gens suspects, il n'y a que des prévenus de délits fixés par la loi," he wrote.

Chapter Three

VOLONTÉ UNE

(a) DIRECT DEMOCRATIC ACTION

IT is not surprising that as a faithful disciple of Rousseau Robespierre was not prepared to recognize the decision of a representative assembly as expressing the kind of popular will which is identical with the general will. Parliaments were in the same category as other vested interests and corporations, although formally emanating from the choice of the people. A representative assembly elected on the basis of a property qualification, such as the Legislative Assembly, was certainly not " of the people ". Without, as he stated, going the whole way with Rousseau, nevertheless Robespierre could not reconcile himself to the idea that an assembly, once elected, even if chosen on a free ballot, was sovereign and its authority unquestionable. The absolute independence of a parliamentary assembly was " representative despotism ". There is always the danger that the people might be afflicted with as many enemies as it had deputies. Robespierre's motion of self-renunciation on the ineligibility of members of the Constituent to the Legislative Assembly was motivated by the fear that if the same people were elected, the Legislative Assembly would become a permanent vested interest.

Robespierre searched for safeguards against " representative despotism ". They were two : constant popular control over the Legislative body, and direct democratic action by the people. Robespierre dreamt of an assembly hall with a public gallery large enough to contain twelve thousand spectators. Under the eyes of so large a sample of the people, no deputy would dare to defend anti-popular interests. On the one hand, Robespierre insisted that any obstacles put in the way of the people in a free choice of representatives were useless, harmful and dangerous. On the other hand, he strongly approved of any rule that was calculated to protect the people from the " misfortunes of a bad choice ", and the corruption of its deputies. At one time Robespierre demanded a fundamental law whereby at fixed and frequent intervals the primary assemblies would be called upon to pass judgment upon the conduct of their deputies. These assemblies were to have the power to revoke their unfaithful representatives. Moreover, once in session, the primary assemblies would act as the sovereign in council, and use the opportunity to express their views on any matter concerning the public good. No power could interfere with the exercise of direct popular sovereignty by the nation in council. " Ce peu d'articles très simples, et puisés dans les premiers principes de la Constitution suffiront pour l'affermir et pour assurer à jamais le bonheur et la liberté du peuple français."

Robespierre fulminated particularly against an alliance between the Legislative and the Executive, which to him could only mean a plot against the people. The exercise of executive powers by an elected body was to Robespierre the worst of all despotisms, an oligarchy. He dreaded most the modern system, where a cabinet emanating from the majority of the assembly works in close touch with, and is supported by, its own party. He was himself later in 1793 to become the father of the theory of Revolutionary government exercised by the Convention through committees, a system, as he put it, as new as the Revolution itself, not to be found in any treatises on political science. With an eye on the Rolandist Ministry, the Incorruptible condemned in severest terms the state of affairs in which party leaders and members of the cabinet manage everything behind the scenes in caucuses and ministerial conclaves. Under such a system the will of the people becomes falsified, and the majorities achieved by such machinations are illegitimate. The laws voted upon in this way represent a fictitious, and not a genuine, expression of the general will. The general will, constant and pure, the sole depositary of which is the people, must neither be arrogated by a party-cum-cabinet plot to perpetuate " representative despotism ", nor become identified with the selfish impulses of ephemeral assemblies. Robespierre expressed impatience with the acceptance of numerical majority in the assembly as sovereign. The general will, the will of the truly popular majority, is not identified with parliamentary majority or minority. The majority in the real sense is where the true general will resides, even if that will happens to be expressed by a numerical minority. There was only one step from this essentially anti-parliamentary programme to the justification

of direct popular action in the name of the sacred principle that
the people have not only a right, but the duty, to resist oppression
and despotism, to rise actively against the plots of government and
treacherous intrigues by unfaithful representatives. " It is vital for
Liberty to be free to exercise reasonable censorship over the acts of
the Legislative body. The National Assembly itself is subject to
the general will, and when it contradicts it (the general will), the
Assembly can no longer continue to exist." The mandatories of the
people have to be placed in a position that would make it impossible
for them to harm liberty. As the people of Paris were nearest to
the seat of power, they and their representative bodies, the Commune
and the Sections, were duty bound to act as the watchdogs of the
millions of people in the provinces. This was Robespierre's attitude
in the crisis of August 10th, 1792, as well as in the events which a
year later caused the exclusion of the Girondist deputies from the
Convention, when the President of the Convention, the Jacobin
Hérault de Séchelles, yielded to the armed insurgents with the words
that the force of the people was identical with the force of reason.

On May 26th, 1793, Robespierre said in his speech at the Jacobin
Club that " when the people is oppressed, and when it has nobody
to rely upon but itself, he would be a coward who would not call
upon it to rise. When all the laws are violated, when despotism
has reached its climax, when good faith and shame are trampled
upon, then it is the duty of the people to rise. That moment has
arrived : our enemies are openly oppressing the patriots ; they
wish, in the name of law, to plunge the people into misery and
bondage. . . . I know of only two modes of existence for the
people : to govern itself, or to entrust the task to mandatories."
The popular deputies who wish for responsible government are
being oppressed. The people must come to the Convention to
protect them against the corrupt deputies. " I declare," exclaims
Robespierre, " that having received from the people the mandate
to defend its rights, I regard as oppressor him who interrupts me,
or refuses me the right to speak, and I declare that alone I put myself
into a state of insurrection against the president and all the members
sitting in the Convention. Contempt having been shown for the
sans-culottes, I put myself into a state of insurrection against the
corrupt deputies." Three days later, again at the Jacobins, Robespierre went further : " Si la commune de Paris, en particulier, à
qui est confié spécialement le soin de défendre les intérêts de cette

grande cité, n'en appelle point l'univers entier de la persécution dirigée contre la liberté par les plus vils conspirateurs, si la commune de Paris ne s'unit au peuple, ne forme pas avec lui une étroite alliance, elle viole le premier de ses devoirs." An uprising of the people follows a pattern and has its technique.

Of the representative institutions of the people of Paris, the Commune and the Sections, only the Commune was an elected and clearly defined body. The Sections were the public meetings of the inhabitants of the various districts. The direct democracy was a casually assembled body of men. The Sections were assiduously attended and dominated by the Revolutionary activists and enthusiasts, in fact by a small minority. At the moment of crisis a Central Revolutionary Committee of the Sections is formed, usually strengthened by provincial activists, *fédérés* who happen to be in Paris. The members of this Insurrectionary Committee are in every case obscure, third- and fourth-rate people. For it is supposed to be an uprising of the anonymous, inarticulate masses. In the background are the Jacobin leaders to direct, give inspiration and define the programme. The Central Insurrectionary Committee of the people in insurrection create a Revolutionary Commune by replacing the old one, or by declaring the existing body to have become Revolutionary. Such a declaration marks, as said once before, the outbreak of the uprising of the sovereign people against oppression. The people are now to exercise directly their sovereign rights. The elected representatives of the National Assembly must stand aside or yield to the will of the represented. This is the pattern followed on August 10th, 1792, and May 31st to June 2nd, 1793. On the earlier occasion Robespierre calls upon his Jacobin friends to " engage their sections to let the Assembly know the real will of the people ; and in order to discover that will, to maintain relations with the popular societies ", that is to say the clubs, where popular opinion is formed.

Robespierre repeats the same call on May 8th, 1793. His speeches on the eve of the two insurrections constitute the political plank of the insurgents, whether they refer to them or not. On August 15th, 1792, Robespierre, who is not a member of the Assembly, heads the deputation of the insurgent people to the Legislative Assembly to remind the representatives of the people that the people is not " asleep ". The popular demands in 1793 to expel the Girondist deputies, to limit the franchise to *sans-culottes*,

to arm *sans-culotte* Revolutionary armies everywhere to watch over
the counter-revolutionaries, and to pay poor patriots for duties performed in the defence of liberty, come straight from Robespierre's
earlier statements. On June 8th, 1793, when an attempt is made
by Barère at the Convention to cancel the emergency state of
insurrection in Paris, Robespierre insists that the insurrection must
be made to spread to the whole country, because the country could
no longer suffer the "disorder that had been reigning". The
popular Revolutionary authorities, the *Comités de surveillance* and
the Revolutionary armies must remain to maintain order, safeguard
freedom and keep the aristocrats in check.

Robespierre did not deny that such direct action by self-
appointed guardians of the people's freedom entailed anarchical
violence. But the attitude of justice of the peace did not befit the
solemn nature of a Revolution and the supremacy of the Revolutionary purpose. Revolutionary events have to be judged by the
Convention "en législateurs du monde", declared Robespierre on
November 5th, 1792, in his speech against Louvet, who tried to
indict him for his part in the events of the last few months, and
accused him of aspiring to dictatorship. A Revolution cannot be
accomplished without Revolutionary violence. It was not possible
"après coup, marquer le point précis où doivent se briser les
flots de l'insurrection populaire". If one particular act of popular
violence and coercion was to be condemned as illegal, then all other
Revolutionary events, the Revolution root and branch, would have
to be declared a crime. "Why do not you put on trial all at the
same time, the municipality, the electoral assemblies, the Paris
Sections, and all those who followed our example ? For all these
things have been illegal, as illegal as the Revolution, as unlawful as
the destruction of the throne and of the Bastille, as illegal as liberty
itself." These were unanswerable arguments, once the people was
recognized as the supreme and permanently active agent in politics.

The "people" became here a vague mystical idea. At one
moment it appears as an avalanche forging ahead, swallowing up
all in its way, acting with monumental ruthlessness. At another
Robespierre presents it as modest, magnanimous and humane,
the depositary of all virtues, schooled in the school of sorrow
and humiliation. No knots of power or nests of influence were
to be left to hamper the march of the people, or distort its self-
expression.

As late as spring, 1793, Saint-Just showed himself still obsessed
with the sacredness of the principle of unlimited popular self-
expression and the fear of governmental power appropriated by a
small group of rulers. The occasion on which he voiced these
sentiments was the discussion on a draft of Constitution submitted
on behalf of the Girondists by Condorcet. The plan contained two
important features : a Legislative Assembly elected indirectly by
departmental councils, and an Executive Council on a direct popular
vote. Both suggestions were rejected by Saint-Just in the name
of the indivisibility of the general will, the only guarantee of a
" vigorous government " and a " strong constitution ", very characteristic and strange epithets for a system under which the Executive was to have no power at all. The Girondist project of an
Executive Council elected directly by the people appeared to Saint-
Just the most dangerous threat of all to the unity of the Republic and
popular sovereignty. The Legislative and the Executive would not
only both be elected, and thus rivals, but the latter, being derived
from direct election, would be endowed with a higher prestige than
the indirectly chosen Assembly. Moreover, whereas in the past the
Ministers were outside the Executive Council, and did not form a
cabinet deliberating together and acting as a collectively responsible
body, the new project laid down that the Executive Council and the
Ministers were to form one and the same body. In short, the
Council was to be an elected, deliberating body, executing its own
decisions. " Le conseil est le ministre de ses propres volontés . . .
sa vigilance sur lui-même est illusoire." Apart from the heresy of
an elected Executive, the elected Ministers enjoying also parliamentary privilege, the people would also be without any guarantees
against them. The Ministers would shield each other through
Ministerial solidarity, and the Legislature would remain without
powers, and indeed, without anything to do, since the Executive
Council was also to be a deliberative council. In two years, Saint-
Just thought, the Assembly would be suspended, and the Executive
Council would reign supreme and without restrictions of a fundamental law. The Council would have enormous powers at its
disposal. Its members would be the true representatives of the
people, the armies would be under its control, all means of propaganda, intimidation and corruption in its hands. Only powerful
and famous men known to each other would be elected to form
in due course a hereditary body of patricians sharing between

themselves the Executive power. All hope for a people's government would have to be given up. There would again be rulers and subjects.

Saint-Just's own plan envisaged an Assembly elected by direct suffrage, and an Executive Council chosen by secondary electoral assemblies, and subordinated to the Assembly. The Executive Council and the Ministers were to be forbidden to form one body, and furthermore the Ministers, who were to be especially appointed, were to be forbidden to form a cabinet, in case they should become a " cabal ". Saint-Just went so far as to forbid the Assembly to divide itself into committees, to appoint special commissions from its own members, except to report on special matters, or to carry out delegated functions. No way was to be opened for the development of partial wills. The general will of the sovereign must not be falsified by distilling or diluting processes. The general will is one and indivisible.

The Jacobin type of democratic perfectionism such as was partly embodied in the Constitution of 1793, especially in regard to plebiscitary approval of laws voted by the Legislative, and to the people's right to resist oppression, was calculated to lead to anarchism : a direct democracy with thousands of sections throughout France in permanent session, bombarding the National Assembly with resolutions, protests, petitions, and above all deputations with the right to address the House ; revoking and re-electing deputies ; a permanent national referendum broken up into small local plebiscites ; an Executive always suspect, and with no power to act ; a Legislative bullied and blackmailed by outside and frequently armed interference ; finally, sporadic outbreaks of popular violence against constitutional authorities ; massacres such as the September massacres of the suspects, with the people's instinct as the sole judge of their necessity and timeliness, and the sole sanction to give them legality and justification.

This democratic perfectionism was in fact inverted totalitarianism. It was the result not of a sincere wish to give every shade of opinion a chance to assert itself, but the outcome of an expectation that the fruit of democratic sovereignty stretched to its limit would be a single will. It was based on a fanatical belief that there could be no more than one legitimate popular will. The other wills stood condemned a priori as partial, selfish and illegitimate. The ancients have already understood, and indeed witnessed, the phenomenon of extreme democracy leading straight to personal tyranny. Modern experience has added one link, the role of the totalitarian-democratic vanguard in a plebiscitary régime, posing as the people. The fervour and ceaseless activity of the believers, on the one hand, and intimidation practised on opponents and the lukewarm, on the other, are the instruments by which the desired " general will " is made to appear as the will of all. Only one voice is heard, and it is voiced with such an insistence, vehemence, self-righteous fervour and a tone of menace that all the other voices are drowned, cowed and silenced. Robespierre was the chief engineer of this type of popular self-expression in the elections to the Convention in Paris during the undisputed dictatorship of the insurrectionary Commune, with " vote par appel nominal ", open voting, ban on opposition journals, publication of names of people who had signed royalist petitions, the scrutiny of electoral lists, and the exclusion of electors and elected thought unorthodox. The result was that only a small minority of the Paris voters recorded their vote, in some sections hardly more than a twentieth of the electorate. Only a tenth voted in the whole of France. The Jacobin Constitution of 1793 was approved by barely two million votes out of the seven entitled to vote. In Paris nobody voted against, in the departments only fifteen to sixteen thousand. It was at once suspended and put into a glass case in the hall of the Convention.

Let the people speak, for their voice is the voice of God, the voice of reason and of the general interest ! Robespierre clung with tenacity to his faith in the equation of liberty and virtue, but even his faith had to give way to the painful realization that this may not always be the case. He thus put up a ferocious and successful fight against an appeal to the people on the fate of Louis XVI, demanding first guarantees that " bad citizens, moderates, *feuillants* and aristocrats would be given no access " to the primary assemblies and would be prevented from misleading and playing upon the tender feelings of the people. For the aim is not to let the people speak, but to insure that they vote well, and bad voters are excluded.

Saint-Just considered that an appeal to the people on the fate of the King would be tantamount to a writ for restoration of the Monarchy. Anti-parliamentarian under the Legislative Assembly, Robespierre became in time a staunch defender of the supremacy of the Convention, especially after the expulsion of the Girondists. He opposed bitterly the suggestion that the Convention should dissolve, after having voted the Constitution of 1793, for the preparation of which it had been elected. The purified Convention (after the expulsion of the Girondists) would be replaced by envoys of Pitt and Coburg, he claimed. At one time a defender of the principle that the Sections should remain in permanent session, he later helped to reverse it. The argument was that after the people had won and obtained their own revolutionary popular government, there was no need any more for direct democratic supervision and vigilance. The permanence of the Sections, which formerly secured such control, would now be an opportunity for counter-revolutionary intriguers and idlers to corrupt public opinion and to plot against the Government, while the good honest *sans-culottes* were away in the fields and workshops. Robespierre came to admit to himself that the people could not be trusted to voice its real will. In his famous confidential Catechism Robespierre declared that the gravest obstacle to Liberty and the greatest opportunity for the counter-revolutionary forces was the people's lack of enlightenment. One of the most important causes of the people's ignorance was the people's misery. When will the people become enlightened ? he asked himself. When they have bread and when the rich and the Government will have ceased to hire perfidious journalists and venal speakers to mislead them.

This line of thought carries with it far-reaching implications, which were to be fully grasped and systematized by Babeuf and the *Égaux*. What in effect Robespierre was saying was that as long as the people were hungry, dominated and misled by the rich, their recorded opinions could not be taken as reflecting the true will of the sovereign. From the point of view of real democracy and the true general will the task was therefore not just to let the people speak, freely and spontaneously, and then to accept their verdict as final and absolute. It was first to create the conditions for a true expression of the popular will. This involved the satisfaction of the people's material needs, popular education, and above all the elimination of evil influences, in other words, opposition. Only after that would the people be called to vote. There could be no doubt about the way they would vote then. In the meantime the will of the enlightened vanguard was the real will of the people.

There was thus no necessary inconsistency between the earlier emphasis on the active and permanent exercise of popular sovereignty and the later dictatorial policies of the enlightened vanguard—

Robespierre and his colleagues. The general will commanded
different attitudes at different times. It spoke every time through
Robespierre.

There was the need to mobilize and to stir the masses in order
to enable the Revolutionary vanguard to carry out the real will of
the people. Once the vanguard had come into power, it must be
given freedom to realize that will in all its purity. The *a priori*
consent of the masses to what the vanguard would do may be taken
for granted, and if so, the perpetuation of popular political activity,
unnecessary in the new conditions, would only, as said before in
another context, give a chance to counter-revolutionary cunning.

(*b*) LIBERTY AS AN OBJECTIVE PURPOSE

The nearer the Jacobins were to power, the stronger grew their
insistence on the conception of liberty as a set of values and not as
merely the absence of constraint. The general will acquired an
objective quality, and the reference to the actual exercise of popular
sovereignty as the essential mode of arriving at the general will came
to be less often repeated.

It is only fair to the Jacobins to emphasize in this connection the
supreme crisis of the Revolution, which they were called upon to
face in 1793. The country was in deadly peril from invasion. The
federalist uprisings in Lyons, Bordeaux, Toulon, Marseilles, Nor-
mandy and elsewhere, the success of the Vendéean revolt, the breakdown of the circulation of commodities, the inflation caused by the
collapse of the *assignats*, the paper money, combined to create an
atmosphere of fanaticism, fear, excitement, suspicion and general
emergency. Yet, these factors, grave no doubt as they were, could
not in themselves account for the régime of terror, without the
permanent totalitarian disposition of Jacobinism. Without the
fanatical, single-minded faith in their embodying the sole truth, the
Jacobins could not have found the courage and strength to build
up and sustain their régime of terror. Without their ever more
narrowly defined orthodoxy, there would have been no need to
brand so many as, and indeed to turn so many into, enemies of the
Revolution. The Terror continued unabated even after the decisive
victories of the Revolution over all its enemies, external and internal,
in October, 1793. It fell to Saint-Just, as *rapporteur* on the most

important issues of the Revolution in the years 1793-4, to start the process of redefining the Revolutionary idea of liberty. His first major pronouncement on this matter was the famous speech on supplies, November 23rd, 1792.

The alarming state of French finances and economy in general was attributed by Saint-Just to the " essor " of liberty that followed the outbreak of the Revolution, and to " la difficulté de rétablir l'économie au milieu de la vigueur et de l'indépendance de l'esprit public. L'indépendance armée contre l'indépendance n'a plus de loi, plus de juge . . . toutes les volontés isolées n'en obligent aucune." Liberty was at war with morality and order. There was a danger of anarchy. To counteract this anarchy of isolated wills, Saint-Just at first resorted to grand invocations of national solidarity and to the argument that the interests of everyone had become so intertwined with the fortunes of the Revolution that its collapse would spell universal doom.

" Il faut que tout le monde oublie son intérêt et son orgueil. Le bonheur et l'intérêt particulier sont une violence à l'ordre social, quand ils ne sont point une portion de l'intérêt et du bonheur public. Oubliez-vous vous-mêmes. La révolution française est placée entre un arc de triomphe et un écueil qui nous briserait tous. Votre intérêt vous commande de ne point vous diviser." Whatever the differences of opinion among the patriots, the tyrants would not take any notice of them. " We win together or perish together." The self-interest of everyone commands him to forget his personal good. Personal salvation is only possible through general salvation. All personal interest and welfare must be sunk in the general pool.

From this appeal to the enlightened self-interest of everyone, Saint-Just comes to the idea of a Republic that represents objective values of its own, and in such an integrated form as to prevent the independence of wills. The Republic envisaged by him would " embrace all relations, all interests, all rights, all duties " and would assure an " allure commune " to all parts of the State. Liberty, the opposite of independence, becomes now " l'obéissance de chacun à l'harmonie individuelle et homogène du corps entier ". This conception is translated into a " République une et indivisible . . . avec l'entière abstraction de tout lieu et toutes personnes ". The unity and indivisibility of the Republic is thus transformed into something that is prior even to the Social Contract. It is an essential

part of the objective general will and liberty, out of the reach of
the transient will of passing mortals. The whole comes before its
components. " A Republic, one and indivisible, is in the very
nature of liberty ; it would not last more than a moment, if it was
based upon a fragile convention between men."

This was another reason for Saint-Just's vehement opposition to
Condorcet's draft of the 1793 Constitution. The Girondist project
envisaged a Legislative elected indirectly by departmental councils,
and not by the " concours simultané de la volonté générale " and
" le peuple en corps ". A deputy elected that way, Saint-Just maintained, would represent only the portion of the people who voted
for him, and not the indivisible nation. All the deputies coming
together as representatives of the fractions of the people would not
constitute a legitimate majority ; they would not express or embody
the general will, but would form a congress, instead of a National
Assembly. The majority in a congress derives its authority from
the voluntary adhesion of the parties. The sovereign thus ceases to
exist, as it is divided. A general will obtained that way is a " speculative ", not a real will. Those who will must do so primarily as
aspects of an indivisible entity, and not as possessors of partial wills.
The nation is an organic, indivisible entity, and not a conglomeration
of mechanically joined particles.

If each department was understood to represent a portion of the
territory, with the portion of the people inhabiting it in possession
of sovereignty over that province, the " droit de cité du peuple en
corps " would become undermined and the Republic would be
broken up by the slightest shock, such as the Vendéean rebellion.
The territorial division was solely a geometrical division for electoral
purposes, not even for administrative reasons. The *a priori* unity of
Frenchmen was the basis and symbol of the unity of the Republic,
not the territory, and certainly not the Government, because this
would mean a Monarchy. Praising Saint-Just's views, one of the
deputies remarked that his draft of the Constitution would make it
possible for Frenchmen to settle down as a French nation, and to
observe their obligations to one another, even if they were evacuated
to a foreign territory.

The instinct for national unity emerged stronger than the logic
of the Social Contract. If the essence of a nation is what Renan was
to call some eighty years later " le plébiscite de tous les jours ", in
other words the active and constantly reaffirmed will to live together

and under the same law, then the right of secession could not be withheld. The Jacobins preached the former, but passionately denied the latter. They had to postulate an *a priori* will to form an indivisible entity, as they were too cosmopolitan and rationalist in their outlook to admit a historic, racial or any other irrational basis for national unity.

This conception of French national unity, when confronted with the Revolutionary attitude to old Europe, was calculated to involve France in one of those permanent wars which spring from a conflict of irreconcilable ideas on relations between nations. Such a war is usually the outcome of the attitude of " heads I win, tails you lose " adopted by a Revolutionary power preaching a new doctrine of international relations, not based on reciprocity. On the basis of the voluntary, non-racial and unhistorical conception of nationhood Revolutionary France, rationalizing her interests and her desire for expansion, claimed—true, not without some hesitation—to have the right to admit into the Republic foreign provinces on her borders, like Savoy, Nice, the cities on the Rhine, Belgium and others, which had expressed freely or had been brought to voice the wish to be united to the French Republic. Coupled with the French proclamations of November 19th and December 15th, 1792, that France would hasten to help any people rising against its King and feudal system, this attitude amounted to an invitation to any foreign commune or province to break away from the body of the nation, the State entity. A partial will was thus set up against the general will of the whole. France was to become the cause and engineer of the disintegration of nations and annexer of their severed parts, in the name of the right of any group to express and act on its general will. At the same time the Convention declared the death penalty for any attempt to divide French territory or to cede any part of the " République une et indivisible ". The implication was that in Republican and democratic France a general national will had already crystallized, while no such will could have crystallized in the countries under the feudal system. Furthermore, as Europe was in any case heading towards a unified free form of government, the beginning might as well be made by joining the liberated parts of Europe to France. It would thus be possible to give them protection, while offering to France, the champion of the unity of free peoples against the dynastic tyrannies which have kept the European peoples divided, an increase of strength in the struggle for universal liberation. This meant endless war with old Europe, without prospect of an agreement on any common basis. No halt was in sight. For it must have soon appeared clear to the more acute Revolutionaries—among them indeed Robespierre— that in fact the free will of men, instead of being a tangible and reliable criterion for nationhood, was in fact very shifting ground. Hence the idea of natural frontiers. Although no doubt part of French tradition, and an expression of a rationalized desire for expanded and safer frontiers, the idea of natural frontiers was meant also to be a safety valve, a signpost to the French themselves, and a kind of assurance to the nations of old Europe that there was a halt to the French claims to the right of annexing peoples who had offered themselves for reunion. France would not go on annexing parts of other states for ever, for she had come to believe in the existence of a national entity, which must not be broken by the partial will of parts. The basis of this national entity was no more the will of the passing generation, but something of a more permanent character—the facts of nature and history, which together have fixed unmistakable frontiers to nations in the form of rivers, mountains and seas. The concomitant of this recognition of a natural and historical basis of national unity was the declaration of non-interference in the internal affairs of other states, the spread of anti-alien feeling and the campaign against foreign agents and spies in France—as a reaction to earlier proselytism.

(c) THE RIGHT OF OPPOSITION; OUTLAWING OF PARTIES

The *a priori* idea of national unity, however, far from serving as a basis for a national reconciliation founded on a common past, gave rise to a process of eliminating from the national body the elements thought to be inassimilable to the new principle of French national existence.

Saint-Just's " Rapport sur la nécessité de déclarer le gouvernement révolutionnaire jusqu'à la paix ", made on October 10th, 1793, was a turning point in this respect.

It is a far cry from that conception of liberty which takes for granted the right of every individual to express his particular will, and to defend his particular interest spontaneously and without external constraint. It is very remote from the confident belief that if everyone forms his will on his interest, the general will would result from a majority of wills. A new principle which " henceforth should never depart from the minds of those who govern " is declared : the Republic " will never be founded till the will of the sovereign has constrained the royalist minority and ruled over it by right of conquest ".

" Depuis que le peuple français a manifesté sa volonté tout ce qui est hors le souverain est ennemi." There was nothing between the people and its enemies but the sword. Those who could not be governed by justice, must be ruled by the sword. " Vous ne parlerez point la même langue, vous ne vous entendrez jamais. Chassez-les donc ! " And he meant it literally, for the plan proposed by him a little later envisaged the eventual expulsion of all suspects, as well as their total expropriation, in other words the total liquidation of a class. Saint-Just invokes the principles of democracy in this connection. " Il leur faut la puissance, qui n'appartient ici qu'à la démocratie." The idea of democracy implied here contains no reference to the right of opposition, to individual liberties or toleration, and clearly revives the ancient Greek view of democracy as the victory of the mass of the under-privileged over the privileged minority, and the suppression of the latter by the former. Severity is an essential element of a free democratic régime, and plays a greater part there than in a tyrannical state.

" There is no government which can preserve the rights of citizens without a policy of severity, but the difference between a free system and a tyrannical régime is that in the former that policy is employed against the minority opposed to the general good, and against the abuses or the negligence of the authorities, while in the latter the severity of the State power is directed against the unfortunates delivered to the injustice and the impunity of the powers."

A weak government was ultimately oppressive to the people, Saint-Just thought. " It is just that the people should in its turn rule over its oppressors ", for " tyrants must be oppressed ". All the wisdom of a government consisted in the elimination of the party opposed to the Revolution and in making the people happy at the expense of the vices of the enemies of liberty. The surest means of establishing the Revolution was to turn it to the benefit of those who support it, and to the destruction of those who fight it.

Robespierre said the same things, and almost in the same words. There were no divergencies between the Incorruptible and Saint-Just, after they were brought together by the latter's election to the Convention. "There are no other citizens in a Republic", wrote Robespierre, "than republicans. Royalists . . . conspirators are nothing but aliens, or rather enemies." Social protection was the due of the citizen. But a citizen was not just everyone born on French soil. Only he was a citizen who was spiritually identified with the substance that constituted French nationhood, the general will. The enemies of the people could not possibly be offered an opportunity of distorting and sabotaging the people's will. Neither the necessity of national unity, which commands men to sink their differences in the face of external danger, nor the idea of the legitimacy of the natural divergencies of opinion had any validity. There were only the people, and the people's enemies.

"Domptez par la terreur les ennemis de la liberté . . . vous avez raison comme fondateurs d'une république. Le gouvernement de la Révolution est le despotisme de la liberté contre la tyrannie." Both tyranny and liberty employ the sword, but the only resemblance between them is that the blade in either hand shines similarly.

What about the right of opposition? Nothing was more calculated to exasperate Saint-Just and Robespierre than this argument, the claim of an opponent to a right to oppose the régime as a right to resist oppression. Resistance to oppression was a sacred right and duty in a tyrannical state, but once the régime of liberty had been established, once the people had come into their own, the claim to resist "oppression" by the new order was mockery or perversity, or sheer selfishness, defiant of the general good.

"Let the people claim its liberty, when it is oppressed, but when liberty is triumphant, and when tyranny has expired, that one should forget the general good in order to kill his country by preference of one's personal good, this is mean villainy, punishable hypocrisy!"

The claim of the aristocracy that its destruction by the people was an act of dictatorship was a revolting abuse of terminology. The people and tyranny!—it was a contradiction in terms. "The people is no tyrant, and it is the people that now reign." "Toutes

les idées se confondent " : a " fripon " condemned to the guillotine
invokes the right of resistance to oppression ! Robespierre fulminated against justice of the people being called barbarism or
oppression. " Indulgence pour les royalistes ! . . . grâce pour
scélérats. . . . Non ! grâce pour l'innocence, grâce pour les
faibles, grâce pour les malheureux, . . . grâce pour l'humanité ! "
It is absurd to say that a free government of the people can be
oppressive because it is vigorous. " On se trompe. La question
est mal posée." Such a government oppressed only what was
evil, and was therefore just. A Republican government rested on
the principle of " vertu " or terror. It was true that force made
no right, but it may well be that it was indispensable for making
justice and reason respected.

Not only traitors, but also the indifferent, the passive, who were
doing nothing for the Republic, must be punished. The people's
cause must be supported as a whole, for those who pick holes are
disguised traitors. " Un patriote soutient la République en masse,
celui qui la combat en détail est un traître. . . . Tout ce qui n'est
pas respect du peuple et vous (Convention) est un crime." As the
aim of an anti-federal government of the people was the unity of
the Republic not for the profit of those in power, but for the
benefit of the people as a whole, no isolationist tendency could be
tolerated in an individual. Such isolationism would be as immoral
in the civil sphere as federalism was in the political sphere.

" Lorsque la liberté est fondée, il s'agit de l'observation des
devoirs envers la patrie, il s'agit d'être citoyen." There could be
no reason and no excuse—as there was in the past—for isolating oneself in order to preserve one's independence. Saint-Just insists
more than once on the difference between liberty and independence
to do evil. For liberty was in the last analysis not freedom from
constraint, but a set of objective and exclusive values. Independence
from these values implied vice and tyranny, bondage to egoism,
passion and avarice. " L'idée particulière que chacun se fait de sa
liberté, selon son intérêt, produit l'esclavage de tous."

According to Robespierre it was wrong to regard terror as pure
repressive violence, resorted to without reference to the general
principles governing a Republic. It was only accentuated justice—
nothing but an emanation from and special facet of the principle of
virtue—not a special principle.

" La terreur n'est autre chose que la justice prompte, sévère, inflexible ; elle est donc une émanation de la vertu ; elle est moins un principe particulier qu'une consequence du principe général de la démocratie appliqué aux plus pressants besoins de la patrie."

Similarly Saint-Just declared that a Republican government had *vertu* as its principle ; if not terror. " Que veulent ceux qui ne veulent ni vertu ni terreur ? " Elsewhere he said that a Revolution needed a dictator to save it by force, or censors to save it by virtue. Virtue, the elusive personal quality, the least tangible of all criteria, was fast becoming the decisive criterion, when the new splits were no longer caused by class differences or royalist loyalties. The doomed wicked were to Robespierre the assassins from within, in the first place, the mercenary scribes (journalists) allied to kill public virtue, to sow discord and to prepare a political counter-revolution by means of a " contre-révolution morale ". Journalists could expect no quarter from the former defender of unrestricted liberty of the press.

The idea of a sole exclusive truth, which is the basis of the rigid and fixed conception of Republican virtue, excludes the possibility of political parties representing honest differences of opinion.

According to Saint-Just it was precisely in a régime of Liberty —such as he claimed to be representing—and one based on absolute truth and virtue, that parties and factions were an anachronism, and a criminal one. Factions had a useful function in the " ancien régime ", they contributed to the isolation of despotism and weakened the influence of tyranny. " They are a crime to-day, because they isolate liberty." Liberty is attained only when the general will can express itself as an entity, as the sole and undivided sovereign deliberating on the common good of the people as a whole.

The curiosity awakened by party controversy, the corruption engendered by party strife, distracted the hearts and minds from the love of country and single-minded devotion to its interests.

" Every party is therefore criminal, because it makes for the isolation of the people and the popular societies, and for the independence of the government. Any faction is therefore criminal, because it neutralizes the power of public virtue. . . . The solidity of our Republic is in the very nature of things. The sovereignty of the people requires that it should be one . . . it is opposed to factions. Every faction is therefore an attempt on sovereignty."

Saint-Just is quite unable to see in the parties an instrument for expressing and organizing the various trends in public opinion. He only sees the people, on the one hand, and the parties conspiring against it, on the other. He called upon the people and the Convention to govern firmly and to impose their will upon the " criminal factions ". The description of the evils of a multiple party system is strikingly reminiscent of the evils nowadays attributed to a single party régime. It deserves to be quoted in full.

" Pride engenders the factions. The factions are the most terrible poison of the body politic, they put the life of the citizens in peril by their power of calumny ; when they reign in a State, no person is certain of his future, and the empire which they torment is a coffin ; they put into doubt falsehood and truth, vice and virtue, justice and injustice ; it is force that makes law. . . . In dividing the people the factions put party fury in place of liberty ; the sword of the law and the assassins' daggers clash together ; no-one dares to speak or to be silent; the audacious individuals, who get to the top in the parties, force the citizens to choose between crime and crime."

As to himself and his friends, Saint-Just would reject with indignation any imputation that they, too, were a party. They were the very people itself. This he declared in his last and undelivered speech in defence of Robespierre. He looked forward in that speech to the day when the Republican Institutions would eliminate for ever all parties, putting " human pride under the yoke of public liberty ", and the " dictatorship of justice ".

He prayed fervently that " the factions may disappear so that liberty alone would remain ". " The fondest prayer a good citizen can pray for his country, the greatest benefaction a generous nation may derive from its virtue, is the ruin, is the fall of the factions."

For after the struggle for unfettered sovereignty of the people had been won, the supreme aim was the unity of will. " Il faut une volonté une," wrote Robespierre in his carnet. " That it should be republican we want republican ministers, republican papers, republican deputies, a republican government." The external war was a mortal malady, but the body politic was ill from revolution and the " division of wills ". Like to Rousseau, a political party was to Robespierre the function of a private interest. " The factions are the coalition of private interests against the general good." For there is such a definite quantity as the general good :

" The concert of the friends of liberty, the complaints of the oppressed, the natural ascendancy of reason, the force of public opinion do not constitute a faction."

Incapable of adapting himself to the idea that differences of opinion were a normal phenomenon and not unnatural, an expression of egoism, perversion, or stupidity, Robespierre was quite shaken at the moment of his greatest triumph, when after the fall of the " factions ", the Girondists, the Hébertists and the Dantonists, he was faced with new strains and new differences. He was appalled at the idea that there should still be differences, and divisions of opinion. He declared that wherever a line of demarcation made itself visible, wherever a division pronounced itself, " là il y a quelque chose qui tient au salut de la patrie ". It was not natural that there should be separation and division among people equally animated by the love for the public good. " Il n'est pas naturel qu'il s'élève une sorte de coalition contre le gouvernement qui se dévoue pour le salut de la patrie." It was to him a symptom of a new malady, because the Convention had of late been voting decrees on the spot. It had been showing unanimity on the sacred principles. There were no more factions. The Convention, with a trained discerning eye, had been going straight ahead and hitting its target unerringly.

The postulate of unanimity as the only natural principle among patriots implied the postulate of unity in action. The question presented itself : how would democracy work, without parties ?

There is no direct answer to this from Saint-Just, but what he had to say on the subject of educating public opinion and organizing the sovereignty of the people clearly re-echoes Rousseauist formulæ and deserves to be quoted in full. It was doubtless the vision of a plebiscitary democracy (or dictatorship), where the people are asked to answer with a clear " yes " or " no " obvious questions, the answer to which could hardly be in doubt. " As all are incessantly deliberating in a free state, and public opinion is affected by many vicissitudes and stirred by caprices and various passions, the legislators must take care that the question of the general good is always clearly put, so that when deliberating all should be able to think, act and speak in the spirit and within the framework of the established order . . . in harmony. It is in this way that the Republic truly becomes one and indivisible, and the sovereign is composed of all hearts carried forward to virtue."

Unless the question was put and answered in this circular

way, society would be delivered to strife, selfishness and anarchy.
Another indication about Saint-Just's ideas on the subject may be
gained from his complaint that the laws and decrees passed by the
Convention had been deteriorating as their projects had ceased to
be the subject of preliminary examination and discussion at the
Jacobin Club.   Clearly Saint-Just thought it inadvisable to have the
Convention without guidance from an extra-parliamentary body of
censors.

(d) THE THEORY OF REVOLUTIONARY GOVERNMENT

Robespierre's answer to the problem is contained in his theory
of the Revolutionary Government, and has the merit of precision.
" J'avoue que mes notions en politique ne ressemblent en rien à
celles de beaucoup d'hommes," he said about his theory.   He said,
as we have seen, that it was new as the Revolution itself, and could
not be found in any of the theoretical treatises.   It was the product
of the Revolution, shaped on its lessons, and a theory that reversed
whatever was left of Robespierre's earlier ideas on the separation
of powers and his enmity towards the Executive.   The function of a
government was according to Robespierre to direct the physical
and moral forces of the nation towards the purpose for which it was
instituted.   Thus while the aim of a constitutional régime was to
preserve the Republic, that of a Revolutionary Government was to
found it.   A constitutional régime can be established only in
conditions of victorious and peaceful liberty.   A Revolutionary
Government implies the war of liberty against its enemies.   One
defends civil liberty, the other public liberty.   A constitutional
Government has as its task the defence of personal freedom against
the encroachments of governmental powers ; a Revolutionary
régime must defend public liberty, embodied in the Revolutionary
Government, against the factions.   It owes protection to peaceful
citizens, nothing but death to enemies of public liberty.   " Ceux
qui les (Revolutionary violent measures) nomment arbitraires ou
tyranniques sont de stupides sophistes ou pervers qui cherchent à
confondre les contraires."   The Revolutionary Government must
have the powers and the machinery to act with rapidity, unen-
cumbered by any legal checks and legal niceties, to mobilize all
forces of the nation, and to hit ruthlessly and powerfully.   This

means that the barrier between the Legislature and the Executive must be broken down so as to insure prompt action. Government action must no longer be slow and complicated as it was in the past, when nothing but informal and casual contact was maintained between the two branches of the administration. Robespierre had moved very far from his savage denunciation of the " intrigues " between the Rolandist Ministry and the Girondist leaders in the Assembly, and from the principle that no deputy could be a Minister of State. What Robespierre was proposing was government by a Committee emanating from the Convention. All executive powers, rendered practically unlimited owing to the Revolutionary character of the Government, were to be handed over to a " faithful commission ", " d'un . . . patriotisme épuré, une commission si sûre que l'on ne puisse plus cacher ni le nom des traîtres ni la trame des trahisons." It was to be a Committee of the most faithful and most ruthless. This was the conception underlying the régime of the Committee of Public Safety and Jacobin dictatorship, a régime designed to make the Revolutionary purpose triumph at all costs, and not to realize liberty in the sense of free self-expression ; a system which replaced the principle of popular choice by the principle of the infallibility of the enlightened few in the central body acting in a dictatorial manner through special agents appointed by themselves.

" The two opposite genii . . . contesting the empire of nature, are in this great period of human history interlocked in a mortal combat to determine irretrievably the destinies of the world, and France is the stage of this redoubtable struggle. Without, all tyrants are bent upon encircling you ; within, all the friends of tyranny are banded in a conspiracy : they will go on plotting, until all hope will have been wrested from crime. We have to strangle the internal as well as the external enemies of the Republic, or perish with her ; and, in a situation like this, your first maxim of policy must be the guiding principle that the people shall be led by reason, but the enemies of the people by terror "—thus spoke Robespierre. War ! The state of war ! This means a state of emergency, above all an atmosphere of " rise and kill him, or he will kill you ". If you credit your opponent with such a fixed resolution, you are free of all obligations towards him, legal, moral or other. Doing justice, observing the code of law, become meaningless ; sheer mockery, when demanded. The supreme law is salvation achieved by the annihilation of the enemy. The war is global ; global, for the theatre of operations is global ; global, because all lives, all possessions and all values are involved, all assets and all means mobilized. This being so, the war has no fixed or limited front. It is not the battlefield alone where the fight takes place. Every preventive action taken to weaken the enemy, to sow confusion in his ranks, to impoverish him or to undermine his morale, to uncover his flank or to deceive and to get him into a trap, is legitimate, is a laudable act ; indeed, a sacred duty. From the point of view of those engaged in the battle on your own side, the fact of war changes the whole scale of values. A war entails direction of the war-operations by a supreme command acting in strictest secrecy, with all possible speed, employing every means of surprise, not hampered by any checks or control ; further-more, by a supreme command composed of men especially, or rather exceptionally, qualified for the task : endowed with the gift of leadership, trustworthy, ruthless, energetic and pure. In short, all emphasis comes to be placed on personal qualities, Robespierre's elusive quality of virtue. The democratic test of election, of preliminary, reiterated and confirmed authorization for the demo-cratic execution by appointed, supervised and responsible leaders of decisions publicly debated, clearly defined and resolved upon, is relegated into the background. It is impossible to debate in public or to prescribe how to act in the heat of battle, under the impact of unforeseen mortal contingencies. The men in the supreme com-mand will know best how to act. Authorization to and control of leaders must make place for implicit trust, *a priori* consent, un-conditional obedience. The relationship between the leaders and the led assumes the character of a personal relationship. However much a salvationist creed may try to ignore the personal element in the realm of pure theory, in so much as in course of time it evolves into a war of the elect against the condemned, it must resort to the personal leader-saviour, endowed with unique qualities, eliciting filial love and obedience from the led. The latter are soldiers in a global struggle. Soldiers do not argue, but carry out orders. Sometimes these orders seem contradictory, often out-rageous, but the soldier must assume that however inexplicable and wrong they may appear in the narrow context surveyable by him, they form part of the grand strategy of the global war, and thus are perfectly logical and desirable moves, when viewed from the point of view of the whole. And so the suspension of personal judgment is a categorical imperative, and the very opposite of characterlessness and moral nihilism.

The personal element becomes all-important for another reason. If the power of the supreme command must be so boundless, its action so rapid and ruthless, placed in wrong hands it will surely become the most terrible power for evil, in proportion to the means at its disposal. " Plus son pouvoir est grand, plus son action est libre et rapide ; plus il doit être dirigé par la bonne foi. Le jour où il tombera dans des mains impures ou perfides, la liberté sera perdue ; son nom deviendra le prétexte et l'excuse de la contre-révolution même. Son énergie sera celle d'un poison violent." Hence the supreme and sacred duty of watching over the men holding the rudder, of purging the supreme command all the time from the contaminated or contaminable. Who will perform the task ? Certainly not the ordinary soldiers. The result would be anarchy. They have not in any case the means of knowing what is going on in the headquarters. It must be the purest of the ensemble at the supreme command, in fact the strongest. This is the reason for Robespierre's maniacal insistence on the personal purity of the leaders of the Revolution, of his obsessive campaign against the " corrupt ". These were in his eyes more dangerous than the open counter-revolutionaries, because they could as it were by one move turn the Revolution into counter-revolution.

Impure, corrupt, was, of course, considering Robespierre's mentality, any one who opposed him or differed from him, or showed an open mind and receptive spirit to things outside the orbit of ascetic Jacobin virtue. Nearly everyone felt in peril, when listening to Robespierre's denunciation of the unnamed impure in the Convention and on the two supreme Committees who must be weeded out, and to Robespierre's " woe, woe to him who names himself ". In the circumstances of war, in face of the almost cosmic stakes, and the titanic powers at hand, the sole means of purging an impure was of course killing him, just as the sole defence by the impure was to kill the accuser. " Il faut guillotiner, ou s'attendre à l'être "—as the shrewd and adroit Barras put it.

A brief outline of the régime of the Committee of Public Safety will bring home the antithesis reached by the Jacobin idea in the course of the Revolution.

(e) JACOBIN DICTATORSHIP

Jacobin dictatorship was an improvisation. It came into existence by stages, and not in accordance with a blue-print. At the same time, it corresponded to, and was the consequence of, a fixed attitude of mind of its authors, intensified and rendered extreme by events.

The *Comité de défense (générale)* set up on January 1st, 1793, was the immediate parent of the Committee of Public Safety. It was made to sit *en permanence* on March 25th. Reorganized and strengthened, it entered on April 6th upon its unbroken and undisputed reign as the Committee of Public Safety. Its duties were to supervise and accelerate the work of the Provisional Executive Council, and it had powers to suspend the orders of the Council and to take any steps it considered necessary for the defence and safety of the country, and to have them executed forthwith by the Council. Although it emanated from the Convention, was responsible to it, and was appointed originally only for executive duties, the Committee of Public Safety soon acquired an absolute ascendancy over the Convention, deprived the Executive Council of all powers, and in fact as well as, in the course of time, in law brushed aside all institutions of elected democracy. On October 10th, 1793, the Executive Council, Ministers, commanding generals and all constituted authorities were placed under its supervision.

The Representatives on Mission, with practically unlimited powers and subordinated directly to the Committee, were the arms of the latter in the provinces. The decrees of April 9th and 30th, 1793, gave them powers to supervise " most actively " the agents of the Executive Council, the armies, army supplies, to prevent sabotage and the squandering of public money, to fight defeatism and attempts on morale, and to keep up the Republican spirit in the army and in the rear. On a motion of Billaud-Varenne on November 18th, 1793 (28 Brumaire), they were granted powers to supervise and overrule local authorities, and to prosecute local officials for defaults, and to replace them without elections, it being implied that the local Jacobin Club would be consulted. Following Danton's intervention of a few days earlier, the Convention on December 4th (14 Frimaire) appointed national agents to the smaller administrative units with similar overall powers as those held by

the Representatives, held directly from the Committee of Public
Safety. These agents were to replace the elected *procureurs*—
syndics of districts and *procureurs de Commune*, and their substitutes.
They were vested with powers of enforcing laws, of tracking
down sabotage and incompetence, of purging the local administration and the local *Comités de surveillance* whose task was to
watch over aliens and suspects. The national agents as "agents
of the whole people" were to replace local representatives brought
to power by "the influence of family fortune" and family ties.
A decree of 5 Brumaire suspended election of municipal bodies
altogether. This extreme form of centralization based upon the
contrast between the oneness of the national interest and the single-
ness of the general will, on the one hand, and the partial character
of the regional units, on the other, reached thus its climax in a
centralized dictatorship of a small body, simultaneously a part of
the Legislative and an Executive. "Le dépôt de l'exécution des
lois est enfin confié à des dépositaires responsables" was Danton's
comment. This dictatorship was a single party dictatorship. Its
laws and decrees clearly envisaged the closest co-operation between
the agents of the dictatorial Committee and the local popular
societies, that is to say, the Jacobins, a network of societies, with no
place in the Constitution or in the official framework of administrative institutions. At the same time all public meetings other than
of Jacobin clubs were forbidden as subversive of the unity of the
Government and tending to federalism. All Revolutionary armies,
which had been raised locally from among the zealots and maintained at the expense of the rich to watch over counter-revolutionaries and to combat federal uprisings, were dissolved, to leave only
the Revolutionary army of the Convention common to the whole
of the Republic. On April 1st, 1794 (12 Germinal), Carnot
moved that a vast country like France could not be governed by a
government which was not in the closest and permanent touch
with the various parts—"ramasse et dirige ses forces vers un but
déterminé". The Committee of Public Safety should therefore
be the organ which does all the thinking, proposes all major measures
to the Convention, and acts on its own in urgent and secret matters ;
a plan that would seem unexceptional to-day to people accustomed
to centralized cabinet government, but extraordinary at the time
it was expounded. On April 2nd the Provisional Executive
Council was abolished. The Committee of Public Safety remained

the supreme and sole executive body with twelve especially appointed commissions under it.

The sample of the sovereign people, Paris, was destined to lose the special position for which the Jacobins had fought so hard against the Girondists, in the advance towards extreme centralization. The law of 14 Frimaire forbade the formation of any central committee of the Sections. All the insurrections and *journées* of the earlier days were hatched in and carried out by the *ad hoc* organized central Committees. To deal a blow against the Hébertists, who were the masters of the Commune, the Sections were forbidden to correspond with the Commune, and were instructed to maintain direct contact with the Committee of General Security, the auxiliary body of the Committee of Public Safety. Only three months earlier (September 5th) the Sectional assemblies had been renovated and given powers to arrest suspects. The same law had fixed two Section meetings per week—which was already a restriction of the principle of permanence—and a salary of forty sous for every attendance so as to attract and enable the right type of *sans-culottes* to be there. Hébert and his friends paid with their lives for the last attempt at a popular insurrection made before 9 Thermidor against the Convention and the Committee of Public Safety, after the Hébertists had been denounced by Robespierre for their violent actions against religious worship.

Hand in hand with centralization went the organization of terror. The vital decrees were passed in the later part of March and early in April, 1793, and were largely due to Robespierre and Marat, the latter having consistently agitated for personal dictatorship "to save liberty by violence". Whole groups of people were outlawed. People who took part in counter-revolutionary riots and persons seen with a white ribbon or other royalist and rebellious insignia were deprived of such legal safeguards as criminal procedure and jury; if apprehended and found guilty, they were to be executed within twenty-four hours. *Émigrés* were outlawed, banished for ever, and their goods confiscated, and enemies of the Revolution and aristocrats were put "hors de loi". The law on the "disarming of suspects" defined as "suspects" not only members of the outlawed classes and their families, like the nobility and refractory clergy, but anyone recognized as such by the authorities. The law on the suspects of September 17th went a step further.

It declared suspect all who had befriended tyranny, federalism and counter-revolution by deed, word or by the way of personal relations ; persons who failed to pay their taxes ; people not furnished with *cartes de civisme* from their Sections ; suspended or dismissed officials ; nobles, their relatives and relatives of *émigrés* ; persons unable to bring evidence of their rightful means of earning a living and of their patriotic conduct in the past. Concierges had earlier been ordered to post the names of the inhabitants of the houses in their charge, and private homes were opened to search. The decree of March 21st set up in every commune *Comités de surveillance*, recruited from the most faithful and charged with general supervision over aliens and suspects, drawing up lists of the latter, and revising the certificates of " civisme ". On March 29th a special law fixed the death penalty for journalists and pamphleteers calling for the dissolution of the Convention, the re-establishment of the monarchy, and attacking the people's sovereignty. On April 1st the parliamentary immunity of deputies to the Convention was suspended.

The Revolutionary Tribunal was properly set up, after having had a fleeting existence as *Tribunal Criminel Extraordinaire*, on April 5th. It was on that day freed from the supervision by the special Conventional Committee, to which its predecessor was subject. Moreover the need for Conventional authorization to start proceedings was waived. Denunciation by one of the established authorities or by an ordinary citizen was to be a sufficient ground, except in case of deputies, commanding generals and similar high dignitaries. The jury was to vote and make its declarations publicly and " à haute voix ". There was no appeal, and the punishments were death and confiscation of property. The month of October, which saw the Republic triumphant on all war fronts, instead of seeing the Terror abate, marked its intensification against the leading political groups and personalities in opposition. The signal event was the trial and execution of the twenty-two Girondist deputies expelled from the Convention on June 2nd, among them Vergniaud, Gensonné, Brissot, Lasource (Roland committed suicide, Mme Roland was guillotined). They were delivered by the Convention to the Tribunal on a unanimous vote, and were sentenced unanimously after proceedings lasting three days, the time thought sufficient for the jury to have their " conscience sufficiently enlightened ", so as to be able to dispense with further examination of evidence and witnesses. Four days were also thought sufficient to enlighten the conscience of the jury on the crimes of Hébert, Momoro, Vincent, Anacharsis Cloots and their friends, sentenced on March 24th, 1794. Danton, Desmoulins, Philippeaux were sent to the guillotine about a fortnight later, also at the end of four days, after the Convention had at the instigation of Saint-Just voted them unanimously " hors des débats ", as guilty of plotting to destroy the Revolutionary Government and restore the Monarchy.

Political centralization focused in the Committee of Public Safety was followed by judicial centralization focused in the Revolutionary Tribunal in Paris. Saint-Just carried, in April, a motion that all persons accused of conspiracy wherever they be should be brought before the Revolutionary Tribunal in Paris. The decree of May 18th (29 Floréal), proposed by Couthon, the third, crippled member of the Robespierrist triumvirate, and executor of the rebellious city of Lyons, suppressed all Revolutionary Tribunals and Revolutionary Commissions outside Paris. Then on June 10th, 1794, came the famous laws of Prairial—suggested by Couthon. They marked the crowning point of the Terror and were based on the axiom that the annihilation of the enemies of the Revolution took precedence over formal justice. Any kind of evidence, material, moral, or verbal " que peut naturellement obtenir l'assentiment de tout esprit juste et raisonable " was declared acceptable as legal evidence, the need for examining witnesses being dispensed with. The right of the defendant to plead before the Revolutionary Tribunal was suspended. The right to denounce conspirators and persons guilty of " incivisme " was accorded to all citizens. The right of delivering suspects to the Tribunal was extended to the two Committees (Public Safety and General Security), the Public Prosecutor, Representatives on Mission and the Convention. The Convention was deprived of its exclusive right of handing over deputies to the Tribunal. This measure sent a shudder down every spine in the Convention. It drove those who felt themselves most menaced, Fouché, Tallien, Barras, Fréron, to desperation, and together with the disagreements between the Robespierrists and their colleagues on the execution of Saint-Just's laws of Ventôse on the expropriation of the suspects and the distribution of their property to poor patriots, brought down Robespierre and his system on 9 Thermidor. Although the Robespierrists were outdistanced in sheer terrorist passion by those who destroyed them, they were nevertheless among the chief apostles of Terror. The redoubtable Bureau de Police, the special and most exclusive department of the Committee of Public Safety, set up to keep a watch and prosecute in the first place civil servants, was presided over by them, especially Saint-Just. As early as August 25th, 1793, Robespierre formulated the philosophy of Terror by demanding that the Revolutionary Tribunal be freed from all encumbrances of old-fashioned legal restraints to pass death sentences, the only type of punishment appropriate in the circumstances of treason.

Jacobin dictatorship rested on two pillars : the fanatical devotion of the faithful, and stringent orthodoxy. The combination of the two was the secret of Jacobin strength, and a new phenomenon in modern political history. Having started as a movement for popular self-expression and permanent debate, to share in joyous communion the experience of exercising popular sovereignty, Jacobinism soon developed into a confraternity of faithful, who must lose their selves in the objective substance of the faith to regain their souls. Submission became in due course release, obedience was turned into freedom, membership to the Jacobin clubs became the outward sign of belonging to the elect and pure, participation in Jacobin fêtes and patriotic rites a religious experience. Inside the clubs there was going on an unceasing process of self-cleansing and purification, entailing denunciations, confessions, excommunications and expulsions. The dictatorship of the Committee of Public Safety was thus no mere tyranny of a handful of men clinging to power and in possession of all the means of coercion, no mere police system in a beleaguered fortress. It rested on closely knit and highly disciplined cells and nuclei in every town and village, from the central artery of Paris to the smallest hamlet in the mountains, composed of men only waiting with enthusiastic eagerness for a sign, no more to express their spontaneous urge for freedom, but their Revolutionary exaltation through obedient and fervent execution of orders from the centre, the seat of the enlightened and infallible few.

In the way of pure improvisation there grew up in Revolutionary France an unofficial organization of French democracy, dupli-cating as it were the official organism and its parts, manning the

Revolutionary armies, and the *Comités de surveillance*, engaging in the task of what Robespierre called "colérer" the *sans-culottes*, that is to say the task of indoctrinating and making them ready to deal with the wicked rich, the federalists and other counter-revolutionaries, often, again as Robespierre urged, especially staying behind, when others had been sent to the front, to watch the rear and fight the internal enemy ; dominating by their ceaseless vigilance all assemblies, managing all elections, providing, as instructed, the right interpretation of all events.

The official dogma claimed that the Jacobins were the people. They could not possibly be regarded as a partial will, as just a party like other parties. Robespierre had said that the "Jacobin society was by its very nature incorruptible. It deliberated before an audience of a few thousand persons so that its whole power lay in public opinion, and it could not betray the interests of the people." Camille Desmoulins had earlier in the Revolution called the popular societies the inquisitorial tribunals of the people. He used the term with fervent approval. What he meant to say was that they were the open forum for ideas to be scrutinized, clarified and purified through free and continuous discussion. Desmoulins lived to realize to the full the horror of the popular inquisition which he so enthusiastically helped to build up. It was in the course of that dramatic clash at the Jacobin Club, when Robespierre, who earlier had half patronizingly, half menacingly admonished him not to be so flexible and volatile in his opinions, called for the burning of Camille's *Vieux Cordelier*, the proofs of which Desmoulins was in the habit of showing to the Incorruptible for approval. "Burning is no answer," whispered the darling of the Revolution.

And so the postulate of plebiscitary popular sovereignty came to fruition in the rule of a small fraction of the nation ; the idea of unhampered popular self-expression in an ever narrower path of exclusive orthodoxy, and a ban on the slightest difference of opinion and sentiment.

It is enough to read the records of the Jacobin Club in the last months before Thermidor, the indicting speeches of Robespierre and Saint-Just or the references given by Crane Brinton in his study on the provincial Jacobin societies to realize to what lengths this process had gone. To have remained silent on some past and half-forgotten occasion, where one should have spoken ; to have spoken where it was better to hold one's peace ; to have shown apathy where eagerness was called for, and enthusiasm where diffidence was necessary ; to have consorted with somebody whom a patriot should have shunned ; avoided one who deserved to be befriended ; not to have shown a virtuous disposition, or not to have led a life of virtue—such and other " sins " came to be counted as capital offences, classifying the sinners as members of that immense chain of treason comprising the foreign plot, Royalism, federalism, bureaucratic sabotage, food speculation, immoral wealth, and vicious selfish perversion. Special lists were drawn up for aspirants to admission and affiliation to elicit answers as to the attitude taken up in the past to, and as to the present appreciation of, every event of the Revolution. The ascendancy of Robespierre appears from the Jacobin records to have become truly religious. A disapproving word, a mere glance from the Incorruptible were enough to ensure the immediate expulsion of any speaker whom Robespierre felt to have gone a little too far, even though only a few seconds earlier the orator had been wildly applauded.

Virtue had been " put on the agenda " to confound the wicked. Robespierre and Saint-Just were the " apostles of virtue ", as the insurrectionary Manifesto of the Commune on 9 Thermidor called them.

It is important to throw a glance at least at the evolution of foreign policy in the Revolution from the angle of the global war for liberty. Similarities between the two spheres, internal and external policy, abound. The Revolution, bred on a humanitarian philosophy, started on a most pacifist note. Men were deeply convinced that the natural state among nations was that of peace. All trouble came from the dynasties in pursuit of selfish aggrandizement. They divide nations and cause all wars. Hence the famous declaration, which the realistic Mirabeau viewed with such scepticism, that France renounces war as an instrument of national policy and expansion. The complex factors, political and psychological, conscious and unconscious, which created in France an almost universal desire for war against old Europe, cannot be analysed here. Clearly, the dynamism of a Messianic creed was spilling over. There was hardly a person among the Revolutionaries who was not, when the war broke out, convinced that France had no wish and would do nothing to subjugate nations and seize their territory. For the Revolution was fighting a common global struggle for the liberation of peoples from the yoke of dynastic tyrannies, and for a harmonious union of nations. When liberating alien territory, France would not interfere with the wishes of the liberated population, and would not impose any régime. But these good intentions were doomed to remain an academic postulate. To free a people, to enable it to make a free choice, what the Revolution proclaimed its duty to do, obviously entailed the immediate abolition of the feudal system, and the introduction of the principle of popular sovereignty. Such an initial step could not be termed non-interference. As the war was global, France could not possibly leave feudal enemies in power and at large to sabotage her war effort and stab her in the back. But also from the point of view of the local Revolutionaries, who found themselves in a situation similar to that of the French Revolutionaries fighting their own counter-revolutionaries, only aggravated by the fact of collaboration with a foreign power, there was the supreme necessity of suppressing the counter-revolutionary enemy by all means. France was shedding her blood, spending her energies and impoverished resources ; she was on the brink of bankruptcy and famine, with inflation running wild—who could demand from her that she should also bear the costs of liberating other peoples ? Indeed, it was only fair that they should pay for their liberation themselves. " The war must pay for itself." The foreign nations must accept the dreaded worthless French *assignat*. The feudal lords, the Church, the rich in general must be soaked. The confiscated feudal property would come into the hands of the lower orders, while the poor would be spared impositions and taxation. Whole classes would thus become vitally interested in the victory of the Revolution, and a tremendous social and economic Revolution would have been achieved : " Guerre aux châteaux, paix aux chaumières " was the famous formula of Cambon. The war is global—this was the underlying thesis of the famous Declaration of November 19th, 1792, that France pledges herself to hasten to assist every people wishing to become free. It was a blank cheque given to any rebellion in any part of the world, and from the point of view of old Europe, an imperialist French provocation designed to foment rebellion everywhere in order to justify French aggression and conquest.

On December 15th came the extension of the November

Declaration. It declared that a liberated population, which failed to adopt the institutions of liberty and popular sovereignty, thereby declared itself a friend of tyranny and an enemy of France in the global war. A time limit was later set for the liberated peoples to show convincingly where they stood. And so the freedom of choosing liberty, which the Revolution set out to give to the nations, became transformed into an obligation to choose liberty. But the French were far from admitting to themselves or to others that they were violating the freedom of the liberated populations. There could be no doubt about the ultimate wishes of the peoples concerned. They were terrorized by their old masters, timid and backward, and they must be freed, without regard to their inhibitions. Popular assemblies must be summoned to adopt by acclamation the institutions of liberty. Naturally, feudal and clerical reactionaries must be excluded and prevented from intimidating the people and falsifying its true will. In Belgium and elsewhere Revolutionary leadership was weak and inexperienced, and the masses under the spell of the Church. French commissars must therefore be sent to arrange elections, and to take charge of affairs, till the liberated people will have given itself a free Constitution, and shown ability to live in accordance with it. The global war, requiring a Revolutionary régime at home, necessitated a similar régime towards the peoples abroad, in order to force the nations to be free : " Ce pouvoir révolutionnaire qui n'est qu'un pouvoir protecteur de la liberté politique à son berceau," as Brissot put it.

In 1790, Burke lamented the disintegration of the French body politic by the spirit of anarchical individualism. In 1796, he stood aghast before a wholly new phenomenon : a State as an " armed doctrine ", quite unlike any ordinary community, whose growth is haphazard, whose movements are hampered by the inertia or resistance of infinite interests, traditions and habits, and " which makes war through wantonness, and abandons it through lassitude ". Revolutionary France " is struck out at a heat . . . systematic . . . simple in its principle ; it has unity and consistency in perfection " ; it is able to mobilize men and resources and to subordinate all to the single principle of its being—" the production of force ", to further the cause of the Revolution. " Individuality is left out of their scheme of government. The state is all in all."

Chapter Four

ULTIMATE SCHEME

(a) THE POSTULATE OF PROGRESS AND FINALITY

-No longer necessary as a defensive weapon, the Terror was gradually becoming an instrument for the enthronement of a positive purpose. This purpose was the natural and harmonious system of society prophesied by the *philosophes*. The existence of such an order was a certainty. It had been on the way since the first days of the Revolution. It would have been there already, if it were not for the selfishness and perversion of some people.

In fact to Robespierre victory in the national war was not the main purpose. He feared a too speedy and too victorious end to the war. It would knock the bottom out of the Terror, as " it is natural to slumber after victory ". The enemies of the people, wishing to detract popular attention from their crimes, were endeavouring to concentrate all eyes on the victories in the external war. But the real victory will be the one which " the friends of liberty will win over the factions ". " C'est cette victoire qui appelle chez les peuples la paix, la justice et le bonheur." A nation does not become illustrious by beating down foreign tyrants and enchaining other peoples. " Ce fut le sort des Romains et quelques autres nations ; notre destinée, beaucoup plus sublime, est de fonder sur la terre l'empire de la sagesse, de la justice et de la vertu." In brief, to enthrone the exclusive Jacobin pattern.

It is vital for the understanding of Jacobinism to remember all the time that the Jacobins sincerely and deeply believed that their terrorist dictatorship, even when maintained for no compelling reason of defence, was nothing but a prelude to a harmonious state of society, in which coercion would become unnecessary. The régime of force was merely a provisional phase, an inescapable evil, at a deeper level and within a broader context no dictatorship at all.

Jacobinism was nurtured on a deep eighteenth-century faith in man, his essential goodness and perfectibility, and on the belief in continuous social progress, at the end of which there was some terminus of social integration and harmony. Not a permanently pessimistic conception of man and society bred Jacobin Terror, but an impatient hope, exasperated by obstacles, which ardent faith refused to acknowledge as natural or inevitable. The mixture of Messianic hope and despairing doubt gives to the Jacobin attitude a peculiar passionate urgency and poignancy. There is grandeur in it, as well as monumental self-deception and *naïveté*.

Robespierre and Saint-Just seem to vibrate with the faith in a short cut to salvation. " It is time to fix clearly the aim of the Revolution and the terminus (terme) at which we wish to arrive," declared Robespierre solemnly in one of his last speeches. He was proposing to " take the universe into confidence about the political secrets of the French people ", and to map out the goal across the maze of pragmatic and so often contradictory moves and incongruous happenings : " idée simple et importante qui semble n'avoir jamais été aperçue ". When laying down the scheme of the Republican Institutions for the Utopia of the future, Saint-Just in the same spirit expressed his astonishment that nobody had thought of the scheme before. He could hardly believe that truths so obvious, principles so salutary, remedies so imperative, measures so practicable, should not have occurred to anybody before. Both he and Robespierre, like most of their generation, firmly believed that legislation was an easy science. All evils and all diversity of régimes were the result of the mistaken view that it was a difficult art. Men's hearts could be formed by laws. Men were meant to realize their destiny and achieve happiness in a harmonious social system, easily brought about by legislation and education. Their faith was, however, checked by the disconcerting and dismal fact that things so obvious, simple and necessary failed to be applied throughout all the centuries of man's career on earth. Robespierre paraphrased Rousseau's famous opening paradox of the *Social Contract*, declaring in his great speech on Religious Ideas that while Nature was telling us that man was born for liberty, the experience of centuries showed him everywhere a slave ; while man's rights were engraved in his heart, his humiliation was writ large across history. Surveying the annals of man, Saint-Just similarly concluded with dismay that " all arts had produced their marvels, only the art of government has produced nothing but monsters ". " D'où vient ce mélange de génie et de stupidité ? " asks Robespierre in reference

to the wonderful progress of the arts and sciences, and man's total
ignorance of the elementary notions of political morality, of his
rights and duties. Robespierre's answer is that all the rulers of the
past, bent upon nothing else than upon retaining their power, had
nothing to fear from scientists and artists, but very much from
" philosophes rigides et défenseurs de l'humanité ". They could
afford to encourage the former, but had to persecute the latter.

The Revolution was in this respect an apocalyptic moment
in history, the most important event in the career of man upon
earth, totally different from such episodes as the Cromwellian and
American Revolutions, outbreaks prompted by local grievances
and driven by limited aims. The French Revolution had as its
aim " to put back the destinies of liberty in the hands of truth which
is eternal, rather than into the hands of men who pass ". This
juxtaposition and this contrasting of an objective and eternal truth
with the passing character of man should be noted. " Vous commencez une nouvelle carrière où personne ne vous a devancés." On
more than one occasion did Robespierre proclaim that Revolutionary France was thousands of years ahead of all other nations.
" All must be changed in the moral and political order," exclaims
Robespierre, and his words are re-echoed by Saint-Just. At the
moment of the Revolution, the world resembled the globe, half of
it was already enlightened, while the other part was still plunged
in darkness. And here faith and desperate anxiety alternate. At
first there was boundless hope. Thus in his speech in the Constituante on the unrestricted freedom of the press, Robespierre
claimed that the time had come for all truths to be spoken out—
" toutes seront accueillies par le patriotisme ". As late as July 9th,
1792, Robespierre hoped that the regeneration of the French people
could be accomplished without bloodshed. After the execution of
the King he still hoped that after this " great exception " the death
penalty would no longer be applied. As late as February, 1793, he
claimed that the new order was already so deeply rooted in French
society that no real reaction was possible. Human reason had been
on the move for quite·a time " slowly and by detours, and yet
surely ", and now the world was witnessing the wonderful spectacle
of " a democracy affirmed in a vast empire ". " Those who in the
infancy of public law and in the midst of servitude have been stam-
mering contrary maxims, did they foresee the marvels accomplished
in one year ? " Quite a different mood is expressed in Robespierre's

last speech, where he confessed to see only dupes and *fripons* in the world, and only very few generous men loving virtue for its own sake and disinterestedly desirous of the people's happiness. A similar sentiment is expressed in a striking passage in Saint-Just's *Institutions Républicaines* written some time in 1794. Its epigrammatic style breathes an uncanny air, the air of the Terror at its height. " No doubt, the time to do good has not yet come. The particular good that one may do is a palliative. We have to wait for a general evil that would be great enough for public opinion to experience the need of proper measures to do good. That which produces the general good is always terrible, or appears bizzare, when started too early. The Revolution should halt at the perfection of happiness and public liberty by the laws. Its tides have no other objectives, they must overthrow all that opposes them." " People speak of the height of the Revolution ? Who will fix it ? There have been free peoples who have fallen from greater heights."

The elation at what had been so miraculously achieved, the amazement at ideas having become flesh, are matched by the anxiety lest men falter, and " intrigue " succeeds in overpowering virtue for generations. It is " now or never ", for in case of failure the reaction would be commensurate to the distance covered by the Revolution, as if the Revolution were about to reach the peak of a sharp slope. If there was no advance to the summit, there would be a headlong fall into the abyss. Passionate faith enmeshed in anxiety and despair breaks forth time after time. Repeatedly Robespierre and Saint-Just declared that this or that decree or purge was the last, the very last, and the one sure to inaugurate the natural order. " If only they had thought of that particular thing, the *Institutions Républicaines*, all the evils might have been avoided, all the crimes would not have happened ! " exclaims Saint-Just

(b) THE DOCTRINAIRE MENTALITY

Here we are face to face with the Messianic doctrinaire as a historic phenomenon. He is a compound of two things, inner fanatical certainty, and what may be called a pencil sketch of reality. The pencil lines represent the external facets of social existence, in fact the sinews of the institutional framework. The flesh of the intangible, shapeless living forces, traditions, imponderables, habits, human inertia and lazy conservatism are not there. They are ignored. Left out of account are also the uniqueness and the unpredictability of human nature and human conduct, which result either from the irrational segments in our being, or from man's egotism. The Revolutionary doctrinaire is convinced that his pencil sketch is the only real thing, that it sums up all that matters. He experiences reality, not as an inchoate static mass, but as a *dénouement*, a dynamic movement towards a rational solution. The amorphous fleshy mass is unreal, and can be brought into shape in accordance with the pencil pattern. It is not something that is, but something that fails to be, that is not yet what it should be. Similarly, human idiosyncrasies and peculiarities that interfere with the rational working of the systematic, abstract pattern are not something that must be taken for granted, but an accident to be prevented, removed or avoided. Nor is the fact that a triumphant doctrine is after all embodied in the living personalities of those in charge, and is thus bound to receive their personal imprint and become distorted, ever noticed. Hence patterns of Left totalitarianism are so universalist in their character, and ignore completely national and local characteristics, just as they seem completely unaware of the problem of the personal element in leadership and oblivious of the place of the actual human personality in the working of politics. It is their nemesis and one of the ironies of history that the personal leader, like a *deus ex machina*, is thrown up by the movement of realization to become its most vital factor and its embodiment, the head of the militant confraternity of the elect in its struggle against all the powers of darkness.

When the Revolutionary doctrinaire is thwarted by the inchoate, " unreal " mass of flesh and the " irrational " egotistic behaviour of men, his impatience turns into exasperation. The resisting forces appear a dumb, stupid mass that will not budge, for no other reason than sheer obstinacy, or—in the case of individuals—perversion and egoism. This resistance appears to the Revolutionary the more baffling and exasperating, because at the great moment of the Revolutionary climax of popular self-expression the enthusiasm appeared to be so general, so active and so single-minded. The fact is that the Revolutionary spasm is in the emotional sense a magnificently simplified formula of existence reduced to a single emotion, as the pencil sketch is in the intellectual sphere. The undiluted Revolutionary ecstasy is of very short duration. Soon men drift back into the morass of obtuse conservatism, selfishness or neutral privacy. The impatience and violence of the rationalist doctrinaire soon turns the initial mass enthusiasm into resentful hostility towards the Revolutionary pattern. It has always happened in modern Revolutions that as the inner dynamism of the pencil-sketch Revolution continued to throw forth ever more extreme doctrinaires, the inarticulate masses grew increasingly more indifferent and hostile to the Revolutionary endeavour. The case of religion in the French Revolution is the classical example of the clash between the rationalist doctrine and the forces of irrational conservatism. No other factor was so fatal to the Revolution as the attack on the Church. The new, ever increasing rigidity of the pattern has always resulted in sharper and sharper clashes, greater fissures and splits at the top. Fanatical dictatorship causes the problem of human egotism to grow more acute in relation to the advance of *Gleichschaltung*. And so it happened that many a Revolutionary who started with and put his trust in the institutions of a pencil-sketch doctrine to solve all problems, hoping that conditions and men would fall in by themselves into the harmonious whole, ended with a desperate determination to create like Moses a new type of man and a new people. At the beginning of the French Revolution there was the Declaration of the Rights of Man, at its height Saint-Just's *Institutions Républicaines*, Robespierre's cult of the Supreme Being and the Lepeletier scheme of Spartan Education, adopted by the Incorruptible after the Revolutionary martyr's death.

The doctrinaire never thinks of the pencil sketch in terms of coercion. It is not intended to interfere with freedom ; on the contrary, it is designed to secure it. Only the ill-intentioned, the selfish and perverse can complain that their freedom is violated. They are guilty of sabotage, refusing to be free, and misleading others. They cannot be given freedom to do their evil deeds, for they are at war with the pattern of freedom that continues to unfold itself till its full realization. Liberty can be restored only after this war has come to an end, only when the enemy has been eliminated and the people re-educated, that is to say, when there will be no longer any opposition. So long as there is opposition there can be no freedom.

" The Revolution will come to an end ", said Robespierre in the Speech on the Principles of Political Morality, " in a very simple way, and without being harassed by the factions, when all people will have become equally devoted to their country and its laws. But we are still far from having reached that point. . . . The Republican Government is not yet well established, and there are factions." The Revolutionary Government has two objects : the protection of patriotism and the annihilation of aristocracy. The goal will never be achieved as long as the factions continue to sabotage the effort. "It will be an impossible thing to establish liberty on unshakable foundations as long as any individual can say to himself : 'if to-day aristocracy is triumphant, I am lost.'" The "institutions sages" of the Utopian pattern can be founded only on the ruins of the incorrigible enemies of liberty. Robespierre used in this context the term democracy. It meant to him, on the one hand, a form of government, and on the other, a social and moral pattern. As a form of government it signified, innocuously enough, a state of things where the sovereign people, guided by laws made by itself, was making by itself all that it could do by itself, and through chosen representatives what it could not do by itself. Robespierre came out strongly against direct democracy on this occasion. There was no need for it any longer ; the people had trustworthy representatives. As a social and moral pattern democracy was the only system capable of fulfilling the wishes of Nature, realizing the destinies of mankind, and making good the promises of philosophy by the enthronement of egalitarian virtue, which is another name for the universal preference of the general interest over the private good, for love of country and equality and the death of egoism. The reign of virtue could not be established as long as there were parties, which were by definition selfish factions. And so to obtain the rule of virtue the war of liberty against tyranny must first be brought to an end, the factions annihilated, and the storm of the Revolution overcome by the Revolutionary Government. "Votre administration doit être le résultat de l'esprit du gouvernement révolutionnaire, combiné avec les principes généraux de la démocratie."

Liberty has however no meaning without freedom to oppose, and without there being anybody to oppose. The vision of un-fettered freedom at the end of the days, and the prophecy of the cessation of the conflict between freedom and duty, in spontaneous obedience without a sense of constraint, turns out to be a fiction, wherever there is an idea of a fixed pattern of things to be enthroned by a sustained effort.

(c) THE REIGN OF VIRTUE

Saint-Just would have passionately repudiated any suggestion of dictatorship as a permanent form of government. It is baffling to read on the same page expressions of the human liberal eighteenth-century spirit, juxtaposed with the most bloodthirsty denunciations. What Saint-Just had to say on power might have come straight from the pen of Lord Acton. " Power is so cruel and evil that if you release it from its inertia, without giving it a direction (règle), it will march straight on to oppression. . . . One wants to be rigid in one's principles, when destroying an evil government, but it is rare that one should not reject the same principles, to substitute for them one's own will, as soon as one comes to govern oneself."

Saint-Just professed to be particularly fearful of a provisional form of government, since it was based upon the suppression of the people, and not on law or natural harmony. It was an invitation to any usurper to establish a tyranny by the promise of peace and order, and an excellent excuse to crush all opposition.

In the Constitutional debate he warned the Convention that even the rights of man and constitutional liberties could become a weapon in the hands of a " gentle tyrant " who had designs on the freedom of the nation.

Not force, but wisdom, should be used in dealing with the people, for the people were essentially good and just, and could be governed without being enslaved or becoming licentious. Man was born for peace and happiness and for life in society. His misery and corruption were the results of insidious laws of domination, and of the doctrine of man's savage and corrupt nature. Having let themselves be persuaded by the tyrants that they would destroy each other if left free, the peoples bent their heads to the yoke of despotism and grew demoralized under its corroding influence.

" Every people is made for virtue . . . it should not be forced, it should be led by wisdom. The French are easy to govern ; they want a mild constitution. . . . This people is lively and suited for democracy, but it should not be worn out too much by the encumbrance of public affairs. It should be governed without weakness, but also without constraint."

Fundamental in all this is Saint-Just's conviction that there was an inherent harmony in society. The task of a government was not to impose its own will or its own pattern upon a society, but to

remove the impediments to that harmony, a purpose for which the
terror had been instituted. Harmony was bound to come into its
own, when all elements of social existence had been put in their
proper place. " Le gouvernement est plutôt un ressort d'harmonie
que d'autorité." The abolition of tyranny was bound to bring man
back to his true nature. " Ôtez la tyrannie du monde, vous y
rétablirez la paix et la vertu." The people would find its happiness
by itself. The Government's task was not so much to make men
happy as to prevent them from becoming unhappy. " Do not
oppress, that is all. Everybody will know how to find his own happiness." A people once infected with the superstitious belief that
they owed their happiness to their Government would not preserve
it for long. Crowds thronging the antechambers of tribunals and
state offices were eloquent evidence of the rottenness of the Government. " C'est une horreur qu'on soit obligé de demander justice."
The private lives of citizens should be interfered with as little as
possible. " The liberty of a people is in its private life ; do not
disturb it. Disturb no one but the evil-doers."

Force should be used only to protect the " state of simplicity "
against force itself, and nothing should be imposed except probity,
and respect for liberty, nature, human rights and the national
representation.

There was meant to be a social order in which men's sentiments
and actions would by themselves set themselves into so harmonious
a pattern that all coercion would be superfluous. With laws true
to his nature, man would cease to be unhappy and corrupt. Evil
having become alien to his interests, justice would become the
permanent and determining interest and passion of all, and liberty
would reign supreme. The Revolutionary task is to make " nature
and innocence the passion of all hearts ". Such a change can be
brought about earlier than people think, declares Saint-Just.

This faith is deeply rooted in the eighteenth-century premises,
reaffirmed by Robespierre in his speeches on the Revolutionary
order. The Revolutionary aim was to vindicate the idea of cosmic
pragmatism on earth, and so arrange things that all that was moral
would also be useful and politic, and what was immoral would be
impolitic, harmful and counter-revolutionary. Robespierre distinguished—in line with Rousseau—two kinds of self-love, one vile
and cruel, which seeks one's own exclusive good in the misery of
others, and the other, which, generous and benevolent, confounds

our well-being with the prosperity and glory of the country. Of the marriage of the natural order and man's virtuous disposition there would be born the identity of the personal and general good. Real democracy would thus come into fruition, since men would be obeying nothing but their own virtuous disposition, and would not need the master, who is indispensable where virtue is not natural and spontaneous. The supreme aim of politics was therefore, as Mably maintained, to direct human hearts, to educate men, to repress the "moi personnel" and the proclivity for small, petty things. According to the direction given to human passion, man could be elevated to the skies or debased to the lowest pit. "Le but de toutes les institutions sociales, c'est de les diriger vers la patrie, qui est à la fois le bonheur public et le bonheur privé."

If politics were to the eighteenth century a question of ethics, the problem of the rational and final social order was a question of attuning hearts. This was the vital discovery made by the Jacobins, after the disappointment with popular sovereignty and its institutions as virtue-releasing forces. The new and continuing disagreements could not, or at least could no longer or not fully, be explained in terms of the conflict between Royalism and Revolution or between ruling and ruled classes, and there were many factors to obscure the social and economic problem.

"A quoi se réduit donc cette science mystérieuse de la politique et de la législation ? A mettre dans les lois et dans l'administration les vérités morales reléguées dans les livres des philosophes, et appliquer à la conduite des peuples les notions triviales de probité que chacun est forcé d'adopter pour sa conduite privée."

All is reduced to a question of morality, and consequently education. All the rest will follow, claims Saint-Just. Objective factors are left out of account, only human consciousness matters. The irrational anti-social, anarchical elements in man are considered accidental ; only the rational and social part of human nature is acknowledged as real and permanent. The former exist, for sure, but can be made to efface themselves before the latter. Man, and consequently society as a whole, may be shaped anew—"Quel est le but où nous tendons ?" asks Robespierre. His long answer may be treated as mere verbiage and turgid preaching. But, once more, Robespierre believed that the vision he was spinning was something attainable, real, and full of precise, compact meaning. "The passage from crime to virtue" to be accomplished by the

Revolution meant to Robespierre a real event, a turning point, a new birth, a definite date, like the passage from a class society to a classless society was to mean to Communist Messianism.

The aim is "the peaceful enjoyment òf liberty and equality ; the reign of that eternal justice, the laws of which are engraved not on marble or stone, but in the hearts of all men, even in that of a slave who forgets them or a tyrant who denies them. We want an order of things where all base and cruel passions would be chained, all the benevolent and generous passions awakened by the laws, where one's ambition would be to merit glory and to serve his country ; where distinctions have no other source than equality itself ; where the citizen is subordinated to the magistrate, the magistrate to the people and the people to justice ; where the country insures the well-being of every individual, and where every individual enjoys with pride the prosperity and glory of his country ; where all souls grow greater through the continuous interchange of republican sentiments, and by the need to merit the esteem of a great people ; where the arts would be the ornament of that liberty which ennobles them, and commerce the source of public wealth and not only of the monstrous opulence of a few houses. We want to substitute in our country morality for egoism, probity for honour, principles for habits, duties for good manners, the empire of reason for the tyranny of fashion, the contempt of vice for the contempt of misfortune ; pride for insolence, greatness of soul for vanity, love of glory for the love of money ; good men for good company, merit for intrigue, genius for *bel esprit*, truth for brilliance . . . a people magnanimous, powerful, happy, for a people amiable, frivolous and miserable, that is to say all the virtues and all the miracles of the Republic for all the vices and absurdities of the Monarchy."

Has there ever been such a state on earth ? Throughout the centuries of uninterrupted tyranny and crime, history knows only of one brief spell of liberty in a tiny corner of the earth—Sparta : " brille comme un éclair dans les ténèbres immenses." This is the key to the understanding of Robespierre and Saint-Just : Sparta as the ideal of liberty.

"Let us beware of connecting politics with moral regeneration —a thing at present impracticable. Moralism is fatal to freedom "— wrote Desmoulins.

For the creation of this ideal Robespierre falls back upon the civil religion and Saint-Just upon a Utopian scheme of moral legislation called by him Republican Institutions. In both cases the motive is despair in the spontaneous will of man as the sovereign agent. More than disillusionment—desperate fear. Man had to be remade.

(d) SAINT-JUST'S "INSTITUTIONS RÉPUBLICAINES"

Saint-Just developed a mystical faith in the power of his Republican Institutions to check man's anti-social arbitrary urges, to regenerate the French people and to reconcile all contradictions in a perfect harmony founded upon virtue. They were to be the crowning of the Revolution, the seal upon the Revolution. " Un état où ces institutions manquent n'est qu'une République illusoire." They were the essence of a Republic, for the superiority. of a Republic over a Monarchy was precisely in this, that the latter had no more than a government, while the former also had Institutions to realize the moral purpose. " C'est par là que vous annoncerez la perfection de votre démocratie . . . la grandeur de vos vues, et que vous hâterez la perte de vos ennemis en les montrant difformes à côté de vous." Clearly, he thought of the Republic in terms if not of the Church, at least of a spiritual community, and of the Institutions as inaugurating the " passage from crime to virtue ". In Saint-Just's last and heroic (undelivered) speech of 8 Thermidor in defence of Robespierre the Republican Institutions appear as the panacea that had fatally been ignored, and which alone, as said before, can save the situation, making all the difference between total damnation and total salvation. The factions will never disappear till the Institutions have produced the guarantees, put a limit to authority and put " human pride irrevocably under the yoke of public liberty ". Saint-Just implores Providence to give him a few days more " pour appeller sur les institutions les méditations du peuple français ". All the tragedy they had been witnessing would not have occurred under their rule. " Ils seraient vertueux peut-être, et n'auraient point pensé au mal ceux dont j'accuse ici." The speech ends with a formal proposal for immediate consideration of the scheme of the Republican Institutions.

Saint-Just's scheme of regeneration was intended to offer a cure for the corroding influence of power and the danger of the substitution of the ruler's personal will for the law as well as to shape a universal pattern of moral behaviour. The proposed Institutions were to lay down so precise and detailed a system of laws that no room would be left for arbitrary human action, or indeed for spontaneity. People would not be obeying men, but laws, laws of reason and virtue, and therefore of liberty. Politics would thus be entirely banished.

"We have to substitute with the help of the Institutions the force and inflexible justice of the laws for personal influence. The Revolution will thus be strengthened ; there will be no jealousies, no factions any longer ; there will be no pretentious claims and no calumny . . . we have . . . to substitute the ascendancy of virtue for the ascendancy of men. . . . Make politics powerless by reducing all to the cold rule of justice."

The Institutions would be a more effective brake on anti-revolutionary tendencies than the Terror. For the Terror comes and goes according to the fluctuations of public opinion and sentiment, and the reaction to terror has normally been an excessive indulgence. The institutional laws would secure "a durable severity".

The Institutions were calculated to make the art of government simpler, easier and more effective. For instance, more wisdom and greater virtue would be needed for the exercise of the office of censorship over conduct—an idea particularly dear to Saint-Just—in a weak government than in a strong one, that is to say, in a régime based upon Institutions. For in a weak government all depended on the character of the men in charge, whereas in a strong régime the laws provided for everything and secured a perfect harmony, in excluding all the unpredictable elements in human behaviour. "Dans le premier, il y a une action et réaction continuelle des forces particulières ; dans le second, il y a une force commune dont chacun fait partie, et qui concourt au même but et au même bien."

In his fear of human egotism and, above all, of the competition between personalities, Saint-Just devised a most paradoxical plan. As there should be fewer institutions and fewer men in charge, and since it was essential that an institution should operate by its own harmony and without being thwarted by the interplay and clash of men's arbitrary wills, it was—he thought—important to reduce the number of people in the institutions and the constituted authorities. In this connection Saint-Just called for a re-examination of collective magistratures like the municipalities, administrative bodies, *Comités de surveillance*, etc., to see whether the placing of " the functions of these bodies in the hands of a single official in everyone of them would not be the secret of a solid establishment of the Revolution ".

Into this context have to be set the nearly identical statements of Barère, Prieur de la Côte-d'Or, Baudot and Lindet, according to which Saint-Just at a joint meeting of the two Committees on 5 Thermidor proposed the setting up of a government by " patriotic reputations (or deputations ?) pending the establishment of the Republican Institutions ". Barère quotes him as saying that it was imperative to hand over dictatorial powers to a man " endowed with sufficient genius, strength, patriotism and greatness of soul . . . sufficiently imbued with the spirit of the Revolution, the spirit of its principles, its various phases, actions and agencies—to take upon himself the full responsibility for public safety and the maintenance of liberty . . . a man enjoying the favour of public opinion and the confidence of the people . . . " " Cet homme, je déclare que c'est Robespierre, lui seul peut sauver l'État," Saint-Just is reported to have said, in the spirit, one may add, of his famous statement—" il faut dans toute Révolution un dictateur pour sauver l'État par la force, ou des censeurs pour le sauver par la vertu ". From both statements there is only a short step to the generalized theory of Revolutionary dictatorship as formulated later by Babeuf and Buonarroti. A dictator " qui puisse répondre . . . du maintien de la liberté . . . "—the dictatorship of Robespierre would have been a " dictatorship of liberty ".

Fearing the competition of men, Saint-Just was thus driven back to the idea of one man. Believing in the power of institutions to achieve everything and to eliminate the rule of men, he had nevertheless to fall back upon the single-mindedness and smooth efficiency secured by a single mind.

Saint-Just got himself involved in the inevitable contradictions presented by the two irreconcilable principles : sovereignty of the people and an exclusive doctrine. While anxious to expel the arbitrariness of man and all opposition by an all-embracing yet exclusive system of laws, Saint-Just was not less keen to preserve the active interest of the people in their own affairs. He abhorred nothing more than the monopolization of public affairs by bureaucracy, ambitious professional politicians and seekers of office. He feared nothing more than the indifference of the masses. He was to see this happen, and to admit to himself that very few people were interested in anything but their private affairs, and that most people took a " lâche plaisir à se mêler de rien ". The magistrates were rapidly usurping the Government as well as the popular societies, destroying the young French democracy, whose very essence was the supremacy of the people and not of officials. " Où donc est la cité ? " he asked himself in despair. " Elle est presque usurpée par les fonctionnaires." A spirit of clique and caucus was abroad. The Terror has frightened away the citizens.

" La Révolution est glacée ; tous les principes sont affaiblis ; il ne reste que des bonnets rouges portés par l'intrigue. L'exercise de la terreur a blasé le crime comme les liqueurs fortes blasent le palais."

Saint-Just's community of the future is placed under the auspices of the Supreme Being. " The French people ", he declares, " recognize the Supreme Being and the immortality of the soul." The temples of the civic religion, where incense would be burnt for twenty-four hours a day, were to be the communal centres of the Republic. All laws were to be announced there and all civil acts—apart from special patriotic fêtes—were to take place there and bear the character of religious rites. Although all cults would be permitted, the external rites other than of the civil religion would be banned.

The Institutions lay down a detailed scheme of a Spartan type for the education of youth by the State. The conduct of young people as of civil servants was to be publicly scrutinized every ten days in the temple. Every person above the age of twenty-five was to declare every year who were his friends and his reasons for breaking friendships. Friends would be held responsible for each other. Disloyal and ungrateful persons would be banished. Prescriptions concerning marriage, military discipline, were similarly Spartan. Solemn patriotic fêtes were to inspire the people with civic piety and national pride.

(e) THE CIVIL RELIGION AND CONDEMNATION OF INTELLECTUALS

Individual spontaneity has thus been replaced by the objective postulate of virtue ; freedom by the (uncoerced) acceptance of obligation ; the idea of liberty by the vision of an exclusive pattern. The other vital value in eighteenth-century philosophy, rationalism, was in the end made to give place to mysticism.

There was always the unresolved ambiguity in the eighteenth century, especially Rousseauist, juxtaposition of the two qualities of the eighteenth-century ideal—its objective, eternal character, and its being engraved in human hearts. The unresolved ambiguity seemed to resolve the question of coercion. Since the objective truth was also immanent in man's consciousness, there was no external coercion in forcing him to follow it. There was also another ambiguity ; on the one hand, the optimistic hope that man (or the people) rendered free, and thus also moral, would see the truth and follow it ; on the other, there was the fear of human arbitrariness and hubris. It soon developed in the case of Robespierre into a distrust of the intellect. We saw him demanding that liberty be put into the hands of " the truth that is eternal ", instead of being in the hands of men who are passing creatures. Robespierre and Saint-Just grew suspicious of the intellect, as well as of wit. The sophisms of the brilliant debater, the flexibility and individualism of the intellectual, appeared no less dangerous than the partial interests in the earlier days of the Revolution. Robespierre began to dream of " a rapid instinct which without the belated help of reasoning " would lead man to do good and shun evil. " La raison particulière de chaque homme " was a sophist, too easily yielding to the whisper of passion and too easily rationalizing it. In one of his last speeches Robespierre made a violent attack on the intellectuals, the men of letters, who had " dishonoured themselves " in the Revolution. The Revolution was the achievement of the simple people carried by their instinct and unsophisticated natural wisdom. " A la honte éternelle de l'esprit, la raison du peuple en a fait seule tous les frais. . . . Les prodiges qui ont immortalisé cette époque ont été opérés sans vous et malgré vous." Any simple artisan had shown more insight into the rights of man than the writers of books, who, nearly Republicans in 1788, emerged as defenders of the King in 1793, like Vergniaud and Condorcet. Robespierre takes up the cudgels for Rousseau of the *Profession de foi d'un Vicaire Savoyard* against the atheism of the Encyclopædists, and declares the battle to be resumed. On his orders the busts of Helvetius and Mirabeau in the Club are pulled down and broken. A war is declared on sophists.

The only power that can still the pernicious sophistic instinct is religion, the idea of an authority higher than man, which is the final sanction of morality. "What silences or replaces this pernicious instinct, and what makes good the insufficiency of human authority, is the religious instinct which imprints upon our souls the idea of a sanction given to the moral precepts by a power that is higher than man."

A crude Voltairian attitude has been read into Robespierre's utterances on the subject. He laid himself open to the charge of opportunist social utilitarianism by his clumsy statement that he was not interested in religion as a metaphysician, but as a statesman and social architect, to whom what was useful in the world and good in practice was true, whatever its metaphysical validity. What Robespierre wanted to say was not that since the populace would not be moved by rational arguments to behave ethically, but by the fear of God, religion had to be simply invented for the sake of the social order. He wanted to say that in the light of cosmic pragmatism factual existence was sufficiently proved by logical and pragmatic coherence. The postulate of justice and meaning in the universal and social order was a sufficient proof of the existence of Divinity. Without Divinity, transcendental reward and punishment, the logical and righteous structure of the universe and society would be without a basis. The absence of such a logical cohesion was unthinkable. God therefore existed, and the soul was immortal. The test of social cohesion was truer and more vital than scientific, philosophical and theoretical tests. The life of a community was too solemn a fulfilment to be tossed about by blind forces, which mete out the same fate to good and bad, patriots and egoists, and leave the oppressed with no consolation, victims of triumphant evil selfishness : "this kind of practical philosophy which, by turning egoism into a system, regards human society as a war of cunning, success as the criterion of justice and injustice, probity as a matter of taste".

Morality is what it is, not because God has ordered it and we have to obey. We do not fulfil ourselves in the fruition of God. The starting point and the sole and final criterion is the existence of men in society ; the absolute postulate, the morality that sustains it. The fully integrated community becomes thus the highest fulfilment, the highest form of worship. Providence hovers over it.

Chapter Five

THE SOCIAL PROBLEM

(a) THE INCONSISTENCIES

THE great dividing line between the two major schools of social and economic thought in the last two centuries has been the attitude to the basic problem : should the economic sphere be considered an open field for the interplay of free human initiative, skill, resources and needs, with the State intervening only occasionally to fix the most general and liberal rules of the game, to help those who have fallen by the wayside, to punish those guilty of foul play and to succour the victims thereof; or should the totality of resources and human skill be *ab initio* treated as something that should be deliberately shaped and directed, in accordance with a definite principle, this principle being—in the widest sense—the satisfaction of human needs. Whereas the latter attitude puts all stress on the injury caused to the weak by the cupidity of those who succeed in monopolizing all the resources, and on the disorder and confusion brought about by the lack of general direction ; the former maintains that State-guaranteed social security would take away all incentive to exertion—the fear of poverty and the hope of gain and distinction— and thus cause a lowering of vitality and a weakening of all productive effort, in addition to the stifling of freedom by centralized regimentation. At bottom the whole debate centres round the question of human nature : could man be so re-educated in a socially integrated system as to begin to act on motives different from those prevailing in the competitive system ? Is the urge for free economic initiative nothing else than rationalized greed or anxiety, bound to die out in an order guaranteeing equal economic well-being, as the Collectivist ideology teaches ?

It has been shown that eighteenth-century thinkers, while holding fast to the idea of a rational, not to say scientific, system of society, fought shy of the latter conception of the social-economic problem, which would appear to have been inherent in the postulate of the natural order. Jacobinism may be regarded as the eighteenth-century attitude on trial. The Jacobin inhibitions on the subject of property and their reluctance to face the social-economic issue on their own general premises were the main cause for the Utopian, mystical character of their vision of the final social order as the reign of virtue. In a sense the evolution of Jacobin thinking on the question of property throughout the Revolution would appear as a gradual liberation from inhibitions, effected under the impact of events, and leading to a total liberation in those post-Thermidorian Jacobins and Robespierrists who joined the plot of Babeuf, and reinterpreted the idea of the natural order into terms of economic communism. The Jacobins were not abreast with the masses in the Revolution. Carried away by the idea of the rights of man and the Revolutionary hope of salvation, and exasperated by famine and shortage, the masses confusedly and passionately clamoured that the Revolution should carry out its promises, that is to say, should make them happy. However anarchical and crude the agitation of the Enragés under the leadership of Jacques Roux and Varlet, however naïve the socialism of such pamphleteers as Dolivier, Lange of Lyons, Momoro and others, the whole social movement in the Revolution derived from the Messianic expectation engendered by the idea of the natural order, and went beyond the spasmodic social protest and the clamour for instant relief. But these agitators, with or without a programme, successful or not as spokesmen of pressure groups, did not make policies. The Revolution was steered by the Jacobins at the vital period.

Their whole thinking dominated by the idea of a rational and natural order, the Jacobins were most reluctant to yield to the view that there was an inconsistency between a rational political-ethical system and free economics. The Revolution forced upon them lessons against their own grain. There was a definite social dynamism in the idea of unlimited popular sovereignty. The poor were the vast majority of the nation, and thus entitled to dictate conditions to the small minority of the rich. The issue received a definite social complexion with the exclusion of the poor from the active political life of the nation. It created the consciousness and sealed the fact of conflict. Moreover, owing to reminiscences of antiquity, the democratic popular ideal was always associated with the social radicalism of the great legislators of ancient Greece and Rome, Lycurgus, Solon, the Gracchi, with the abolition of debts owed to landlords, redistribution of land, and in general the rule of the poor over the rich. Moral asceticism had always glorified the austere virtues of the poor, and condemned the vices of wealth. The fact also was that as soon as the feudal system was abolished and the rule of wealth affirmed, the propertied classes, the bourgeoisie and the richer peasantry, having well benefited from the sale of confiscated Church property, began to wish for a halt to the Revolution. They felt their property and their new gains in danger of attack from Revolutionary dynamism. While they were turning against the Revolution, the Revolution was becoming more and more identified with the poor and propertyless, above all in the mind of Robespierre. And yet, the Jacobin attitude remained ambiguous and inconsistent to the end. The incongruities in it were only finally resolved in Babouvism. And so almost ironically the chain of laws and decrees which led to the establishment of an economic dictatorship, which violated every principle of private property and free economics, was started by the Convention on March 18th, 1793, with the unanimous vote of the death penalty against anyone proposing the *loi agraire* or any plan "subversive of landed, commercial and industrial property". As late as November, 1792, Saint-Just proclaimed in his famous and most gloomy speech on Supplies his dislike of "lois violentes sur le commerce". He came out firmly in favour of free trade, and suggested that the Convention should place freedom of trade "sous le sauvegarde du peuple même", although he made the reservation that unrestricted economic liberty, "une très grande vérité en thèse générale", may require some reinterpretation in the context of the evils of Revolution. There was also the necessity of teaching virtue to a people demoralized by the crimes of the Monarchy. A year and four months later, on February 26th, 1794 (8 Ventôse, an II), Saint-Just made the meaningful statement that in the social domain the force of circumstances was leading the Revolution "à des résultats aux-quels nous n'avons pas pensé". He was proposing the confiscation of all the possessions of the suspects and their distribution to the poor on the ground that the right to property was conditional on political loyalty. In the last few months or weeks before their downfall the Robespierrists began dimly and reluctantly to perceive that their rational and final system, to have any meaning and to last, must carry with it a corresponding change-over in the social and economic conditions. And so on the very eve of his execution (7 Thermidor, July 25th, 1794)

Saint-Just coupled together in a flicker of comprehension the idea of the Institutions with a Revolutionary social programme : " créer des institutions civiles et renverser l'empire de la richesse ". But, as will be shown, even in this resolve there were inherent reservations that were calculated to vitiate the general postulate.

(b) CLASS POLICY

Political rather than social considerations gave rise to Jacobin class orientation. Thus Saint-Just arrived at the conclusion that the Revolution was menaced by a fatal contradiction between the Revolutionary form of government and social realities. He discovered that the wealth of the nation was to be found in the main in the hands of the enemies of the Revolution. The working people, the real supporters of the new régime, depended for their existence on their enemies. The interests of the two classes being irreconcilable, the outcome could only be a class policy favouring the class supporting the Republic, and carried out at the expense of the possessors of wealth. To Saint-Just such a policy came to mean the realization of democracy.

Robespierre's thinking evolved in a similar way. His famous *Catechism* opens with the question, " What is our aim ? " His answer is—the execution of the Constitution in favour of the people. " Who are the enemies ? " The answer is—the vicious and the rich, who are the same. To the question on the possibility of a union of the popular interest and the interest of the rich and (their) government, Robespierre gives the laconic answer " never ". The last question and answer was crossed out by the Incorruptible, but the very fact of it having been jotted down shows where his thoughts were wandering. In another of Robespierre's notes we read that all internal dangers came from the bourgeoisie. In order to defeat the bourgeoise " il faut rallier le peuple ". The people must be paid and maintained at the expense of the rich : paid for attendance at public assemblies, armed and maintained as Revolutionary armies out of special levies on the rich whom they were to watch, finally subsidized and provided for by the Government at the expense of the producers and merchants. These were the premises of the economic dictatorship which came into being alongside the political terrorist dictatorship in 1793, and to the emergence of which

Robespierre and Saint-Just made a substantial contribution, although in a way only yielding to the violent pressure of the Enragés and the inescapable necessities of the situation : war, inflation and economic disintegration.

The first series of decrees were issued on May 4th, 1793, after the assembly of Paris mayors and municipal officers had declared the people in " a state of revolution " till supplies had been secured, and demanded fixed prices for corn and what amounted to an abolition of the corn trade, in so far as mediation between producers and consumers was concerned. The decrees of the Convention ordered producers to make declarations on their produce, under penalty of confiscation. Private houses and stores were opened to search. Corn and flour were to be sold only on the public market. A " prix maximum " was fixed. A forced loan of a milliard francs, the first of the enforced loans and levies on the rich, was launched. On July 27th, 1793, on a motion of Billaud-Varenne (his *Éléments de Républicanisme* deserve attention as an exposition of Jacobin social philosophy alongside of Saint-Just's *Institutions Républicaines*), the Convention voted the famous decree on the suppression of food speculation. This law put an end to freedom of trade and secrecy of commerce in practically all commodities except luxury articles. It was followed by a decree on the *greniers d'abondance*, which turned all bakers into State employees, although it failed to build up the State granaries. On September 29th came the law on the " general maximum ", fixing prices of all commodities and wages, to be supplemented, at least in Paris, by a system of rationing. In forcing sellers to sell at a loss, and without compensation, the law was no less a class measure than the progressive tax, the forced loans, the special levies on, and requisitions from, the rich, all designed to pay for the war and to maintain the poor. More than that, it was calculated to reduce small tradespeople and artisans to the position of wage earners. In fact, on 15 Floréal a decree was passed allowing for the mobilizing of all engaged in the production and circulation of goods of prime necessity. Penalties were provided for shirkers as guilty of conspiracy. On October 22nd, the three-man Commission des Subsistances was appointed to take over the economic dictatorship of the whole of France, and to put an end to the alleged sabotage and incompetence of the local authorities, who had been in charge of the execution of the economic decrees till then. From this there was only one step to the nationalization of industries.

The idea was not indeed quite absent from the minds of those responsible for the social policies of the Revolution. So Chaumette urged the Convention " to concentrate its attention on raw materials and factories, in order to place them under requisition by fixing penalties for those holding or manufacturing goods who allow them to be idle ; or even to place them at the disposal of the Republic, which has no lack of labour to turn them all to a useful purpose ". As a Representative of the people on mission Saint-Just displayed an example of dictatorial action and class policy at their highest. He would order houses of speculators, defaulters against the " maximum " and hoarders to be razed to the ground, he would requisition in eight days 5,000 pairs of shoes and 15,000 shirts (" déchaussez tous les aristocrates "), order the Mayor of Strasbourg to deliver on the same day 100,000 livres of the levy imposed upon the rich for the benefit of the poor patriots, war widows and war orphans ; he would have the richest individual who had not paid his share of the nine million enforced loan within twenty-four hours exposed on the guillotine for three hours ; double and treble the amount to be paid for any delay ; seize in twenty-four hours 2,000 beds, requisition all overcoats, and so on.

(c) FUNDAMENTAL QUESTIONS

A class policy provoked by a Revolutionary and war-time emergency may be nothing more than an empirical *ad hoc* policy and need not entail deliberate and planned shaping of the social and economic life *in toto*. There are, however, clear indications that Robespierre and Saint-Just felt themselves, however reluctantly, driven beyond such empiricism in the direction of integral planning in accordance with a definite principle. Thus in his speeches on Supplies and on the Declaration of the Rights of Man (1793) Robespierre made the emphatic distinction between the old ways and the postulate of a new deal in the economic sphere, which would correspond to the great political change-over that had taken place. Robespierre objected to the approach of the Convention to the problem, on the grounds that it accepted as the highest authority the contradictions and vagaries of former royal ministers. The legislation of the first two Revolutionary Assemblies on this subject had been in the old style, because the interests and the prejudices which were the basis of their policy had not changed. The defenders of hungry citizens and the spokesmen of the poor were in the eyes of the earlier Assemblies dangerous agitators and anarchists. The Assemblies and their governments employed bayonets to calm alarms and to still famine. Their idea of unrestricted freedom of commerce put a premium on bloodsucking. It was an essentially incomplete system, because it had no bearing upon the " veritable principle ". What was this principle? It was that the question of supplies must be considered not from the angle of commerce, that is to say of the rich and the ruling classes, but from the point ·of view of the livelihood of the people. The distinction is of capital importance. It may make the difference between free economics and planned society. The awareness of the necessity of a fundamental principle is what matters most here. Thus in his speech on the Declaration, dealing this time not with trade but with the more fundamental problem of private property, Robespierre declared : " posons donc de bonne foi les principes du droit de propriété." It was the more necessary as prejudice and vested interest had combined to spread a thick fog over the issue. It was in connection with the social problem that Saint-Just declared that those who made Revolutions by halves were digging their own graves, and spoke of the " quelques coups de génie ", which were still needed to save the Revolution, to make a " true Revolution and a true Republic ", and to render democracy unshakable, and Robespierre admonished the Assembly to remember that they were starting a new career on earth, " où personne ne vous a devancés ". Re-echoing Robespierre, Saint-Just spoke in the fragments on the Republican Institutions of the need of a " doctrine which puts these principles into practice and insures the well-being of the people as a whole ". He reached this conclusion from another angle as well. He had realized the insufficiency of ethics and politics alone to insure a rational order. The enthronement of Republican *vertu* must proceed on a par with social and economic reform. These matters, he realized, " were analogous, and could not be treated separately ". The French economy, shattered by inflation and war, could not be stabilized, without the triumph of morality over avarice. At the same time moral reform could not be initiated in an atmosphere of general distress, and a pauper would never make a self-respecting proud citizen. " Pour réformer les mœurs il faut commencer par contenter les besoins et l'intérêt." The Revolution could never be securely established as long as the poor and unhappy could be incited against the new order. The fundamental principle postulated by the Robespierrists referred to a postulate which was not concerned with the expansion of economic activity and the increase of wealth—values not much in favour with them, but with economic security for the nation, which in fact came to mean the masses. Robespierre declared that the wealth of a nation was essentially common property, in so far as it supplied the pressing needs of the people. Only the surplus may be considered as individual property, to be disposed at will, speculated with, hoarded and monopolized. From this point of view food must be regarded as being outside the sphere of free trade, because it concerned the people's right to and means of preserving their physical existence. Freedom of trade in this case would be tantamount to the right of depriving the people of their life : freedom of assassination. It mattered little whether non-essential goods had a free market, were hoarded and sold at a high price, for the lives of the people were not dependent on them.

It was quite natural for Robespierre to reject the view that property was made sacred and legitimate by the mere fact of its existence, its being established and time-honoured. There was a need for a moral principle as a basis for the idea of property. Private property was not a natural right, but a social convention. A declaration consecrating all established property as natural would be a declaration in favour of speculators and the rich, and not for man and the people. The right of property must at least (like the more sacred, because natural, right to liberty) be restricted by the rights and needs of others. Property is a right to enjoy and dispose of that portion of the national wealth which is guaranteed by the law. Any possession or traffic violating the security, liberty, existence and property of others is illicit and immoral. The poor and propertyless had a sacred claim on society to a livelihood in the form of employment—the 1848 right to work—or social assistance. This was the debt the rich owed to the poor. This debt should be shed through progressive taxation, which would also tend to level possessions and incomes. For as Robespierre had said in an early speech on the right of bequest, the Social Contract, far from promoting inequality, must be designed to counteract the tendency towards inequality and strive to restore by all means natural equality.

It is vital to realize that what was meant here was not the right of the unfortunate pauper to charity and the duty of the Government to come to his assistance, but the idea that the needs of the poor were the focus and foundation stone of the social edifice. " The bread given by the rich is bitter," declared Saint-Just. " It compromises liberty ; bread is due to the people by right in a wisely regulated State." Economic dependence of man on man stands condemned. The State must remove it. The State has the authority to employ, make changes and dispose of all the goods and assets which make up the nation's wealth, if private property is ultimately no more than a concession made by the State. Saint-Just threw out a number of slogans which were to become the catchwords of Babeuf. " Les malheureux sont les puissances de la terre, ils ont le droit de parler en maîtres aux gouvernements qui les négligent." The welfare of the poor was the primary task of government. " The Revolution will not be fully accomplished as long as there is a single unhappy person and pauper in the Republic." Very significantly Saint-Just, usually the least cosmopolitan of the Revolutionary leaders, strikes a solemnly propagandist note when dealing with the social problem. " Que l'Europe apprenne que vous ne voulez plus un malheureux ni un oppresseur sur le territoire français, que cet exemple fructifie sur la terre, qu'il propage l'amour des vertus et le bonheur ! Le bonheur est une idée neuve en Europe ! " This idea of happiness, seized upon by Babeuf and nineteenth-century successors of Jacobinism up to 1848, was in its defiant tone new and upon a totally different plane from the right to happiness of Locke and the fathers of the American Constitution, as well as from the right to social assistance recognized in the famous Report of the Duc de la Rochefoucauld in the Constituent Assembly. Saint-Just introduced a new and additional consideration to the analysis of the question of private property. He added to Robespierre's moral and social arguments a political consideration. The right to property, as said before, became for him conditioned on political loyalty. One who had shown himself an enemy of his country, that is to say a counter-revolutionary, had no right to possess property. Only the man who had contributed to the liberation of the fatherland had rights. The property of the patriots was sacred, but the possessions of the conspirators " sont là pour tous les malheureux ". The practical and immediate application of this principle were Saint-Just's famous *lois de Ventôse* on the confiscation of the property of the suspects and its distribution among the poor patriots, the carrying out of which was prevented by the events of Thermidor, but which was designed to bring about a vast transfer of property, indeed a social revolution. And yet, the main feature of Jacobin thinking on the social problem was its lack of coherence. The Jacobin attitude shows unmistakable signs of embarrassment throughout. It has often been suggested that the more " socialist " utterances of Robespierre and Saint-Just were mere lip-service, designed to counteract the agitation of the Enragés, and paid by men who were at heart typical representatives of the bourgeoisie. This was not really the case. Robespierre's statements expressing an anti-bourgeois class policy are to be found in his confidential notes, not intended for publication. Words of appeasement and reassurance directed to the possessing classes, in an incidentally nonchalant and contemptuous tone, appear in Robespierre's public utterances, but have no counterpart in his *carnet*. If a person's most genuine sentiments are those which he keeps to himself, it follows that not Robespierre's socialism but his conservatism is to be taken as an expression of opportunism. This does not, however, exhaust the case.

What is quite clear is that neither Robespierre nor Saint-Just felt themselves to be part and parcel of the proletarian class fighting for its liberation against the propertied classes. On occasion Robespierre, it is true, could adopt a vocabulary not far removed from the language of the Enragés : if the people are hungry and persecuted by the rich, and can get no help from the laws which are supposed to protect them, they are justified " in looking after themselves " against the bloodsuckers. He had nevertheless nothing but words of condemnation for the tactics and temperament of the Enragés, " who would cut the throat of any shopkeeper because he sells at high prices ". He considered them crazy anarchists and tools of a counter-revolutionary conspiracy.

The Robespierrist point of departure was not class consciousness, but the idea of social harmony based on the egalitarian conception of the rights of man. The aim was not the triumph of one class and the subjugation of the other, but a people where class distinctions have ceased to matter. The upper classes constituted a factor violating these principles, and had therefore to be brought to their knees. The mass of the people was thought to have no anti-social interests. It was virtuous and free from hubris and the vices engendered by wealth. Hence, on the one hand, what may be called the patronizing attitude of Robespierre and Saint-Just towards the proletariat and, on the other, their anxiety not to drive things to a breaking point. In a characteristic passage of a late speech, Saint-Just expressed his impatient disapproval of people of the artisan and working class who, instead of sticking to their jobs like their honest hard-working fathers, had completely yielded to their passion for politics, were thronging to public meetings and hunting for political jobs. In one of his last speeches and some time after the promulgation of the Laws of Ventôse, Saint-Just urged upon the Convention the necessity of calming public opinion on the question of the security of property, especially ecclesiastical and *émigré* property bought recently from the State. " Il faut assurer tous les droits, tranquilliser les acquisitions ; il faut même innover le moins possible dans le règne des annuités pour empêcher de nouvelles craintes, de nouveaux troubles."

Robespierre felt a good deal of embarrassment that he, the moralist contemptuous of money, was being driven to make money appear the decisive factor in the social order. In this embarrassment there was, of course, also an element of fear, and a subconscious wish to evade the issue. He reassured the " âmes de boue ", the haves, that there was no need for them to become alarmed for their property. The *sans-culottes*, following eternal principles and not considering the " chêtive marchandise " a sufficiently lofty aim, did not ask for equality of goods, but only for an equality of rights and an equal measure of happiness. Opulence was not only the prize of vice, but its punishment. " L'opulence est une infamie," said Saint-Just. The children of a righteous and poor Aristides, brought up at the expense of the Republic, were happier than the offspring of Crassus in their palaces, taught Robespierre. Robespierre feared damning the propertied class as a whole, and without reprieve, for the sole sin of owning wealth. What mattered was the disposition of a man. In the good old tradition of Catholic homiletics Robespierre taught that a man may own much wealth, and yet not feel rich. He opposed on occasion a motion whereby members of the Convention would have to declare their fortune. He would not agree that that was the final test of patriotism. The test was a lifelong dedication to virtue and the people. Not even the visible signs of service, such as taxes paid, and guards mounted—Pharisaic phylacteries—were the criterion, but the disposition externalized in a general and continuous attitude. A very elusive test indeed. On one occasion Robespierre declared that " La République ne convient qu'au peuple, aux hommes de toutes les conditions, qui ont une âme pure et élevée, aux philosophes amis de l'humanité, aux sans-culottes ". He condemned the factions who had just suffered their doom for having tried to frighten the bourgeoisie with the spectre of the agrarian law and worked to separate the interests of the rich from those of the poor, by presenting themselves as the protectors of the poor. The ultimate test was virtue ; only, while the people were virtuous almost by nature (and definition), the rich must make a great effort.

Saint-Just endeavoured to give a more concrete meaning to virtue in the social sense. He declared labour an integral part of virtue, and idleness a vice. There was, according to him, a direct relationship between the amount of labour and the growth of liberty and morality in a country. The idle class was the last support of the Monarchy : " promène l'ennui, la fureur des puissances et le dégoût de la vie commune." It must be suppressed. Everyone must be compelled to work. Those who do no work have no rights in a Republic. " Il faut que tout le monde travaille et se respecte."

(*d*) ECONOMIC RESTRICTIONISM AND INDIVIDUALISM

The postulate of a definite principle for the management of the economic life of the nation voiced by Robespierre and Saint-Just, although suggesting an effort at overall planning and direction by the State, turns out to be something very remote from State owner-ship of the means of production, or collectivism. It envisages social security and the economic independence of the individual, guaranteed and actively maintained by the State. It is a mixture of restrictionism and individualism. It denies freedom of economic expansion out of fear of inequality and out of asceticism, and yet is motivated by a secret wish to restore freedom of trade. Robespierre rejected complete equality of fortune quite emphatic-ally as a chimera, and a community of goods as an impracticable dream, running counter to man's personal interest. The *loi agraire* was a phantom invented by the knaves to frighten the fools.

The problem of social security was not to Saint-Just a question of the dole and charity, not even of pensions, but of legislation to prevent poverty. Man was not born for the alms-house, but to be

a contented and independent citizen. In order to be so, everyone
ought to have land of his own to till. Land should be provided for
everyone, either through the expropriation of the opponents of the
régime, or from the large State domain especially built up for the
purpose. Only invalids should be placed in a position of receiving
charity. The duty of the State was to give to all Frenchmen the
means of obtaining the first necessities of life, without having to
depend on anybody or anything but the laws, " et sans dépendance
mutuelle dans l'état civil ".

Security must be accompanied by equality, it too enforced by
the State with the help of restrictive laws. There must be equality.
There should be neither rich nor poor. A limit to the amount of
property owned by one person would have to be fixed. Only those
would be considered as citizens who possess nothing beyond what
the laws permit them to own. Excessive fortunes would be gradually curtailed by special measures, and their owners would be
compelled to exercise severe economy. Indirect inheritance and
bequests should be abolished. Everyone should be compelled to
work. Idleness, hoarding of currency and neglect of industry
should be punished. Every citizen would, in the scheme of the
Institutions Républicaines, render an account every year in the
communal Temple of the use of his fortune. He would not be
interfered with unless he used his income to the detriment of others.
Gold and silver, except as money, would never be touched in
Saint-Just's Utopia. No citizen would be allowed to acquire land,
open banks or own ships in foreign countries. Austerity in food
and habits was to be observed. For instance, meat was to be
forbidden on three days of the *decadi*, and to children altogether up
to the age of sixteen. The public domain, at Rousseau's advice
made as large as possible, was to serve as a national fund to reward
virtue and to compensate victims of misfortune, infirmity and old
age, to finance education, to give allowances to newly married
couples and, as said before, to offer land to the landless.

" Land for everybody "—this, if anything, sums up the Jacobin
social ideal : a society of self-sufficient small-holders, artisans and
small shopkeepers. The combination of a small plot of land and
virtue would secure happiness. Not the voluptuous happiness of
Persepolis, but the bliss of Sparta. " Nous vous offrîmes le bonheur
de Sparte et celui d'Athènes de la vertu . . . de l'aisance et de la
médiocrité . . . le bonheur qui naît de la jouissance de nécessaire

sans superfluité . . . la haine de la tyrannie, la volupté d'une cabane et d'un champ fertile cultivé par vos mains . . . le bonheur d'être libre et tranquille, et de jouir en paix des fruits et des mœurs de la Révolution ; celui de retourner à la nature, à la morale et de fonder la République . . . une charrue, un champ, une chaumière à l'abri de la lubricité d'un brigand, voilà le bonheur." Land ownership was in Saint-Just's reactionary Utopian vision the sole guarantee of social stability, personal independence and virtue.

The reform envisaged in the Laws of Ventôse on the confiscation of the property of the suspects and its distribution to poor patriots was to be a first step in the direction of an overall reform designed to give land (or some property) to everyone. The latter idea was formulated in the *Institutions Républicaines* written in Pluviôse, that is to say, before the Laws of Ventôse. There is no reference in the Institutions to the right to property being conditional on political allegiance. It would therefore be legitimate to conclude that the Ventôse project was not merely another act of repression taken against the suspects or an *ad hoc* demagogical measure designed to take the wind out of the sails of the Enragés, but was meant as a part of a comprehensive social programme. It was appreciated as such by contemporaries as well as by the Babouvists.

There is one aspect in Saint-Just's doctrine of " land for every-body ", which had failed to receive the attention it deserves, and which goes to prove two important things. The first is the fact that however Utopian and fanciful the plan, it originated at least partly in the realities and difficulties of the hour, above all in the crisis in food supplies. Secondly, on closer scrutiny the plan, while *prima facie* bearing the character of a State-planned overall reform, turns out to be a policy designed to create the conditions for free trade. This is the measure of Jacobin inconsistencies and grave inner difficulties in the matter of property and economics.

The exposition of the reasons for the establishment of a society of small-holders in the *Institutions Républicaines* begins with the difficulties in the circulation of corn. Easy circulation is essential where few owned property and few had access to raw materials. In his inveterate dislike of restrictions on trade and deep reluctance to accept the fixing of " maximum " prices by the State, Saint-Just declared that grain would not circulate where its price was fixed by the Government. If it was "taxed" without a reform of conduct, avarice and speculation would be the result. In order to reform conduct, a start must be made to satisfy needs and interests. Everyone must be given some land.

Should there be a distribution of land on the lines of a *loi agraire*, on the principle that the State had the power to change all property relations as it pleased ? No. Even the Laws of Ventôse did not contain an attack on the principle of private property as such, but made it conditional only on political allegiance. Apart from his genuine faith in private property, Saint-Just was too much of a responsible statesman, too vitally interested in the success of the sale of national property and the policy of *assignats*, the Revolutionary paper money, which had the national property as its cover (ecclesiastic, *émigré* and other confiscated property) and upon which the fate of the régime depended, to frighten the potential purchasers of national property into believing that their property was insecure and might be taken away from them.

But Saint-Just himself gives the clue to his intentions in the famous sentence found among his papers : " ne pas admettre partage des propriétés, mais le partage des fermages."

It appears that notwithstanding his desire that everyone should have some landed property in order to be happy and free, the redistribution of land was less important to him than its breaking up into small units of cultivation, units not necessarily held as an inalienable property, but as " fermages " on rent. The multiplication of such units seemed to Saint-Just the best guarantee of the free circulation of grain and of its reasonable price. The greater the number of sellers, the fewer the buyers, the better the supply, the lower the price. This reasoning is already to be found in Mably, the bitter opponent of free trade in grain, and in an article by Marat of September 5th, 1791, which must have influenced Saint-Just, and which reveals striking similarities with Saint-Just's treatment of the subject. Marat suggested that landowners should be forced to divide their large property into small-holdings, without the Government resorting to the *loi agraire* and to a redistribution of land. Marat's explanation of his plan would probably fill in the details of Saint-Just's thinking. Both seemed to be primarily concerned with the actual crisis of supplies, and the problem of satisfying the needs of the poorer classes. Neither of them liked the idea of keeping prices down by the law of maximum, for such a law in the opinion of both was calculated to ruin the producers and to discourage agriculture. A remedy was to be found in the law of supply and

demand. Since the price of a commodity was determined by the
proportion of buyers to sellers, it was essential to multiply the
number of farmers. Many journeymen could be transformed into
small farmers. The number of sellers of agricultural produce
would be immensely increased, and the number of buyers pro-
portionately diminished. A healthy equilibrium and prosperity
would be restored. Marat insisted that the State and not the landowners should have the power to select the farmers. State control
of leases was probably also envisaged by Saint-Just.

Moreover, Marat envisaged a very large State domain which
would farm out to landless peasants. In terms similar to those of
Saint-Just (about the correlation between the social realities and the
form of government) Marat thought that his plan would bring the
civil order nearer to the natural order by a greater facility of cultivation and a more equal distribution of the fruits of the land. In
addition, it would re-establish the balance between the price of food
and the price of manufactured goods, and finally abolish all mono-
poly in the fruits of the land. The more farmers there would be,
the fewer the journeymen, and thus the wages of the journeymen
would increase. On the other hand, the more farmers, the greater
the competition in the sale of produce. Furthermore, the people
on the land, assured of their needs, would be interested in getting
the best value for their surplus " and the free trade in corn would
be restored by itself ". It was this freedom of trade which most of
the leaders of the Revolution were grieved to be compelled to
restrict, and which, finally, by devious ways and State interference,
they hoped to restore.

PART III
THE BABOUVIST CRYSTALLIZATION

Que ce gouvernement fera disparaître les bornes, les haies, les murs, les serrures aux portes, les disputes, les procès, les vols, les assassinats, tous les crimes ; les tribunaux, les prisons, les gibets, les peines, le désespoir que causent toutes ces calamités ; l'envie, la jalousie, l'insatiabilité, l'orgueil, la tromperie, la duplicité, enfin tous les vices ; plus (et ce point est sans doute l'essentiel), le ver rongeur de l'inquiétude générale, particulière, perpétuelle de chacun de nous, sur notre sort du lendemain, du mois, de l'année suivante, de notre vieillesse, de nos enfants et de leurs enfants.

BABEUF

Je vous ferai donc, malgré vous, s'il le faut, être braves. Je vous forcerai à vous mettre aux prises avec nos communs adversaires . . . Vous ne savez point encore comment et où je veux aller. Vous verrez bientôt clair à ma marche ; et, ou vous n'êtes point démocrates, ou vous la jugerez bonne et sûre.

BABEUF

Chapter One

THE LESSONS OF THE REVOLUTION
AND OF THERMIDOR

(a) THE MESSIANIC CLIMATE

ON October 26th, 1786, Dubois de Fosseux, secretary of the Arras Academy, wrote to François-Noël Babeuf, then twenty-six, " arpenteur-géometre " and " feudiste " at Roye, that he had got hold of the " most extraordinary and most original pamphlet " called " *The Forerunner* of total world transformation through ' aisance ', good education and general prosperity for all men, or *A Prospectus* of a patriotic memoir on the causes of the great misery that exists everywhere and on the means of extirpating it radically ".

This was only one item in a typical eighteenth-century correspondence of intellectuals on books, philosophical subjects, social problems and practical affairs. The spirit that prevails in the correspondence is one of great hope and faith in the progress of enlightenment, in " that modern philosophy, of the righteous man (Rousseau) . . . so conforming to the rights of mankind . . . which is the honour of our century and which will inevitably secure the complete happiness of the generations to come... upon the debris of the fatal prejudices, cruel fanaticism and dangerous superstition ".

Both correspondents agree on the universal significance and validity of the new philosophy : it should form the basis for a universal code for the whole of mankind. " Ou il n'y a point de morale démontrée," writes Dubois, " ou elle doit être une, comme il n'y a qu'une géometrie." Dubois expresses a deep admiration for Montesquieu, and apologizes for his own audacity, but he cannot accept the view that what is just in the North can be unjust in the South. Climatic differences may necessitate diverse medical treatment, but they do not affect jurisprudence. In this spirit Babeuf in a letter of March 21st, 1787, formulates a problem :

with the sum of the knowledge at humanity's disposal, what would
be the state of a people whose institutions would establish the most
perfect equality among men, establish that the land should belong
to nobody in particular, but to all together, and that all should be
in common, including the products of all types of industry? Could
such institutions be considered as authorized by the natural laws?
Would such a society be able to exist, and would the arrangements
for absolutely equal distribution be practicable? Babeuf adds that
these questions had not been formulated without his having much
wider views on the subject, and Dubois describes them, in his
reply, as "highly important, meriting much reflection and susceptible of being treated in a very satisfactory manner".

Coming back to the "extraordinary pamphlet", Dubois reassures his friend that he has searched "with the greatest attention"
for an indication that its author "meant it all as a joke", but was
unable to find any such sign. The academician devotes therefore
quite a few letters to the detailed plans put forward in the pamphlet
about food, dress, lodgings, religion, sanitary arrangements and
education in the proposed Utopia. Babeuf declares himself ready
to be one of the first settlers in the New Republic.

Thus did the two men indulge in a *jeux d'esprit*, and compete
in finding subjects for exercises in essay writing as a pastime.

Hardly more than two years later the Revolution broke out and
released a chain of events and changes undreamt of by the most
audacious philosophers. Babeuf in the following way described the
impact of these events upon his attitude to political ideology :

" Electrified by the intervention of an unexpected disposition of
things, they conceived the reasonable possibility of contemplating
the application of the theories which only a little time before they
did not flatter themselves to have been treating in relation to their
own time."

" Leur âme, dès-lors enflammée de tout le courage nécessaire,
leur montrant·praticable le projet d'envahir des mains du crime
les éléments de parfaite justice."

Similarly, Buonarroti wrote that before the French Revolution
had exhibited the extraordinary spectacle of several millions of men
proclaiming and sealing with their blood " those eternal truths
which in former times had been known to a few philosophers ",

the design of setting the people in motion by the sole force of these truths might have appeared chimerical. But the unbelievable had actually happened.

In his polemic against what may be called the Reformist views of Antonelle, Babeuf declared that after the destruction of so many institutions and customs regarded before as unalterable, the sweeping away of the institution of private property, that last remaining vestige of the old order, which makes all the difference between an evil and a perfect society, was no more an unattainable dream. The argument that society had grown too corrupt for perfect equality, or that the price of such happiness would be an upheaval too terrible to contemplate, had lost all validity. For never had there been a more favourable disposition on the part of the people to a total Revolution than the state of popular consciousness begot by events since 1789.

The Revolution altered the course of Babeuf's life. In an autobiographical note written in 1794 he said about his profession : " avant la Révolution archiviste et géomètre. Depuis la Revolution, propagandaire de la liberté et défenseur des opprimés."

He said about himself that the Revolution had " spoiled him furiously ". He had become completely incapable of pursuing any profession except " publicisme ", and " matters concerning legislation ". Politics and meditation on the true principles of law and their execution had become a matter of such irresistible attraction that he began to think that that was his " unique vocation ".

This state of fascination was due to some "défaut inhérent à notre nature " ; " cet orgueil ", "cette sorte de vanité intime ", which tells him and those like him that they are " better than many of their brethren " and are called upon to proclaim the " terrible mystery ", and to regenerate the world to its " greatest advantage ".

He is convinced that this overwhelming sense of mission is not just an error or illusion, or vain ambition. Has he not renounced all advantages, has he not been living like an anchorite, defying prison, persecution, as well as the mockery of the fools and the corrupt who had treated him as insane ?

Here we have it all : that disposition, that quality of mind—a complex mixture of ideas, mystical faith, volition, passion, emotion,

Messianic hope and error—that has for a hundred and fifty years been among the most important factors in the destinies of mankind ; the faith in a single and final cause of and answer to all evils the world over ; the belief that the secret has at last been found, that humanity is heading in an irresistible march for some denouement, a violent break-through to a preordained, perfect and ultimate scheme of things.   Prophets emerge to call people to prepare for the Day of Judgment, and orders of priesthood—parties—spring up to organize the preparations.   The encounter between a Messianic political creed and the masses revives phenomena, precedents for which could only be found in the religious-social movements of the past, and carrying with them terrible possibilities of mass tyranny.

Whatever may be said against exaggerating the innovations brought about by the Revolution, it is beyond dispute that the temper described here was wholly a new product of the Revolution. The Revolution linked together the abstract ideas of a few philosophers with the inarticulate masses, whom the " ancien régime " kept apart, principally because it had no room for the intermediaries —political parties.   A vibration that shows as yet no signs of coming to rest was thus begun.

The postulate of salvation, inherent in the Revolution, evolved only gradually into a vision of the fall of the mighty and rich, and the rise of the poor and the downtrodden to inherit the earth. Babeuf was the culmination of it.   Early in the Revolution he assumed the name Camille, in 1795 he dropped it for the name Gracchus.   The reason given by Babeuf was that in the meantime his " démocratisme s'est épuré ".   He had become aware of the gravity of Camille's error in building a temple to Concord and concluding an agreement between the patricians and the plebeians. The latter had been deceived as they would always be, for no social peace between the two classes was possible.

This appeared to the Babouvists to have been the lesson of the Thermidorian reaction.

(b) THE LESSONS

The events since the 9 Thermidor ran counter to the underlying faith in the inevitable advance towards ever wider popular and social democracy. The almost plebiscitary and direct democracy of 1793 was replaced by a system of census. The poor, " as the ignorant who are unfit to rule the instructed ", were disfranchised. Boissy d'Anglas, in his report on the Constitution of 1795, declared that " all social order rests on the preservation of property ", and that a country governed by the propertyless would be in a state of nature.

The Constitution of 1793 affirmed that the people or any part of the people had the right and duty to revolt against oppression. Jacobin practice and the Constitution of 1793 envisaged legislative referenda, and the people's right of veto against the decisions of the Legislative Assembly. Implicitly they accepted the direct democracy exercised by the immense network of the popular societies, above the heads of the Legislative Assembly through a system of intercommunications, petitions and other means of expression and pressure. True, the direct democracy of year II was a dictatorship. It was, however, a dictatorship of the popular masses.

The new bourgeois and conservative régime not only restricted popular sovereignty, freedom of speech and discussion, it also deprived the masses of the social and economic benefits derived from Robespierre's dictatorship. The Committee of Public Safety had pursued confiscatory policies, fixed compulsory prices, organized and enforced production, sales and deliveries, established the *livre de bienfaisance* of social assistance, resorted to special and gratuitous grants to the poor—all with the avowed aim of maintaining the poor and conducting the war by soaking the rich. The Laws of Ventôse on the expropriation of the suspects and the distribution of their possessions to poor patriots had, as shown above, the character of a social reform of a more permanent significance than the State's intervention in the working of the economic machine, an intervention necessitated by the gravest emergencies, and only resorted to with reluctance. The Constitution of 1793 had earlier proclaimed the social rights, which became the rallying point of all the radical movements up to 1848 : the right to happiness, that is to say, the right to work and to social assistance.

The post-Thermidorian régime abolished price control, allowed prices to shoot up, let inflation run wild, and saw the speculators grow richer and richer. Government war projects, conducted till then in a manner assuring the employment of as many workers as possible, returned to free enterprise, and the number of workers was consequently drastically reduced. The gratuitous distribution of supplies to the poor was so curtailed as to be practically discontinued. The national administration of hostels, hospitals and *maisons de bienfaisance* came to an end. A terrible famine among the working classes was the outcome of these changes. The régime followed the principle that the social problem was no problem for State action.

(c) BABEUF

Babeuf's Messianic longings fed on deep personal misery. He put all the intensity of his anguish into the vision of a general redemption, which would bring a sudden release from all material and spiritual torment. He was a possessed and hunted being, yearning for repose.

To follow the story of his life is to experience a hardly ever relieved sense of dismay, mingled with acute embarrassment. The restless, indeed convulsive activities in the service of the " grand secret ", the " terrible mystère ", are unfolded to the accompaniment of a ceaseless and horrible dirge : the whining of starved children and their crushed mother. And Babeuf was much too good a husband and too tender a father to play the role of a Don Quixote of the Revolution. With the personal misery and the passionate dedication to an ideal there went a passion for self-dramatization, a deliberate acting for history, that cannot fail to evoke a feeling of revulsion. He had an inflammable imagination, a quite uncontrollable pen, and a capacity for becoming intoxicated with words that at times make it difficult to take him seriously.

His restlessness verged on madness. At times he appears to be simply tossed about by a flux and reflux of emotion. He was not of a masterly or commanding personality.

Babeuf's emotionalism and the fact that he dealt with people on incompatible levels made him very trying and often dangerous. " Moi qui me trouve si déplacé auprès de la plupart des hommes de ce siècle "—he said about himself. This incompatibility was a source of perpetual misery and disappointment to him. When cast down from his " glorious " poses by a rude blow, he would in most cases fail to react consistently. He would too often behave in an ambiguous, confused, if not cringing manner. In spite of declaring himself a new Achilles with " the pride of guaranteeing himself able to pulverize . . . Atlas and all the giants ", he was not made of heroic stuff at all. He was too wordy for that.

François-Noël Babeuf was born on November 23rd, 1760, the oldest son of an ex-soldier who became a village labourer, and who in deepest misery maintained an inordinate pride and sense of importance. Babeuf never received any systematic education. At the age of fourteen he started earning his bread and helping his family in distress. He became a *feudiste*, a clerk engaged in tracing feudal claims. Babeuf was later to say in a passage ringing with genuine eloquence that it was among the dust of old charters and contracts that he had learned the fraud and robbery in which all property claims originated. Babeuf's native Picardy had a long tradition of social radicalism. It was the scene of some of the cruellest outbursts of medieval Jacquerie. Calvin hailed from his district, as well as Saint-Just and Saint-Simon.

In his capacity of *feudiste* Babeuf, not unlike Voltaire and Rousseau, had to go through some humiliating incidents with the aristocracy, resulting from the ambiguity in the relationship between an educated plebeian and the ancient aristocracy. The outbreak of the Revolution turned Babeuf into a *déclassé*. *Feudistes* were no longer needed. He witnessed the early days of the Revolution. His fascination with the spectacle was boundless, and was to last till his execution as martyr of the Revolution. The first two years of the Revolution were spent by Babeuf in feverish activities as agitator, journalist and pamphleteer, always more violent and more extreme than everybody else. He edited the *Correspondant Picard*, wrote pamphlets, participated in storming châteaux and burning government offices. He organized protest strikes, boycotts, petitions and collective refusals to pay the feudal dues that remained. He saw himself as the defender of the oppressed, one of " hommes . . . exagérés, moroses, extravagants, propres à troubler l'ordre et la tranquillité publique " with an " air gêné et sauvage . . ." " like Rousseau ". He served several prison sentences for his efforts of " revolutionizing " the people.

After the fall of the Monarchy there came for Babeuf a period of office. He was elected administrator of the Department of the Somme, Assistant-Secretary and Secretary of the Electoral Assemblies of the Department and of Montitier respectively, and also member of the Comité de Règlement, where he had to deal with national and émigré property. But now, when all seemed to suggest a reasonable status in life, a steady income and an opportunity of useful activity, came the catastrophe. For reasons never explained Babeuf, acting, as alleged, on the suggestion of the President of the district, scratched out one name and substituted for it another in a document of ownership of national property, on January 30th, 1793. He was immediately suspended and charged. He escaped to Paris to reach the very depths of misery, while his family remained behind on the brink of starvation. Three children had already died of hunger and disease. " Rousseau, trop sensible Rousseau," Babeuf exclaims, " the idea of finding thyself one day unable to provide for the needs of thy children broke thy heart ; thou couldst not support them, and thou abandonedst them therefore from their birth to the cares of the Government. This abandonment—I can understand it, thou didst not know thy children ; but, tell me, wouldst thou have abandoned them at that age when the first signs of their intelligence, the first movements of their souls, make them so interesting ?   O my son of seven years, so faithful a copy of the good, the innocent Emile ! Oh ! No, I could never abandon thee."

Rousseau could never be forgotten. When trying to obtain a post, Babeuf reassures his future employer : " I have the character of a philosopher. I reflect, I meditate as much as Rousseau did in his time. Like him the search for means of effecting general happiness is my constant study." On top of it he adds : " Je suis laconique comme un Spartiate . . ." Exasperated by his poor wife's letters, Babeuf tells her " die, if 'tis your pleasure ". Like the Jacobins and the Enragés, he says, the love of the Revolution has killed any other love in him, and made him " hard as the devil ". In Paris Babeuf lived on private charity till influential people obtained for him a place in the Paris Food Office, although his case was still pending. He soon became involved in a quarrel with his superiors, whom he accused of plotting famine. On August 23rd, 1793, Babeuf was sentenced by the Criminal Court at Amiens to twenty years. Arrested, and released, rearrested and released again, he succeeded eventually in having the sentence squashed in July, 1794, after the case had gone through several instances. The 9 Thermidor arrived. It was the end of a régime with which Babeuf was in sympathy. It was his special misfortune to have become an outcast during a régime which was likely to offer him great opportunities. The general opening of a new chapter by 9 Thermidor meant also a new beginning for Babeuf. Before that date Babeuf was no more than an obscure provincial agitator with a stigma attached to his name. After 9 Thermidor he becomes a widely read journalist, editor of the Paris *Journal de la Liberté de la Presse*, and an anti-Robespierrist.

By the end of 1794 Babeuf returned to the pure creed of Robespierrism, to become the apostle of egalitarian Communism and the soul of the plot to which he gave his name. He paid the supreme penalty. On the eve of his execution, in agony from the wounds which he inflicted on himself after hearing the verdict, he wrote : " Je ne vécus et respirai que pour la justice et le bonheur du peuple."

(d) BUONARROTI

Babouvism as a theory and legend owes probably more to Philipe Buonarroti than to Babeuf. Buonarroti's extraordinarily beautiful and magnetic personality, his apostolic activities, finally his History of the Babouvist Conspiracy, at once a most reliable account and an excellent exposition of the doctrine, were among the most potent and inspiring forces in the seething Revolutionary underground of Europe in the first half of the nineteenth century. They exercised a profound influence upon budding socialism. Buonarroti was made of quite different stuff from Babeuf. He was a descendant of Michelangelo, and the son of a Tuscan noble, who was well connected with the court of the future Emperor Leopold II. He received a very solid and many-sided education. He fell early under the influence of eighteenth-century French philosophy. "J'agis, je parlai, j'écrivis conformément à ces principes," he wrote. Stirred to his depths by the outbreak of the Revolution, Buonarroti left in October, 1789, his native country for Corsica. There he edited journals, and was soon appointed to head the office dealing with Church affairs and national property. He struggled bitterly with the local reactionaries and was deposed and expelled by a counter-revolutionary uprising. He returned to become at once engaged in a bitter struggle against Paoli. Appointed as first National Commissioner at the local tribunal, he was then made chief of propaganda in connection with an abortive

French invasion of Sardinia. The plan failed, but Buonarroti was given the opportunity of playing the role of the Rousseauist Legislator on the small island of Saint-Pierre, renamed Ile de l'Égalité.

On May 27th, 1793, the National Convention decreed Buonarroti's naturalization as French citizen and paid tribute to his services. While in Paris, Buonarroti entered into close relations with the Jacobin leaders and was a frequent guest at Robespierre's lodgings. During the last months before Thermidor, Buonarroti was active in the South of France. He was attached to the armies fighting on the Italian front and in charge of various important administrative, political and educational activities. He was also engaged in preparing plans for the invasion and "republicanization" of Italy and Corsica, then in the hands of the British. After 9 Thermidor Buonarroti was imprisoned at Plessis. Released from there, he joined the Conspiracy of Babeuf as one of its chiefs. After having served his prison sentence and gone into exile, he became the high priest of egalitarian Communism in Europe.

It was the purest brand of idealism that turned Buonarroti into an egalitarian and Communist. If ever there was a Robespierrist, it was Buonarroti, with his unshakable faith in *vertu*, his opposition to materialism, in spite of his acknowledged indebtedness to Helvetius, his belief in the Supreme Being and the civil religion. But unlike the dreary tight-lipped Master, Buonarroti had no personal grudge against the world or people. His person and life were surrounded by that romanticism of the first half of the nineteenth century, which speaks to us through a Delacroix and a Victor Hugo. There was about him an air of generous solemnity. An Italian by birth, he became an ardent French patriot, but remained deeply concerned with and involved in the struggle for the Risorgimento. But not one particular country was his fatherland. His true fatherland was the Revolution, and Buonarroti looked upon France as the Messiah of the Revolution. The signal and the lead must come from Paris. This brought him into conflict with the young rising prophet Mazzini. Another disagreement drove them apart again on a point of Messianic significance. The old conspirator could not conceive the Day of Judgment without fire and gnashing of teeth. Dictatorship and terror were, in his opinion, the inescapable necessity of the Revolution. Mazzini's profound faith in the Italian people led him to believe that with the outbreak of the

Revolution a wave of brotherly love would sweep Italy, so that there would be no need to constrain anybody. Buonarroti also objected to Mazzini's contacts with the Italian upper classes. He could not agree to a struggle for national liberation, which was not at the same time a social uprising. In the end, Buonarroti excommunicated his opponent.

Buonarroti was the prototype of those Revolutionary prophets who were to spend the major part of their lives in prison or exile, with the police of half Europe in concerted pursuit of them ; men made of steel, never broken by torture, never weakened by failure or indifference, never enticed by allurements ; members, or rather leaders, of an international confraternity with hidden cells, illegal papers, secret meeting places, mysterious rites and symbols, waiting in a ceaseless vigil for The Day.

When the 1830 Revolution allowed him to return to Paris after an exile of thirty-three years, he appeared to his contemporaries as an almost supernatural apparition. Nestor of the Revolution, he acted from then on like the chief of a Party, sending out instructions, receiving reports, gathering round him every active Revolutionary, among them Voyer d'Argenson, of the famous family, Charles Teste, Trélat, editor of the *National*, Hareau, Raspail, Louis Blanc and finally Auguste Blanqui. With their help he reorganized the Charbonnerie Démocratique Universelle. His pupils worshipped him like a god. In the last few years Buonarroti became still more secretive than ever. His passion for conspiracy and Revolutionary symbolism was unabated. He deprecated all haste and premature Revolutionary outbreaks, whether initiated by Mazzini, the Société des Droits de l'Homme or by the strikes in Lyons, in 1833. Buonarroti died on September 17th, 1837. His funeral turned into one of those famous republican manifestations, which looked like thunder presaging the gathering storm of the Revolution.

Shortly before his death Buonarroti told Trélat : " I am going to rejoin soon those virtuous men who have set such good examples." He did not, of course, mean the saints of the Church. He meant Lycurgus, Gracchus, Rousseau, Robespierre and the like. The nineteenth century was already changing the face of the earth, an unprecedented industrial development was gathering momentum, but Buonarroti still lived in 1793 and 1796. In a fervent *apologia* for Robespierre, Buonarroti said in the hearing of the Italian Morini : " The peoples are advancing towards that goal . . .

equality . . . the sole institution able to satisfy all needs, to direct our useful passions, to chain the dangerous ones and to give society a régime free, happy, peaceful and stable. But I shall not see it, for sure. Let it suffice if I have always kept my faith alive and unaltered, and that nobody can accuse me of inconsistency."

Chapter Two

THE BABOUVIST SOCIAL DOCTRINE

(a) EQUALITY AND THE SOCIAL CONTRACT

THE Babouvists were " terribles simplificateurs " *par excellence*, fanatically sure of there being a sole and all-explaining principle of social existence. They believed this to be human equality. Their postulate of equality took no cognizance of the variety of human experience and historic realities, and refused to acknowledge either the uniqueness of men and situations or the irrational element in human behaviour.

The philosophical basis of the concept of equality was, according to Buonarroti, to be found in man's intuitive recognition of every individual of the human species as equal, in the sympathy and pity evoked in every one of us by the suffering of our fellow-men, and " in the spirituality of the thinking principle ". " This principle, which constitutes to him alone his entire human self (tout le moi humain), being indivisible and pure, and always derived from the same source, is necessarily equal in every individual of our species." In other words, reason, which is the essential characteristic of man, is equally present in all, while the varying abilities and talents of different individuals are accidents, which do not alter the essential sameness of human spirituality. Furthermore, these accidents are primarily the result of circumstances and opportunities. The differences of ability and talent have also been enormously exaggerated by vested interests.

The life and experience of all mankind are confined within an essentially identical circumference of wants, desires and affections : " the want of food, the desire of procreation, self-love, pity, sympathetic affections, the disposition to feel, to think, to will, to communicate our ideas, and understand those of our companions, and to conform our actions to rules ; hatred of constraint and love of freedom."

These natural rights emanating from the natural law of equality

were the basis of the Social Contract. The Contract intended to
create a system of institutions which would preserve natural equality,
and prevent the undeniable inequalities—physical or spiritual—
from asserting themselves. The essence, the " elixir ", of Rousseau's Contract was that all should have enough, and nobody more
than enough. It was for the State to create the necessary institutions
for equitable distribution. The State was also to be vested with the
power " to restrain within just limits the riches and power of
individuals . . . by subjecting all citizens equally to the laws
emanating from the whole ", and compelling all hands to work.
According to Buonarroti it was Mably—Babeuf would rather say
Morelly—who first found that " the science of politics reduces
itself to the art of effectually stifling these passions " of avarice and
ambition, in order to make good the pledge of common happiness
contained in the original Contract of society.

In this version of the Social Contract the emphasis is clearly not
upon the guarantee given to the free initiative of the individual,
but upon the power and tasks of the State. Liberty, to Buonarroti,
" resides in the power of the Sovereign, which is the entire body
of the people, to carry out an impartial distribution of goods and
pleasures ". The individual is no more than an employee and
pensioner of the State. Buonarroti goes still further. He claims
that Rousseau also wished the State to be the spiritual guide and
master of man.

" This social order subjects to the will of the sovereign people
the acts and properties of each individual, encourages the acts which
are useful to all, proscribes those which only flatter the vanities of
the few, develops, without predilection or partiality, the reason of
each citizen, substitutes for base cupidity the love of country and
glory, and constitutes the whole of society into one vast, peaceable
family in which each member is subject to the will of the whole, but
no member to that of another."

The State, and not the unfettered mind of the individual, is the
source of social as well as moral progress.

Logically such an attitude should take as its starting point an
a priori principle or some purpose outside and above man's will.
The paradox of Babouvism like that of Jacobinism was the individualist basis of their collectivist philosophy. Babeuf declared
the happiness of man, or common happiness, to be the sole purpose
of society : " le type inattaquable de toute vérité et de toute justice

. . . en entier la loi et les prophètes." But what kind of happiness is envisaged here ? Security, " the enchained fate ", the removal of all hazards. Were it not for the suffering from insecurity experienced by Babeuf and those with him, their creed could certainly have been described as lacking in courage.

(b) VISION OF HISTORY AS HISTORY OF CLASS STRUGGLE

The Babouvist vision of history is a grand simplification determined by the postulate of a single principle. The whole drama of history appears as enacted between the moment of the violation of original equality and its restoration at some preordained future hour. It can be summed up as the story of avarice. Babouvist treatment of the subject is strongly reminiscent of medieval preaching, leans heavily on Rousseau's *Discourse on Inequality* and on Mably's ascetic socialism, and at times gives the impression of being a crude prototype of Marxist analysis.

The violation of the terms of the original Social Contract resulted in a situation where " the most foolish, the most vicious, the most feeble, and the least numerous have been enabled to overburden with painful toils and duties, and to deprive of their natural liberty the great majority of the strongest, most virtuous and even best instructed men ". This change can be traced back to a single factor, the acquisitive spirit. No objective factors working for a class differentiation—like changing modes of production—are as yet perceived. Nor would the part played in the desire to increase wealth by the impulse for a higher culture be admitted. The " haves ", identified with idlers, are always vicious. Their wealth is never admitted to be a reward for merit. The oppressed poor are always righteous and good. Manual labour is the only real contribution to prosperity. The role of managers and experts—their age had not yet come—is seen as secondary, and their claims are treated with contempt and anger as pretentious and immoral.

The legal and educational system, the moral outlook, indeed the whole *Weltanschauung* of existing society, are depicted as a superstructure deliberately built up by avarice to secure its reign of pillage. First came the institution of private property, then heredity, after that, in the wake of feudalism, primogeniture and the feudal theory about the divine right of overlords to exploit their vassals. To justify class distinctions in the bourgeois world false notions were spread about the intrinsic superiority of one profession over another, and claims were made for preferential treatment for alleged higher abilities. " As if various people had different stomachs." Commerce is described by Babeuf as the worst poison of the social body, while it should be its lifeline. It keeps the first—and real—producers in want of necessities produced by them. The merchants are engaged in a permanent conspiracy against the consumer class : they raise and lower prices at their will, create artificial shortages or gluts, deceive the public by false advertisements, and plot together to reduce the wages of the workers.

State laws and taxation were framed with the view to depriving the dispossessed of every means of rising from their degradation. They give the lie to the claim that the poor are free to sell or to withhold their services. The rich, being masters of their industry, are in a position to dictate conditions ; since they have all necessities at their disposal, they can impose the law upon the " proletarians ", who are in no position to bargain.

Babeuf speaks of the " bizzare codes " praised as works of prudence and equity, which bear the unmistakable imprint of acquisitive passion on them.

False teachings were spread to make the iniquitous system appear as the only natural order. Respect for private property was declared to be the rock of the social order ; the coexistence of exploitation and oppression was proclaimed to represent social harmony ; the resentment of the oppressed, subversion. No limits were set to the ravages and wiles of the acquisitive spirit. The success of sharp practices was acclaimed as the triumph of skill and good luck, while the poor were made to believe that their misfortune was due not to greed's usurpation, but to inefficiency and bad luck. Even the satisfaction of a sense of grievance was not allowed to the oppressed. The " haves " finally convinced themselves of the naturalness of this order : that " superiors " should live at the expense of " inferiors ". They grew callous and indifferent to the sufferings of their starving fellow-men. All ethical instincts were corroded by avarice, jealousy, perversion, unrest, war and social troubles. The decay of the species had set in. " La société est une caverne. L'harmonie qui y régne est un crime." " Que veut-on parler de lois et de propriétés ? Les propriétés sont le partage des usurpateurs, et les lois l'ouvrage du plus fort," exclaims Babeuf.

Society is thus being torn by an incessant, although mostly silent, civil war, which the dominant classes are anxious to ignore or to gloss over. There are, however, rare moments when the silent struggle changes into an open war. This happens " quand les extrêmes se touchent ", when all the wealth of society becomes monopolized in the hands of a small minority, while the number of the dispossessed, who have nothing to lose, swells to embrace the vast majority of the nation. And so the climax of the system means its undoing. The complete destruction of the natural order of equality is the beginning of its restoration. " L'ordre naturel peut-être défiguré, changé, bouleversé, mais son entière destruction tend à le reproduire."

Such moments, writes Babeuf in his dithyrambic style, have been prophesied in the Apocalypses of History, the Book of the Times. The masses suddenly become aware that they have come of age. They begin to claim their rights " en qualité d'hommes ", no more willing to be tutored by self-appointed, unworthy mentors ; defiant of the superstitious teachings and deliberately misleading principles, with the help of which the " haves " had been keeping them down. In such circumstances the unifying framework of national unity explodes. The poor love their country, but if a property qualification bars them from the exercise of their right to popular sovereignty, they have every right to declare that they recognize no duties without rights, no obligation to obey laws in the framing of which they had no share. Deprived of active citizenship rights, they owe no allegiance to the State. It is enough for them to sit down " bras croisés " to paralyse the life of the nation by a general strike.

The people demand the complete fulfilment of the conditions of the Social Contract, that is to say, a general restitution of all that has been stolen and usurped. The torrent of the people's wrath is then let loose and no dam would contain it.

To quote Babeuf's own words : " For there are moments when the last consequences of these murderous social laws result in the universality of riches being swallowed up by a few ; when the peace, which is the natural state when all are happy, becomes unavoidably disturbed ; when the masses are no longer able to carry on, finding everything outside their grasp, encountering nothing but pitiless hearts in the caste which has grabbed all ; these facts shape the epoch of those great revolutions, determine those memorable periods foretold in the Book of Time and Destiny, when a general upheaval in the system of property becomes inevitable, and when the revolt of the poor against the rich becomes an inevitability that nothing could prevent."

(c) THE INTERPRETATION OF THE FRENCH REVOLUTION

The French Revolution was taken by the Babouvists to mark the beginning of an apocalyptic hour in mankind's history.

Babeuf and Buonarroti submit the French Revolution to an analysis designed to prove that its course represented the unfolding of an objective pattern, which, when near completion, reached self-awareness. They postulate a certain dynamism in the Revolution, which if allowed to run out its preordained course would not have stopped before attaining the foretold system of perfect equality, if not precisely Communism. " C'est là où se repose toujours un peuple lorsqu'il est parvenu à améliorer sa Constitution sous tous les autres rapports." It " alone offers a reasonable boundary to the Revolution, which would be a crime if, changing the mere form of oppression, it left the multitude in servitude aggravated by false hope, consolidated by the increased number and perversity of oppressors ".

The French Revolution appears as a lesson in class struggle, a struggle in the beginning unconscious, then fully conscious, between the two forces, the two social classes, in the Robespierrist tradition equated with virtue and immorality. The class of the rich, guilty of selfishness and tainted by privilege, is immoral, whereas the party standing for equal rights for everyone, and the rehabilitation of the poor, represents virtue.

A certain inconsistency in Babeuf's view on the origins of the Revolution is not without interest. At one time he describes 1789 as one of those apocalyptic moments in history, when the accumulation of oppression and calamities give to the " ébranlement majestueux " of the people an urgency that cannot be resisted. Another time, in a rather thoughtful article, he wrote that it was not so much oppression as national pride that caused the outbreak of the

Revolution. Compared with other countries, the situation in France before 1789 was less unbearable. The French would not however be outdone by the United States and Holland, where a struggle for freedom had achieved the triumph of popular sovereignty.

The earlier days of the Revolution were marked by great unanimity. The motive was not virtue, but ambition, the hope of gain and power. The " rich and vicious class ", having weakened the Monarchy and the feudal caste, and gained all the advantages it could, was determined to put a stop to the Revolution. But then something unexpected happened.

Virtue, that is to say, the national interest as a whole, equated with the interest of the most numerous, while quite weak in the first Assemblies, gained a number of fervent adherents in the third, the Convention. Although these were in a minority in the Assembly itself, the quality of their ideals and the support of the masses rendered them most formidable, and made them powerful enough to face the large number of profiteers of the Revolution.

And so the two parties began to face each other in the full knowledge of what divided them.

" L'un qui veut le bien pour le seul appât de la gloire, l'autre qui veut le mal pour l'avantage honteux de faire son bien personnel." Both parties may have desired a Republic, but one wished her to be bourgeois and aristocratic, while the other, believing itself to be the real maker of the Revolution, wished the Republic to be popular and democratic.

The one party wanted a " Republic of one million ", the million of the enemies, overlords, exploiters, oppressors and bloodsuckers of the other twenty-four millions, to continue to enjoy all privileges, leisure and superfluities, while reducing the vast majority of the nation to the status of slaves and helots. The other party wanted a Republic for the twenty-four millions who have " laid her foundations and cemented it with their blood, who feed, sustain, provide all the necessities to their fatherland, defend it and die for its safety and glory ". This party was not contented with equal rights and " equality in the books ", but strove to have " l'honnête aisance " legally guaranteed, equal satisfaction of needs, and all the social advantages secured.

The representative of virtue was Robespierre, at times quite isolated in the midst of his colleagues and the factions. As early

as 1791 Babeuf saw in him a secret or at least potential adherent—
" en dernier résultat "—to the idea of the *loi agraire*. The factions,
knowing the virtuous disposition of the masses and aware of the
identity of their interests with the strictest precepts of eternal justice,
endeavoured to deceive the people by paying lip service to the
people's cause and dangling before the eyes of the people only the
image of justice.   Robespierre alone sincerely strove to give the
people the reality of freedom.

Babeuf and his followers are the heirs of Robespierre and Saint-
Just, who themselves were the first executors of the perennial
philosophy of such prophets of the just social order as Minos,
Lycurgus, Plato, the " Lawgiver of the Christians ", the " Jew Jesus
Christ ", Thomas More, Montesquieu, Mably, Morelly (Diderot),
Raynal and, above all, Rousseau, all prophets of virtue and equality,
in contrast to the preachers of—in Buonarroti's special version—
the " system of egoism ", the English economists.

Babeuf is the second Gracchus, carrying out the Incorruptible's
testament, enacting the last act of the Revolution.   With this vital
difference, that while the first Gracchi, Robespierre and Saint-Just,
had been groping in the dark and improvising, not fully conscious
of their aim and its practicability, without a proper organization
and programme, in the midst of personal divergencies and heterogeneous ideas, and were thus able to achieve only " des résultats
imparfaits et définitivement nuls ", the Babouvists are not only
richer in experience of success and failure, but superior in the
precision of their aim, the full consciousness of its significance and
in the possession of the necessary organization and single-mindedness for its achievement : " de marquer d'avance un point unique
où, sans partage, sans modifications, sans restrictions, sans nuances,
vous tendrez tous ; et d'être circonscrits dans un cercle étroit
d'hommes vertueux, isolés de tout ce qui pourrait opposer des vues
divergentes et contradictoires, de tout ce qui ne serait point capable
de se confondre dans le sentiment un et parfait de l'apogée du bien."

The Babouvist is the last lap of the Revolution, of the permanent
Revolution, in that it intends to inaugurate at last an era of real
and not of " speculative and derisive equality ".   In that lies its
difference from all Revolutions that have preceded it.   This unrestricted equality is equated with the greatest happiness of all and
with the " certainty of never being deprived of it again ".   *The
Manifesto of the Equals* written by the poet Sylvain Maréchal, an

atheist and communist of long standing, expresses this state of consciousness : " The French Revolution is but the forerunner of another revolution, far more grand, far more solemn, and which will be the last. . . . Never was a more vast design conceived and put in execution. At distant intervals in the history of the world it has been talked of by some men of genius—by a few philosophers—but they spoke of it in a low and trembling voice. Not one of them has had the courage to speak the whole truth. The moment for great measures has arrived. Evil is at its height ; it has reached its maximum, and covers the face of the earth. Chaos, under the name of politics, has too long reigned over it. Let everything revert to order, and resume its proper place. . . . The days of general restitution are come. Weeping families come and seat yourselves at the common table provided by Nature for all her children."

(d) THE EVOLUTION TOWARDS COMMUNISM

It was not without some justification that Babeuf felt that he was standing on the shoulders of the prophets of the past and the leaders of the Revolution, and that he was seeing further and clearer. Not only had the Revolution taught him to dare, it had, he thought, also offered a lesson.

The earliest and constant element in Babeuf's thinking was the general and very vague idea that it was incumbent upon society to secure everybody's existence, in his nomenclature a " honnête médiocrité ", neither less nor more than enough : " portion égale ". On the eve of the Revolution he had come to think that this could best be done if all property was put into a common pool, and the State was given the power to carry out an equal distribution, without according preferential treatment to any class or profession. Babeuf had found that Rousseau " rêvait bien " in the *Discourse on Inequality*, but that the author of the extraordinary brochure " rêve mieux " : if all men are absolutely equal, nobody should possess anything in particular, be more or less rich, or esteemed better than his fellow-men. Moreover, Babeuf adds in a characteristic fashion : Rousseau would like to send us back to the woods, to let us dwell under an oak and drink from the nearest brook, while the Reformer was offering four decent meals a day,

" elegant dress " and " charming houses ".   " C'est là avoir bien
su concilier les agréments de la vie sociale avec ceux de la vie naturelle
et primitive."

During the Revolution Babeuf looked for a time to the *loi
agraire* for a solution of the social problem.   In the Physiocratic
fashion he was still inclined to regard landed property as the real
wealth of society.   The *loi agraire* propagated by him was not
Communism, but State ownership of the land, the land parcelled
out to cultivators as life-long holdings.   The actual life-long holders
of the allotments were to be forbidden to sell or alienate them.
This prohibition was considered essential for the prevention of
inequality and the accumulation of holdings in single hands.   Babeuf
calculated that as France had about 66,000,000 hectares of arable
land, eleven *arpents* would be allotted to each family.

But the *loi agraire* embraces more than the redistribution of
the land and the abolition of inheritance.   It connotes " la réclamation des premiers droits de l'homme, du pain honnêtement assuré ",
" le pain de l'esprit, et le pain du corps ", the right to expect from
society work, and social assistance in case of infirmity and old age,
as well as equal and free education, health service and gratuitous
justice.   In other words, the *loi agraire* means social security,
with the land as its guarantee.   Moreover, Babeuf is anxious to
state that apart from the new land régime and the system of social
insurance, the framework of economic pursuits should remain intact.   Except for the inalienable patrimony, security against needs,
" all that is concerned with human industry would remain in the
same state as at present ".

In his first letter to Coupé in 1791 Babeuf went much further.
He spoke obliquely of the " stipulation . . . immédiatement
sanctionée par la mise en commun de toutes les resources indéfini-
ment multipliées et accrues au moyen d'une organisation savamment
combinée et du travail général sagement dirigé ".   Babeuf did not
elaborate the point further.   If ownership of all resources and the
organization of all production by the State are the essential features
of socialism, then this is a socialist programme.

At this stage Babeuf still considers the social problem primarily
within the context of natural law and natural rights.   The background of the discussion is the controversy on the meaning of the
right to property in the Declaration of Rights : Did it state the
inviolability of private property ?   Did it intend private property

rights to be restricted by the needs of others and the community as a whole ? Or did it imply the right of the propertyless to demand some property from society ? Clearly, the immense unsettling of the property system by the seizure and sale of ecclesiastical property also influenced Babeuf's thinking. In a pamphlet written soon after the 9 Thermidor, *Du Système de dépopulation*, purporting to be an exposure of the horrors of the Robespierrist Terror, Babeuf claims that the Terror was actually a weapon for the achievement of a social transformation. The social programme attributed by Babeuf to Robespierre was built upon a Malthusian assumption that the soil of France was unable to provide enough for all the twenty-five million of its inhabitants, especially as most of the land was concentrated in the hands of a minority, while the large majority were propertyless. A drastic reduction of the population and a redistribution of the land into small, but sufficient and equal, holdings were called for. According to Babeuf, Robespierre expected the population to be greatly reduced by the Terror, the war and the internal uprisings. He planned to achieve a redistribution of the land by the liquidation of the landowning class. Its members would be, if not killed off, forced to " execute themselves " in time, and in their own interest. The Government would seize their property as a prelude to the State ownership of all property, which would initiate the restoration of the conditions of the original Social Contract. Babeuf is in sympathy with the social aims he ascribes to Robespierre. He refuses, however, to accept the Malthusian premise and Terror as a weapon of social policies. If the soil of France does not grow enough for all, then the remedy should be an all-round reduction of the standard of living by means of persuasion.

The war, inflation, the breakdown of the machinery of the free adjustment of supply to demand, and the ensuing misery of the poorer classes, contributed to make the social problem a matter of the highest immediate urgency. The terrible situation of the masses seemed to justify Babeuf's contention that formal political rights are meaningless without social guarantees. The masses, he claimed, had been cheated out of any benefits from the Revolution by high-sounding and empty phrases.

The emergency measures taken by the Government to regulate the flow of supplies and distribution were described by Babeuf as poor palliatives. Sporadic interventions, hand-to-mouth action, were not enough to solve the problems. " Il faut qu'elles le soient par les bases fondamentales du Contrat Social." The State must take over the whole organization of production, distribution and consumption. The whole population would become at once State employees, and State pensioners, producers and consumers at the same time. All produce would be directed to common stores, and distributed from there to centres of consumption in fixed quantities. Workers and industries would be organized in unions. An overall, annual plan would fix quotas. There would be no more blind groping. All industry would be totally nationalized and commerce would disappear altogether. No longer would the welfare of the people be delivered to hazard or the greed of exploiters. There would be no need to cheat, deceive or hoard, no need to fear unemployment or bureaucratic chicanery. A scientific system would have placed the lives of the people " à l'abri de vicissitudes ". Moreover, once the system is set going, the supervision of its working would become reduced to a matter of simple arithmetic, comprehensible to anybody with elementary education.

At this stage Babeuf repudiates the *loi agraire* as stupid. The idea of transforming France into a chessboard of small and equal holdings is ridiculed as chimerical, and condemned as calculated to engender new inequalities.

The demand for a *loi agraire* is described in the *Manifesto of the Equals* as a crude and instinctive desire of veterans for immediate reward, not based on any wider principle. " We want something more sublime, more equable ", a community of goods : " déproprairiser toute la France ", and not a reparcelling of her soil.

What gives Babeuf the certainty that his plan of State organization of production and consumption is no chimera ? The experience of Revolutionary France at war : the organization of supplies for a force of 1,200,000 divided into twelve widely dispersed fronts.

Buonarroti's account of the discussions in the Secret Directory brings out very strikingly the way in which the lessons of the Revolution forced Communist conclusions upon the Babouvists. There were no differences on the ultimate aim, a régime of equality. People differed on ways and means. Amar, the ex-member of the Committee of General Security, wished to pursue the Jacobin policy of levelling incomes by spoiling the rich with the help of high taxation, compulsory contributions and requisitions. Others went further, suggesting laws to prevent accumulation of wealth, ostentatious living and luxury. But Buonarroti, Félix Lepeletier, himself a wealthy man, and Darthé, all faithful disciples of Robespierre and Saint-Just, insisted that all these measures were ramparts too feeble to dam the torrent of the competitive spirit. The requisitions, taxes and contributions were properly resorted to during the Revolution to avoid a breakdown, and to defeat the vicious designs of the rich, but they could not form part of the habitual order of society, without assailing its existence. To leave the present order of private property and competition intact, and yet to attempt to hamper its working by repressive exactions, would result in grave difficulties. Assessments could never be certain. There would always be the risk of taking away necessities. Proprietors, left with the burden of cultivation and production, while being exposed to confiscatory taxation and requisitioning, would simply have no incentive to carry on. The sources of production would dry up. If trade were left free, nothing could prevent a secret accumulation of money, which would certainly turn to speculation.

It was, characteristically, Robert Lindet, ex-member of the Committee of Public Safety, who had been in charge of food supplies in 1793–4, who came out strongly in favour of full-fledged Communism. But Lindet's development from regimented egalitarianism to pure Communism need not appear so astonishing. A letter of a Montagnard *député suppléant* of 1793, reproduced by Mathiez, shows strikingly how this chain of thought was becoming fixed already in 1793. Grenus of Mont Blanc thus writes in November of that year : " I believe that the principles of ' maximum ' lead us to a system of common ownership (Communauté), which may be the only means of preserving Republicanism, as it destroys personal ambition that fights incessantly against equality, and directs all our faculties towards general well-being. You will see that in order to establish the ' maximum ', it will be necessary to set up national stores to receive the surplus of foods and manufactures (surplus of what is consumed by the producer—' l'excédent des consommations et des fabriques '), to be after that distributed in equal shares. We thus arrive on the threshold of a system of common ownership, where everyone brings the product of his industry into the common pool so that it may be distributed to all. This will strike you as very doctrinaire (très systématiquement philosophique). But consider the strength that will accrue to the Republic from the union of all the personal ambitions. I will say more. It will prove the perfection of equality and liberty. I cannot conceive of a Republic in any other way. This is not that *loi agraire*, which would not last more than twenty-four hours from the moment that you give to personal ambition free play. Common ownership—this is the great principle of the Republic. One may be thought a fool for saying this at present. But we shall come to it, and it will be put on the agenda, or I am very much mistaken. And from that moment will start the true moral and political regeneration."

We are here in face of what is commonly called distributive socialism (or communism). It has been argued that as this is the essence of Babouvist Communism, Babouvism could for that reason hardly be considered as the parent of modern Communism. In the Babouvist scheme the individual producer works by himself and brings the surplus or the whole of his produce to the common pool, from where every consumer receives his equal share. Modern Communism, it is said, does not derive from the idea of natural rights, but is a conclusion drawn from objective developments in the sphere of economic production. These developments were by scientific socialism recognized as leading irresistibly to collectivist forms of economic and social organization. From this point of view modern Communism is held to be an entity, the birth of which can be exactly fixed. The thesis of this study, however, is that this allegedly distinguishing mark of modern Communism is by no means so essential, because modern Communism partakes of a more comprehensive unity, more comprehensive in time as well as in what this unity encompasses. The essential feature of this wider unity is the postulate of an exclusive social pattern based on an equal and complete satisfaction of human needs as a programme of immediate political action. The economic justification or definition of this postulate is a matter of secondary importance, a distinguishing mark of a subdivision of a larger species.

Furthermore, we have in fact seen Babeuf writing in his first letter to Coupé (August 20th, 1791) of an " organization savamment combinée et du travail général sagement dirigé ", after all resources have been pooled together. In his letter from the Arras prison to Germain of four years later (July 28th, 1795) Babeuf says that while everyone would in his scheme remain in his present occupation, all workers would be classified according to the type of their work. Society would have exact information of what everyone is doing so that there was no under- and no over-production. Society will determine the number of people that should be employed in one particular branch. All would be apportioned to the needs of the present hour and to the requirements of the future, in the light of the probable increase of population. " All real needs will be exactly investigated and fully satisfied thanks to the swift transport of goods to all localities and all distances." " Will industry perish, because it will no more be exposed to proceed blindly, to take risky adventures, to err by fortuitousness or over-production ? Will it go under, because it will be intelligently directed and stimulated in accordance with the needs and well-being of all ? " asks Babeuf of those who claim that common ownership and economic collective planning would destroy industry. If this plan, naïve and crude as it may be, does not amount to a scheme of collectively organized production, it would be difficult to see what does. Few would maintain that the idea of such an organization could not occur or would have no meaning, if it was not suggested by the existence of a central source of industrial power or productive energy, making possible or even necessitating forms of mass production.

The individual owes the State the totality of his strength and means, in the absence of private property—all the labour of which he is capable. The principle of absolute equality extends not only to advantages and enjoyments, but also to burdens and contributions to the common pool. All competition should be forbidden. A person who is able to do the work of several should be considered a " social pest " and annihilated as a public danger. " La folie meurtrière des distinctions de valeur ", which demands higher reward for talent, is a crime. To each according to his needs, which should in all cases be equal, and modest. For whatever one has above what he actually needs is the result of theft from others, and from the common pool. " Aucune raison ne peut faire prétendre une récompense excédant la suffisance des besoins individuels," wrote Babeuf.

The political justification of the extreme position taken up by Babeuf is to be found in his polemic with Antonelle, referred to above. The ex-marquis and former member of the jury which condemned the Girondists, while extolling Communism as the only just and ideal régime, maintained that the evil institution of private property had struck its roots too deep in modern society and had corrupted men too thoroughly. People could not even appreciate the excellence of egalitarian Communism. An attempt to bring it about was fraught with unspeakable dangers, civil war and endless bloodshed. All that could be hoped for, in the circumstances, was a degree of supportable inequality, and laws against avarice and ambition. He advocated, therefore, a Reformist programme.

Babeuf replied that the Revolution had shown that palliatives and half-justice would be of no avail. They would only intensify the evil. Negotiations and compromises would only kill the revolutionary energy of the masses, and strengthen the domination of the oppressing classes. "La caste friponne de million (against the twenty-four millions) le marchandera, elle temporisera, et elle tâchera de ne rien fixer." Babeuf condemns the policy of "perfecting the imperfect", and giving a new lease of life to tottering evil. "Qu'au contraire le peuple exige une justice entière, il est obligé alors d'exprimer sa toute-puissance ; et au ton dont il se prononce, aux formes qu'il déploie, tout cède nécessairement : rien ne lui résiste ; il obtient tout ce qu'il veut . . . qu'il doit avoir."

The moment at hand was one of "sociabilité prête à se dissoudre". The masses had experienced changes once thought unthinkable. They had seen through the great fraud of the old system. They now are animated by a Revolutionary impetus that refuses to prop up the crumbling framework. Babeuf and Buonarroti reject the theories of the "organic depravation" of mankind making total regeneration impossible. The feared upheaval would be no worse than the permanent civil war which has been raging unabatedly throughout the ages. The "happy catastrophe" is inevitable.

To some Babouvists the discovery of Communism was an illumination. Amar, at first an exponent of moderate policies, was given to read a—lost—book or memorandum by Debon on the evils of the private property system. "He appeared smitten, as it were," records Buonarroti, "by a beam of light. At the first enunciation of this system he became its enthusiastic defender . . . no longer thinking of aught else than to justify and propagate its principles." Characteristically Debon is described by Buonarroti as having spent his whole life "in the study of public evils, and having grasped better than anyone else Robespierre's ideas".

Bodson, an old Hébertist and ex-member of the Commune, wrote : " Je me rallie aux principes de la sainte égalité. Pour leur propagation, les plus pénibles privations me seraient des délices." Young Germain had mystical trances after his conversion in the Arras prison.

Whether actually willed by the people or not, the Babouvist doctrine claimed absolute and exclusive validity. " Where is the man," exclaims Babeuf, " who could be so mad " as to reject—as an insufficient incentive to human effort and emulation—" this guarantee of never being in want ", this promise of " prospérité commune ", " inépuisable mine du bien-être individuel à perpétuité ". The Babouvist programme was nothing but the affirmation of the natural order. It was sure to give a new heart to man. All possibilities of crime, discord, ambitious scheming or ill will would be removed. Babeuf describes in these words the millenial vision of the order to come. " Let that government make disappear all frontiers, fences, walls, locks on doors, all disputes, trials, all theft, murder, all crime ; all Tribunals, prisons, gallows, torture, jealousy, insatiability, pride, deceit, duplicity : finally all the vices. No more (and this is, no doubt, the most essential) of the ever gnawing tooth of the general restlessness, of the personal perpetual anxiety of every one of us, about our lot of to-morrow, next month, next year, in our old age, the fate of our children and their children . . . Guarantee to every one of its members a state of stable felicity, the satisfaction of the needs of all, a sufficiency inalterable, independent of the ineptitude, immorality or ill-will of those in power."

Once private property is removed, the spring of all vices and evil passions will be dried out, and all means of doing harm gone. Men would begin to act on different incentives than in the past. The men chosen to run the affairs of the community for a fixed period would simply have no interest in perpetuating their power, as it would give them no advantages over others.

Chapter Three

THE STORY OF THE PLOT OF BABEUF

(a) THE PREHISTORY OF THE CONSPIRACY

THE seeds of the Conspiracy of the Equals were sown in the political prisons which held the Jacobins taken captive after the unsuccessful uprisings of the 12 Germinal and 1 Prairial. These prisons became a kind of political academy.

The prisoners were released after the abortive Royalist coup of 13 Vendémiaire. By this amnesty the Government wished to repay the Left for its help in quenching the Royalist revolt. The Left—Robespierrists, Hébertists, Enragés and Jacobins in general —were in a grave difficulty. The Government, especially Barras, was emphasizing the Royalist danger and inviting the Left to become reconciled to a conservative Republic. Many of the "amnistiés" entered Government service willingly, or because poverty left them with no choice. Some were able to accommodate their consciences, without much pain, others consoled themselves with the hope of working for the egalitarian ideal from inside. The Moderates declared themselves men of 1789. The Irreconcilables raised the rallying cry of "Bread and the Constitution of 1793". Some of these moved still further to the Left, to Communism, but even those who would not go so far welcomed and encouraged the vigorous and effective propaganda against the régime conducted by the extreme Left, especially Babeuf in his *Tribun du Peuple*, which was the successor of the more moderate *Journal de la Liberté de la Presse*.

The Left had no proper organization. Its members were in loose touch with each other, met casually in cafés and parks, indulging in general discussions. The Jacobin Club had been dissolved. The Constitution of 1795 forbade affiliations and correspondence between societies, prohibited the election of permanent officers and fixed conditions of admission and eligibility. It also banned collective petitions and closed meetings. The popular societies were to be no more than casual Hyde Park gatherings to listen to a soap-box speaker.

During the liberal period soon after the Vendémiaire events, the Directory allowed the Society of the Panthéon, called the "Réunion des amis de la République", to be founded, and to become a rallying centre for the Left. The Government hoped to be able to control the Society through its agents.

The Society proceeded without permanent officers, rules of procedure, registers or minutes. It was a very loose body. The meetings were held in the ancient refectory of the nuns, and, when this hall was occupied, in the Convent's vault or crypt, "where", in the words of Buonarroti, "the dim paleness of the torch light, the hollow echoes of their voices, and the constrained positions of the persons present, either standing or seated on the ground, impressed on them the greatness and the perils of their enterprise, as well as of the courage and prudence it required".

The Société de Panthéon became the scene of a tug of war between Left extremists and Government agents. When its discussions became too menacing, the Government ordered General Bonaparte to close it down, on 1 Ventôse, an IV.

(b) THE STORY OF THE PLOT

While the Society was carrying on its activities, efforts were being pursued to organize a nucleus for political action. The first attempt was made in Brumaire, an IV, at a meeting attended by Babeuf, Buonarroti, Darthé, Fontennelle, and Julien de la Drôme, the younger. A masonic association was suggested. Others thought of a Committee of Insurrection. No decisions were reached. A number of other attempts to create a secret nucleus followed. The most important was the establishment of a Central Committee in the house of the old Conventional Amar. It was dissolved soon owing to the grave suspicion with which the extreme Robespierrists treated Amar, one of the architects of the Incorruptible's fall. Babeuf had in the meantime escaped an arrest and gone into hiding, from which he continued to publish the *Tribun du Peuple*. The Secret Directory Committee of the Conspiracy of the Equals was finally organized in the first days of Germinal, an IV. Its original members were Babeuf, Antonelle,

Sylvain Maréchal and Félix Lepeletier, to be soon joined by Buonarroti, Darthé and Debon. The structure of the Conspiracy will be described presently. The Secret Directory engaged in vigorous anti-government propaganda, without at first having fixed a definite date for insurrection.

Events were however hastening the outbreak of the insurrection. On the 27-8 Germinal, an IV, were issued a series of draconic laws threatening the death penalty for criticism of the régime in speech and writing, for suggesting the re-establishment of the Constitution of 1793 (or the Monarchy), for incitement to seize property, public or private, for advocacy of a new distribution of property (the agrarian law), for demanding the dissolution of the existing authorities and for similar offences.

For a moment the Equals saw their opportunity in what appeared an imminent mutiny of the Légion de Police, stationed at Grenelle. The Legion was saturated with Babouvist propaganda and was seething with unrest. The conspirators hoped to utilize this force as the spearhead of the insurrection. Unexpectedly the Legion surrendered and was disbanded. The most compromised deserted and went into hiding in the houses of the Equals. They were a welcome military nucleus, but their restlessness, coupled with the nervousness of the Babouvist militants, was threatening to cause a premature outbreak.

A joint meeting of the political Secret Committee and the Military Committee on 11 Floréal ordered the Military Committee to make the final preparations for the insurrection. A proposal of alliance with the Royalists was rejected, although the Royalists were for the moment considered less detestable than the " Sénat " : " ils nous servent." Similarly, a plan to assassinate the Directors, suggested by a young officer in charge of the guard at the Directory, was not accepted. The Act of Insurrection was ready, so were the banners. Further action was held up by an important and for a while unresolved problem. Having independently formed an organization with a view to an insurrection, the former Montagnard deputies, who had been expelled from the Convention, made an offer of fusion with the Equals. The original founders of the Conspiracy disliked the idea intensely. They distrusted the ex-Conventionals. Furthermore, a fusion, as will be shown, added a further complication to the unresolved problem of the aim of the Conspiracy : return to the 1793 Constitution and pre-Thermidorian legality, or a total Communist revolution? After a good deal of wrangling an understanding was reached on the basis of a compromise to be referred to. In the *post scriptum* to the circular letter to the Chief Agents Babeuf expressed the hope that on the day of the insurrection the pressure of the masses would neutralize the influence of the Montagnards. The fusion was concluded at a joint meeting of the representatives of the two parties on the 17 Floréal. Robert Lindet, Félix Lepeletier, Javogues and others represented the Montagnards.

The Government was all the time aware of the brewing trouble. On 15 Floréal, Grisel, a government agent, who succeeded in worming his way into the innermost councils of the Conspiracy, offered Carnot, the then presiding member of the Directory, all the information that was wanted.

In the meantime Carnot's colleague, Barras, the consummate trimmer, entered into contact with the Equals. Barras was anxious to build up a force on the Left upon which he could rely against his colleagues on the Directory. He invited Germain, one of the military leaders of the plot—he sent his official carriage to fetch him—sounded him on what was going on, and urged him to prevail upon the Equals to behave as " true patriots ", and rally round him against the Royalists, *émigrés* and reactionaries. Barras offered to put himself, with his staff, at the head of the insurrection or, failing that, to place himself as a hostage in the Faubourg St. Antoine The Conspirators made no answer to Barras's overtures, and Babeuf denounced them in the forty-second number, the last, of the *Tribun*.

A meeting of the Insurrectional Committee was held on 20 Floréal. " L'impatience était générale et extrême . . . la chute de la tyrannie était certaine . . . dispositions militaires mûrement concertées."

Next morning the police seized the headquarters of the Conspiracy, while the leaders were at work on the post-victory manifestos. Babeuf, who since he had gone into hiding had been the virtual secretary of the plot, was there, as well as Buonarroti. " Why do you obey your masters ? " Babeuf asked the officer who came to arrest him.

Encouraged by Barras's agents—twenty-four thousand francs were actually given—the Equals at large made a desperate attempt to induce the garrison at Grenelle to launch a joint attack on the Directory. The troops answered with fire, killing or dispersing the assembled crowd. The ring-leaders were seized and tried by a special military court. Thirty-one were sentenced to death, twenty-four to deportation, more to various prison sentences.

This was not yet the end of the drama. The trial before the High Court of Vendôme was to come. It sentenced Babeuf and Darthé to death, and the other leaders to imprisonment on a lonely island off the Breton coast.

Although Carnot is quoted by his son as saying that the Equals had a very good chance of seizing power, and although Mathiez maintains that the Plot was very important in that it made a coalition between the Thermidorians in power and the Jacobins no more possible, the Conspiracy was in effect only a tiny episode from the point of view of the broad course of the Revolution. Its significance, however, for the evolution and the crystallization of ideas, and as an historic myth, could hardly be exaggerated.

Chapter Four

DEMOCRACY AND DICTATORSHIP

(a) THE DEFINITION OF DEMOCRACY

THE Babouvists considered their goal not only absolutely right, but inevitable. It being so, how could their attitude fit in with the dogma of the people's sovereignty, and the sacred right of every individual to express his will and to participate in the exercise of sovereignty? Clearly, the sovereignty of the people could not in this case mean the unreserved acceptance of the spontaneously expressed will of the people, and for that matter of the individual, as the final and decisive criterion. If the goal is inevitable, what difference does it make whether it is actually willed or not by all or even by the majority? Or does it mean that it is inevitable that all or most should will it? Once the goal is achieved in its all-solving form, to what extent could it still be subject to the wishes or moods of men?

In his letter to Coupé in 1791 Babeuf looks forward to a Constitution which would be framed in such clear, detailed and precise definitions that no diverse interpretations, sophisms, ambiguities or cavilling would be possible. Not only would nobody have any interest in tampering with the Constitution, but on the contrary, respect for it would become a religion, " la foi salutaire de la raison de l'humanité ". The people would rather be killed than allow such a Constitution to be violated, after they had experienced its blessings. And as to the possibility of sabotage by a refractory minority, the majority will always know how to deal with such a perverse group, even one employing the greatest energy and all possible astuteness.

One single true will is postulated, a will that must and would be willed in a condition of freedom from selfishness, ignorance, prejudice, vice and evil influences. Such a will must be presumed, or engendered by the proper handling of the conditions in which the people are called to will. This is the essence of Babouvist democracy.

The Babouvists referred to themselves as democrats *par excellence*, and used the word democracy as an ennobling term, and slogan. They clearly felt the need to define the concept. Buonarroti distinguishes between the pre-revolutionary conception and the Revolutionary usage of the term democracy. Before the Revolution it signified a form of government where the whole people were exercising the functions of government. Obviously an unreasonable system. Through the application to the exercise of sovereignty of a term previously used for the executive power, a State has, since the Revolution, come to be called democratic, where every citizen contributes directly to the formulation of the laws. Democrats, however, do not simply demand universal franchise. Conscious of and " revolted by the corruption, misery, and especially the ignorance which holds the multitude in bondage, often making it unable to exercise the inalienable natural rights ", they demand laws of simplicity and equality to relieve misery and to secure the development of intellectual faculties. Democracy, in brief, is " that public order in which equality and good morals place all the people in the same condition to exercise legislative power usefully ".

Without these, formal democracy and popular sovereignty are a fraud. The equality of votes is rendered illusory by the inequality of assets enabling some to exercise an undue influence in society. A democracy such as " according to pure principles " it should be, " c'est l'obligation de remplir, par ceux qui ont trop, tout ce qui manque à ceux qui n'ont point assez ". The deficit of the latter is nothing but the theft of the others. The establishment of a democracy is in effect a process of restitution of all that was stolen from the poor by the rich ; before all, the return of the lost old tatters and furniture, as Babeuf put it.

Formal freedom and formal equality, what is considered the freest form of government, would in the established order of things benefit only those who can live without work. The poor have no time to attend assemblies or to get the necessary information. This enables the governments to make a show of democratic sovereignty, for it is confined to the wealthy classes. " How would they act, if the people, taking them at their word, were to moot the question of their own usurped distinctions, and demand of them to descend to their proper level ? "

What is, after all, the value of all the laws, if they do not result in getting the great mass of the nations, " the poor, out of their profound misery " ? Without restoring the totality of human rights to the indigent, a government, even if it gives assistance to the poor, is no more than a Charity Committee based on repressive laws.

Among the Notes of Babeuf one ends with " salut en démocratie, oui en démocratie, car l'on entend les porteurs de sac et des blanchisseurs dire : nous sommes souverains ". Babouvist writings speak of French democracy not in the sense of a political system, but as of a class, rather a class with a definite class consciousness. Democracy is a stage beyond mere republicanism and superior to it. It is the class in march towards perfect happiness : " the purest and most perfect of systems."

" Des hommes qui ne veulent pas pour le peuple un demi bonheur, qui en veulent le maximum, qui ne souffrent aucune atteinte à ses droits, à son indépendance, qui ne tolèrent aucune restriction à sa liberté."

His evolution from a believer in class reconciliation into a partisan of class struggle was, as we saw, explained by Babeuf as a purification of his " démocratisme". Babouvism is " la dernière expression du parti démocratique . . . et se différencie . . . de toutes les autres . . ."

(*b*) ANTI-PARLIAMENTARY, PLEBISCITARY IDEAS

Yet, political democracy, in spite of all its shortcomings, is recognized as embodying a social dynamism. With the help of proper propaganda and extreme popular forms, this dynamism is bound to become operative.

In his second letter to Coupé in 1791 Babeuf says that universal, direct and equal franchise, the people's veto on the decisions of the Assembly, open debates, the elimination of Committees, the adoption of the principle that each Assembly is a *Constituante*, not bound by any decisions taken or fundamental laws adopted by earlier Assemblies, the removal of the means test for office and the National Guard—all such measures must lead to a demand for a *loi agraire*. The masses are bound to vindicate the totality of their rights, and the measures suggested will give them the power to exact their rights by their sheer numbers as well as by intimidation.

"La plénitude des droits de l'homme, principe qu'on peut toujours invoquer et professer hautement sans courir de danger." And so the first line of attack on the social system could and should confine itself to the political plane, the final aim being the *loi agraire* : "Et ce but est le but unique où tendront toutes les institutions de la terre, lorsqu'elles vont en se perfectionnant " "loi agraire . . . est le corrollaire de toutes les lois." Without this accomplishment no Revolution can be considered complete and no Constitution as deserving its name.

Babeuf believed that Robespierre and Petion, adherents to the *loi agraire* at heart, pursued a similar line, waiting for public opinion to mature for the *loi agraire*. Babeuf is not prepared to wait passively. He wants to set up a party in and out of the National Assembly with a precise and detailed programme and tactics. He has little liking for or confidence in parliamentary representation. He wants therefore to enable the electorate, or rather party, through the instrument of the electorate, to check and overrule the actions of the Assembly. Babeuf wants a party of "firm and solid heads, imbued with all the force of the great principles, methodical and tactical (tacticiennes) minds . . . capable of conceiving the vast ' ensemble ' of a good plan of constitution and of following it up point after point, without tolerating the slightest change in its physiognomy or direction . . . capable of turning all the obstacles, and of foiling by skilful manœuvring all the plots and intrigues of the party of iniquity, of avoiding surprises and traps, of finding in one word apropos and clear-sightedly the right tactics in every situation ".

Not having any hope of election to the Assembly, and being convinced of his powers of persuasion, Babeuf suggests to Coupé the creation of a parliamentary group, of which he himself would be the extraparliamentary leader and policy maker, while Coupé would be its spokesman in the Chamber. Very strikingly foreshadowing party procedure of the future, Babeuf lays down preliminary consultations on every question with a view to formulating the policy to be pursued and the answers to any possible objections. Also the distribution of roles in the debate was to be settled in advance. In this way adherents to the same ideology would never be found contradicting each other and compromising themselves. "As to the principal speaker, he and myself being always at one in our principles, it is evident that whatever he was to receive from me it would be exactly as if he had derived it from his own resources ; only that he will be completely freed from ' travail de cabinet ', which would become my exclusive task."

Babeuf makes no concrete suggestions about building up an extraparliamentary, national party organization. At the same time he wishes to subordinate the elected Legislature to the strictest control by the electorate, and to the people's power of veto, in other words to the direct French democracy. He intends, furthermore, to restrict its power of legislation by a stipulation of momentous significance that no modification of the Constitution tending to restrict liberty and equality could be proposed. " Ne seront discutées que les propositions ayant pour but leur extension."

Who is to decide whether a proposal is likely to restrict liberty and equality ? The sovereign people, its appointed or self-appointed guardians of orthodoxy, that is to say the active agitators of Babeuf's party creating an atmosphere of intimidation and violent denunciation.

Not only is the sovereignty of the Legislature thus rejected by this canon of the supremacy of the direct democracy, but ultimately also that of the people : for there are things which even the people cannot do. In appearance every Assembly is sovereign and un-fettered by the decisions of its predecessors. Every Assembly is a *Constituante* ; the people are free at any moment to change its laws. But only in one direction. The Assembly cannot legislate any-thing which cannot be annulled by the people, even its internal disciplinary rules and rules of procedure not excluded. All must be submitted to the people's consent. Without these precautions, the liberty of the tribune may be stifled for the benefit of a faction, argues Babeuf. Every deputy is revocable by his constituents at any time. He is to give a monthly account of his activities to his constituency. Every canton will have a body of seven Curators of Liberty, and every department twenty-one of them. These bodies meet every three months to examine reports of their deputies, and to decide whether they have faithfully carried out their man-dates. The deputy will not be allowed to plead : his report is his plea. As long as liberty has not struck deep roots, not everyone will be eligible for curatorship. Too many are still backward and steeped in old prejudices. " Il faut donc prévoir et se prémunir contre les défections." Curators can be elected only from among citizens who have reached twenty-five years of age, live from the product of their labour, exercise an independent profession, and hold no government job. Nothing is said here about political reliability of the curators, but it may be taken as implied that they should come from Babeuf's flock. Other considerations could not be regarded as disqualifying. For Babeuf insists with much vehemence on the absolute imprescriptible and equal right of every person to exercise his citizen rights in shaping national sovereignty, to belong to the National Guard and be eligible for office. Above all, there should be no withdrawal or suspension of such rights for people who had been declared insolvent. He pleads fervently on behalf of people who have no time to look after their own affairs because of their preoccupation with the public welfare in a spirit of " sublime disinterestedness and self-denial ". " Qui s'absorbe exclusivement dans les rêves de bonheur pour la patrie, pour l'humanité, court grand chance de ruine," as the lives of great men of antiquity, and his own troubles, can witness.

The exercise of sovereignty must take place in the greatest possible publicity. The Assembly must contain the largest possible galleries for the public. All deliberations must be held in public, for committees are centres of intrigue where factions prepare their plots against the liberties of the people. The people must have the unrestricted right and opportunity to express its will in the form of petitions. A special Bureau de Petitions is to be established to receive, classify and forward the petitions to the Assembly. The Bureau is to meet daily to hear all petitions read aloud, and to inform the petitioner that his petition is under consideration. No petition is sent directly to the Bureau. All are sent through the local municipality to the local deputy, who under a penalty of twenty years of penal servitude must forward them to the Bureau. Extracts from the petitions are printed daily and presented to the Assembly.

Ultimately the Legislature would have only the right to initiate legislation, but not to decide upon it. There must be a fortnight's warning before any project could even be discussed. There must be three debates at intervals of ten days. The decree can only be drafted on the forty-fourth day. It is then sent to the municipalities for sanction or veto by the people by means of petitions. The counting of the petitions would take place within six months. All these cumbersome provisions are claimed by Babeuf to be necessary to safeguard that all views, interests and wills are taken into account, and that no other will but the people's prevails. But such plebiscitary, direct democracy is—as said elsewhere—the preliminary of dictatorship or dictatorship in disguise. It is an invitation to a totalitarian party in opposition to whip up agitation, to " organize " the discontent or the will of the people, by engineering mass petitions, manifestations, and pressure from below ; and an encouragement to a totalitarian party in power to engineer referenda and mass resolutions of support. It could not be done otherwise. For where full unanimity is postulated, there is no escape from the imposition of a single will.

(c) CAN THE PEOPLE BE TRUSTED?

For ultimately Babeuf trusts the people no more than he trusts the National Assembly. As early as 1786 Babeuf expressed his grave doubts about the " manie de la pluralité des voix ", and complained of the preponderance of stupid majorities. He was complaining that those whose views were above the heads of the multitude were being treated as innovators and " gens à système ". The innate indolence of the people leads them to prefer the things they know and to which they are accustomed. For every change means an effort and a disturbance. " La majorité est toujours du parti de la routine et de l'immobilité, tout elle est inéclairée, encroutée, apathique. . . . Ceux qui ne veulent pas marcher sont toujours les ennemis de ceux qui vont en avant, et, malheureusement, c'est la masse qui s'opiniâtre à ne pas bouger."

Above all, the attitude of the masses at and after Thermidor seemed to the Babouvists a proof that the vast majority of the people cared for nothing but to be left in peace to pursue their own occupations. The fact that the masses, the vast majority of the nation, allowed the power and rights gained by them to slip out of their grasp, and let themselves become dominated by a minority class, appeared as a grave warning and challenge. It was, above all, a source of bitter disillusionment. Babeuf wrote that the ardent friend of liberty, who is ready to sacrifice himself for the people, feels discouraged and ready to give up his task : the people have nearly convinced him that they are incapable of " arriving at this precious liberty, and of conserving it, when they had already obtained it ". The masses were ready to obey anybody who was

able to keep the peace, and were quite prepared to welcome back
the Monarchy. Some even sighed after the fleshpots of the *ancien
régime*. They would overlook any violation of principles, which
were so abstract as to be fictitious to them. So many ambitious
agents were active to keep the people in ignorance of their rights
and power, or to mislead them by empty verbiage.

"The philosophers that desired to effect the happiness of their
enslaved, unhappy and ignorant fellow-citizens, have been generally
rewarded by death upon the vulgar accusation of ambition, hypo-
critically urged by crafty enemies of equality." Buonarroti, the
author of these words, is worried by the general philosophical
problem of passing on to the masses a deep conviction which,
though corresponding to absolute truth, is beyond most people's
grasp. In antiquity, Buonarroti says, legislators were wont to
resort to religion or religious fiction, determined to astonish rather
than to persuade. This could not be done—"whether fortunately
or unfortunately, I cannot tell"—in modern times. Buonarroti
does incidentally say that the conspirators thought of preaching
their doctrine as a dogma of the natural religion, since it was founded
upon the unshakable and true principles of the natural religion and
reason. The problem appeared to Buonarroti still more difficult
than to Babeuf, because of his preoccupation with *vertu*. What
was to Babeuf a question of happiness, was to Buonarroti a problem
of *vertu*. Babeuf was exasperated by the people's inability to
see the great principles and their own ultimate interests, whereas
Buonarroti was hurt by the selfishness and lack of any spirit of self-
sacrifice in the masses. The original pure religion of Christianity,
he thought, might have wrought a change in the hearts of men, had
it not been so distorted by power-seeking impostors. "Such
morals (of true Christianity) were irreconcilable with materialism
which influences people to consult in their conduct only their own
direct interest, and to make a mockery of all virtue." The Thermidorian régime, in particular, had been a reign of shameful rapacity
and egoism. Even those—complained Buonarroti—who only a
little while ago were ready to renounce all they had, were now
clinging to their possessions with all the passion of petty proprietors.

Should therefore those who know the people's true interest
ignore the people altogether? To act with no reference to the
wishes of the people and the sacred principle of popular sovereignty
was unthinkable.

(d) THE IDEA OF THE ENLIGHTENED VANGUARD

In order to maintain the reference to the will of the people, it was claimed that backward, inarticulate and immature as the people might be, there could be no doubt as to the secret wishes of the masses. The people could not fail to recognize their rights, strength and interests, if those were clearly explained to them by proper leaders. When one day a violent shock awakens the people from lethargy, they will be ashamed of having been inactive for so long. There need thus ultimately be no conflict between the action of a self-appointed enlightened vanguard of the people, and the principle of popular sovereignty. This theory was also the basis of the Babouvist philosophy of Revolution. The theoretical problem of Revolution was complicated by two ultimately contradictory principles held by the Equals : that arrogation of sovereignty was a crime justifying anybody's taking justice into his own hands and instantly killing the usurper ; and that the right to resist oppression was the sacred right and duty of the people, indeed of any portion of them. Since an act of Revolution was not only resistance, but an attempt to seize power, it was difficult to argue that the act of Revolution did not constitute an usurpation of sovereignty. It was perpetrated without popular authorization after all. Such an authorization was regarded by the Babouvists as by no means indispensable. The people were generally too slow to recognize that their rights were being violated, and still slower in rising against oppression, lulled and deceived as they were by the oppressors. " C'est aux vertus les plus rares, les plus courageuses qu'appartient l'initiative de l'entreprise de venger le peuple." A fraction of the people, even a single person, may recognize the necessity of revolt, and, acting on this, call upon the people to rise. What about the anarchy, the lawlessness that might result from such a blank cheque to Revolution ? The Babouvist reply contained more than one argument. The first was a highly optimistic one : no Revolutionary act would carry with it the masses, if the motive was impure or imaginary. A Revolution breaks out only when vicious institutions have driven the most useful members of society to desperation, and compelled them to seek a violent change.

An articulate authorization was thus not necessary. There was an authorization and challenge in the very order of things. Society was founded to secure happiness for all. As long as this had not been done, as long as there existed inequality, and consequently oppression, and as long as men's faculties and freedom were being stifled, there was a permanent right to Revolution. As to the last Revolution, clearly it had not yet come to an end ; it had not yet run out its course, for it had brought no universal happiness. " Ou bien, si la Révolution était finie, elle n'aurait été qu'un grand crime." The same line of argument was valid in regard to the objection to revolting against a legitimate government accepted by the people. A people may accept in apparent freedom a vicious constitution, which ignorance and deceit may prevent it from recognizing as tyrannical. But more than that. A legitimate authority presupposed a constitution as perfect as can be made by men, a constitution embodying all the known principles of social justice, guarantees of freedom and popular sovereignty. A constitution from which these were absent could not give rise to a legitimate government. And, after all, the Constitution of 1795 had not been accepted by a majority in universal suffrage. The 1795 Constitution had rejected the fundamental principles of full popular sovereignty, of universal and equal instruction and " l'aisance de chacun ". What therefore might constitute a crime in a free régime where the people were free to voice their wishes, was a sacred duty in the existing régime of oppression, especially to the zealots of the people, endowed with courage, clear-sightedness, virtue and energy.

Whatever may be said objectively about these views and their dangerous implications, the prosecution at the trial of Vendôme, like Robespierre's opponents in similar circumstances, found it extremely difficult to indict them, without condemning the great Revolution as a whole. The prosecutor did not consequently condemn the phenomenon of Revolution as such, but resorted to a doubtful distinction : a Revolution was sacred and legitimate as when in 1789 it was the whole people who made it under a free and spontaneous impulse, and with a " truly general will ". But if only a faction rose to destroy the peace and a legitimate government, then it was a crime. How could one prove the universal character of the Revolution of 1789 ? And what about the Revolutionary journées, which by no stretch of imagination could be described as carried out by the whole people ?

That there was no contradiction between the idea of a party of the vanguard and the idea of the general will, and that the general will was not the spontaneously expressed will of individuals, but something that ought to be willed, and that must be imposed if necessary—Babeuf claimed to have learnt from no less a person than Robespierre, who—Babeuf quotes him with approval—taught that " true lawgivers ought not to subordinate their laws to the corrupt morality of the people for whom they are destined, but they ought to be able to restore the morality of the people by their laws, first to base these on justice and virtue, and then to know how to surmount every difficulty in order to impose them upon men ". That did not mean that the leader or leaders should take no notice of the people, while preparing their "regeneration". The masses must be brought in. Their interest must be roused. They must be made to vibrate with activity. But it was not for them to determine policies, to assert their will. It was unthinkable that the leaders should be treated by the people as men simply charged with executive tasks. The leaders, and not the masses, were to make the wheels turn. The essence of Revolutionary democracy is precisely in the obedience and loyalty of the masses to their leaders. " I shall make you brave," wrote Babeuf, " if necessary in spite of yourselves. I shall force you to get to grips with our common adversaries. You do not know yet how and where I want to march. You will soon see clearly my direction, and either you are no democrats or you will judge it right and sure." The attitude of the leaders to the led was visualized by Babeuf as a mixture of pity, contempt and love. " L'indignité des hommes ne devait pas l'arrêter dans sa pensée de régénération, qu'il fallait avoir pitié d'eux et les rendre dignes de la liberté."

The masses could not, however, be trusted even with the choice of leaders, at least early in the Revolution. The people may feel vaguely the necessity of social reform, but have not the sagacity to choose the proper leaders to carry it out. The choice must be left to those whose love of equality, whose courage, devotion and clairvoyance, qualify them for this most important function, in short, the party of the vanguard. From a merely theoretical question the problem became an urgent and practical issue, once the plan of a coup was launched. Buonarroti says that although the Secret Directory of the plot was confident that " the union of authority and wisdom " embodied in the vanguard could by themselves achieve the goal, it felt that even the best intentioned power in the world would be unable to guarantee the complete success of the efforts, without the affection and concurrence of the people. But apart from expediency, there was also the principle of the sacredness of popular sovereignty. Somehow it had to be made certain that the élite was not acting arbitrarily, but in accordance with the will of the people. It was not quite enough to assume that the élite knew better what the people wanted than the people themselves ; to proceed without much worrying about the people at present, in the hope that, once placed before a *fait accompli*, the people would enthusiastically acknowledge that what had been done for them was exactly what they had always wanted. The Babouvists claimed to abhor the idea of their being a band of " criminal conspirators working in darkness ". They were not a handful of factious plotters moved by the desire for gain or " insane fanaticism ". They wished to achieve their goal through the progress of " raison publique et de l'éclat de la vérité ". That meant work on public opinion : propaganda. Babeuf boasted to have discovered that nothing mattered more in a Revolution than the finding of a sure means of directing and sustaining " le bon esprit public ". " Car c'est avec l'opinion qu'on remue tout.''

The Babouvists firmly believed that the leaders of a Revolutionary party must not isolate themselves from the masses. Nothing was in their opinion more calculated to bewilder and dishearten the people than their leaders' esoteric behaviour and secret plotting. Tortuous Machiavellism, secrecy and dissimulation of leaders, were most harmful to the Revolutionary cause. There should be full-mouthed propaganda, which would reach everybody, and not esoteric teaching. The isolation of a handful of activists, claiming to act for the welfare of the people, without the active support of popular opinion and popular force, is stupid, inept and detestable. All the inconveniences of open propaganda are offset by the confusion and apathy of the people, if left without guidance and with no sense of purpose. The Babouvists could never make up their minds on the major problem of policy : whether their aim should be a violent coup carried out in the deepest secrecy by a small group of plotters, or a movement to enlighten and educate the masses for Revolutionary action. They were incapable of making the choice between victory by surprise and the imposition of a Revolutionary scheme of things on the one hand, and the triumph of enlightenment in all hearts and a Revolution by consent, at least of the masses, on the other.

The latter way appeared too long. The leaders would, Babeuf claimed, be arrested in the early stages of agitation, and the forces of reaction would do all in their power to fill the masses with horror of the Revolutionary message and its party. A violent coup, on the other hand, without the people being prepared for it, may have the most disastrous consequences. The Revolutionaries would appear in the eyes of the people as brigands and murderers. The teachers and guides appointed by the " haves " to defend their usurpation, and to keep the masses in ignorance, would start a violent campaign against the rebels. The multitude, bewildered, deceived, agitated and frightened, taken by surprise and unable to reflect and to grasp the significance of the revolt, would throw themselves upon their saviours and destroy them, and with them the hope of a Revolution and salvation for many generations to come. The victorious rulers would do all to perpetuate the memory of the unsuccessful coup as an odious, " delirious extravagance joined to an atrociously criminal scheme to destroy every reasonable and just order ". The real intentions of the conspirators would never be known.

Babeuf proposed therefore a middle course. After a period of most intensive propaganda, the rebels should perpetrate a coup in a thoroughly indoctrinated area, and immediately proceed to carry out the reforms advocated by them. This would be received with enthusiasm by the local zealots, and the example would have an electrifying effect upon the neighbouring provinces. " Ainsi s'étendrait graduellement le cercle des adhésions " to the " plebeian Vendée ". The growth would be rapid, but not too rapid for the need of properly consolidating every new extension, in accordance with the laws of equality. The essential point was not to fail, and to be properly understood.

For the obvious advantages offered by the capital, Paris was chosen to serve as the Vendée Plébéienne, the place in which to start the insurrection by seizing the nerve centre of power. In later years Buonarroti explained the differences between Babeuf's and Owen's approach. Owen envisaged the creation of small voluntary socialist communities, whose example would be followed by increasing numbers, till the final triumph of socialism, whereas Babeuf taught the conquest of the central artery of power. Such

a conquest would make possible the imposition of the desired
régime upon the whole country. In his explanations Buonarroti
is again anxious to pay "all possible homage" to the principles
of popular sovereignty. Considering the impossibility of collecting the votes of the whole of France, "the only means of
rendering to the sovereignty of the people all the homage compatible with circumstances" was to invest the insurgents of Paris
with the power of electing the provisional national authority.
The devotion of the people of Paris to the cause of the Revolution,
and the courage displayed by them in the past and likely to be
displayed in the course of the insurrection, strengthened their title
to serve as sample and exponent of the sovereign will of the nation.
As to the possible objection to the usurpation of power, it being a
sacred duty to destroy tyranny, this duty was incumbent on the
people of Paris before every other section of the nation ; for they
were nearest the seat of tyranny. The overthrow of tyrannical
power being incomplete, without the setting up of a provisional
authority, the people of Paris were called upon to establish one
which would be "as conformable, as actual circumstances may
allow, to the principles of national sovereignty".

(e) THE THEORY OF REVOLUTIONARY DICTATORSHIP

In theory the moment of the destruction of the old Government
should bring the sovereign people into their own. For the unrestricted sovereignty of the people was the purpose of the planned
Revolution. Yet, if the people were not mature enough to make
the Revolution, how could they be trusted to exercise their sovereign
rights properly ?

The experience of the French Revolution, declares Buonarroti,
had shown that in the beginning of a Revolution, "it is of less
consequence, even as regards (and for the sake of) the real popular
sovereignty itself, to busy ourselves in collecting the votes of a
nation, than to make the supreme authority fall by the least arbitrary
means possible, into hands that are wisely and vigorously
Revolutionary ".

A people fresh from a tradition of oppression would not be
capable of selecting its leaders. A constitutional régime based
upon primary assemblies and a legislative body could not be brought

into existence at once. It would be folly to leave the nation for an instant without guidance. The exercise of sovereignty in such circumstances would be a mere fiction.

" This difficult task (of seeing the Revolution through) can belong only to certain wise and courageous citizens, who, strongly impregnated with the love of country and of humanity, have long before fathomed the sources of public calamity—have disenthralled themselves from the common prejudices and vices of their age—have shot in advance of contemporary intellects, and who, despising money and vulgar gestures, have placed their happiness in rendering themselves immortal by ensuring the triumph of equality." Babeuf used in the same connection the expression " dictature de l'insurrection ", demanding it for those who had taken the initiative in the uprising.

Formal democracy is thus rejected, and no incompatibility between the aim of establishing democracy and dictatorial means is conceded. " To what ", asks Buonarroti, " can we reasonably attribute the loss of democracy and of liberty in France, if it be not to the diversity of views, to the opposition of interests, the want of virtue, of unity, and of perseverance in the National Convention ? " A strong and irresistible authority animated by a single will is needed to establish equality in a corrupt society. Had the French had the wisdom to " invest a man of Robespierre's stamp with a dictatorship . . . the Revolution would have attained its veritable end ".

The interval between the insurrection and the establishment of a constitutional order was all-important. Formal democratic principles would require the provisional authority to summon immediately the primary assemblies to elect a Convention. But real democracy made the prolongation of this interval imperative. For a mere change in the form of public administration and of the men in power was not an end in itself. Useful and durable laws were the purpose : a social transformation. " And though the Secret Directory was not ignorant that the mode in which the law is emitted and executed may exercise some influence on the institutions to be established, history and the French Revolution had forewarned it that the certain effect of inequality of condition is to divide the citizens, to create opposing interests, to foment hostile passions, and to subject the multitude (whom it renders ignorant, credulous, and the victims of excessive labour) to a small number of informed and crafty men, who, abusing the preference acquired by their address, apply themselves afterwards only to preserve and strengthen, in the distribution of goods and advantages, the social order that exclusively favours themselves." The task was therefore not just to let the people vote and exercise their sovereignty, but to enable them to exercise it " effectively ", and not " in mere fiction ".

In other words, the task before any voting took place was to erect a " Revolutionary and provisional authority " capable of removing the people " for ever from the influence of the natural enemies of equality, and of restoring to it the unity of will necessary for the adoption of Republican institutions ". The people had to be prepared to vote in the way they should vote. To make this still easier and safer the provisional authority should carry out the double function: of proposing to the people a plan of legislation simple and suited to ensure to it equality and the real exercise of its sovereignty ; and of dictating provisionally the preparatory measures necessary " to dispose the nation to receive it ". The elimination of opposition and intensive education and propaganda were the two cardinal tasks.

Of whom should this Revolutionary authority or dictatorship be constituted, this " extraordinary and necessary authority, under which a nation may be put in full possession of liberty, in spite of the corruption which had resulted from its old bondage, and the traps and hostility of internal and external conspirators against it " ?

Was it to be a dictatorship of one or more ? Emanating from the insurgent leadership ? Imposed upon, accepted by or chosen by the insurrectionary people of Paris ? And was it to act as an Executive, without there being any legislative body? These questions were in a sense only a part of a much more fundamental issue, which, as hinted before, was never fully clarified. On the one hand, the Equals were claiming to aspire to sweeping away the past in its entirety, and to the erection of a totally new and permanent order. On the other hand, they proclaimed themselves the heirs of the régime illegally abolished on 9 Thermidor, and declared as their aims the return to the Constitution of 1793, and the abolition of the post-Thermidorian Government of usurpers and violaters of the rights of the people. In the first case, the insurgents could think themselves free from any constitutional or legal restrictions, but not if they adopted the latter attitude. One of them, Amar, insisted that the proper course would be to recall the Montagnard deputies who had been expelled from the Convention, and who were themselves engaged—as said before—in preparations for an insurrection to restore the pre-Thermidorian régime, and to recognize them as the only legal Convention fit and empowered to assume the government of the country.

It was natural for the Montagnards to insist on their constituting the sole legal legislative authority and popular representation until a new Convention was elected. Any unconstitutional addition of deputies not elected on a universal ballot to their body was bound to be regarded as an encroachment of popular sovereignty. In the same way the orders which the Secret Directory of the insurgents planned to have executed on the outbreak of the insurrection were regarded by the Montagnards as tantamount to a violation of the rights of the people. For instance, they bitterly opposed as unconstitutional the plan to distribute the dwellings and possessions of counter-revolutionaries to the insurgent people on the day of the insurrection. They claimed that these could never be conceded as of right to the people, and that, at most, the distribution should be regarded as an exceptional and unique act of generosity. The Montagnards could not treat the Secret Directory as the provisional government or even allow the people of Paris to nominate it, or members of it, as a government. The task and the rights to elect an executive had to be returned to the Convention. At most, the Montagnards were prepared to promise to nominate some members of the Secret Directory to the Executive Council.

One way of resolving this dilemma of legality and Revolutionary procedure might have been the proclamation of a dictatorship of one man acting on behalf of and for the good of the people, without being hampered by any legislative authority. The plan was suggested by Darthé and Bodson, an old disciple of Marat, but it had been previously discarded. No suitable candidate presented himself. Dictatorship was too reminiscent of monarchy. There was always a possibility of abusing dictatorial power, and popular opinion would not have approved of personal dictatorship, in view of the prejudices against it. Babeuf was very much against it, possibly because, knowing that he would not be chosen, he did not wish to see anybody else vested with the supreme authority. A compromise between legality and Revolution was reached on the question of the Revolutionary Convention. The people of Paris were to elect a new Convention consisting of the Montagnard seventy deputies and of one deputy for each department elected from a list of democratic patriots presented by the Committee of Insurrection. The deputies would thus be out-voted. But the insurgent Equals, although their intention was " to speak to the people without reservation or equivocation, and to pay the most striking homage to its sovereignty ", could not leave to the new Convention unhindered freedom, or rather could not completely trust the Convention to see the work of regeneration through alone. A small body with the exclusive power of legislative initiative, and vested with exclusive power of executing the decrees proposed by it and adopted by the Convention, seemed indispensable. That this body should be composed of the most trustworthy democrats, that is to say, exclusively of members of the Committee of Insurrection (the Secret Directory), appeared obvious, notwithstanding the expected objections that the Committee was animated by an ambition to monopolize power and to perpetuate itself. It was, however, asked whether any formal arrangement was necessary, whether the majority of the conspirators in the new Convention and their intimate relations with each other would not suffice " to impart to the laws the spirit of their enterprise, and to raise to supreme executive power magistrates worthy of exercising its function " ? After many hesitations, relates Buonarroti, it was decided to ask the insurgent people to confide the initiative and the execution of the laws exclusively to the Committee of Insurrection.

The Convention was to be merely a rubber stamp, as the Executive was to have the exclusive power of initiating legislation ; an Executive not chosen by the Legislative, but nominated by the insurgent people, that is to say, the self-appointed faithful.

For the essential thing was, once more, not to let the people be free to act as they like, but to have the right thing done, as understood by those who claim the virtue of knowing what is exclusively right and good for the people.

The real Revolution is not carried out solely by the enthronement of what is right by a vanguard conscious of its knowing and representing the ultimate wishes of the people. The Revolution has to reckon with the fact that in a social transformation the losers will never reconcile themselves to the loss, even if the loss is decided upon by a majority. The strength and ruthlessness of the losers made them formidable, so that the people has to choose between

" the annihilation of certain conspirators on the one hand, and the inevitable ruin of popular rights on the other ". It is, as Buonarroti and Babeuf recognized, a question of ends and means, and of the end justifying the means. The use of force is a sacred though painful duty in the light of the *a priori* promise that the losers will never accept defeat as final. " Neither mercy nor amendment was to be expected from exasperated pride." The losing class must therefore be annihilated.

" To pretend to establish justice and equality, without employing force, amongst a people of whom great numbers had contracted habits and pretensions irreconcilable with the well-being of the rest of society and with the just rights of all, is a project as chimerical as it is seductive in theory. To undertake such a reform, and then to halt at the firmness it requires, is but to avow one's cowardice and want of foresight." It is worse : it is to sacrifice the safety of the whole to the vices of a small number. Moreover, the necessary violence was only a small measure of compensation and punishment for ages of crimes, which made Revolutionary violence unavoidable. Popular insurrections have in the past been put down in terrible blood baths. " Why did not the parties that are pleased to exaggerate what they call the excesses of the French Revolution prevent their occurrence, by the voluntary abandonment of their iniquitous pretensions which were the whole and sole cause of them ? "

In a régime of equality those who represent privilege and anti-social interests and habits are " manifestly " placed outside " the pale of popular sovereignty ", and national unity, indeed outside the law. The rapidity and strength of the popular " thunder ", if employed at an early stage and effectively, is calculated to spare the much more terrible miseries of prolonged civil war.

" Every advance towards equality prevents the recurrence of an infinity of afflictions, and opens an immense field to the benedictions of the emancipated millions, which, though less noisy, cannot be counterbalanced by the selfish murmur of a handful of corrupt usurpers, whom, for their own true happiness, as well as for that of the whole of Commonwealth, and of all posterity it is necessary to lead, by consent or force, to more reasonable sentiments." It is the holy violence which saves the corrupt from the violence of their selfish passions.

As Babeuf declared before the Tribunal : " I liberated then my thought from all particular consideration, and I judged as an inevitable evil the yoke to be imposed upon some castes which have for centuries been able to impose theirs on this precious multitude ; I thought, furthermore, this repression to be no more than a feeble compensation for the reprisals, and the long drawn out oppressive treatment meted out by them to the people ; I considered also this struggle as a war which, in its purpose, was more beneficial than any in history."

The ex-general Rossignol, conqueror of the Bastille, and one of the military leaders of the Conspiracy, declared that he would have nothing to do with the insurrection if " heads do not fall like hail ", and if the insurrection is not to inspire a terror that would make the universe tremble. For there would have been no need for this insurrection had this policy of making heads fall like hail been followed in the past.

The suppression of the defeated class is not the only justified case of violence. An hour of crisis, where unity of purpose and single-minded execution are essential, equally justified the elimination of ideological or tactical opposition. This is the burden of Babeuf's *apologia* of Robespierre's dictatorship " diablement bien imaginé ", and best calculated to make democracy triumph, as " Robespierrism is democracy ", " and these two words are absolutely identical ".

" Ce dernier pouvait avoir à bon droit l'orgueil d'être le seul capable de conduire à son vrai but le char de la Révolution." " Even this man of initiative, this man who must have been conscious that he was the only capable leader, must have seen that all these ridiculous rivals, however good their intentions may have been, would trammel and spoil everything. I suppose him to have said : ' Let us cast all these intrusive trifles under the extinguisher, good intentions and all ' ; and to my mind he was right. The salvation of 25,000,000 men cannot be weighed against consideration for a few shady individuals. A regenerator must take broad views. He must mow down all that impedes him, all that cumbers his path, all that might hinder his safe arrival at the goal he has set before him. Knaves or fools, presumptuous or greedy for fame, it is all the same thing and is much the worse for them ! "

True, such ideas, says Babeuf, might have carried even him away. But what would this matter, " si le bonheur commun fût venu au bout " ?

Does not this mean the abandonment of the postulate of the

dictatorship of the idea or group for the dictatorship of a man ?
Yes, and no.   For, as hinted before, Robespierre is the embodiment
of the cause of the people, and not a personal tyrant, and Robespierre
is not a party, but the people.   " Le robespierrisme atterre de
nouveau toutes les factions ; le robespierrisme ne ressemble à
aucune d'elles, il n'est point factice ni limité.   Le robespierrisme est
dans toute la République, dans toute la classe judicieuse et clair-
voyante, et naturellement dans tout le peuple."
   Not the form, but the content, matters.

Chapter Five

THE STRUCTURE OF THE CONSPIRACY

(a) ORGANIZATION AND PROPAGANDA

WE may now attempt a summary examination of the structure of the Babeuf plot and of the plan of the coup, against the background of their ideological premises. The Secret Directory of Public Safety, or, as it was alternatively called, the Committee of Insurrection, was the supreme authority of the Conspiracy. It consisted of just over half a dozen people.

The Committee as first constituted was hardly more than a seminary of political science, in which, " after unravelling the causes of the calamities that afflict nations, they at length arrived at the knowledge of determining with precision the principles of social order the best calculated, in their belief, to deliver mankind from them, as well as to prevent their recurrence ". Clearly, the Committee was a forerunner of those Revolutionary groups of the nineteenth and twentieth centuries to whom the elaboration of the Revolutionary doctrine was a matter of no less importance than the Revolutionary coup itself. Buonarroti describes the aim of the Committee as finally constituted as " a resolution of binding to a single point the scattered threads of democracy, for the purpose of directing them towards the re-establishment of popular sovereignty ".

The Directory divided Paris into twelve *arrondissements* directed by twelve Chief Agents. Contact between the Directory and the Chief Agents was maintained by Intermediary Agents, of whom there was in fact only one, Didier, who owing to his exceptional merits was allowed to have a seat in the Secret Directory itself. The work of the Directory was shrouded in the deepest secrecy. The Chief Agents did not know the names of the members of the supreme body, and maintained no contact with each other. The Intermediary Agents (or agent) received daily notes from the Directory, instructions and orders with a mark to prove their authenticity, to circulate them among the Chief Agents. The task of the latter was to carry out the instructions of the Directory ; to foster and direct the public mind ; to distribute journals, pamphlets and leaflets ; to arrange for posters to be posted on the walls by the special brigades of bill-stickers ; to select and direct open-air speakers, called "groupers" ; to infiltrate into and direct clubs, societies and much frequented cafés ; to send reports about the state of public opinion ; to collect and convey information about stores of arms, food and other commodities ; to suggest names of reliable men, with a capacity for leadership ; to prepare lists of dangerous persons ; to spy on the police and government departments ; and, of course, to organize the local militants for action.

The instructions of the Directory insisted that the Agents should do their work with the minimum of outward self-assertion, without appearing to be the leaders. " Let us sacrifice the vanity of appearing to advantage to the glory of being really useful " . . . and to the inner consciousness of being the " invisible instrument by which great springs of action are moved " is said in one circular. Blind obedience and unreserved surrender were demanded from the Agents. " Remember that you no more belong to yourself " is said in one instruction. " All those whom the Revolution had requisitioned will have to answer to the fatherland for every action and every moment of their life. There can be no conspirators by half. Woe to him who misuses the confidence put in him."

The journals of the Conspiracy were to serve as a " mariner's compass ". The " thermometer of energy " of the masses was to be adjusted strictly to the " temperature " of the journals ; the impetus of the people to be quickened or slowed down accordingly.

Although the main instructions of the Secret Committee expressed preference for small groups meeting informally in private houses, and imperceptibly evolving into well-disciplined cells, the main work of propaganda was done in cafés, in parks and in the public squares, where workers liked to assemble after work. Women did signal service, especially among the troops. The pretty Sophie Lapierre bewitched soldiers and civilians at the much frequented Café des Bains Chinois, built in a bizarre pseudo-Chinese style. There she sang patriotic songs, the refrains of which were taken up by the guests. " On levait son verre en l'honneur de la Liberté et de l'Égalité. On s'échauffait mutuellement."

Propaganda among the troops and the police was supremely

important. In this respect the Secret Directory wished to exploit the war weariness of the soldiers, and even their cowardice. It was not enough to appeal to the patriotic sentiment alone. All " the passions of those precious men " had to be stirred and utilized. The coward who feared the front-line or hated leaving his family and dear ones might be turned into a valiant soldier of the Conspiracy. The perils of the front were to be exaggerated. The soldiers were to be " caressed " and coaxed by promises and solicitude.

There were five special agents for action among the troops and police. Darthé and Germain were the superintendents. Grisel, the agent-provocateur who betrayed the plot, and who was one of the most active military agents, contributed to lowering the tone of the propaganda in the Army. It acquired through him a particularly vulgar and repulsive character. But this was in line with his judgment on the type of soldier under the Directory régime. In an interesting report to the Secret Directory, he pointed out that the old idealistic volunteers had disappeared. Those who remained were recruits kept in the Army by force. They were longing to see the end of the war, regarding themselves as conscripts to hard labour. Others were professional soldiers thinking of little else than their promotion. The former must be promised early release, the latter spoils. The soldiers would be quite unreceptive to and even suspicious of the ideas of equality. Hardly ten per cent could write or read. Grisel suggested drink as the most persuasive means of winning over the troops: "monterait adroitement leurs esprits à la hauteur nécessaire." Money was wanted for that. This commodity was in very short supply. The only rich member of the Conspiracy was Felix Lepelletier, but he was less helpful than expected. The only substantial contribution came from the Dutch Minister in the form of two hundred and forty livres. " Cette révolution n'est point entreprise par des milords," says one instruction. The reports of the Chief Agents contain complaints that the patriots of their regions are mostly poor. Only a few could make the necessary sacrifices, offer hospitality to provincial comrades or contribute to the costs of printing the journals and leaflets.

The more open the propaganda and the more open the threats of an imminent uprising became, the lesser grew the hope of taking the Government by surprise.

Babeuf almost desired the Government to know that a coup was being prepared. He hoped the Directory would take fright. It was enough if the names of the leaders remained unknown, he said, in spite of the air of utmost secrecy which it had been decided to maintain. "It would be folly to pretend to conceal . . . our hostile intentions under pretence of disarming their vigilance," wrote Babeuf in *A pressing word to the patriots*, to warn them not to be deceived by the Government's attempts to cajole them with the pretence of popular policies. The plan of the coup was long known to the Government. "I oppose to them not masked, but open batteries. The geese, the cacklers, the fools of the faction of the Prudents will say, perhaps, that it would be better policy to cover ourselves with some disguise. . . . It is no longer by surprise that we either can or wish to vanquish it, but in a manner more worthy of the people—by open force."

What was the force at the disposal of the Secret Directory? Buonarroti reckons that apart from the "vast number of ardent friends of the Revolution", "without counting the very numerous class of workmen, whose discontent and impatience were breaking out in all directions", the Secret Directory could rely on an army of seventeen thousand. This force was composed of four hundred "revolutionaries of Paris", one thousand five hundred pre-Thermidorian officials dismissed by the Directory, one thousand "democratically minded" gunners stationed in the capital, six thousand one hundred men of the Legion of the Police, one thousand reliable men from the provinces, one thousand five hundred grenadiers of the Legislative Assembly, one thousand men, that is to say the whole corps of Invalides, and five hundred each, military personnel in detention and ex-officers. Apart from the arms and munitions in the possession of the reliable military units and the party militants, the conspirators counted on seizing the armouries, arsenals and food stores with the help of their guards.

All these calculations were wildly exaggerated. As subsequent events were to show, no reliance could be placed on the troops, although the plotters were almost sure that even the all-important artillery regiment of Vincennes was ready to join the insurrection. As to the masses, the time when the militant Revolutionary masses were highly organized and permanently on the alert—in the Commune, Sections and the popular societies, in the heyday of the Revolution—had gone. The early state of exhilaration had given place to a mood of disillusioned weariness. There is enough internal evidence to show that in the last few days before the planned outbreak (and collapse), Babeuf and his friends became very nervous and conscious of the inadequacy of their preparations. They urged the Chief Agents to restrain the impatience of the militant rank and file, to avoid a premature outbreak.

(b) THE PLAN OF THE INSURRECTION

The signal of the insurrection was to be given by the tocsin and trumpets, following the reading of the Act of Insurrection, the Revolutionary proclamation of the Insurrectional Committee of Public Safety. The Act, starting with the words "the Democrats of France, considering that the oppression and misery of the people are at their height", declared the people in insurrection against tyranny, with the aim of re-establishing the Constitution of 1793. All the crimes of the régime and the vices of the Constitution of 1795 were enumerated in the proclamation. It further called upon the people to proceed from all points " in disorder as it may be ", with any weapons they could lay hands upon, to the points of assembly. Six Revolutionary generals, distinguished by their tricolour ribbons on their hats, were to command the three " regular " insurrectional divisions. They were subordinated to one com-mander-in-chief. The people were to carry banners proclaiming the sacred right to insurrection, death to the usurpers of the people's sovereignty, the restoration of the Constitution of 1793, and of the régime of Liberty, Equality and Happiness. All city barriers were to be immediately closed and movement on the Seine stopped ; all entry into and exit from the capital suspended, except for incoming food. The insurrectional troops and the people, deliberately mixed up, were to proceed from the assembly places to the National Treasury, Post Office, Ministries and other centres of government and administration, and to seize them. The government troops were to be invited to come over to the insurgents, and rumours were to be spread that they had done so. In case of their refusal, and of an attack by them on the people in insurrection, barricades were to be set up. The streets were to be closed, and men, women and children called to pour stones, boiling oil and water from the roofs upon the army columns.

The Act of Insurrection declared the dissolution of all existing authorities in the face of the sovereign people resuming its rights

and powers. The various documents contain somewhat contradictory instructions about what should be done to the members
and supporters of the existing administration. The need for " a
great example of justice, capable of terrifying " and " inspiring
salutary dread ", and of " withdrawing the working classes from
the influence of the Government " was taken for granted.

Moreover, it was also thought essential to whip up the passions
of the people and to egg them on to commit acts from which no
retreat was possible. To quote the characteristic instruction : " It
is infinitely essential and even of capital importance that some such
acts should take place. All reflection on the part of the people is
to be prevented. It is essential that they should first commit acts
which would prevent any retreat."

While the Act of Insurrection and some other instructions speak
of an immediate trial of the members of the Directory and the two
Councils by an especially appointed Commission, and in the presence
of the people, on the capital charge of usurping popular sovereignty,
another instruction (the incriminating words were erased, but nevertheless are legible) orders the killing (" tuer ") of the five members
of the Directory, the seven Ministers, the general of the Army of
the Interior and his staff, the temporary commander and his staff,
and " faire main basse sur tout ce qui s'y rendrait " in the hall of
the Five Hundred. The charge would have in any case meant the
death penalty. The one material difference between the instruction on instant killing and that on bringing to trial is in the fact
that in the latter case there is a stipulation of the people's right of
mercy in regard to errors of the past redeemed by services to the
insurrection.

All instructions agree on the absolute necessity and duty to kill
any deputy, administrator, judge, officer, indeed any government
functionary trying to oppose the insurgents or to exercise his
authority. " Toutes autres exterminations seront déterminées par
de nouveaux ordres." Also foreigners found in the streets, leaders
of the Vendémiaire uprising, or anybody beating the alarm were
to be put to death. Similarly merchants who failed to declare their
stocks of food were to be executed. Bakers refusing to bake, and
wine merchants to distribute their wine, were to be " accrochés à la
première lanterne ". The Directors were to be buried under the
ruins of their palaces. It is to be assumed that the people listed in
the files of the conspirators as enemies would also have been put

out of the way. Eloquent and " energetic patriots " as well as placards and leaflets were to " colérer le peuple ". The instructions also order the employment of the " pathetic and persuasive eloquence of women " on the soldiers, to whom they were to present " civic crowns ", while exhorting them " by all the powerful considerations they know so well to employ ".

The plan of the Conspiracy laid great emphasis upon the importance of giving immediate satisfaction to the people by instant distribution of commodities. All stores and stocks of food, clothing, shoes, vehicles, horses, etc., were to be seized and distributed at public places, or employed by the insurrectionary authorities. All bakers were to be requisitioned to bake and distribute bread gratis on account of future compensation. All dwellings and movables of émigrés, " conspirators " supporting the " tyrannical government " and of all " enemies of the people " were to be seized and distributed to the poor defenders of the Revolution. The effects of the poor pawned at the Monts de Piété were to be returned without payment. Exiled or proscribed patriots were to be compensated from the confiscated spoils of the people's enemies.

Buonarroti claims " that it would be wrong to consider the promise of a grand distribution of goods " as contrary to the spirit of the community at which it was sought to arrive. The main point was to succeed, and the Secret Directory felt " neither too much restraint, nor too much precipitation ". The act of immediate distribution was to give the people an earnest of the imminent fulfilment of their long-deferred hopes, without unduly alarming those who were not as yet believers in complete communist equality. The momentary distribution of goods did not, Buonarroti assures us, mean either total expropriation or a policy of parcellation (instead of Communism). In fact, the Insurrectionary Act placed all property, public and private, under the safeguard of the new National Assembly ; of course, only temporarily, and only with the implication that the property of patriots alone deserved respect. This was in line with the conception underlying the Robespierre-Saint-Just Laws of Ventôse, as was the decision to carry out the distribution of the milliard worth of national property which had been promised to the " defenders of the fatherland ". Communism had to come by degrees. The masses were first to be won over by distribution of spoils, and the whole foundation of respect for property shaken.

THE STRUCTURE OF THE CONSPIRACY

After having "broken tyranny" and resumed "their rights received from nature", the people of Paris were to be asked to approve a decree giving the new Government powers to bring about a new social system based upon the principle of absolute equality, the universal obligation to work, and the unrestricted right of the nation to dispose of all property on French soil. These instructions were to be framed as orders for the amelioration of the Constitution of 1793 and a prompt execution of the laws designed to secure permanent equality, liberty and happiness. The new Government was to render an account to the nation on the execution of this decree not later than in a year's time.

This was the compromise between the two legal positions : the one that the people were called upon to conclude a new Social Contract upon the *tabula rasa* of the past, and only on the basis of natural rights and the people's unlimited sovereignty ; and the other that all that was intended was to restore the illegally abolished régime of before 9 Thermidor, upon the basis of the Constitution of 1793. The latter principle was adopted, but the amelioration of the 1793 Constitution was ordered.

A similar line was followed in regard to the setting up of new authorities. We have already spoken of the compromise whereby the new Assembly was to consist of the seventy Montagnard deputies who had been expelled from the Convention, and one deputy per department chosen by the "sovereign people of Paris" from a prepared list. The sovereign people was at the same time to be asked to approve the decree that the Insurrectionary Committee should remain in power till the complete success of the uprising, and till "regenerating laws" had been "drawn up in such a manner as not to leave a single poverty-stricken citizen in the State". In principle, all authorities were to be reconstituted "as they were before 9 Thermidor". In each section three members of the old Revolutionary Committee, who had preserved themselves "les plus purs", were to take the initiative in restoring the pre-Thermidorian institutions. All pre-Thermidorian functionaries were ordered to return to their posts under the threat of being declared traitors and executed. The Insurrectional Committee seems to have reserved for itself the appointment of authorities in the capital. Upon the reconstituted authorities were grafted special agents, or rather Commissars to departments and districts, with overall authority and the task of making the new spirit prevail. They were to be apostles of the new dispensation. Before being appointed, they would have to declare what they possessed.

A special seminar was contemplated to train propagandists and leaders, and to work out the new ideology. Special lists of old pre-Thermidorian activists and " energetic patriots " who qualified for leadership had been prepared in time. They were to be given a free hand to take all measures required by the situation. All who had not been active in the insurrection were to be disarmed, except *sans-culottes*, for their passivity was to be attributed rather to lack of instruction than ill will. All pre-Thermidorian prisoners were to be sent back to prisons. Exception would be made in the case of some who would voluntarily agree " to restrict their wants to the bare minimum of necessities " and to give up the surplus to the people.

Those who would be so rash as to refuse, as well as suspect foreigners and all persons arrested as a result of the insurrection, would be sent to what could not be called by any other name than concentration camps, " islands . . . converted into bridewells, or places of correction . . . hard labour in common with other convicts . . . rendered inaccessible . . . having administrations directly subject to the Government . . . ", in order to " terrify and disconcert " those who might be tempted to cause bloodshed. Malcontents would, furthermore, be made to give a hand to the effort of national regeneration, " forced as they would be, however reluctant, to seek in it their only means of safety ".

The fighters of the insurrection, soldiers, would be allowed to return home after victory, but it was expected that they would volunteer to stay in the people's army. They would be properly compensated. The next of kin of the fallen were to receive pensions, and their children were to be adopted by the Republic. New National Guards would be organized at the earliest date. " A theatrical display of banners as if descending from the clouds " was to constitute the grand pageant of the inauguration of peace in the regenerated Republic. " In the midst of applause . . . hundred times repeated you will see the insurrection march instinctively to its natural destination."

What would have been its natural destination ? In his *History of the Conspiracy*, Buonarroti gives a detailed answer to this question. No less competent historians than Mathiez and Lefebvre have seriously questioned the historical value of Buonarroti's remarkably full description of the ultimate plans of the Equals. Buonarroti wrote his book many years after the events. There is no way of confronting his account with authentic material from the days of the Conspiracy, and finding out how much of his subsequent ideas he read into the minds of his companions of 1796, and to what extent he was led to systematize into a coherent blueprint vague and unco-ordinated suggestions and schemes. Nevertheless, the unquestioned faithfulness of his reconstruction of events which actually took place and are confirmed by other direct or circumstantial evidence gives Buonarroti's account of the ultimate plans a very strong claim to authenticity.

Whatever importance one may attach or deny to the special details of the institutional framework of the Babouvist city of the future as painted by Buonarroti, Babeuf's letters to Coupé and Germain, the last numbers of the *Tribun*, and the documents seized by the police leave little doubt that a fully-fledged communist and democratic-totalitarian city was envisaged by the plotters. The image of such a city was a part of the myth bequeathed by the Babeuf Conspiracy —through Buonarroti—to the faithful of the Revolution in the nineteenth century. As we are in this work primarily interested in the shaping of the religion and myth of Revolutionary political Messianism, we have to give to Buonarroti's picture of his heavenly city a place of honour as one of the important elements, along-side others, in the nascent religion of the totalitarian-democratic Revolution.

Chapter Six

THE ULTIMATE SCHEME

(a) POLITICAL ORGANIZATION

ESSENTIAL in the thinking of the early totalitarians was the refusal to take the people as it was for granted ; the people, that is to say, the sum total of the given generation, the good and the bad, the advanced and the backward, with their wishes, enlightened or otherwise. It would be wrong to say that therefore the idea of the people was restricted to the " elect " only, and to a minority. The mass of the people were taken to be the people, or at least as qualified to become the people; a minority was considered to be beyond redemption, a dangerously corrupting influence, and deserving annihilation. The Robespierrists saw in the people a community of virtue, of virtue strongly coloured by a social tinge. The Babouvists went a step further : to them the people was a community of equals (the essence of virtue is equality, and the absence of avarice) and, still further, a community of propertyless workers. The aim of the Revolution and post-revolutionary legislation was to give birth to the regenerated people, the true people, by the total elimination of the unredeemable minority, and the proper education of the remainder.

The emphasis on the correlation between virtue, democracy and communist equality is the peculiar contribution of Babouvism, and its advance upon Robespierrism. Without communist equality there could, in its view, be no democracy, and *vice versa*. The object of legislation is, as said before, to place the whole people in a position to exercise their sovereignty usefully and effectively, to give them the means of really being sovereign. This could be achieved only in a régime of perfect equality. Then, and only then, would all the elements tending to distort and obscure the real will and interests of the people have disappeared. The decisions of the people would then be enlightened decisions, and as such they would never run counter to equality, for the people, in the possession

232

of knowledge and in freedom from constraining pressures, would never legislate against themselves. Over the deliberations of the people would then preside that spirit of unanimity which, according to Babouvism, is the mark of true democracy. For a healthy people and a healthy democracy are only those in which there is no "diversity and no opposition of interests". A nation may be always pronounced corrupt whenever there exists "in its bosom a class of persons who have formed for themselves pretensions irreconcilable with the well-being of the whole, or of the other component parts". A single unequal individual contradicts and breaks the unity of a people.

The granting of sovereign rights is thus no end in itself, for it will have achieved nothing, without the preparation of the people for the proper exercise of these rights. More than that, so long as the conditions for the proper exercise of sovereignty do not yet exist, it is not only futile, but dangerous to put no restrictions on the exercise of the sovereign rights by all and sundry. These conditions include, once more, the elimination of the unredeemable minority, the establishment of perfect equality, and the spiritual regeneration of the people.

"Upon the consolidation of those institutions . . . (the economic ones especially) . . . depended the accomplishment of the Revolution and complete exercise of popular sovereignty." In other words, "the day on which the people should enter the peaceable enjoyment of equality would have been that on which it would be able to exercise in all its plenitude the right of deliberating on its laws as consecrated in the Constitution of 1793". In the early stages there could therefore be only a partial execution of the Constitution, gradually enlarged. "Till then the sovereign power was to be rendered to the people only gradually, and according to the progress of the new ways." In other words, the people would assume their democratic rights only after the elimination of all opposition, and the complete saturation of the people with communist ideas.

The real citizens of the people of the future will not be just anybody born and living within the territory of France, but only those comprised in the National Community, which, as far as its economic organization is concerned, would constitute at the same time the National Economy. All outside it would be treated as strangers. The essential qualification of membership would be participation in the productive effort of the nation, labour. Intellectuals could be admitted only on their presenting a certificate of "civisme", that is to say political reliability. A law would determine the date after which no one would have the right to exercise political and civil rights who was not a member of the National Community. This preparatory operation once consummated, the nation would have existence only in those participating in the Community. But even then no one would be automatically born into the National Community. The Community would have to be joined by a solemn act of contract. Buonarroti describes the ceremony of the granting of citizenship in truly Rousseauist terms.

"On stated days, young men of the requisite age, and after completing the degrees of civil and military instruction prescribed by the laws, should have come to demand of the assembled citizens the inscription of their names on the register. After the deliberation of this assembly, the nature of the social compact would have been explained, the rights it confers, and the duties it imposes on the candidates, who would have been called upon to declare whether they consented to become a part of French society on conditions they had heard, and in which they had been instructed by their education. The recusants, if any, would have been forthwith banished for ever from the Republic, and accompanied to the frontiers, after being provided for a certain time with the necessaries of life. As to the others—those consenting to the conditions—they would have contracted a solemn engagement with the sovereign people by virtue of which they would have received the tokens of their new condition. Clothed by the magistrates in the costume of the citizens, they would have been saluted as French citizens, and their names inscribed in the civic register borne in pomp in the midst of the people ; then would each new citizen have been presented with a military coat and a complete suit of armour with his name engraved thereon, to the end that the fear of being dishonoured by losing it, might render him more resolute in battle, and engage him to defend at the cost of his life whatever his country confided to his care."

The nation is not the aggregate of men, women and children but a confraternity of faith. Moreover, in the true Rousseauist tradition, the individual receives his very personality, and any rights he may possess, from the Social Contract alone.

Babouvist democracy is not quite the organization of the

totality of the citizens for the purpose of giving them the means of expressing their will and having it executed. Its essential feature is the distrust of parliamentary representation—again in the spirit of Rousseau—and the introduction of checks on the Assembly, consisting of the people's power of veto, and a special popular tribunate or senate as the guardian of orthodoxy.

There would be three types of Assemblies of Sovereignty : the Assembly of Sovereignty (consisting of the assemblies in the communes and sections), the central Assembly of Legislators (that is to say, the National Assembly) and the Body of the Conservators of the National Will elected from the Senates, the special committees of censors of orthodoxy in every local assembly. The Conservators are the people's tribunate against the Legislators' encroachments upon the sovereignty of the people. Any law or decree adopted by the National Assembly must go back to the Assembly of Sovereignty for approval, amendments or veto. The Assemblies of Sovereignty transfer petitions and projects of law to the National Assembly through the body of the Conservators.

There were diverse opinions, reports Buonarroti, as to what should happen in the case of a definite usurpation of the people's rights by the Assembly of Legislators. Some suggested that the Body of Conservators should have the right of an immediate appeal to the people ; others wished the Conservators to have the power of suspending the decrees of the National Assembly till the people had had an opportunity of asserting its will. So great was the distrust of an elected assembly which holds the power of legislating and executing its own decisions at the same time, that there was a suggestion that Parliament should be divided into two separate sections, one for drafting legislation and the other for executive functions. Buonarroti stresses the advantages of having several organs of legislation, and the dangers inherent in a single chamber from the spirit of faction.

The Conservators and the Senates were to be old men of high merit, proved defenders of the rights of the people. As, however, the old men of the day were still too deeply steeped in the prejudices of the past, the test for membership of that august body would be not age plus service, but political reliability. Only the most devoted and deserving, and above all the most orthodox, exponents of the cause of equality would be elected. There would thus be an institution of guardians of political orthodoxy who could always appeal to

236 THE BABOUVIST CRYSTALLIZATION

the people against the National Assembly. Moreover, the deputies would be held responsible for their opinions.

There would be not only institutional checks on the Legislators in the form of rival and controlling bodies, but the contents of legislation would be circumscribed in advance. There would be some inviolable principles which even the Assemblies of Sovereignty could not touch, without the danger of dissolving society, such as " vigorous " equality, popular sovereignty, the institution of the State, and the Constitution of Authority. There would be fixed periods for the review, and if necessary the revision, of the Constitution. These periodic assemblies would appoint a small committee of " sages " to make the formal proposals for revision. Apart from this arrangement, especially appointed Commissars would at fixed dates review the state of the nation, and make suggestions for extirpating abuses.

The Executive Council would have the status and be appointed in the way prescribed in the Constitution of 1793, but its members would be under a stronger supervision. There would be of course an immense body of civil servants in a State which had taken over the whole system of production and distribution. In a sense, everybody would, as a State employee, be a civil servant. There was no reason to be alarmed by the spectre of a swollen body of functionaries, say Babeuf and Buonarroti. Every magistrate would have to go through all grades in the Service, without exemption from any. Moreover, every candidate would have to pass the test of " civisme " and go through an examination of his *mœurs* by a censor. Furthermore, in view of the most detailed and rigid circumscription of duties and rights, civil servants would not be in a position not to act in conformity with the people's will. In general, in a system of equality, the art of government and administration would be so simplified, and so much reduced to simple arithmetic, that anybody could perform the tasks of government. No exclusive class of expert civil servants would thus be necessary, and the danger of usurpation by such a specialized group would not arise. In the beginning only the most politically reliable revolutionaries would be selected for civil service jobs so that a truly republican spirit could be created. Later on, the system of national education and the general atmosphere of permanent debate would be a natural training of youth for State service.

(b) ECONOMIC COMMUNISM

The Grand National Economy was the name for the Babouvist organization of production and distribution, which when properly set up would leave no room for private property, nor indeed for any people not comprised in the organization.

The Grand National Economy was to be set up gradually, till it had assumed the ownership of all that could be owned publicly or privately on the soil of the Republic. As State property would be declared at once : all national property not sold up to 9 Thermidor ; all the possessions which were liable to confiscation according to the Laws of Ventôse ; all properties forfeited by a decision of the courts ; buildings occupied or owned by public, health, educational and charitable services ; all houses seized on the day of the insurrection from the rich enemies of the people and given to the poor patriots ; property voluntarily abandoned by its owners ; lands uncultivated or neglected ; usurped possessions of those who enriched themselves during the Thermidor reaction. As there would be no inheritance or bequests, the property of deceased would naturally revert to the Grand National Economy.

The rich would be exhorted to yield their possessions " with good grace " in good time, obeying the imperious voice of justice, to spare their country convulsions, and themselves a long train of calamities, and to restrict themselves to simple living, by a generous abandonment of their superfluities to the people. There would be no direct expropriation by a stroke of the pen. There would be a " policy to determine people to proscribe property from necessity and from interest " in such a way that the rich should not be able to get any pleasure, power or consideration out of their wealth. They would be oppressed under the weight of oppressive taxes, shut out from the administration of public affairs, deprived of all influence, unable to procure for themselves any extra services or enjoyment, as all the energies previously employed in the service of wealth would now be given to public works and national culture. " Despised . . . a suspected class of foreigners, they will either emigrate, by disposing of their effects, or will hasten to seal, by their voluntary adhesion, the pacific and universal establishment of the community." People of both sexes guilty of "incivisme", indolence, luxury and loose living, and of thus setting a bad example, would be put to forced labour. Their property would be seized by the National Economy.

Small traders, petty shopkeepers, small proprietors, peasants, workers and journeymen oppressed by fatigue, insecurity, insufficient wages and privations would gladly respond to the invitation to join the Grand National Economy and to exchange their precarious existence for the security of a decent living.

" Let us create the Grand National Economy . . . prevent coxcomb witlings from coming to disturb it by sophisms and exaggerations, force all the ramifications of authority to march in the sense of equality, dry up every source of pride displaying the illusions of deceitful pomp ; let us render gold more onerous to its possessors than sand and stones ; let us strike the first blows with boldness and firmness and then leave it to man's natural desire for happiness and wisdom, to complete, by progressive changes, so sublime an enterprise." The Grand National Community or Economy would soon amalgamate with the entire nation, and the nation would have existence only in those participating in the Community. " A happy change of opinion . . . would have been the infallible consequence of such a reformation." The day would soon have arrived, when obligation and restraint might be without danger substituted for exhortatory example and the force of necessity. " Then and from that time the word proprietor would begin to signify something barbarous or outlandish to the French." There would, in short, come the leap from the realm of necessity into the realm of freedom. Avarice would be dethroned for ever, and in consequence society and men would be subject to psychological and social laws different from those of the past.

The Grand National Community is based upon the principle of everyone's right to happiness and obligation to work. While abundance is the object of general labour, only absolutely equal and modest shares and enjoyments are admissible. " Whatever is not communicable to all ought to be severely retrenched ", and a general " honourable mediocrity " will be the aim. The State is the sole proprietor, employer and provider of all needs. Nobody may enjoy anything not assigned to him by the Grand National Community. There would be common meals in each commune. All money would be abolished. As early as possible salaries would begin to be paid in kind according to one's wants. Anyone receiving money or hoarding money or commodities would be severely punished. One would be able to receive one's common rations only in one's place of domicile, except in cases of removal authorized by the authorities. Transport throughout the Republic would be carried on by *corvées*, specially of young people, who would thus be given a chance to get to know and to love their country and all its various regions. Dirty work would be done as fatigues in rotation. All foreign trade would be carried on by the State, and no private individual would be allowed to trade abroad ; and in general the trade with foreign states would be limited to absolute necessities unobtainable at home. For the import of foreign commodities enhances luxury and has always a demoralizing effect. This is the pure milk of Rousseau and Mably.

The Administration of the Grand National Economy would be centralized and nationwide, with local sub-divisions. The creation of small territorial units of production and consumption on a basis of self-sufficiency was considered highly undesirable. The wealth of every province belongs to the whole nation, and the national wealth is there to be enjoyed by every unit. The surpluses and shortages of the various departments should cancel each other out. One of the chief aims of the National Economy was also to foster national cohesion and solidarity.

The National Economy was to be placed under the legal direction of the Supreme Administration of the State. The whole Republic was to be divided into regions, which comprised contiguous departments with similar types of production. The departmental administration was to be subordinated to the regional division, and so on.

The smallest territorial units would have an economic organization based upon trade unions, or as Buonarroti calls them, classes—professions. Each trade union appoints magistrates of its own to direct works, execute orders of the municipal administration and to set an example of zeal. Representatives chosen by the trade unions would form a trade unions council, which would be accredited to the municipal administration to advise it on all matters concerning distribution, mitigation and improvement of labour. The municipal administration regulates conditions in every branch of production and class of workers, while the Supreme Administration would be concerned with the provision of machines, labour-saving devices and the general protection of labour. The Supreme Administration would have the power to condemn to forced labour men and women guilty of anti-social behaviour, idleness, love of luxury and dissolute living, and to displace workers in accordance with national needs.

240 THE BABOUVIST CRYSTALLIZATION

" There arises in the administration of a very extended society a certain complexity puzzling to persons who consider the thing superficially : but at bottom the whole affair is one of simple calculation, susceptible of the most exact order and regular operation, since cupidity being deprived of all aliment by the establishment of the institutions in question, there would be no longer any occasion to fear the losses incessantly caused, under the existing order of things, by the competition of rival chiefs, and the plunder of their subordinates."

And so, once again, all the economic administration, based upon perfect, all-embracing and unifying planning, would become reduced to simple calculation ; and with the security of future wants, all anxieties, greed and corroding feelings would subside. With the abolition of private property, which had annihilated all the advantages of the social state, " each individual will feel how much he is interested in the well-being of all his associates. The science of government, which the collision of so many opposing interests renders at present so very intricate, is reduced by the system of community to a single calculation, scarcely beyond the capacity of anyone."

(c) SPIRITUAL COHESION

A Community of sentiment was the main aim and the only guarantee of success in other fields, the political as well as the economic. Such a community would come into being with the disappearance of all taste for inequality and privilege on the one hand, and by the growth of a sentiment of spontaneous and loving affirmation of the new order on the other. Constraint would then become unnecessary.

" The masterpiece of policy consists in so modifying the human heart by education, by example, by reasoning, and by the attractions of pleasure, as to cause it never to form any other desires than those which tend to render society more free, more happy and more durable. When a nation reaches this point, it has good manners, then are duties, the most painful, discharged with alacrity and pleasure. A spontaneous obedience is yielded to the laws ; the limits imposed on our natural independence are regarded as blessings ; reasonable propositions encounter no opposition, and there prevails throughout the body politic a unity of interest, of will, and of action."

It was, in the first place, imperative to counteract any spirit of federalism and isolationism in the various districts, especially the ones better favoured by nature. It was supremely important to prevent these from feeling themselves as separate entities, independent of and indifferent to the fate of the rest ; and to make them feel that their prosperity depended on others, and could be preserved and increased only by a harmonious communion of the whole country in will and action.

This could be achieved chiefly by the reciprocity of benefits, the suitable co-ordination of the productive efforts of the various parts, and by the knowledge of the advantages of social order. " When the inhabitant of the south shall know how useful to him are those of the north, by the enjoyments they procure him, by the importance of the district they defend, and by the fraternal sentiments engendered in them by the conformity of manners and laws, he will feel his soul aggrandized, he will admire the social mechanism by which so many millions of men conspire to render him happy, and he will be convinced that, for the very sake of his equality which he cherishes, it is necessary that, overstepping the limits of his commune, it should comprise the whole extent of the Republic."

This is the Jacobin speaking, the preacher of " République une et indivisible ".

But economic or political isolationism cannot be effectively combated, if spiritual isolationism is to be given free rein.

" Shall the human mind be left," asks Buonarroti, " to rave without guide and without curb through the vast fields of imagination ? Shall it be left to introduce into society, under pretence of polishing and ameliorating it, an infinity of fictitious wants, of inequalities, of disputes, of false ideas of happiness ?   Or shall limits be imposed on industry, by banishing from the homes of education everything that is not strictly necessary to the well-being of the Republic ? "

It was desired to " deliver their fellow citizens from the constraints of superfluous wealth, and from the love and enjoyments which enervate men, and are of no value, except on account of the distinctions of which they are signs ".

The Equals were anxious about the evils that flow from the refinement of the arts, and mindful of Rousseau's and Mably's theory that morality and liberty had never existed together with brilliance of the arts and sciences. Intellectual and artistic refinement breed taste for superfluities, frivolities, claims of distinction, superiority and privilege. They feed vanity and a desire for notoriety. Eloquent vanity develops a dangerous and seducing eloquence, " deluding credulous honesty ". The Equals wished therefore " to divest false science of all pretext of escaping its share of the common duties, of all opportunity of flattering pride . . . and of seducing the passions with the idea of an individual happiness foreign to that of the rest of society ".

Only socially useful subjects were to be taught. Theology, for instance, would have to go, and so would jurisprudence, to a large extent rendered superfluous by the abolition of private property. The stoppage of special remuneration would soon cure " the mania for displaying small wit, and for writing books ". Only the sciences and arts necessary for service to and defence of the country were essential. No claims for pre-eminence, intellectual or moral, could be admitted, not even to a genius, against the strictest equality. " The prudent limitation of human knowledge . . . connaissances . . ." was the most solid guarantee of social equality. The knowledge of reading, writing and arithmetic was to be sufficient. In the houses of education the works of art and handicraft were to be limited to objects " easily communicable to all ", and the pretended elegance, " pomps and delicacies of tyrants and slaves " were to be replaced by rustic simplicity.

The press, an invaluable weapon against tyranny and usurpation of sovereignty, the best means of disseminating ideas and knowledge, had different functions to perform in the new society. Individual property having been abolished, and all pecuniary interest having become impossible, it was necessary to adopt means of deriving from the press all the services to be expected, " without risking calling in question the justice of equality, and the rights of the people, or delivering the Republic to interminable and disastrous discussions ".

" La presse devait être sévèrement renfermée dans le cercle des principes proclamés par la société."

No one may express opinions directly contrary to the sacred principles of equality and of the sovereignty of the people. All writings on the form of government, and on its administration, were to be printed, and sent to all the libraries upon the demand of an assembly of sovereignty, or of a prescribed number of citizens above the age of thirty. No writing about any pretended revelation would be allowed. In fact, only those writings would be printed and distributed which would gain the approval of the Conservators of the National Will as useful to the Republic. Already in 1792 Babeuf protested against the theatre of Amiens for continuing to give performances of plays savouring of the " superstitions " and " perversities " of the *ancien régime*. " You can't serve two masters "—wrote virtuous Babeuf. In an age of reason and liberty, the theatre should express the enlightened sentiments of the new era and guide the people. In a scurrilous note Babeuf attacked the Revolutionary Abbé Gregoire for complaining about the damage done to the Cathedral of Chartres : " one of the old turpitudes." Babeuf advised the abbé to go to bed.

Although preaching an anti-intellectual philosophy and Spartan austerity of life, the Babouvists were not insensitive to the objection that their egalitarian system was calculated to kill the arts. One of the reasons for the rejection of Sylvain Maréchal's *Manifesto of the Equals* by the Babouvist Directory was the slogan " perish all the arts, and let equality reign " in the *Manifesto*. The Babouvist answer to the challenge was the distinction between individual austerity and collective magnificence, between the arts that have a universal appeal and the esoteric, or in their vocabulary frivolous, eccentricities or indulgences, for which they had nothing but condemnation. They were insistent on the " essor " of the sciences and the arts that would result from the national regeneration, accompanied as it would be by the immense expansion of the public, and the disappearance of the pressure of want or desire for lucre in the case of the creative artist and scientist.

The arts and sciences would in general become social functions and instruments for evoking collective experiences. They would lose the character of individual self-expression, and their purpose would no more be to thrill the individual's perception in his solitary communion with the work of genius. But they would acquire a new and solemn significance under the influence of the regenerating spirit and in the service of the Republic, " conformable to the grand sentiments which an immense association of happy beings should necessarily give birth to ", whereas, in the existing conditions, the masses, utter strangers to the fine arts, would not even perceive any decay of culture.

In the hoped-for system . . . " some crafts, it is true, whose productions only serve to relieve the ennui of a very small portion of parasites, and to pump enormous masses of money into their hands, would give place to others which would augment the well-being of the great mass of society. But where is the man who could regret this happy change ? The sciences and the fine arts once relieved from the goad of ever-pressing, ever-crippling want, the man of genius would no longer have any other stimulus than the love of glory, and, soon shaking off the yoke of flattery, and of selfish Mæcenas-like patrons, his only object would be the prosperity of the social body. To frivolous poems, to architecture of bad taste, to pictures without interest, we should see succeed temples, and sublime porticos whither the sovereign people (at present worse lodged than our brute animals are) would repair to imbibe, in the monuments and works of philosophy, the doctrine, the example, and the love of wisdom."

The Utopian and Spartan character of the Babouvist collective city is best exemplified in the ideology of " back to the land ". The Rousseauist, not less than Robespierrist, Buonarroti saw in great cities and capitals " symptoms of public malady, an infallible forerunner of civil convulsions ". The evils of the old régime were to him indissolubly interwoven with the huge cities, which have condemned one portion of the people to overwhelming toil, and the other to demoralizing inaction. The countryside has been crushed, the cities overcrowded. The latter became seats of " voluptuous pleasure " of the rich, the source and manifestation of most glaring inequality, greed, envy and unrest. Agriculture should be restored to its ancient primacy and glory. " Agriculture and the arts of first necessity, being the true nutritive supports of society, it is to the scene of these occupations that men are called by nature to live, whether it be to till the soil, or to furnish the agriculturists with commodities and recreations." Buonarroti fully acknowledges the contribution of the capitals to the progress of the Revolution, and admits that " they might still be made to render effectual aid towards establishing a real social order, provided wise and upright minds could attain the directing power of their movements ". But what is desirable is to make their unwieldy conglomerations disappear, by scattering their inhabitants over the country to live in healthy smiling villages of simple, but agreeable, architecture.

Paradoxically the cosmopolitan Babouvist creed preached extreme national isolation. But it did so in the interest of the World

Revolution : to safeguard the regenerated people " against the contagion of pernicious examples which might otherwise enervate the force of manners, and the love of equality ". Buonarroti says that the Conspirators wished to raise " barriers bristling with obstacles " between France and the world, obstacles to be lowered only to political refugees, " persecuted friends of liberty ", seeking asylum and a spiritual home in France. All rigours were to be applied to foreigners wishing to introduce frivolities and alien fashions. All foreigners would be strictly supervised, and in some cases even interned.

"This precaution in regard to foreigners ", says Buonarroti, "was dictated not by a malevolent spirit of isolation, but by the desire of better discharging the offices of humanity and fraternity, which all states owe to one another . . . in the recovery and defence of their natural rights." France's mission was to shine as a " brilliant example " of the realization of the ideal of equality. " So great a blessing could not be communicated by the force of arms ", because of the invasion, violence and domination it implied. Armed proselytism was thus renounced. The world was to be taught by example. It was important to ward off carefully from the new social order everything that might retard or prevent its establishment ; and to exclude rigidly from the French territory " that crew of foreigners which hostile governments would not have failed to pour in upon it, under the colour of philanthropy, for the perfidious purpose of sowing discord and creating factions in it ". Free intercourse with other states would not be entered upon so long as they had not adopted the principles of France. Until then the latter would have seen only dangers for herself, in their manners, in their institutions and particularly in their governments. Buonarroti tells us that it was planned to let the French people adopt a costume that would distinguish them from all other nations.

In matters of religion, Rousseau and Robespierre were the oracle. Faith in the Supreme Being, the immortality of the soul, the civil religion, reward and punishment after death, was considered the foundation of civil society. The citizen must recognize and fear an infallible judge of his thoughts and secret actions, beyond the reach of the earthly power. He must also be convinced that eternal bliss would be the reward for devotion to humanity and country. Although the sanction of religion was necessary for the maintenance of morality, the " so called " revealed religions were

considered maladies to be extirpated gradually. The pure religion
of the Gospel might have served the purpose, but the follies and
the stupidities of the Biblical stories and the commentaries have
made it impossible. There remains therefore the natural religion,
with its two principles, that of an omnipotent will presiding over the
universe, and that of future life, " principles derived from nature,
reason and social necessities ". Atheism was for Buonarroti, as for
Robespierre, identical with immorality and cynicism.

"Le décret qui mit la vertu et la probité à l'ordre du jour
fut . . . un coup de foudre," declares Buonarroti in an *apologia*
for Robespierre's religious policy. Equality was " the only dogma
agreeable to the divinity ". As to worship, he wished it to be limited
to respect for the Social Compact, to the defence of equality, and to
certain public festivals. " Les dogmes religieux doivent être la
sanction de l'ordre social . . . et le culte doit se confondre avec
les lois."

It is the ideal of the ancient *polis*.

Since education in the widest sense was the most potent, indeed
decisive, factor in creating and maintaining the community of spirit
in the new Republic, the Republic was the sole judge of the instruction to be given to youth. The education of the youth could no
more be left to the " exclusive and egoistic régime of family ".
" Plus d'éducation domestique, plus de puissance paternelle."
" Dans l'ordre social conçu par le Comité, la patrie s'empare de
l'individu naissant pour ne le quitter qu'à la mort." Again the
purest Rousseau, though not the Rousseau of the *Emile*.

Love of the native land must be made the predominant passion.
By education the legislator would be able to render all affections of
family and kindred subordinate to this sentiment. Having imbued
only " sentiments analogous to the principles of state, they would
have been accustomed to refer to the country—the mistress of all—
every beauty and perfection they witnessed, and to attribute to her
sacred laws, their wealth, their well-being, and their pleasures.
Living constantly together, they would soon learn to co-mingle
their happiness with others, and removed from the contagion of
self-interest. . . ."

Education should eradicate all instincts of avarice and love of
distinctions, and fully call into being the natural goodness of human
nature. It must be national, common and equal on the Spartan
model, designed to foster the force and agility of the body, the

goodness and energy of the heart, and the development of the spirit. The sexes would be rigidly separated. The education of girls would endeavour to kill the spirit of coquetry, and to check the early impulses of sex. Military education, obligatory for every male youth, would form a school of citizenship.

The system of education would be under the supervision of an office, composed of " vieillards blanchis dans les fonctions les plus importantes ". There would be a special seminary for teachers.

As to the contents of Republican education, and spiritual life in general, Buonarroti lays very great stress on the nationalization of leisure. Individual leisure, and the improper use of leisure, appear to him as the greatest enemies of the system of equality and the community of spirit. Leisure must not be given up to voluptuousness or " ennui ", and yet the State must not give the impression that there was constraint in spending one's leisure. " The skilful legislator attaches the people to them (the national leisure occupations) by their own free choice." Education would do the trick. The object of the leisure occupations is " to fortify soul and body ", " to close without restraint all avenues to corruption ", " to shed a charm upon every moment of life, to develop the enthusiasm of virtue, and to render his country the dearest of earthly abodes to each citizen ".

Patriotic and semi-religious festivals on the ancient model would be multiplied. They would be devoted to the Divinity, the memory of great men, " wonders of the social system ", the departure of the young to the army, their return, the passing away of distinguished citizens, and other similar civic occasions. They would inspire courage, love of liberty, and make corruption appear hateful. Then there would be the four classes of frequent citizen assemblies : of the sovereign power, the military order, instruction and censorship (or love of virtue). The latter would pass judgment upon the life and morals of magistrates, young people, the deceased and indeed everybody. The greatest influence in these assemblies would be reserved for old men. Every deceased would be judged whether he deserved public honour or not. The children of those found unworthy would be prohibited from bearing the names of their fathers.

CONCLUSIONS

TOTALITARIAN democracy, far from being a phenomenon of recent growth, and outside the Western tradition, has its roots in the common stock of eighteenth-century ideas. It branched out as a separate and identifiable trend in the course of the French Revolution and has had an unbroken continuity ever since. Thus its origins go much further back than nineteenth-century patterns, such as Marxism, because Marxism itself was only one, although admittedly the most vital, among the various versions of the totalitarian democratic ideal, which have followed each other for the last hundred and fifty years.

It was the eighteenth-century idea of the natural order (or general will) as an attainable, indeed inevitable and all-solving, end, that engendered an attitude of mind unknown hitherto in the sphere of politics, namely the sense of a continuous advance towards a *dénouement* of the historical drama, accompanied by an acute awareness of a structural and incurable crisis in existing society. This state of mind found its expression in the totalitarian democratic tradition. The Jacobin dictatorship aiming at the inauguration of a reign of virtue, and the Babouvist scheme of an egalitarian communist society, the latter consciously starting where the former left off, and both emphatically claiming to do no more than realize eighteenth-century postulates, were the two earliest versions of modern political Messianism. They not only bequeathed a myth and passed on practical lessons, but founded a living and unbroken tradition.

Totalitarian democracy early evolved into a pattern of coercion and centralization not because it rejected the values of eighteenth-century liberal individualism, but because it had originally a too perfectionist attitude towards them. It made man the absolute point of reference. Man was not merely to be freed from restraints. All the existing traditions, established institutions, and social arrangements were to be overthrown and remade, with the sole purpose of securing to man the totality of his rights and freedoms, and liberating him from all dependence. It envisaged man *per se*, stripped of all those attributes which are not comprised in his common humanity. It saw man as the sole element in the natural order, to the exclusion of all groups and traditional interests. To reach man *per se* all differences and inequalities had to be eliminated. And so very soon the ethical idea of the rights of man acquired the character of an egalitarian social ideal. All the emphasis came to be placed on the destruction of inequalities, on bringing down the privileged to the level of common humanity, and on sweeping away all intermediate centres of power and allegiance, whether social classes, regional communities, professional groups or corporations. Nothing was left to stand between man and the State. The power of the State, unchecked by any intermediate agencies, became unlimited. This exclusive relationship between man and State implied conformity. It was opposed to both the diversity which goes with a multiplicity of social groups, and the diversity resulting from human spontaneity and empiricism. In Jacobinism individualism and collectivism appear together for the last time precariously balanced. It is a vision of a society of equal men re-educated by the State in accordance with an exclusive and universal pattern. Yet the individual man stands on his own economically. He conforms to the pattern of the all-powerful State inevitably, but also freely. Communist Babouvism already saw the essence of freedom in ownership of everything by the State and the use of public force to ensure a rigidly equal distribution of the national income, and spiritual conformity.

Man was to be sovereign. The idea of man *per se* went together with the assumption that there was some common point where all men's wills would necessarily coincide. The corollary was the tendency to plebiscitary democracy. Men as individuals, and not groups, parties or classes, were called upon to will. Even parliament was not the final authority, for it was also a corporate body with an interest of its own. The only way of eliciting the pure general will of men was to let them voice it as individuals, and all at the same time.

It was impossible to expect all men, especially those enjoying a privileged position, to merge their personalities immediately in a common type of humanity. Unlimited popular sovereignty was expected to offer to the unprivileged majority of the nation, that is to say to men nearest the idea of man *per se*, the power to overrule the minority of the privileged by vote, and if necessary by direct, coercive action. This conception of the sovereignty of the people was inspired not so much by the desire to give all men a voice and a share in government as by the belief that popular sovereignty would lead to complete social, political and economic equality. It regarded, in the last analysis, the popular vote as an act of self-identification with the general will. This conception of popular sovereignty asserted itself as soon as it began to be seen that the will of the majority would not necessarily be the same as the general will. So the seemingly ultra-democratic ideal of unlimited popular sovereignty soon evolved into a pattern of coercion. In order to create the conditions for the expression of the general will the elements distorting this expression had to be eliminated, or at least denied effective influence. The people must be freed from the pernicious influence of the aristocracy, the bourgeoisie, all vested interests, and even political parties so that they could will what they were destined to will. This task thus took precedence over the formal act of the people's willing. It implied two things : the sense of a provisional state of war against the anti-popular elements, and an effort at re-educating the masses till men were able to will freely and willingly their true will.

In both cases the idea of free popular self-expression was made to give place to the idea that the general will was embodied in a few leaders who conducted the war with the help of highly organized bands of the faithful : the Committee of Public Safety governing in a Revolutionary manner with the help of the Jacobin clubs, and the Babouvist Secret Directory supported by the Equals. In the provisional state of Revolution and war, coercion was the natural method. The obedience and moral support given by a unanimous vote bearing the character of an enthusiastic acclamation became the highest duty. The suspension of freedom by the legalized violence of Revolution was to last till the state of war had been replaced by a state of automatic social harmony. The state of war would go on until opposition was totally eliminated. The vital fact is that the Revolutionary suspension came to be regarded by the survivors and heirs of Jacobinism and Babouvism as far from having come to an end with the fall of Robespierre and the death of Babeuf, and the triumph of the counter-revolution. In their view the Revolution, although overpowered, continued. It could not come to an end before the Revolutionary goal had been achieved. The Revolution was on, and so was the state of war. So long as the struggle lasted the vanguard of the Revolution was free from all

allegiance to the established social order. They were the trustees
of posterity and as such were justified in employing whatever means
were necessary to the inauguration of the Millennium : subversion
when in opposition, terror when in power. The right to Revolution
and the Revolutionary (provisional) dictatorship of the proletariat
(or the people) are two facets of the same thing.

Extreme individualism thus came full circle in a collectivist
pattern of coercion before the eighteenth century was out. All the
elements and patterns of totalitarian democracy emerged or were
outlined before the turn of the century. From this point of view
the contribution of the nineteenth century was the replacement of
the individualist premises of totalitarian democracy by frankly
collectivist theories. The natural order, which was originally conceived as a scheme of absolute justice immanent in the general will
of society and expressed in the decisions of the sovereign people,
was replaced by an exclusive doctrine regarded as objectively and
scientifically true, and as offering a coherent and complete answer
to all problems, moral, political, economic, historical and æsthetic.
Whether approved by all, by a majority, or by a minority, the
doctrine claimed absolute validity.

The struggle for a natural and rational order of society soon
came to be considered as a conflict between impersonal and amoral
historic forces rather than between the just and the unjust. This
tendency was confirmed by the increasing centralization of political
and economic life in the nineteenth century. The organization of
men in the mass made it far easier to think of politics in terms of
general movements and disembodied tendencies. Nothing could
be easier than to translate the original Jacobin conception of a
conflict endemic in society, between the forces of virtue and those
of selfishness, into the Marxist idea of class warfare. Finally, the
Jacobin and Marxist conceptions of the Utopia in which history was
destined to end were remarkably similar. Both conceived it as a
complete harmony of interests, sustained without any resort to force,
although brought about by force—the provisional dictatorship.

As a conquering and life-sustaining force political Messianism
spent itself in Western Europe soon after 1870. After the Commune, the heirs of the Jacobin tradition abandoned violence and
began to compete for power by legal means. They entered parliaments and governments and were incorporated by degrees into the
life of the democracies. The Revolutionary spirit now spread east-

wards until it found its natural home in Russia, where it received
a new intensity from the resentment created by generations of
oppression and the pre-disposition of the Slavs to Messianism. Its
forms were modified in the new environment, but no entirely new
patterns of thought or organization were created in Eastern Europe.
The vicissitudes of the totalitarian democratic current in nineteenth-
century Western Europe and then in twentieth-century Eastern
Europe are intended to form the subject of two further volumes of
this study.

The tracing of the genealogy of ideas provides an opportunity for
stating some conclusions of a general nature. The most important
lesson to be drawn from this enquiry is the incompatibility of the
idea of an all-embracing and all-solving creed with liberty. The
two ideals correspond to the two instincts most deeply embedded
in human nature, the yearning for salvation and the love of freedom.
To attempt to satisfy both at the same time is bound to result, if not
in unmitigated tyranny and serfdom, at least in the monumental
hypocrisy and self-deception which are the concomitants of totalitarian democracy. This is the curse on salvationist creeds : to be
born out of the noblest impulses of man, and to degenerate into
weapons of tyranny. An exclusive creed cannot admit opposition.
It is bound to feel itself surrounded by innumerable enemies. Its
believers can never settle down to a normal existence. From this
sense of peril arise their continual demands for the protection of
orthodoxy by recourse to terror. Those who are not enemies must
be made to appear as fervent believers with the help of emotional
manifestations and engineered unanimity at public meetings or at
the polls. Political Messianism is bound to replace empirical thinking and free criticism with reasoning by definition, based on *a priori*
collective concepts which must be accepted whatever the evidence
of the senses : however selfish or evil the men who happen to
come to the top, they must be good and infallible, since they
embody the pure doctrine and are the people's government : in
a people's democracy the ordinary competitive, self-assertive and
anti-social instincts cease as it were to exist : a Workers' State
cannot be imperialist by definition.

The promise of a state of perfect harmonious freedom to come
after the total victory of the transitional Revolutionary dictatorship
represents a contradiction in terms. For apart from the improb-
ability—confirmed by all history—of men in power divesting

themselves of power, because they have come to think themselves superfluous; apart from the fact of the incessant growth of centralized forms of political and economic organization in the modern world making the hope of the withering away of the State a chimera ; the implication underlying totalitarian democracy, that freedom could not be granted as long as there is an opposition or reaction to fear, renders the promised freedom meaningless. Liberty will be offered when there will be nobody to oppose or differ—in other words, when it will no longer be of use. Freedom has no meaning without the right to oppose and the possibility to differ. The democratic-totalitarian misconception or self-deception on this point is the *reductio ad absurdum* of the eighteenth-century rationalist idea of man ; a distorted idea bred on the irrational faith that the irrational elements in human nature and even " different experiments of living " are a bad accident, an unfortunate remnant, a temporary aberration, to give place—in time and under curing influences—to some uniformly rational behaviour in an integrated society.

The reign of the exclusive yet all-solving doctrine of totalitarian democracy runs counter to the lessons of nature and history. Nature and history show civilization as the evolution of a multiplicity of historically and pragmatically formed clusters of social existence and social endeavour, and not as the achievement of abstract Man on a single level of existence.

With the growth of the Welfare State aiming at social security, the distinction between the absolutist and empirical attitude to politics has become more vital than the old division into capitalism and social-security-achieving socialism. The distinctive appeal of political Messianism, if we leave out of account the fact of American laissez-faire capitalist creed, it, too, deriving from eighteenth-century tenets, lies no more in its promise of social security, but in its having become a religion which answers deep-seated spiritual needs.

The power of the historian or political philosopher to influence events is no doubt strictly limited, but he can influence the attitude of mind which is adopted towards those developments. Like a psychoanalyst who cures by making the patient aware of his subconscious, the social analyst may be able to attack the human urge which calls totalitarian democracy into existence, namely the longing for a final resolution of all contradictions and conflicts into a state of total harmony. It is a harsh, but none the less necessary task to drive home the truth that human society and human life can never reach a state of repose. That imagined repose is another name for the security offered by a prison, and the longing for it may in a sense be an expression of cowardice and laziness, of the inability to face the fact that life is a perpetual and never resolved crisis. All that can be done is to proceed by the method of trial and error.

This study has shown that the question of liberty is indissolubly intertwined with the economic problem. The eighteenth-century idea of a natural order, which originally shirked the question of a planned rational economic order, assumed full significance and began to threaten freedom only as soon as it became married to the postulate of social security. Is one therefore to conclude that economic centralization aiming at social security must sweep away spiritual freedom? This is a question which the progress of economic centralization has rendered most vital. This volume does not presume to answer it. Suffice it to point out that liberty is less threatened by objective developments taking place as it were by themselves, and without any context of a salvationist creed, than by an exclusive Messianic religion which sees in these developments a solemn fulfilment. Even if the process of economic centralization (with social security as its only mitigating feature) is inevitable, it is important that there should be social analysts to make men aware of the dangers. This may temper the effect of the objective developments.

NOTES

INTRODUCTION

Section 1 : *The Two Types of Democracy, Liberal and Totalitarian, pp.* 1-3

There exists no special and systematic study on the subject of this work ; neither a theoretical treatise on the main thesis of the present essay, nor a historical investigation into the emergence and growth of what will be called here the totalitarian trend of democracy. The keenest perception of the current and of its vital significance is to be found in some of the—considering the early date—prophetic utterances of *Alexis de Tocqueville*. The motto of this book comes from De la Démocratie en Amérique, 4ème partie, ch. vi, Œuvres Complètes, Paris 1864, Vol. III, p. 519. Relevant references will be found in *J. P. Mayer*, Political Thought in France from the Revolution to the Fourth Republic, London 1949, and by the same author, Prophet of the Mass Age, A study of Alexis de Tocqueville, London 1939.

The great liberal thinker was obsessed by the phenomenon, and—as he himself confessed—still incapable of a systematic presentation of it. It is therefore important to distinguish clearly between the various aspects of the problem, and to realize what Tocqueville perceived, and what he failed to foresee. The author of American Democracy was observing the steady growth of State power and egalitarian centralism. Their combination, in his view, threatened to create a Leviathan that would swallow up all the intermediate powers, and turn the *gleichgeschaltete* individuals—atoms—into soulless State employees and pensioners. He saw in this trend an objective, irresistible process. This objective character of the development must be clearly distinguished from democratic-messianic totalitarianism as a creed, which sees in perfect equality, State ownership and in a uniform spiritual pattern the fruition of the ideal of liberty. For to Tocqueville, as to *Lord Acton*, equality was incompatible with liberty, just as to *Reinhold Niebuhr* in our time social security seems to exclude freedom. An opposite view is represented by *R. H. Tawney*, Equality, London 1931. We shall return to the question in the Conclusions.

When we speak of the coexistence of the two phenomena, but not in their purity, and use the term " towards totalitarian democracy ", what is meant is that up to the October Revolution totalitarian democracy was not a coherent pattern, a régime, but an ideological current, which having emerged in the French Revolution, asserted itself through Revolutionary movements and violent outbursts, such as for instance the Paris Commune in 1871. Furthermore, within the ranks of totalitarian democracy a process of fissure, elimination and purification was going on throughout the nineteenth, and well into the twentieth, century, till the crystallization and the enthronement of the final pattern in our own days. As for liberal democracy, here again, while it is legitimate to say that the development towards liberal democracy started in the French Revolution, it was not until the last third of the nineteenth century that in France, England and elsewhere, liberal democracy—as a programme and as a régime—received its definite shape, with freedom of the individual, universal suffrage and equality of rights. The real and vital line of demarcation at the present moment is, as will still be elaborated in the Conclusions, between absolutism and empiricism in politics. From this point of view the Social-Democrats, for instance, whatever the degree of their Marxist and Socialist dogmatism in the sphere of economics, are politically and spiritually on the side opposite to the Communists, together with Capitalists, Conservatives and Liberals, although in the past they, and others with them, may have believed themselves to be on the same side as the Communists. This has been the result of the process of elimination, reduction and purification which both trends have been going through.

The logical positivists, in the first place Bertrand Russell, The Practice and Theory of Bolshevism, London 1949 ; Philosophy and Politics, London 1947 ; and K. R. Popper, The Open Society and its Enemies, London 1945, have been examining the philosophical aspect, although not the historical, psychological and social side of the distinction.

A French scholar at the end of the nineteenth century, Alfred Espinas, La philosophie sociale du XVIIIᵉ siècle et la Révolution, Paris 1898, set out to show that Babouvist Communism was the logical outcome of eighteenth-century ideas. He dealt however—especially as far as the eighteenth-century philosophy and the Revolution are concerned—only with one aspect, namely the element of Socialist anti-property collectivism. He left out, when analysing eighteenth-century philosophy and the Revolution, the political issue altogether, and failed to show the convergence of the various elements into a coherent and compre-

hensive totalitarian pattern. The debt we owe him must nevertheless be acknowledged.
Stimulating ideas with more or less direct bearing on our subject can be found in some more recent books ; thus *E. H. Carr*, The Soviet Impact on the Western World, London 1946 ; Studies in Revolution, London 1950, show a strong awareness of the continuity of the Revolutionary trend in modern European history ; *Elie Halévy*, L'Ére des tyrannies, Études sur le socialisme et la guerre, Paris 1938 ; Histoire du socialisme, Paris 1948, are most stimulating on the question of the tension between the liberal and centralist tendencies in socialism ; *Karl Mannheim*, Ideology and Utopia, London 1936, is an important contribution on the morphology of ideas and movements ; *Bertrand de Jouvenel*, Du Pouvoir, Histoire naturelle de sa croissance, Genève 1945. In his acute awareness of the irresistible growth of the centralized power of the State, Jouvenel is a spiritual descendant of Tocqueville. Light is shed on the subject indirectly by *H. J. Laski*, Reflections on the Revolution of our Time, London 1943 ; Faith, Reason, and Civilization, London 1944 ; *Martin Buber*, Paths in Utopia, London 1949 ; *Graham Wallas*, Human Nature in Politics, London 1948 ; and the various works of *Reinhold Niebuhr*.

A few quotations from Stuart Mill must suffice to illustrate the difference between the liberal and absolutist approach. *J. S. Mill*, On Liberty and Considerations on Representative Government, ed. R. B. MacCallum, Oxford 1946—" Men and Governments must act to the best of their ability. There is no such thing as absolute certainty, but there is assurance sufficient for the purposes of human life." " As it is useful that while mankind are imperfect there should be different opinions, so it is that there should be different experiments of living ; that free scope should be given to varieties of character, short of injury to others ; and that the walks of different modes of life should be proved practically, when anyone thinks fit to try them. It is desirable, in short, that in things which do not primarily concern others, individuality should assert itself. Where not the person's own character, but the traditions or customs of other people are the rule of conduct, there is wanting one of the principal ingredients of human happiness, and quite the chief ingredient of individual and social progress." " No wise man ever acquired his wisdom in any mode but this, nor is the nature of human intellect to become wise in any other manner," ibid, pp. xvii–xviii, xx.

Section 2 :   The Eighteenth-Century Origins of Political Messianism ;
The Schism, pp. 3-6

It will be realized that for the purposes of this work the connected
discursive reasoning by great individual thinkers through a chain of
closely following syllogisms is less important than patterns of thought
and feeling. Furthermore, the inner cohesion of the various systems of
thought or the sequence of ideas are less important in this context than
the diffusion of ideas, and, furthermore, than the manner in which they
moulded the consciousness, the way of thinking and feeling of those
ordinary people of the intelligentsia, artisan class, small government
employees and others like them, who afterwards were to form the cadres
of the Jacobin activists.

Nothing could surpass the acuteness and clarity of the analysis of
ideas by *Elie Halévy*, The Growth of Philosophical Radicalism, London 1949 ; or the elegance and wit with which *Basil Willey*, The
Eighteenth-century Background, Cambridge 1940, shows the inter-
dependence of ideas ; or the depth of insight revealed by *Ernst Cassirer*,
Die Philosophie der Aufklärung, Tübingen 1932, much as their approach
differs from the one adopted in this study.   Yet none of them succeeded
in grasping and conveying the flow of consciousness, the rhythm produced
in people who fell under the spell of ideas, as did *Carl Becker*, The
Heavenly City of the Eighteenth-century Philosophers, New Haven 1932,
and of course *A. de Tocqueville*, L'ancien régime et la Révolution,
Paris 1859, and incidentally *Hypolite Taine*, Les Origines de la France
Contemporaine, Vol. I, L'ancien régime, Paris 1876.   Neither has
Daniel Mornet, Les Origines Intellectuelles de la Révolution Française,
Paris 1933, and La Pensée française au XVIIIème siècle, Paris 1926,
been very successful in that, although he has done very much indeed
to describe the diffusion of ideas, and to analyse the statistical data.
Even his excerpts from diaries leave the impression of an essentially
mechanical procedure.   "Les Origines" are nevertheless a capital contribution, and *Philippe Sagnac*, La Formation de la société française moderne,
Paris 1945, leans heavily on Mornet's work.   Works of a general
descriptive nature on the political ideas of the eighteenth century,
which deserve to be mentioned and to which the author is in some
measure indebted, are : *Henri Sée*, L'évolution de la pensée politique en
France au XVIIIème siècle, Paris 1925 ; the same author's, La France
économique et sociale au XVIIIème siècle, Paris 1933 ; *Marius Roustan*,
The Pioneers of the French Revolution, London 1926 (translated from

the French); *Kingsley Martin,* French Liberal Thought in the Eighteenth Century, London 1929; *Felix Rocquain,* L'Esprit révolutionnaire avant la Révolution, 1715–89, Paris 1878.

A word should be said about the use of the terms "eighteenth-century philosophy" and "eighteenth-century philosophers" (or *philosophes*) in this work. It is certainly not intended to lump all eighteenth-century thinkers, of all the various countries, the various periods and schools of the hundred years, into one mass. We are concerned primarily, if not exclusively, with the French *philosophes* ; in the second place, with those of the second part of the century ; and still more narrowly, with those who shaped the Revolutionary mood and spirit and who, when all reservations are made, do deserve, in our opinion, to be considered as speaking for the ˙eighteenth century. It goes without saying that it would be inadmissible to treat Montesquieu in the same way as Morelly, to speak of Voltaire in the same breath with Rousseau and Sieyès. The reservations alluded to refer, of course, to the controversy on the element of *a priori* doctrinaire thinking on the one hand, and the empirical regard for facts, on the other, in eighteenth-century thought. *Mornet,* in the cited works, and still more *E. Carcassonne,* Montesquieu et le problème de la Constitution Française au XVIIIème siècle, Paris 1927, have tried to revise the admittedly distorted picture painted by Taine and others of eighteenth-century thought, and to bring into relief the awareness of facts and of the value of experience among the writers of the time. But Carcassonne himself had to admit that the nearer we get to the French Revolution, the more prevalent, not to say universal, becomes abstract and dogmatic thinking, and that in the more strictly political field. The call for reform through the resumption of the thread of French constitutional tradition, or of what was, like in England earlier, alleged to be the true national tradition, gives way to an absolutist approach, based on abstract, universal ideology, and desirous of a clean and total sweep. This had much to do with the emergence of new social forces. Earlier in the century, and on the eve of the Revolution, especially at the time of the Revolution nobiliaire, which according to *Albert Mathiez,* La Révolution Française, Paris 1922–7, and *Georges Lefebvre,* Quatre-vingt neuf, Paris 1939, preceded the Revolution of the Third Estate, the nobility, wishing to recapture its old position as a partner in the government of France or to gain a position similar to that of the English aristocracy, quite naturally tended to invoke the constitutional tradition of France, allegedly broken by royal absolutism. (See also

P. Sagnac, La Formation, etc.)   The rising bourgeoisie had no particular
reverence for that tradition, and no reason to have any attachment to it.
No wonder that the bourgeoisie based its claims on the absolute and
abstract principles of the natural system and egalitarian natural rights,
not content with the type of liberty, the division of powers (with the
nobility having an Upper Chamber), and safeguards against royal
despotism postulated by the nobility.   From the political and social
angle, the history of the intellectual struggle of the second part of the
eighteenth century is the story of this evolution.   Moreover, if the
significance of a current is estimated by the criterion of historic influence,
the absolutist trend won the day.   Its representatives were best known
and have remained the best remembered thinkers of the time, whatever
the number of obscure publications, or quotations from more illustrious
authors, of the opposite camp one may be able to collect.   As *Mornet*
points out, clerical apologists ceased altogether to count in the latter part
of the century for instance.   *Carcassonne*, pp. 616 f, 669 ; *Mathiez*, pp.
18 ff. ; *Lefebvre*, pp. 36 ff. ; *Mornet*, Pensée, pp. 98 ff, 150–216 ; Origines,
pp. 205–66, 469 ff.

Much has been written on the social ideas of the eighteenth century,
mostly, however, in order to trace the beginnings of socialism in them.
Espinas's book is a case in point.   He sees in the eighteenth-century social
philosophy a message of socialism, indeed communism, pure and simple.
The paradox stressed here is alien to him.   *André Lichtenberger*, Le
socialisme au XVIIIème siècle, Paris 1898, is an example of a most patient
and laborious compilation, designed to collect " hints ".   His conclusions
are not Espinas's.   Into this category would also fall *Maxime Leroy*,
Histoire des idées sociales en France, de Montesquieu jusqu'à Robespierre, Paris 1946 ; *H. J. Laski's* The Socialist Tradition in the French
Revolution, London 1930.   His Rise of European Liberalism, London 1936, is an interesting contribution for the connection between
liberalism and the defence of property.

Max Beer, An Enquiry into Physiocracy, London 1939, like *Charles
Gide* and *Charles Rist*, A History of Economic Doctrines, London 1948,
is interested in physiocratism as an economic doctrine.   A more
comprehensive presentation of the theory and movement is very
necessary.

Similarly desirable would be a study on the reaction of the liberals,
such as Mme de Staël, Benjamin Constant (there is an article on Mallet du
Pan from this point of view by *A. Passerin d'Entrèves*, in the Cambridge

Journal, Vol. I, 1947) to 1793 and Jacobin Terrorist dictatorship. While the counter-revolutionary ideological answer by men like Burke, Joseph de Maistre, Bonald, Gentz, Adam Müller and others has been made into a subject of much study, for instance by *H. J. Laski*, Authority in the Modern State, 1919, the liberal reaction of fright, but not of total condemnation, has been quite neglected. The capital work of *Henry Michel*, L'idée de l'état, Essai Critique sur l'histoire des théories sociales et politiques depuis la Révolution, Paris 1896, is still a classic and alone in its field.

Section 3 : *Totalitarianism of the Right and Totalitarianism of the Left, pp. 6–8*

The analysis of the Left or " progressive " conception of man in the eighteenth century will be found in the coming chapter, and in the next two volumes as far as the later period, till our own day, is concerned. On the idea of man held by Right totalitarianism *Friedrich Meinecke*, Weltbürgertum und Nationalstaat, Studien zur Genesis des deutschen Nationalstaates, München und Berlin, 1915. *Michael Oakeshott*, The Social and Political Doctrines of Contemporary Europe, Cambridge 1929. *Raymond Aron*, L'homme contre les tyrans, Paris 1946. *Carl Schmitt*, Der Leviathan in der Staatslehre des Thomas Hobbes. Sinn und Fehlschlag eines politischen Symbols, Hamburg 1938 ; the same author's Die Diktatur von den Anfängen des modernen Souveränitätsgedankens bis zum proletarischen Klassenkampf, München und Leipzig, 1921. Schmitt was the main theoretician of the National Socialist philosophy of law.

It is difficult to avoid mentioning *Hobbes* in this connection. Would it be right to father him with one or both of the totalitarian trends ? The answer is in the negative, in our view. Hobbes's grandiose conception of the State Leviathan is a purely legalistic, static framework, with no element of purpose in it, except that of maintaining order, or rather preventing chaos. It contains no ideal. It is a theory of despotic dictatorship, but not of a totalitarian system. Now all the forms of modern totalitarianism point to some ideal, whether this ideal is an objective of supreme value such as the State and the race ; or the essentially individualist ideal of human freedom and happiness achieved by equality, in other words, by the imposition of a uniform and exclusive pattern, and the subordination of the actual, concrete man to the image of what he should be. This does not mean that Hobbesian elements are wholly absent from the two major trends under discussion.

What Right totalitarianism has in common with Hobbes is the low, and even cynical, estimate of human nature, at least in the common run, as distinct from those destined to lead. Of a deeper and subtler kind are the affinities between Hobbes and totalitarians of the Left. The peculiar slant of Hobbes's thinking is, if one may use this expression, thinking " by definition ". When Hobbes demands the total surrender of man to the State-Leviathan, and then denies not only the right of the individual to resist oppression, but even the possibility of real oppression by the State, he implies the premise that in a State worth its name, unjust oppression would be unthinkable, impossible. And if it nevertheless occurs, well, the State is a State no longer. It is like the famous definition of treason as treachery that has failed ; for if it had succeeded, it would no more be treason. Rousseau's State cannot possibly oppress its members, for it would have no more cause to do that than man has to hurt any of his limbs wilfully, and nothing happens in nature without cause. His sovereign by the mere fact of his being is what he should be. These statements are in direct line with Hobbes's thinking " by definition ", just as is the dogma that a Workers' State cannot by definition be guilty of aggression or oppression.

Another reason for Hobbes's startling doctrine is the assumption that once the joints of the social order are loosened, all the dams holding back the flood of anarchy are destroyed. To Hobbes any form of inconvenience or even hardship suffered under the order-preserving Leviathan is the highest form of freedom—freedom connoting security —in comparison with the endless misery and oppression, which would ensue from anarchy. This is the second peculiarity of Hobbes's thinking, common also to the totalitarians of the Left. It is the exclusion of shades, of diluted colours and mixed quantities from between the positive and the negative, the white and the black, the " is " and the " is not ". There is either total order or complete chaos, a capitalist or a socialist world. *Tertium non datur*. When one ceases to be what it is, or is supposed to have been, it becomes at once its opposite. Between the two there is war to a finish. Hobbes's war in the state of nature, as well as in the state of chaos after the dissolution of government, is a war of all men against all men, not a war between collective forces. The modern totalitarians of the Left think in terms of war between collective entities. A state of chaos to be replaced by a harmonious order is a postulate of paramount importance in their thinking. To return to totalitarianism of the Right. Apart from its postulate of an ideal, it diverges still further from Hobbes in two more respects. It sanctifies the peculiar national spirit, shaped by racial or national idiosyncrasies and history. This element is quite alien to Hobbes's purely legal and mechanical structure. Modern totalitarianism of the Right, in the second place, involves the stirring of the masses to active participation, not indeed as a rationally determining factor, but as a force acting under the impact of a collective emotion in a uniform manner. This constitutes an advance not only upon Hobbes, but also upon the essentially reactionary (the modern totalitarian trends are rather perverse, but they could hardly be called reactionary) doctrines and trends which emerged in France and in Germany (political romanticism) after the French Revolution, and quite recently in Vichy France, and preached a form of authoritarianism based on theocratic premises, historic paternalism, the national spirit, and—occasionally—on the metaphysical affirmation that " what is " is "what should be", the Logos of history. In these teachings the masses had no place at all. *Thomas Hobbes*, Leviathan, ed. Oakeshott, Oxford, 1946, pp. 21, 38, 60, 63 ff., chs. xiii–xv, xvii–xviii.

Section 4 : Secular and Religious Messianism, pp. 8–11

Ernest Troeltsch, The Social Teachings of the Christian Churches, London 1931. *Paul Alphandéry*, Les idées morales chez les hétérodoxes latins au début du XIIIème siècle, Paris 1903. *Ernst Benz*, Ecclesia spiritualis. Kirchenidee und Geschichtstheologie der franziskanischen Reformation, Stuttgart 1934. *Herbert Grundmann*, Religiöse Bewegungen im Mittelalter, Berlin 1935. *J. L. Talmon (Flaiszer)*, The Doctrine of Poverty in its religious, social and political aspects as illustrated by some movements of the twelfth and thirteenth centuries. Ph.D. Thesis, University of London, 1943.

Some of the problems, or rather dilemmas, antinomies and impasses of the Puritan Revolution show an astonishing similarity to those of the French Revolution during the Jacobin phase. To mention only one with a direct bearing upon the subject of this study : one of the most important tenets of the Puritan Revolution, common to all parties and groups, was the principle of, if not exactly popular sovereignty, at least Constitutional legality based upon a freely elected Parliament. Not less cherished a principle, indeed the supreme objective value of the Revolution, was freedom of conscience and toleration. It was clear to all that a freely elected parliament would come out against religious freedom. And so the alternative to "letting the people speak" spontaneously and freely, and accepting their verdict, whatever it proves to be, as final, was to have a government by and parliament of the "godly", the fifth-monarchy men or others like them; and to have freedom of conscience imposed by force. Democratic legality ceased thus to be the supreme test, and in its place came the elusive, indefinable quality of "godliness" and virtue, the only judges of which were to be ultimately the "godly" themselves. Now the believers in the rule of the "godly" were the most fervent preachers of the rights of man (or Englishman) and democratic popular sovereignty. The way out of the dilemma was to think of man not as he actually, though unfortunately, is, but of man as he should be. The bad actual men, that is to say those outside the fold, had to be refused the attribute of humanity. You cannot be tolerant towards those who reject toleration, the counter-revolutionaries, Roman Catholics of course in the first place.

J. R. Tanner, English Constitutional Conflicts of the Seventeenth Century, 1603–1689, Cambridge 1928. S. R. Gardiner, The First Two Stuarts and the Puritan Revolution, 1603–1660, London 1874. G. P. Gooch, Political Thought in England from Bacon to Halifax, London 1915; the same: English Democratic Ideas in the Seventeenth Century, ed. H. J. Laski, Cambridge 1927, deal with this aspect. On the social aspect of these impasses see David W. Petegorsky, Left-Wing Democracy in the English Civil War, London 1940; William Haller and Godfrey Davies, The Leveller Tracts, 1647–1653, New York 1944; A. S. P. Woodhouse, Puritanism and Liberty, being the Army Debates from the Clarke Manuscripts, London 1950.

Section 5 : Questions of Method, pp. 11–13

See Note on Section 2 of Introduction.

PART I. THE EIGHTEENTH-CENTURY ORIGINS OF POLITICAL MESSIANISM

CHAPTER I. NATURAL ORDER: THE POSTULATE

Section (a)—The Single Principle, pp. 17–21

Morelly, Code de la Nature, ed. E. Dolléans, Paris 1910, preface ; pp. 5, 7, 9 (the violated code of nature), 14 (the eventual impossibility of being vicious), 12, 13 (tout intelligent ; automate), 63 (point d'intégrité). All that is known, and it is next to nothing, of Morelly is contained in *Dolléans's* Introduction. It was *La Harpe* who wrote a book to refute the Code, in which he attributed the authorship of the book to Diderot. Morelly had earlier written a poem called La Basiliade, 1753, a Utopian vision of an ideal communist society. The *Marquis d'Argenson*, French Foreign Minister in the years 1744–7, and a writer of unusual views, called the Code de la Nature, " the book of books ", far superior to *Montesquieu's* Esprit des Lois ; Cambridge Modern History, Vol. VIII, pp. 33, 16 ; *Kingsley Martin*, pp. 242 ff., and *André Lichtenberger*, Le Socialisme au XVIIIème siècle, pp. 104–28, devote some space to Morelly.

C. A. Helvetius, De l'Esprit, Discours II, ch. xvii, in Œuvres Complètes d'Helvetius, Paris 1795, Vol. I, pp. 314 ff., 323 ; De l'Homme, Section IV, ch. xiv, Œuvres, Vol. III, pp. 348 ff ; Section VIII, ch. xxvi, Œuvres IV, p. 199 f ; Section X, ch. vii, Œuvres, IV, pp. 354 ff. On Helvetius see *Albert Keim*, Helvetius, sa vie et son œuvre, Paris 1907 ; on Helvetius' contribution to utilitarianism—*Elie Halévy*, Growth of Philosophical Radicalism, pp. 3, 4, 18 ; on his materialism— *G. V. Plekhanov*, Essays in the History of Materialism, London 1934, pp. 79–164 ; the same author, In Defence of Materialism, the development of the Monist view of history, London 1947, pp. 27 ff ; on Helvetius' ethics—*V. I. Guerrier*, L'Abbé de Mably, moraliste et politique, Étude sur la doctrine morale du jacobinisme puritain, et sur le developement de l'esprit républicain au XVIIIème siècle, Paris 1886, pp. 20 ff.

P. H. D. Holbach, Système de la nature, ed. Diderot, Paris 1821, preface, Vol. I, ch. i, p. 13 ; ch. iv, pp. 58 ff ; ch. v, p. 72 f. ; ch. xii, pp. 267 ff. ; Système social, ou principes naturels de la morale et de la politique. De L'influence du gouvernement sur les mœurs, London 1774 ; Vol. II, ch. ii, p. 35 ; ch. v, p. 64 f. ; Vol. I, ch. ii, pp. 19 ff., 29 ; Vol. III, ch. xii, pp. 151 ff. On Holbach see *W. H. Wickwar*, Baron d'Holbach, London 1935 ; *Plekhanov*, op. cit., pp. 3–75 ; pp. 27 ff. ; *H. Lion*, Les idées politiques et morales de Holbach, Annales Historiques de la Révolution Française, 1924, Jan., pp. 42–63, July, pp. 356–70 ; *G. H. Sabine*, A History of Political Theory, London 1937, deals with both Helvetius and Holbach, pp. 563 ff. *Kingsley Martin*, pp. 178 ff.

Gabriel Bonnot de Mably, De la Législation ou principes des Lois, Lausanne 1777, Vol. I, p. 43 ; Doutes proposés aux philosophes économistes sur l'ordre naturel et essentiel des sociétés politiques, Kell 1789, pp. 2 ff. ; De l'Étude de l'histoire, Mastreicht 1778, pp. 20 f. 137, 302 ; Les Droits et les Devoirs du citoyen, Kell 1789, p. 143 ; Phocion's Conversations : or the relation between morality and politics (Eng. trans.), London 1769, pp. 19, 21 f. Further references will be found in Note on ch. iv of this part. Because of his tedious style, Mably has repelled historians and critics, notwithstanding his considerable influence on the Revolutionary generation. The best study on him is still *Guerrier*, op. cit. ; more recent works on Mably are *E. A. Whitfield*, Gabriel Bonnot de Mably, London 1930, a critical summary of his ideas. *Georg Müller*, Die Gesellschaft und Staatslehren des Abbés Mably und ihr Einfluss auf das Werk der Konstituante, 1932.

Condorcet, Outlines of an historical view of the progress of the human mind (Eng. trans.), London 1795, pp. 242 ff., 254 ff., contains a classical summary of what may be termed the eighteenth-century liberal religion of progress. The passages on the new æsthetic laws which would come into existence in response to the diffusion of culture and art among the masses deserve special attention, ibid., pp. 305, 310 ff. Consult *Jules Delvailles*, Essai sur l'idée de progrès jusqu'à la fin du XVIIIème siècle, Paris 1910, as well as the works of *Becker*, Heavenly City, pp. 45, 53, and *Willey*, Eighteenth Century, pp. 155 ff.

J. J. Rousseau, ed. C. E. Vaughan, The Political Writings of Jean Jacques Rousseau, Cambridge 1915, Vol. I, pp. 296 (Fragments, L'état de guerre), 168 (Discours sur l'inégalité), 141 (Discours), 462 (first version of Contrat Social) ; Vaughan's Introduction in Vol. I, pp. 13, 29, 31. Other references, those designed to illustrate the shift of reference from nature to will, see below. It is true that Rousseau's letter to Mirabeau the older (the Physiocrat), Vaughan, Vol. II, pp. 159 ff., like *Mably's*

Doutes, written to refute *Lemercier de la Rivière*, L'Ordre naturel et essentiel des sociétés politiques, 1767, contain some sharp talk against the Physiocratic attempt to treat human situations in the spirit of geometrical theorems, and there is also the well-known passage at the beginning of Book II, ch. viii, of the Social Contract about the builder who must take into account the special circumstances. Viewed, however, against the background of their teaching as a whole, these asides of Rousseau and Mably are no more than debating points, or tribute paid to the challenge of historical geography. *Rousseau*, Vaughan, Vol. I, pp. 297, 307 ; Vol. II, p. 3, 82 ff., 387.

Robespierre, Rapport 18 Pluviôse, an II ; *Charles Vellay*, Rapports et Discours, Paris 1910, pp. 324 ff. The letter of *Salle* to Dubois Crancé is quoted by *Georges Lefebvre* in his Lectures on the French Revolution, 1944–5, La Convention, tome I, p. 25, issued by Centre de Documentation Universitaire, Paris. On the ideological and spiritual preparation of the Revolution, besides the authorities already mentioned, *E. Champion*, Esprit de la Révolution Française, Paris 1887 ; *Bernard Fay*, The Revolutionary Spirit in France and America, London 1928, have proved suggestive.

Section (b)—The Secular Religion, pp. 21–4

Morelly, pp. 42 ff. ; *Helvetius*, De l'Esprit, Discours II, ch. xxiii, Œuvres, Vol. I, pp. 376 ff. ; ch. xxiv, pp. 383 ff. ; ch. xvii, p. 322 ; De l'Homme, Section II, chs. ix–xv, Œuvres, III, pp. 49, 64, 70, 86 ; Section IX, ch. vi, Œuvres, IV, p. 237 f.

Holbach, Système de la nature, preface, Vol. I, ch. i, pp. 7 ff. ; ch. viii, pp. 119 ff.; ch. ix, pp. 148 ff. ; ch. xii, pp. 267 ff., 287 ff.; Système Social, Vol. I, ch. iii, pp. 29, 31 ; ch. vii, pp. 69 ff. ; ch. iv, p. 45 ; ch. xv, pp. 187 ff. ; Vol. II, ch. i, p. 7 ; Vol. III, ch. viii, p. 88 f.

Condorcet, pp. 34 ff., 64 ff., 77 f. (" War will continue to be waged as long as there shall exist priests and kings upon earth ").

Mably, De la Législation, Lausanne 1777, Vol. II, pp. 159, 194, 200, 204, 208, 221 ff. ; as it is Mably's most comprehensive work, it contains also the most comprehensive treatment of the religious question. Mably's Phocion had a deep influence on the Jacobin puritans. Passages in Robespierre's famous speeches to be referred to, especially Idées religieuses, *Vellay*, pp. 359 ff., are almost copied verbatim from Mably. " I wish all men were fully persuaded of this important truth that there is another life, in which Providence . . . will punish vice and reward virtue. This doctrine which stands founded on the divine justice, which our reason rejoices in, and which is so adapted to our wants, is terrible only to our passions" (Phocion, p. 123), "Il doit être le premier garant du pacte que les hommes ont fait en entrant en société, et ce n'est que sur la foi de cette garantie . . . que les hommes peuvent compter sur la foi de leurs concitoyens. Il reste consolateur de tous ceux qui sont opprimés par la justice humaine, et que leur innocence pourra rendre heureux au milieu des malheurs, s'ils peuvent appeler de la méchanceté ou de la sottise des hommes au tribunal de la sagesse divine." Atheism is " plus funeste aux hommes que la guerre, la famine et la peste ", atheists " qui croient qu'un même sort attend les gens de bien et les méchants après la mort " (Guerrier's quotations, pp. 63, 66). With all his hatred of atheists and even deists (as he did not believe in a pure religion of the heart, without any external forms), Mably's point of departure in the question of religion was his opposition to Malebranche, who maintained that any type of love for a creature for its own sake was a derogation from the love for the Creator, who must be the sole and exclusive object of our love, the created things being only an extension of the Creator. " Le meilleur moyen de mériter la faveur du ciel, c'est d'être utile aux hommes " (Guerrier, pp. 61–62).

Saint-Just and Mably, Annales Révolutionnaires, Vol. I, p. 345.

Rousseau : all attention is usually focused on the chapter on the Civil Religion, in the Contrat Social, L. IV, ch. viii, and on the Profession de Foi du vicaire Savoyard, ed. P. M. Masson, Fribourg 1914, because indeed they represent the two opposite poles. But the other writings of Rousseau on the matter have also to be considered : his letter to Voltaire, Vaughan, Vol. II, pp. 163 ff. ; the letters to Usteri, ibid., pp. 166 ff. ; lère Lettre de la Montagne, ibid., pp. 169 ff. ; reference in the Projet de Constitution pour la Corse, Vaughan II, p. 297 (Introduction). In the letters referred to in this Note the view that citizenship of a state excludes membership to the human kind or Christian fraternity is expressed by Rousseau in the most extreme form.

Seldom has so much ingenuity and such stupendous industry been lavished on so untenable a thesis as in the case of P. M. Masson, La Religion de J. J. Rousseau, Paris 1916, in order, as Albert Mathiez in reviewing the book, Annales Historiques de la Révolution Française, Paris 1922, said, to make of Rousseau a Father of the Church. We cannot elaborate the point further, and for a detailed description of the controversy on the religion of Rousseau we refer the reader to Albert Schinz, La Pensée religieuse de Rousseau et ses récents interprètes, Paris 1927 ; the same author's État présent des travaux sur J. J. Rousseau, Baltimore 1941. Compare *Ch. W. Hendel*, Jean Jacques Rousseau, Moralist, London 1934 ; *H. Höffding*, Jean Jacques Rousseau and his Philosophy, London 1930. *Diderot's* saying, that philosophical morality must prove itself superior to religious ethics, is quoted by *Becker*, op. cit., p. 80.

Section (c)—Apriorism and Empiricism, pp. 25-7

Morelly, pp. 23, 36 ; *Helvetius*, De l'Esprit, Discours III, ch. xxvii, Œuvres, Vol. II, pp. 220 ff. ; De l'Homme, Section I, ch. xiii, Œuvres, III, pp. 70 ff. : Section IV, ch. xi, p. 340 ; Lettres d'Helvetius au président de Montesquieu ;. et à M. Saurin on the Esprit des Lois, Œuvres, V, pp. 208 ff., 217 ff. ; l'Examen critique de l'Esprit des Lois par l'auteur De l'Esprit, analysed by *A. Keim*, Helvetius, pp. 165-77, and constituting Helvetius's notes on the margin of the manuscript of the Esprit des Lois. Their authenticity has, however, been lately seriously questioned by *R. Koebner*, The Authenticity of the Letters on the Esprit des Lois attributed to Helvetius (Bulletin of the Institute of Historical Research, Vol. XXIV, No. 39, May 1951), who maintains that they were forged in 1788 for electoral purposes.

Holbach, Système Social, Vol. III, ch. i, pp. 6 ff. ; II, ch. i, p. 11 f. ; I, ch. xi, p. 117. "Les lois naturelles . . . sont celles qui découlent immédiatement de la nature de l'homme, indépendamment de toute association" (Vol. II, p. 11) ; Politique naturelle, London 1773, Vol. II, p. 10 ; *Plekhanov*, Essays in the History of Materialism, p. 30.

Mably, Droits et Devoirs, p. 202 : Montesquieu . . . idées fondamentales de son système sont fausses ; Étude de l'histoire, pp. 97 ff. ; De la Législation, Vol. I, p. 27 : "Ils vous diront gravement que des lois bonnes au dixième degré de latitude ne valent plus rien sous le trentième . . . qu'importent des plaines, des montagnes . . . pour décider des lois les propres . . ."

Helvetius, Lettre au président de Montesquieu, Œuvres, Vol. V, p. 212, main objection is that Montesquieu offers a justification and alibi for all the vested interests of priests, obscurantists, nobles and other privileged groups when affirmin gtheir "naturalness" . . ., ibid., p. 215 ; Lettre à M. Saurin, ibid., pp. 217-20.

Rousseau. Vaughan, Vol. II, p. 147 (Emile, L. V) ; Vol. I, pp. 439, 462 (first version of C.S., L. I, ch. v). See also Note on ch. i, section (a). On the Kantian quality of Rousseau's regulative ideas and the distinction between a point of view or a central idea and a dogmatically assumed reality, see *Höffding*, op. cit., p. 106 ; *Cassirer*, Rousseau, Kant, Goethe, Princeton 1945. On the postulate of a self-contained and coherent *Weltanschauung* and adverse criticism of the English system—*Helvetius*, De l'Esprit, Discours I, ch. xvii, Œuvres, Vol. I, p. 323, and above all his two letters just quoted ; *Holbach*, Système Social, Vol. I, ch. iv, p. 45 f. ; II, ch. v, pp. 64 ff. (antiquity is there criticized for the absence of a Monistic outlook).

Condorcet, pp. 86, 88 f., 91, 234, 263 f., 266 f., 19. " Errors occasioned by the more general one of mistaking as the man of nature him who exhibited in his character the actual state of civilization, that is to say man corrupted by prejudices, by the interest of factious passions, and by social habits ", p. 91 ; (*Mably*, in De la Législation, Vol. I, pp. 84 ff., and *Morelly* resort to a similar sort of argument, when trying to refute the view that without the profit motive man would not work at all) ; against doling out rights, which ought to be universal and equal, in alleged accordance with climate and size of country, and then erecting institutions to perpetuate the created inequality (p. 234) ; long quotation in text, p. 230 ; *Delvaille*, Essai . . . progrès, pp. 670–707 ; on Sieyès, see Note on Part II, ch. i, section (*a*) ; on Diderot's *a priori* thinking see *Becker*, op cit., 104 ; on Montesquieu's dependence on it, ibid., p. 114, and *Champion*, op. cit., p. 9. Compare *Taine*, *Espinas*, *Tocqueville*, op. cit., passim.

CHAPTER II. THE SOCIAL PATTERN AND FREEDOM (HELVETIUS AND HOLBACH)

Section (a)—Identity of Reason, pp. 28–31

Philosophical premises in regard to cognition : *Helvetius*, De l'Homme, Section I, ch. x, Œuvres, Vol. III, p. 63 f. ; Section II, ch. xix, p. 225 : A common dictionary for the whole of mankind . . . to confound " all those fools . . . who under the name of metaphysicians. . . ." " Then the propositions in morality, politics, becoming as susceptible of demonstration as the propositions of geometry, men will all have the same ideas . . . all of them will necessarily perceive the same relations between the same objects " ; Section II, ch. xxiii, pp. 246 ff.—" There is no truth not reducible to a fact." De l'Esprit, Discours III, ch. xxvi, Œuvres, Vol. II, p. 216 f. ; Discours I, ch. vii,

Œuvres, I, p. 171 ; *Holbach*, Système social, Vol. I, ch. i, p. 18 : " la
vérité est la conformité de nos idées avec la nature des choses " ; *Condorcet*, p. 26. *Michel*, op. cit., p. 67 f. : on *Rousseau's* general will as a
Cartesian idea. R. *Hubert*, Les sciences sociales dans l'Encyclopédie,
Paris 1923, pp. 166 ff.

Nature of man distorted by evil institutions created by vested interests
—*Morelly*, pp. 9 ff., 16, 26, 31, 52, 65, 70, 84 ; *Helvetius*, De l'Esprit,
Discours II, ch. xxiv, Œuvres, I, pp. 383 ff. ; De l'Homme, preface,
Œuvres, III, pp. 5–12 ; Section IV, ch. xi, Œuvres, III, p. 338 ; *Holbach*,
Système Social, Vol. I, pp. 6 ff., 9 ff., 45, 51 ff., 187 ; II, p. 5 f. ; Vol. I,
p. 55 : " En partant de l'homme lui-même on trouvera facilement la
morale qui lui convient. Cette morale sera vraie, si l'on voit l'homme
tel qu'il est . . . principes . . . evidents . . . capables d'être aussi
rigoureusement démontrés que l'arithmétique ou la géometrie " ;
Système de la nature, Vol. I, preface ; ch. i, pp. 1–15 ; ch. vii, p. 265 ;
II, ch. ix, p. 250 ; I, ch. ix, p. 169 ; *Mably*, De la Législation, Vol. I,
p. 43 f.

Power of education ; essential equality of man permits the rearing
of genius ; the Legislator as educator—*Helvetius*, De l'Esprit, Discours III,
ch. xxx, Œuvres, Vol. II, pp. 245 ff. ; Discours II, ch. xvii, Vol. I,
pp. 322 ff. ; Discours II, ch. xxii, Œuvres, I, pp. 370–99 ; De l'Homme,
Section II, ch. i, Œuvres, III, pp. 106 ff. ; Section I, ch. i, Œuvres, III,
pp. 24 ff. ; chs. xii–xix, pp. 67–86 ; *Holbach*, Système Social, Vol. I,
pp. 7 ff., 13, 47 ff., 59 ; Vol. III, pp. 5 ff. ; Système de la nature, Vol. I,
ch. vii, pp. 110 ff. ; ch. ix, pp. 169 ff., 175 ff. ; *Mably*, De la Législation,
Vol. II, p. 31 : " Rien n'est impossible à un Législateur, il tient, pour
ainsi dire, notre cœur et notre esprit dans ses mains ; il peut faire des
hommes nouveaux " ; *Rousseau*, Confessions, L, IX ; Œuvres, Vol. VIII,
ed. Hachette, p. 288 ; Vaughan, Vol. II, p. 3 ; Vol. I, p. 248 (Économie
polit.). See *Becker*, op. cit., pp. 65, 138.

Section (b)—Self-interest, pp. 31–4

Self-interest, the general interest and cosmic pragmatism—*Morelly*,
pp. 26, 59, 70, 84 ; *Helvetius*, De l'Esprit, Discours I, ch. iv, Œuvres,
Vol. I, pp. 163, 165 ff. ; Discours II, ch. ii, pp. 182 f. ; ch. xxiv,
pp. 383–98 ; De l'Homme, Section IV, ch. i, Œuvres, III, p. 300 ; ch. x,
p. 332 f. ; ch. xii, pp. 341 ff. ; ch. xiv, pp. 348 ff. ; *Holbach*, Système
Social, Vol. I, pp. 17 ff., 55 f., 58 ff., 62 f., 68, 166, 158 ff. ; Système de la

nature, preface, Vol. I, ch. ix, pp. 160 ff. ; ch. xii, pp. 267 ff., 282 ff., 287 f. ; ch. xv, pp. 374 f., 386, 396 f. ; ch. xvii, p. 422 ff.

The action of the Legislator to ensure artificial harmony—*Morelly*, pp. 20, 31 ; *Helvetius*, De l'Esprit, Discours II, ch. xvii, Œuvres, Vol. I, pp. 219–29 ; ch. xxiv, 394 ff. ; ch. xv, p. 308 ; Discours III, ch. iv, Œuvres, II, pp. 34 ff. ; ch. xvi, 148 ff. ; ch. xxiv, p. 199 ; Discours II, ch. xxii, Œuvres, I, p. 375 : " The whole study of the moralists consists in determining the use that ought to be made of those rewards and punishments, and the assistance that may be drawn from them, in order to connect the personal with the general interest. This union is the masterpiece which moralists ought to propose to themselves. If citizens could not procure their own private happiness without promoting that of the public, there would be none vicious but fools. All men would be under the necessity of being virtuous, and the felicity of nations would be of benefit to morality."

Helvetius, De l'Homme, Section IV, ch. xiii, Œuvres, Vol. III, p. 347 f. ; Section X, ch. vii, Œuvres, IV, p. 354 f. ; Section XI, ch. vi, pp. 238 ff. ; Section VI, ch. xvi, pp. 54 ff. ; Section IX, ch. i, Œuvres, IV, 207 ff.

Holbach, Système de la nature, Vol. I, ch. ix, p. 169 f. ; ch. viii, p. 119 f.

Mably, Droits et Devoirs, pp. 16 ff., 28 f., 40 ; De la Législation, Vol. I, pp. 28 ff., 34, 43, 55, 84 ; II, p. 89 f. ; Doutes, p. 248 ; *Guerrier*, pp. 30 f., 36 ff.

Halévy, Growth, pp. 17, 8 f., on the distinction between natural and artificial harmony ; *Basil Willey*, Eighteenth, etc., pp. 155–67, on Holbach. The Physiocrats—*Lemercier de la Rivière*, L'Ordre naturel et essentiel des sociétés politiques, ch. xxi, t. I, pp. 265 ff.

Mirabeau, the older : " Il s'agit aujourd'hui de faire que l'intérêt personnel et physique de chaque homme devienne le lien des hommes entre eux et le mobile de tous leur rapports. On sait assez que cet intérêt, s'il n'est éclairé, est la pomme de discorde qui sépare les hommes et les rend enemis les uns des autres. Toute la science législative et politique, tout le grand œuvre des amis des hommes consiste donc à les éclairer tous sur la nature de cet intérêt personnel, sur les principes qui l'établissent, sur les conséquences qui l'étendent et le lient aux autres intérêts et par suite à l'intérêt général, et enfin sur le point de réunion auquel tous les intérêts humains aboutissent—" *Guerrier*, p. 44 ; see also *Sée*, Évolution, pp. 203–13.

Section (c)—The Natural Order, the Legislator, and the Individual, pp. 34–7

Helvetius, De l'Esprit, Discours II, ch. xxiv, Œuvres, Vol. I, p. 385 (quotation) ; De l'Homme, Section IV, ch. xi, Œuvres, III, pp. 333 ff. ; ch. xiii, pp. 345 ff.

The liberal tenets—*Helvetius*, De l'Homme, Section I, ch. xiii, Œuvres, III, pp. 70 ff. ; *Holbach*, Système Social, Vol. II, pp. 8 ff., 13 f., 21, 42 ff. ; III, pp. 27 ff. ; Système de la nature, Vol. I, ch. ix, pp. 170 ff., ch. xii, 272 f., 281 ff. ; ch. xvi, pp. 370 ff. In Politique Naturelle, London, 1773, Holbach, as in his other writings, appears as what may be called a moderate bourgeois liberal ; he has a more comprehensive political philosophy than Helvetius. See *H. Lion*, Les idées, etc., op. cit.

Mably, Droits et Devoirs, p. 10 f. : " Les hommes sont sortis des mains de la nature parfaitement égaux, par conséquent sans droits les uns sur les autres et parfaitement libres . . . ne dicte qu'une seule loi, c'est de travailler à nous rendre heureux . . . " ; p. 11 : " tout appartenait à chacun d'eux ; tout homme était une espèce de monarque qui avait droit à la monarchie universelle." A striking illustration of the inner connection between extreme individualism and communism ; see *Espinas*, op. cit., p. 112 f. ; *Rousseau*, Économie Politique, Vaughan, Vol. I, p. 252 f., as well as the Discours sur l'Inégalité, passim.

The perfected State (and freedom to reason)—*Morelly*, p. 48 ; *Helvetius*, Lettre à Montesquieu, Œuvres, Vol. V, p. 215 : there are only two forms of government, the good and the bad : De l'Homme, Section IX, ch. iv, Œuvres, Vol. IV, pp. 231 ff., 238 f. " Now supposing this legislation the most proper to render the people happy, what means are there to secure its perpetual duration ? The most certain would be to order preceptors in their instructions and magistrates in their public discourses to demonstrate its excellence ; which being once established, the legislation would be proof against the inconstancy of the human mind ; whatever be the pretended inconstancy of the human mind, when a nation is made clearly to perceive the reciprocal dependence between their happiness and the preservation of their laws, their inconstancy is sure to be restrained. Every wise legislation that unites private and public interest and founds virtue on the advantage of each individual is indestructible. But is such legislation possible ? Why not ? The horizon of our ideas is every day extended ; and if legislation, like the other sciences, participates in the progress of the human mind, why despair of the future felicity of mankind ? Why may not nations as they become every age more enlightened, one day arrive at that

plenitude of happiness of which they are capable ? It is not without
pain that I quit this hope" (pp. 231–8). We shall see in Part III,
ch. i, section (a), how this hope affected Babeuf, Buonarroti. On
authenticity of Helvetius's two letters see Note on ch. i, section (c).
Helvetius, De l'Homme, Section IX, ch. i. Œuvres, Vol. IV, pp. 209 :
Section IX, ch. vi, ibid., p. 238 f.
On the Physiocrats—see E. *Sée*, L'évolution de la pensée, pp. 208 ff. ;
Lemercier de la Rivière, ch. viii, tome I, p. 94 f. : "Il est donc nécessaire
que l'opinion soit eclairée et par conséquent la pensée soit libre, que
toutes les opinions soient permises" ; *Mably*, Droits et Devoirs, pp. 28–
31 ; *Rousseau*, see Note on ch. i, section (a) ; Note on Introduction,
section (4) ; first version of Contrat Social, Vaughan, Vol. I, p. 471 ;
Emile, L. V., Vaughan, Vol. II, p. 151. ; C. S., L. I, ch. vii : "the
sovereign power need give no guarantee to its subjects . . . the sovereign
power by virtue of what it is, is always what it should be".

CHAPTER III. TOTALITARIAN DEMOCRACY (ROUSSEAU)

Section (a)—The Psychological Background, pp. 38–40

The Index volume (XIV) of the Hachette edition of Rousseau's
Œuvres, Paris 1908, gives all the references in regard to the use of the
term Nature. It may be suggested that Nature in the sense of the final
and predestined stage of development, and not as the erstwhile state, is an
Aristotelian idea at bottom. On eighteenth-century conception of
Nature, see *Basil Willey*, op. cit., pp. 14, 55, 205 ff., 241 ; pp. 3–18.
Helvetius, Man, preface ; *Holbach*, Système Social, Vol. III, p. 63 ;
Morelly, pp. 9, 52, 65, and numerous references given in former Notes.
With *Mably*, as shall be seen, Note on section (c) of ch. iii, it is a
different matter because he, like Rousseau, laboured under a deep sense
of sin. Human inadequacy postulated the need of salvation through an
effort to overcome it and to throw off the entanglements into which
evil human institutions and instincts excited by them have got man.
See E. *Cassirer*, Das Problem Rousseau, Archiv für Geschichte der
Philosophie, Vol. XLI, Nos. 112–3, 1932. The first version of the Contrat Social has a line saying that all virtues come from social contact ; on
the same page another line states that all vices are born from social

contact, Vaughan, Vol. I, p. 449; II, p. 145 f. (Emile, Livre IV); II, 387 (Considérations sur la Pologne); p. 139 (Emile, Introduction); Vol. I, pp. 15, 17, n. 3, 27, 29, 324; Social Contract, L.IV, ch. vii; " unnature ", " unité numérique " (Vaughan, Vol. II, 145).

" Forcé de combattre la nature ou les institutions sociales, il faut opter entre faire un homme ou un citoyen ; car on ne peut faire à la fois l'un et l'autre." The context is the idea of the mutually exclusive qualities of members of the society of mankind, and citizenship of a State (Vaughan, Vol. II, p. 144). " De ces contradictions naît celle que nous éprouvons sans cesse en nous-mêmes. Entraînés par la nature et par les hommes dans des routes contraires, forcés de nous partager entre ces diverses impulsions, nous en suivons une composée qui ne nous mène ni à l'un ni à l'autre but. Ainsi, combattus et flottants durant tout le cours de notre vie, nous la terminons sans avoir pu nous accorder avec nous, et sans avoir été bons ni pour nous ni pour les autres " (p. 147). A multitude of references from the Confessions, Rousseau's letters and autobiographical writings could be brought to illustrate the question of the dual Rousseau.

On the question of unity or inconsistency in Rousseau, see *Albert Schinz*, op. cit., who expounds the theory of a " Rousseau classique" and a " Rousseau romantique "; *Cassirer*, op. cit. ; *Lanson*, Histoire de la Littérature française, Paris 1912, pp. 773–804 ; *Hendel*, J. J. R., Moralist ; *Höffding* ; and others. Schinz surveys the various theories.

Section (b)—The General Will and the Individual, pp. 40–2

Liberty and the general will—*Rousseau*, C.S., L. I, chs. vi–viii ; L. II, ch. iv, ch. vii, ch. xii ; L. IV, ch. i. ; Vaughan, Vol. I, pp. 328 (Fragments), 338 ; Écon. Polit., Vaughan, I, pp. 241 ff. ; *Diderot*, Droit Naturel, Encyclopédie, Vol. XI, pp. 371 ff. ; *Rousseau*, first version of C.S., Vaughan, I, pp. 452, 457, 460 f. ; *Holbach*, Système Social, Vol. II, p. 21, uses the term volonté générale, as well as *Montesquieu* in one place in the Esprit des Lois.

The literature on the general will is inexhaustible ; of those consulted for this work the following deserve to be mentioned : *T. H. Green*, Lectures on the Principles of Political Obligation, London 1895 ; *Bernard Bosanquet*, The Philosophical Theory of the State, London 1920 ; *G. del Vecchio*, Über Grundgedanken der Politik Rousseau's, Archiv für Rechts- und Wirtschaftsgeschichte, Band I, H. 1, pp. 1–16 ; *Sabine*, op. cit. ;

Alfred Cobban, Rousseau and the Modern State, London 1934 ; *A. Schinz*,
La pensée de Rousseau ; *Hendel*, Rousseau, Moralist ; *H. Michel*, L'idée
de l'état, pp. 67, 68 ; *Carl Schmitt*, Die Diktatur, pp. 116 ff. ; *Léon
Duguit*, Jean Jacques Rousseau, Kant et Hegel, Revue de Droit public et
de la science politique en France et à l'Étranger, 1918, pp. 94 ff., and
Vaughan's introductions.

To become before the law what the law was intended to make them
—*Rousseau*, C.S., L. II, ch. vii ; Vaughan, Vol I, p. 324 (Fragments) :
" Celui qui se croit capable de former un peuple doit se sentir en état
de changer, pour ainsi dire, la nature des hommes. Il faut qu'il trans-
forme chaque individu, qui est par lui-même un tout parfait et solitaire,
en partie d'un plus grand tout, dont cet individu reçoive en quelque
sorte sa vie et son être, qu'il mutile, pour ainsi dire, la constitution de
l'homme " ; Écon. Polit., Vaughan, I, 245 ; II, p. 426 ; " Car la Loi
est antérieure à la justice, et non pas la justice à la Loi '—C.S., II, IV ;
Vaughan, I, p. 494.

It is very important to distinguish, and to bear in mind, the various
layers of Rousseau's thought, and the particular flavour of his associations
of ideas. There is the Cartesian level, there is the eighteenth-century
context, there is the romantic premonition, and finally, or perhaps before
all, the recollection of classical antiquity. The latter is particularly
important in regard to Rousseau's idea of liberty and the dignity of
citizenship. The Revolutionary spirit was in full accord with antiquity
in the horror common to both of personal dependence of man on man.
The principle of honour was not to have a superior, as *Lord Acton* put
it in his Lectures on the French Revolution. This did not entail in the
least a horror of dependence on the State, the collective person. On
the contrary. In the words of *Rousseau*, Contrat Social, trans. Cole,
p. 48 : " each citizen would then be perfectly independent of all the rest,
and at the same time very dependent on the city ". *Benjamin Constant*,
in an essay of comparison between the ancient and the modern idea
of liberty (one would be inclined to say Anglo-Saxon conception),
Cours de politique constitutionelle, 1818–20, Paris 1861, Vol. II, p. 549,
pointed out that whereas to the Moderns liberty suggests freedom from
State interference, and from the pressure of prevailing collective patterns
of thought and feeling—in a word, privacy (like to J. S. Mill)—the ancient
idea of liberty connoted above all the active and equal participation of
the citizen in the shaping of the sovereign will, in the exercise of active
citizenship rights ; not so much his freedom, as his dignity as a member
of the sovereign. This was far from implying privacy or the liberal

escape from the State; quite the reverse. *Tocqueville*, in *L'Ancien Régime*, has remarked that unlike the Anglo-Saxon critic of his government, the opponent of the *ancien régime* did not so much criticize the State for its interfering with the individual's activities and oppressing him, as for doing nothing for him, obliged as the State was to look after all and everything. *Acton*, Lectures Fr. Rev., London 1910, p. 15 f.

Section (c)—The General Will, Popular Sovereignty, and Dictatorship, pp. 43-8

Rousseau, Contrat Social, L. II, chs. ii–iv, vi–vii ; L. III, chs. i–ii ; L. III, chs. xii–xviii ; Économie Politique, Vaughan, Vol. I, pp. 241–4, 247, 248, 255 f ; Emile, Vaughan, II, p. 152 ; Lettres de la Montagne (IV), Vaughan, II, 201 ; Contrat Social, first version, Vaughan, I, pp. 452, 462, 476 (" savoir l'interroger à propos "). " As long as several men in assembly regard themselves as a single body, they have only a single will which is concerned with their common preservation and general well-being. In this case, all the springs of State are vigorous and simple and its rules clear and luminous ; there are no embroilments or conflicts of interests ; the common good is everywhere clearly apparent, and only good sense is needed to perceive it. Peace, unity and equality are the enemies of political subtleties. . . . A State so governed needs very few laws ; and, as it becomes necessary to issue new ones, the necessity is universally seen. The first man to propose them merely says what all have already felt, and there is no question of factions or intrigues or eloquence in order to secure the passage into law of what every one has already decided to do, as soon as he is sure that the rest will act with him. . . . But when the social bond begins to be relaxed and the State to grow weak, when particular interests begin to make themselves felt and the smaller societies to exercise an influence over the larger, the common interest changes and finds opponents : opinion is no longer unanimous ; the general will ceases to be the will of all ; contradictory views and debates arise ; and the best advice is not taken without question. . . . Does it follow from this that the general will is exterminated or corrupted ? Not at all ; it is always constant, unalterable and pure ; but it is subordinated to other wills which encroach upon its sphere. Each man, in detaching his interest from the common interest, sees clearly that he cannot entirely separate them ; but his share in the public mishaps seems to him negligble beside the exclusive good he

aims at making his own. Apart from this particular good, he wills the
general good in his own interest, as strongly as any one else " (C.S, L. IV,
ch. i), trans. Cole, pp. 90, 91.

" Pour qu'une volonté soit générale, il n'est pas toujours nécessaire
qu'elle soit unanime, mais il est nécessaire que toutes les voix soient
comptées " . . . " toute exclusion rompt la généralité " (Vaughan, Vol.
II, p. 40, n. 1).

" La volonté générale est rarement celle de tous "—first version of
C.S., Vaughan, Vol. I, p. 462 ; " la volonté générale est toujours droite,
il n'est jamais question de la rectifier, mais il faut savoir l'interroger à
propos ", ibid., p. 476 ; " If, when the people, being furnished with
adequate information, held its deliberations, the citizens had no com-
munication one with another, the grand total of the small differences
would always give the general will, and the decision would always be
good. But when factions arise, and partial associations are formed at
the expense of the great association, the will of each of those associations
becomes . . . particular in relation to the State : it may be said that
there are no longer as many votes as there are men. . . . It is therefore
essential, if the general will is to be able to express itself, that there
should be no partial society within the State, and that each citizen should
think his own thoughts " (C.S., L. II, ch. iii, trans. Cole, pp. 25, 26).

On the exhilarating experience of sharing sovereignty, C.S., L. III,
ch. xv. Here is a case illustrating the transformation of Rousseau's
thought from individualist rationalism into collectivism of the organic
and historical type. The cognizant being who wills freely is being
transformed into a product at first of teaching and environment, then
of historic forces, past traditions, and finally of the national spirit.
Similarly the general will, a truth to be discovered, is being transplanted
by the idea and experience of patriotism into the common heritage
with all its peculiarities. Here is the branching out of Rousseau's contribution into two currents, into the rationalist-individualist and eventually collectivist of the Left on the one hand, and the irrational nationalist
ideology of the Right, with its affinities with German political romanticism, Fichte, Hegel and Savigny, on the other. The shift towards
nationalism takes place in *Rousseau's* Considérations sur le Gouvernement
de Pologne. Here are a few illustrations : " Éducation . . . forme
nationale . . . C'est l'éducation qui doit donner aux âmes la forme
nationale, et diriger tellement leurs opinions et leurs goûts, qu'elles soient
patriots par inclination, par passion, par nécessité. Un enfant, en ouvrant
les yeux doit voir la patrie, et jusqu'à la mort ne doit plus voir qu'elle.

Tout vrai républicain suça avec le lait de sa mère l'amour de la patrie : c'est-à-dire, des lois et de la liberté. Cet amour fait toute son existence ; il ne voit que la patrie, il ne vit que pour elle ; sitôt qu'il est seul, il est nul ; sitôt qu'il n'a plus de patrie, il n'est plus ; et s'il n'est pas mort, il est pis" (Vaughan, Vol. II, p. 437). "De l'effervescence excitée par cette commune émulation naîtra cette ivresse patriotique qui seule sait élever les hommes au dessus d'eux-mêmes, et sans laquelle la liberté n'est qu'un vain nom et la législation qu'une chimère" (ibid., p. 492). There (p. 507) Rousseau speaks with bitterness of the indifference of the Moderns to "objets moraux et sur tout ce qui peut donner du ressort aux âmes". This is a far cry from the prevailing mechanical and legalistic conceptions of State and Nation. Cf. Vaughan, Vol. II, pp. 428, 431 ff, 437, 445, 497 f. See on this A. Cobban, Rousseau, pp. 151 ff. ; T. H. Green, Lectures on Political Obligation; A. Osborne, Rousseau and Burke, London 1940.

Green saw also quite early the totalitarian implications of the general will in regard to engineering elections. The quotation at the end of section comes from C.S., II, ch. vi, trans. Cole. p. 34.

Holbach, Système Social, Vol. II, pp. 48, 52 ff., 68 ff. ; Letronne, quoted by Tocqueville, L'Ancien Régime, p. 269 ; Morelly, p. 51 (actually all forms of government are to him, as to Harrington, the expression of the prevailing property relations) ; Helvetius, Lettres à Montesquieu (Œuvres, Vol. V, p. 213), à Saurin (ibid., p. 217) : "vos combinaisons de pouvoirs ne font que séparer et compliquer les intérêts individuels au lieu de les unir. L'exemple du gouvernment anglais vous a séduit. Je suis loin de penser que cette constitution soit parfaite." Very strikingly Helvetius lays all the emphasis on the social implications of the theory of checks, intermediaries—it was designed to secure the privileges of the aristocracy anxious to place itself between King and people— instead of the constitutional aspect of the problem. Trial of John Horne Tooke, 17–22, XI, 1794, State Trials, XXV, pp. 590–2. Mably, disconcertingly enough for a fanatically egalitarian Communist, but not surprisingly for a planner of laws for a society in state of sin, in Doutes, pp. 85, 175 ff., 180, 185 ; Étude de l'Histoire, pp. 345 f., 348, 367 ; De la Législation, Vol. II, p. 44 f., lays all emphasis on the necessity of consulting all the various interests, classes and trends so as to enable them to cancel each other out, and to isolate despotism. "Toutes les classes réunies . . . parviennent à connaître la vérité par le secours de la discussion" (Doutes, p. 85 ; Étude, p. 345).

On the Physiocrats, see E. Sée, Évolution, pp. 203–213 ; Guerrier,

Mably, pp. 143 ff; "Une multitude ne peut être législatrice, car elle se compose d'individus dont les intérêts et les droits sont inégaux et opposés les uns aux autres, et qui se trouveraient être à la fois juges et partis. D'ailleurs, c'est une grande erreur de considérer la nation comme un corps . . . (*Sée*, p. 207) ; legal despotism based on infallible evidence "écarte absolument l'arbitraire et rend impraticables dans les souverains, comme dans les magistrats, les abus de l'autorité, qui troubleront l'administration de la justice" (p. 210). "A l'égard des lois naturelles . . . les préceptes de notre raison . . . si simples, si claires, si lumineuses qu'il suffit de les présenter aux hommes pour qu'ils y acquiescent, à moins qu'ils ne soient dérangés . . ." (*Mably*, Droits, p. 143).

Quesnay : "que l'autorité souveraine soit unique et supérieure à tous les individus de la société et à toutes les entreprises injustes des intérêts particuliers. . . . Le système des contreforces dans un gouvernement est une opinion funeste qui ne laisse apercevoir que la discorde entre les grands et l'accablement des petits" (*Guerrier*, p. 144).

Lemercier de la Rivière, L'ordre naturel, chs. xiv-xxi, pp. 100-65, and in subsequent chapters argues against "despotisme arbitraire" as distinct from "despotisme légal".

Section (d)—The General Will as Purpose, pp. 48-9

On the adventures of Rousseau's general will through the French Revolution see references in later parts. Consult *D. Williams*, The Influence of Rousseau on the French Revolution, English Hist. Rev., 1933, Vol. XLVIII, pp. 414-30.

Benjamin Constant, op. cit., argues against an unnamed publicist who thought that a single man (clearly Napoleon) could embody and express the general will.

In Économie Politique (Vaughan, Vol. I, p. 247) *Rousseau*, notwithstanding his insistence on the vital importance of direct and constant participation of all in the shaping of the general will, says that there may be no need for too frequent assemblies, "car les chefs savent assez que la volonté générale est toujours pour le parti le plus favorable à l'intérêt public, c'est-à-dire, le plus équitable, de sorte qu'il ne faut qu'être juste pour s'assurer de suivre la volonté générale". This means assumed consent, or popular approval by acclamation. Quotation on suspension of government during people's assembly from C.S., L. III, ch. xiv, trans. Cole, p. 81. On the Législateur, C.S., L. II, chs. vii-x.

Another curious development of *Rousseau's* thinking deserves passing notice. The personal Legislator of Rousseau appears like a *deus ex machina*. On the whole Rousseau, like a typical doctrinaire of the Left, remains always in the realm of principles. His citizens and magistrates are mere ciphers. Different is the procedure of a thinker like *Burke*. When coming, in the Reflections on the French Revolution, to assess the significance of the work of the National Assembly, the most important question he believes to be for his purpose is to analyse the composition of the Assembly, the type of man sitting in it, his background, education, profession. The question of politics is how people act and behave, and not how principles are interconnected, for the truer they are, Burke says, metaphysically, the more false are they in life. It is one of the remarkable phenomena that doctrines which put all their hope in principles, and ignore the peculiarities of men, end in conjuring up a personal saviour, whereas the empiric Anglo-Saxon approach as exemplified by Burke, though leaving very much to man's discretion, and being greatly interested in the statesman as man, has no recourse to the saviour-leader. We shall return to this point. *E. Burke*, Reflections, ed. Selby, London 1910, pp. 44 ff.

CHAPTER IV.   PROPERTY (MORELLY AND MABLY)

Section (a)—Premises and Conclusions—the Discrepancy, pp. 50-2

On the discussion on the element of socialism in the eighteenth-century philosophy—see Note on section (*c*), ch. i. The retreat is exemplified in the most striking form by *Sieyès*, see Note on Pt. II, ch. i, section 1, and *Condorcet*, 328 ff, as these two thinkers wrote under the impact of events, and were not merely theorizing in vacuo. Early in the eighteenth century *Recueil de Passerau* wrote: " Le gouvernement démocratique est celui où toute l'autorité est au peuple et où les hommes sont égaux en noblesse, en puissance, en richesses ; pour tel effet il faut que tous les biens appartiennent à la République qui les dispensera en bonne mère selon les besoins. Si on laisse entrer dans la société les paroles meum et tuum, la ruine est inevitable. On ne doit jamais tolérer ces expressions : mon bien, etc.", *Henri Lion*, Les idées d'Holbach, Annales Historiques de la Révolution Franç., 1924, Vol. I, p. 363 f. *Espinas* grasped well the socialist potentialities of the individualist idea of natural rights, pp. 115 ff.

The State as instrument of exploitation—*Helvetius*, Lettre à Montesquieu, Œuvres, Vol. V, p. 215 ; De l'Homme, Section VI, ch. v, Œuvres, IV, pp. 21 ff. ; ch. vii, p. 30 f ; chs. viii–x, pp. 33–43 ; Section VIII, ch. iii, Œuvres, IV, p. 137 ; *Morelly*, p. 37—" all these evils " ; *Helvetius*, Œuvres, IV, p. 127 (ed. 1781, London) ; *Lichtenberger*, Le Soc., p. 264. Love of money incompatible with love of virtue—*Helvetius*, De l'Homme, Section VI, chs. xii–xv, Œuvres, IV, pp. 44–54 ; ch. xvi, pp. 55 ff ; *Diderot*, Législateur, Encyclopédie, 1782, Vol. XIX, pp. 755 ff. *Rousseau*, Discours sur l'inégalité, Pt. II, Vaughan, Vol. I, pp. 169, 180 ff. ; and the famous Note i, pp. 202–7 ; *Helvetius*, De l'Homme, Œuvres, Londres 1781, p. 127 (quoted by *Lichtenberger*, Le Socialisme au XVIIIème siècle, p. 264) ; *Espinas*, 95. The community as owner of all goods—*Rousseau*, C.S., L. I, ch. ix ; Emile, L. V, Vaughan, II, p. 152 ; C.S., first version, L. I, ch. v, Vaughan, I, p. 466 f. ; Corse, Vaughan, II, pp. 337 ff., 344 ff.

Sacredness of property—*Rousseau*, Économie Politique, Vaughan, I, pp. 259 ff., 265, 273 ; *Helvetius*, De l'Homme, Section X, ch. vii, Œuvres, Vol. IV, p. 357.

The middle class is the core of society—*Rousseau*, Économie Politique, Vaughan, Vol. I, p. 254 : " C'est sur la médiocrité seule qui s'exerce toute la force des lois " ; *Mably*, Droits et Devoirs, p. 344—" la modération bourgeoise qui est l'âme et l'appui de la liberté "

Section (b)—Morelly, the Communist, pp. 52–4

Morelly, pp. 76, 15 f., 60, 63, 37, 48 (the evil effects of property), 31 (autorité sévére), 44–5 (forcing man back to his true nature), 57, 63 f. (Theodicée ; point d'intégrité), 94 ff. (political organization), 104 f. (spiritual totalitarianism). See *Lichtenberger*, Social. au XVIII, pp. 104–28.

Section (c)—Mably and Ascetic Virtue, pp. 54–8

Mably became a moralist out of disgust with contemporary diplomacy, a knowledge of which he had acquired in his youth as Secretary to his kinsman Cardinal Tencin, the Minister, *Guerrier*, p. 16.

The sense of sin—*Mably*, Droits et Devoirs, p. 180 ; De la Législation, Vol. I, pp. 13 ff., 19, 231, 238 ; property bred avarice—Doutes, pp. 11 ff., 45 ; Droits, 170 ff. ; Étude de l'Histoire, p. 23 ; Législation, I, pp. 14,

80 f., 114 ; the reign of passions—Doutes, p. 17 ; Législation, I, pp. 28–9 ;
no equality without communism—Doutes, p. 194 ; Droits, pp. 171, 176 ff.
(*Whitfield*, Mably, pp. 71–82, 198), 180 ; Étude de l'Histoire, pp. 23 ff.,
31 f. ; Législation, I, pp. 55, 71, 78 ff., 85 ff. ; sacredness of property in
the state of sin—Étude, pp. 367 ff. ; Législation, I, pp. 114, 117 f. ; the
anarchy of passions and determinism—Droits, pp. 28, 31 ; Législation, I,
p. 27 ; fixed quantity of mediocre happiness—Phocion, pp. 23, 65 ; Étude
de l'Histoire, pp. 31, 33, 48, 75, 81, 85, 87 ; Législation, I, pp. 13, 47, 126 ;
ascetic morality enforced by law—Phocion, pp. 46, 53 f., 62, 83, 201 ;
Législation, I, p. 228 ; denial of civilization—Phocion, pp. 51, 105 ff.,
116, 123, 176 ; Législation I, p. 141 ; low estimate of man—*Whitfield*,
Mably, pp. 59 (253), 99 ; *Rousseau* on freedom—Corse, Vaughan,
Vol. II, pp. 350 ff.

Section (d)—Restrictionist Economics, pp. 58–65

" La propriété ouvre "—*Mably*, Législation, I, p. 147 ; " a curb "—
Rousseau, Corse, Vaughan, Vol. II, pp. 337–8 ; 310 f., 314 ff., 319, 325,
348, 351. ; Économie Politique, ed. Vaughan, I, pp. 254 ff. ; I, p. 8
(Introduct.).

Mably on restrictions on property : Loi agraire—Étude de l'Histoire,
pp. 369 ff. ; Phocion, pp. 106, 167, 178 ; Législation, I, p. 147 (restrict
right of succession ; heirless property to be divided among the poor) ;
Rousseau : " neither so rich . . . "—first version of C.S., L. II, ch. vi,
Vaughan, I, p. 497.

Industrial and commercial development condemned—*Mably*, Étude
de L'Histoire, pp. 73–4 ; Législation, I, p. 142 ; *Rousseau* on agriculture—
Économie Politique, Vaughan, I, p. 255 ; Corse, Vaughan, II, pp. 320–7 ;
Holbach—Système Social, Vol. III, p. 76—" possesseurs de terres qui
seuls . . . sont les vrais citoyens ", " la terre est la vraie base d'un État ".

Robespierre—in A. Aulard, Société des Jacobins, Vol. V, pp. 630 ff. ;
Large cities—*Rousseau*, Corse, Vaughan, II, p. 318 ; *Holbach*, Système
Social, Vol. III, p. 84 (" moyens de corruption ") ; all wars ; " négociants avides " ; " la tranquillité "—*Holbach*, Système Social, III, pp. 76–8,
84–5 ; *Mably*, De la Législation, Vol. I, pp. 42, 142, 158 ; Observations
sur l'Amérique, Œuvres, Vol. VIII, pp. 440–1 ; Droits et Devoirs, p. 168.

" Rien n'est plus . . . "—*Holbach*, Système Social, Vol. III, p. 81 ;
" imaginary needs . . . désirs extravagants "—ibid., pp. 76 ; 81, 84 ;
Helvetius, De l'Homme, Section VI, chs. viii, ix, Œuvres, IV, pp. 33 ff.,

38 ff. ; *Mably* on artisans—Étude de l'Histoire, p. 301 ; The disfranchisement of a class—Étude, pp. 299 ff. ; Phocion, pp. 102–3, 105 ; Droits et Devoirs, p. 79 (espèces d'esclaves) ; *Whitfield*, Mably, pp. 81–139 ; Du Cours des Passions, p. 167 ; Législation, II, p. 59, I, pp. 238–9 (social orders ; the lower classes to be treated gently) ; " La modération bourgeoise "—Droits et Devoirs, p. 344 ; *Holbach* on disfranchise—Système Social, II, pp. 53, 54 f, 65 (" police sévère " to keep populace in check) ; III, pp. 44–5 (humane sympathy for the poor ; system blamed) ; *Mably* on control of corn trade and foreign trade—Calvin's Geneva —Législation, I, p. 158 ; " essentiellement contraire ", " engourdir "— Législation, I, pp. 119, 126 ; " encourage avarice under pretext "— Droits et Devoirs, p. 168.

Mirabeau the younger on industry—*Jean Jaurès*, Histoire Socialiste de la Révolution Française, ed. Mathiez, 1922, Vol. II, p. 284.

PART II. THE JACOBIN IMPROVISATION

CHAPTER I. THE REVOLUTION OF 1789—SIEYÈS

Section (a)—The Revolutionary Attitude, pp. 69–73

Monographs on Sieyès are : *J. H. Clapham*, The Abbé Sieyès, London 1912, written under the inspiration of Lord Acton (preface) ; *Paul Bastid*, Sieyès et sa pensée, Paris 1939. We are concerned here only with Sieyès on the threshold of the Revolution. The evolution of his thinking in his later years, especially after 9 Thermidor, and his part in bringing about the Bonapartist Consulate are outside our scope. It may not, however, be out of place to suggest a dialectical connection between Sieyès's passion for Constitution and blue-print making and his propensity for authoritarian personal régimes. See further remarks below.

A. de Tocqueville, L'Ancien Régime, 1859, pp. 233 ff ; *Lord Acton*, Lectures on French Revolution, on the importance political theorists acquired at the time. *Mornet*, Les Origines Intellectuelles,—pp. 314 ff., library inventory. It is interesting to compare two extreme views, of two contemporary witnesses, of *Mallet du Pan* in Mercure Britannique, saddling the *philosophes* with all the responsibility for what happened in the Revolution, and of *Mounier*, who denied them all influence on the Revolution, *Cambr. Mod. Hist.*, Vol. VIII, p. 1.

The writings of *Sieyès* relevant to the subject and analysed here are : Qu'est-ce que le Tiers État ?—ed. Champion, Paris 1888 ; Vues sur les moyens d'exécution, Paris 1789 ; Essai sur les privilèges, ed. Champion, Paris 1888 ; Sieyès's dogmatism—Vues, pp. 33–4 ; 30 (effroyable expérience) ; Tiers État, p. 73 ; Vues, p. 29 (l'art plus hardi) ; Tiers, pp. 61 ff. ; Vues, p. 29 (Britain) ; " c'est que le despotisme a partout commencé par des faits " (Vues, p. 27) ; " c'est l'erreur qui est nouvelle auprès de l'ordre éternel des choses" (Vues, p. 26) ; Revolutionary attitude—Tiers, pp. 56 ff., 72 ; 78 ("Inutilement, le tiers état attendait-il du concours de toutes les classes, la restitution de ses droits politiques et la plénitude de ses droits civils ; la peur de voir réformer les abus inspire aux deux premiers ordres plus d'alarmes qu'ils ne sentent de désirs pour la liberté.

Entre elle et quelques privilèges odieux, ils ont fait choix de ceux-ci. Leur âme s'est identifiée avec les faveurs de la servitude. Ils redoutent aujourd'hui ces états généraux qu'ils invoquaient naguère avec tant d'ardeur. Tout est bien pour eux ; ils ne se plaignent plus que de l'esprit d'innovation ; ils ne manquent plus de rien ; la crainte leur a donné une constitution "). Scission—Tiers, p. 83.

A. Mathiez, La place de Montesquieu dans la pensée politique du XVIIIème siècle, Annales Historiques de la Révolution Française, 1932. Prevention of old forces' return—Tiers, pp. 40 ff., 71. This is an opportunity to point out a further potentiality in Sieyès's thinking : the idea of exercising a check upon the way of voting is the father of Sieyès's post-Thermidorian plan of a Constitutional Jury, a body of censors of the national will, having the right to a final testing, above the Legislative Assembly. G. Lefebvre, Les Thermidoriens Paris, 1946, pp. 170 ff.

Section (b)—Popular Sovereignty, pp. 73–5

The suspension of all laws and institutions by the people in assembly, Tiers, p. 73, constituting the very act of Revolution, goes back of course to Rousseau, see Note on section (d), ch. iii, Pt. I.

The Extraordinary Assembly—Tiers, pp. 68–73 ; Vues, p. 51. Who is the nation ?—Tiers, pp. 72, 86–88, 74 (volontés individuelles), 77 ; 80 (Estates general) ; Tiers, pp. 28–34 (the nobles of Franconia).

Here is a further pointer to future developments. Although Sieyès speaks with much vehemence on the sacredness of human rights, he is in fact more impressed by competence, power, than by bare natural right. This is vital for the defence of the property census for elections, see next Note ; and it goes some way to explain the ease with which Sieyès was able to switch over from democratic principles to the support of authoritarian competence in politics.

Equality—Privilèges, pp. 4, 9–14 ; Tiers, p. 88 (simile of globe). On the dictatorial character of the juridical Revolution propounded by Sieyès—Albert Mathiez, La Révolution française et la théorie de la dictature, Revue Historique, 1929, J. CLXI, pp. 304–15, reprinted in Le Directoire, Paris 1934, pp. 1–17.

Section (c)—Property, pp. 75-9

Sieyès—Tiers, pp. 89 (n'enfle), 88 (globe) ; Vues, pp. 11, 13 ; " La liberté du citoyen consiste dans l'assurance de n'être ni empêché, ni inquiété dans l'exercise de sa propriété personnelle et dans l'usage de sa propriété réelle. La liberté du citoyen est la fin unique de toutes les lois " (Vues, p. 11). " Propriété personnelle, ce premier de tous les biens, de tous les droits, sans lequel les autres ne sont qu'illusoires " (p. 13) ; Privilèges, p. 2, very much like the formulæ of Locke and Rousseau on the Social Contract ; uneasy reflection—Tiers, p. 38 ; active, passive citizens—Préliminaire de la Constitution Franç., p. 20 ; *Jaurès*, Hist. Soc., Vol. II, p. 10 ; " Tous les habitants d'un pays doivent y jouir des droits de citoyen passif ; tous ont droit à la protection de leur personne, de leur propriété, de leur liberté, etc., mais tous n'ont pas droit à prendre une part active dans la formation des pouvoirs publics ; tous ne sont pas citoyens actifs. Les femmes, du moins dans l'état actuel, les enfants, les étrangers, ceux encore qui ne contribueraient en rien à soutenir l'établisse-ment public ne doivent point influer activement sur la chose publique. Tous peuvent jouir des avantages de la société ; mais ceux-là seuls qui contribuent à l'établissement public sont comme les vrais actionnaires de la grande entreprise sociale. Eux seuls sont les véritables citoyens actifs, les véritables membres de l'association." (Préliminaires, p. 21.)

The fear of undermining respect for property was the main theme of the opposition in the Debate on the Declaration of Rights and on the seizure of Church property—*Aulard*, Hist. Polit., pp. 39 ff. ; *Jaurès*, Vol. I, pp. 341 ff. ; II, pp. 70 ff.

CHAPTER II. BALANCE OR REVOLUTIONARY PURPOSE—UNDER THE CONSTITUTIONAL MONARCHY

Section (a)—Legality and the Supremacy of the Revolutionary Purpose, pp. 78-80

The standard works on the French Revolution utilized for this part are *Alphonse Aulard*, Histoire politique de la Révolution Française, Paris 1901 ; *Albert Mathiez*, La Révolution Française, Paris 1922 ;

J. M. Thompson, The French Revolution, Oxford 1944 ; *E. Lavisse*, Histoire de la France Contemporaine, La Révolution, T. I (P. Sagnac), T. II (G. Pariset), Paris 1920 ; Cambridge Modern History, Vol. VIII— French Revolution, Cambridge 1904 ; *Louis Villat*, La Révolution et l'Empire, 1789–1815, Paris 1936 (Clio, Vol. 8) ; *Lord Acton*, Lectures on the French Revolution, London 1910 ; *Georges Lefebvre*, La Révolution Française (Peuples et Civilisations, Vol. XIII), Paris 1930 ; *Daniel Guerin*, La lutte de classes sous la première République, " Bourgeois et Bras nus ", 1793–7, Paris 1946 ; *Jean Jaurès*, L'Histoire Socialiste de la Révolution Française, ed. A. Mathiez, Paris 1922.

Aulard, pp. 49 ff, offers the fullest analysis of the legislative work of the National Assembly from the point of view of the basic ideological principles ; *Jaurès* is very comprehensive for the social problem as revealed in the debates on the electoral census and on ecclesiastical property ; brings very long extracts and quotations, which are real gems.

Jaurès, Vol. II, pp. 1, 7, points out that in the debate on franchise not one deputy so much as enquired what would be the number of the disfranchised. About the weakness and paucity of reaction to the disfranchisement, all historians are agreed. *Aulard*, p. 70 ; *Thompson*, French Revolution, p. 124.

Mathiez, Directoire, pp. 2 ff., 17 f., 19 f.—on the dictatorial break-throughs in the Revolution ; *Mathiez*, Rev. Franç., Vol. II, p. 1, and *Villat*, La Révolution et l'Empire, p. 159, consider the events of August 10th and the subsequent developments as the real Revolution. On the coup of August 10th and the dictatorship of the Commune, see *P. St. Claire Deville*, La Commune de l'an II, Paris 1946. It is a study in totalitarian Revolutionary dictatorship exercised by what may legitimately be called the Soviet of the capital. *Gerard Walter*, Le problème de la dictature jacobine, Annales Historiques de la Révolution Française, November 1931, pp. 515–29.

The attitude of the upholders of the idea of legality and balance is illustrated by *Barnave* (*Mathiez*, Rev. Franç., Vol. I, p. 175) in the debate of July 15th, 1791, on the flight of the King : " je place ici la véritable question : Allons-nous terminer la Révolution, allons-nous la recommencer ? Vous avez rendu tous les hommes égaux devant la loi, vous avez consacré l'égalité civile et politique, vous avez repris pour l'État tout ce qui avait été enlevé à la souveraineté du peuple, un pas de plus serait un acte funeste et coupable, un pas de plus dans la ligne de la liberté serait la destruction de la royauté, dans la ligne de l'égalité : la destruction de la propriété." The opposing attitudes of the Girondists and Jacobins are brought out in the two pronouncements of the two opposing leaders, *Vergniaud* and *Robespierre*, in a form that is almost poignant, in the Debate of April 10th, 1793. As we shall have many opportunities of analysing Robespierre's attitude and shall refer to many of his speeches, we quote here only Vergniaud. " Nous, modérés ? . . . Si, sous prétexte de révolution, il faut, pour être patriote, se déclarer le protecteur du meurtre et du brigandage, je suis modéré. Depuis l'abolition de la royauté, j'ai beaucoup entendu parler de révolution. Je me suis dit : il n'y en a plus que deux possibles : celle des propriétés ou la loi agraire, et celle qui nous ramènerait au despotisme. J'ai pris la ferme résolution de combattre l'une et l'autre et tous les moyens indirects qui pourraient nous y conduire. Si c'est là être modéré, nous le sommes tous car nous avons voté la peine de mort contre tout citoyen qui proposerait l'une ou l'autre. J'ai beaucoup entendu parler d'insurrection, de faire lever le peuple, je l'avoue, j'en ai gémi. . . . Si l'insurrection a un objet déterminé, quel peut-il être ? De transporter l'exercise de la souveraineté dans la République. Donc, ceux qui parlent d'insurrection veulent détruire la représentation nationale ; donc ils veulent remettre l'exercice de la souveraineté à un petit nombre d'hommes ou la transporter sur la tête d'un seul citoyen " (quoted in *Lefebvre*, La Révolution Française, Cours de Sorbonne, La Convention, Vol. II, pp. 7, 8).

Vergniaud seems to be up against something that he cannot grasp. What is it that they want ? The Revolutionary purpose as a socialist ideal ? The Montagnards have abjured any attempt on property. Sovereignty of the people ? The Convention and its non-Montagnard majority had been elected on universal suffrage. After all that has been written on the differences and the lack of difference between the Girondists and the Montagnards, the real and all-determining one is that the latter, at least their Robespierrist wing, were driven by a Messianic urge-and vision, however vague, while the former lacked at that time already the sense of Messianic urgency and thus simply could not understand Robespierre, and thought him and his followers hypocrites, knaves and fools.

Jeanbon de Saint-André offers the Jacobin answer, in a letter to Barère of 26/III/1793—" La chose publique, nous le disons expressément, est prête à périr, et nous avons presque la certitude qu'il n'y a que les remèdes les plus prompts et les plus violents qui puissent la sauver. Quand on annonça pour la première fois, au sein de la Convention, cette vérité salutaire que nous étions une assemblée révolutionnaire, on eut la douleur

de la voir maladroitement ou perfidement méconnue. Des hommes
que nous n'avons pas besoin d'inculper, surtout dans l'intimité d'une
correspondance confidentielle, nous demandaient alors : ' Où voulez-
vous donc nous mener ? que reste-t-il à détruire ? La Révolution est
achevée et l'instrument révolutionnaire doit être brisé.' L'expérience
prouve maintenant que la Révolution n'est point faite, et il faut bien
dire ouvertement à la Convention nationale :   ' Vous êtes une assemblée
révolutionnaire.' . . . Nous sommes liés de la manière la plus intime
au sort de la Révolution, nous qui avons voulu la consommer. . . . On
ne pardonnera ni à vous ni à nous d'avoir voulu la liberté pure et sans
mélange, et nous devons conduire au port le vaisseau de l'État, ou périr
avec lui . . ." (*Villat*, pp. 205-6). Jeanbon de Saint-André frankly
and painfully admits that only a minority supported the Revolution.
The conclusion as to the necessity of the imposition of the Revolutionary
pattern on the hostile or indifferent majority by a militant minority was
inescapable.

Section (b)—Jacobinism—Mental and Psychological Elements, pp. 80-3

On Jacobins the monographs are : *Crane Brinton*, Jacobins, New York
1930 ; *Gerard Walter*, Histoire des Jacobins, Paris 1945 ; the same author,
Le problème de la dictature Jacobine, op. cit.

Brinton's work is a remarkable essay in the anatomy of a political
party.   The author seems to have chosen the Namier method of collating
statistical data, of group treatment, and sample comparisons for the
description of the structure of the Jacobin movement and their party
life.   The author's natural inclination to draw comparisons between the
Jacobins and the American political parties caused him often to misjudge
the peculiar spirit of Jacobinism.   *Gerard Walter*, admired as he may be
for his conscientiousness, industry as a collector of material, is not really
a historian, as has already been remarked by *J. M. Thompson* in his
review of *Walter's* Robespierre, in the English Historical Review, 1948.

Charles Vellay, Discours et Rapports de Robespierre, Paris 1908,
p. 326, Rapport sur les principes de morale politique qui doivent guider
la Convention, 18 Pluviôse, an II, 5 Février 1794)—" Nous voulons " ;
Robespierre, Défenseur de la Constitution, Nr. IV, pp. 174-5 : " Voilà
l'état de ce grand procès que nous plaidons à la face de l'univers. . . .
Qu'il juge entre nous et nos ennemis, qu'il juge entre l'humanité et
ses oppresseurs.   Tantôt ils feignent de croire que nous n'agitons que

des questions abstraites, que de vains systèmes politiques ; comme si les premiers principes de la morale, et les plus chers intérêts des peuples n'étaient que des chimères absurdes et de frivoles sujets de dispute." See precisely this accusation, the letter of the Girondist Salle to Dubois-Crance, in Note on section (a), ch. i, Pt. I.

"Eternal Providence has called you forth, only you since the beginning of the world to re-establish on earth the empire of justice and freedom, in the midst of the liveliest lights which have ever shone upon public reason, in the midst of almost miraculous circumstances which it has pleased it to bring about in order to give you the power of securing man his happiness, his virtues and his dignity"—(Vellay, p. 93) proclaimed Robespierre as early as in the debate on the marc d'argent on August 11th, 1791. The Revolution, he thought in 1789, had in a few days produced greater events than the whole previous history of mankind—Correspondance de Maximilien et Augustin Robespierre, G. Michon, 1926, p. 17 ; Lettre à ses Commettants, Nr. IV, ser. 1, p. 199. "Une conscience"—Robespierre, Vellay, p. 45 ; Buchez et Roux, Histoire parlementaire de la Révolution Française, Vol. X, pp. 28 ff. Answer to Guadet—Buchez et Roux, Vol. XIII, p. 445.

On Robespierre the outstanding biography is by J. M. Thompson, Robespierre, Oxford 1935 ; Gerard Walter, Robespierre, Paris 1946 ; R. Korngold, Robespierre, the First Modern Dictator, London 1937. Bibliography on Robespierre as statesman and thinker, see below. Robespierre's self-pity and sense of mission—Réponse à Brissot, Vellay, p. 170 : "Le ciel qui me donna une âme passionnée pour la liberté et qui me fit naître sous la domination des tyrans, le ciel qui prolongea mon existence jusqu'à règne des factions et des crimes, m'appelle peut être à tracer de mon sang la route qui doit conduire mon pays au bonheur et à la liberté ; j'accepte avec transport cette douce et glorieuse destinée" ; Vellay, pp. 381 ff. (Robespierre's last speech and apologia) ; Aulard, La Société des Jacobins, Paris 1889–97, Vol. II, p. 533 (nous mourrons tous avant toi !"—exclaims Desmoulins in the midst of delirious enthusiasm) ; Vol. III, p. 576 ; IV, pp. 573 f., 592 ; V, pp. 213, 251 ff., 245 ; VI, p. 154.

Saint-Just—Charles Vellay, Œuvres complètes de Saint-Just, Paris, Vol. I, p. 349 ("I have been ") ; II, p. 504 (" mœurs douces "—suicide) ; II, p. 494 ("J'ai laissé ") ; II, p. 305 (indictment of Danton) ; II, p. 76 (sword) ; II, pp. 377, 507 (idyllic).

Barère believed that Saint-Just " cut on a more dictatorial model, would have finished by overthrowing Robespierre and putting himself in his place . . . he was deeper and a cleverer revolutionist than Robespierre " (*Bertrand Barère*, Memoirs (Eng. trans.), London 1896, Vol. II, p. 139 ; IV, pp. 333 ff.) ; *E. N. Curtis*, Saint-Just, Colleague of Robespierre, New York 1935, p. 346. Similarly *Levasseur de Sarthe* says that from his first-hand knowledge he would " dare to affirm that Saint-Just had a larger part in them (the events) than Robespierre himself. He was " the more terrorist of the two " (*René Levasseur de Sarthe*, Mémoires, Bruxelles, 1830, Vol. III, p. 73—*Curtis*, translation, ibid.) ; *Levasseur*, Vol. I, p. 223.

Vellay's Œuvres complètes de Saint-Just, in two volumes, is a very handy collection and contains all that is relevant to our purpose. There is a spate of books on Saint-Just, mostly of a hagiographic character. The best recent study is *E. N. Curtis*, Saint-Just, Colleague of Robespierre, New York 1935. *D. Centore-Bineau*, Saint-Just, Paris 1936, and *P. Gignoux*, Saint-Just, Paris 1946, do not add very much to the painstaking, detailed work of *E. Hamel*, Histoire de Saint-Just, Bruxelles 1860. A serviceable survey is *P. Deroncle*, Saint-Just, ses idées politiques et sociales, Paris 1937. Useful is also *Crane Brinton*, The political ideas of Saint-Just, in Politica, 1934, Vol. I., No. 1 ; *S. B. Kritschewsky*, Rousseau und Saint-Just, Ein Beitrag zur Entwicklungsgeschichte der sozial-politischen Ideen der Montagnards, Berne 1895, deals with a special aspect. *J. M. Thompson's* profile of Saint-Just in Leaders of the French Revolution, Oxford 1929, is highly readable. *P. Tahard*, Le révolutionnaire idéal selon Saint-Just, Europe 1939.

Sources for *Robespierre* used in this work are : *Charles Vellay*, Discours et Rapports de Robespierre, Paris 1908 ; *A. Vermorel*, Œuvres de Robespierre, Paris 1886 ; *Albert Lapomeraye*, Œuvres de Robespierre, Paris 1834 ; Défenseur de la Constitution par M. Robespierre (period of Legislative Assembly) ; Lettres de M. Robespierre à ses Commettants, in 2 series (period of Convention) ; *E. B. Courtois*, Rapport fait au nom de la commission chargée de l'examen des papiers trouvés chez Robespierre et ses complices, Paris 1795 ; Papiers inédits trouvés chez Robespierre, Saint-Just, etc., supprimés ou omis par Courtois, Paris 1828 ; Le Carnet de Robespierre, in *Mathiez*, Robespierre Terroriste, Paris 1921 ; Correspondance de Maximilien et Augustin Robespierre, ed. G. Michon, Paris 1926 ; *Alphonse Aulard*, La Société des Jacobins, Recueil de documents pour l'histoire des Jacobins de Paris, Paris 1889-97 ; *Buchez et Roux*, Histoire parlementaire de la Révolution Française, Paris 1834-8 ; the *Croker* collection of Robespierre pamphlets at the British Museum ; *L'Ancien Moniteur* (réimpression de), Paris 1840-5 ; *Archives Parle-*

mentaires, J. Movidal et E. Laurent, Paris 1867. The most recent studies on Robespierre as a political thinker are by *Alfred Cobban*, The political ideas of Maximilien Robespierre during the period of the Convention, English Historical Review, January 1946 ; the same author's Fundamental Ideas of Robespierre, E.H.R., Jan. 1948 ; *Richard Schatz*, J. J. Rousseau's Einfluss auf Robespierre, Leipzig 1905 ; *Thompson's* Robespierre ; *A. Mathiez*, Autour de Robespierre, Paris 1925 ; the same author, Robespierre Terroriste, Paris 1921 ; same, Girondins et Montagnards, Paris 1930 ; same, Études Robespierristes, Paris 1917, are indispensable. *Thompson* gives in the first pages of his Robespierre a detailed bibliography, with special reference to the materials to be found in the British Museum.

Section (c)—The Definition of the General Will, pp. 83–6

Robespierre's hand is recognizable in the circular sent by the Jacobin Club in Paris to the popular societies which instructed them to draw up lists of patriotic citizens worthy of public office, excluding any persons who are " cold, egotistical or indifferent to the republic, revolution ", for such men " would have been condemned to death by the law of Athens ; in our country they are condemned to political death by public opinion "—*Thompson*, Robespierre, Vol. II, p. 107.

Robespierre, Défenseur de la Constitution, Nr. IV, p. 163—the duty of every citizen ; Saint-Just, L'Esprit, *Vellay*, Vol. I, pp. 342 ff—on volonté générale ; I, pp. 327, 304—Liberté ; Comp. *Mably*, Phocion, p. 84, Note ; Robespierre, *Vellay*, p. 31 ; 175 (" La majorité veut le bien ; mais elle ne connait ni les moyens . . . ni les obstacles . . . ainsi l'opinion publique s'énerve et désorganise ; la volonté générale devient impuissante et nulle ") ; Saint-Just's later definition—*Vellay*, Vol. I, pp. 428, 429 (" cette liberté ").

Section (d)—The Idea of Balance—Saint-Just, pp. 86–90

Robespierre, *Vellay*, p. 93—purpose ; Saint-Just, *Vellay*, Vol. I, pp. 264 (coalisé), 265 (French and English), 277, 281 (chef d'œuvre), 274 f. (checks), · 266 f., 272 (equality), 285 (property), 271 (the disfranchised), 265 (ancient and modern liberty), 315 (death penalty) ; 344.

Section (e)— Robespierre and the Revolutionary Purpose—the Idea of the People, pp. 90–7

Popular self-expression—Robespierre, *Vellay*, pp. 31, 96, 97 (l'intérêt du peuple), 257 (pour être bon), 317 ; Défenseur, Nr. IV, p. 173 ; *Buchez et Roux*, Vol. V, p. 186 (" nous sommes au moment où toutes les vérités peuvent paraître, où toutes seront accueillies par le patriotisme) ; X, p. 5 (" tout être collectif ou non qui peut former un vœu a le droit de l'exprimer ").

Dignity of man—*Vellay*, pp. 258–61, 70, 96–99 ; Défenseur, Nr. IV, p. 169 ; XII, pp. 591–2 ; Lettre à ses Commettants, I, Ser. 1, pp. 13 ff. ; Government a standing plot—*Vellay*, pp. 257 f. (l'ambition), 55 ; Lettre à ses Commettants, I, Ser. 1, p. 7 ; VII, Ser. 2, p. 338 f. ; I, 2, p. 52 f.; Jacobins, Vol. IV, p. 84 ; Tribunate—*Vellay*, p. 261 f.

Principle of elections—*Vellay*, p. 20 ; *Buchez et Roux*, Vol. VI, p. 227 (bishops to be elected by clergy and laymen) ; free press— *Vellay*, p. 31 ; death penalty—*Vellay*, p. 70 ; Protecting the people from governments—*Vellay*, p. 259 f. ; Lettre à ses Commettants, I, Ser. 2, p. 53 ; " C'est dans la vertu " ; British system—*Vellay*, pp. 12 ff., 261, 93 (" des aggrégations d'hommes plus ou moins eloignés des routes de la raison et de la nature, plus ou moins asservies, sous des gouvernements que le hasard, l'ambition ou la force avaient établis ") ; Robespierre and constitutional measures ; Royal inviolability—*Vellay*, pp. 79 ff ; veto—*Buchez et Roux*, Vol. II, p. 451 ; III, p. 98 ; Royal prerogatives— *Buchez et Roux*, VI, p. 67 ; military matters—*Buchez et Roux*, VIII, p. 256 ; IX, p. 339 ; *Croker*, Vol. IV, pp. 8–13, 35, 46, 51–3 ; popular riots and collision between authorities and people—Défenseur, Nr. IX, p. 488 ; *Croker*, IV, p. 35 ; *Buchez et Roux*, IX, p. 243 ; Jacobins, I, p. 62, II, pp. 305, 316, 490 ; III, p. 320 ; IV, p. 84.

Against corporations—Jacobins, III, p. 320 (" un corps armé distinct des citoyens ") ; *Buchez et Roux*, Vol. VI, p. 227 (episcopal elections) ; Défenseur, IV, pp. 181 ff. ; *Croker*, IV, pp. 8–13, 46 ; Nat. Guard, *Vellay*, pp. 5, 7 ; 21 (jury ; to be paid) ; People—" J'entend par le peuple généralité des individus qui composent la société " (*Buchez et Roux*, IX, p. 340) ; Social split—" J'ai entendu déjà distinguer le peuple et la nation . . . pour moi ces mots synonymes "—*Vellay*, p. 231 ; *Vellay*, pp. 5, 7, 20, 23, 235 ; Franchise—*Vellay*, pp. 89 ff., 102 f ; Right of petition for poor—*Buchez et Roux*, X, p. 5 ; proprietors, men— Défenseur, IX, pp. 500–1 ; Gardes nationales—*Vermorel*, pp. 185 ff ; " On veut diviser la nation en deux classes, dont l'une ne semblerait armée

que pour contenir l'autre, comme un ramas d'esclaves toujours prêts à
se mutiner ! Et la première renfermerait tous les tyrans, tous les
oppresseurs, toutes les sangsues publiques ; et l'autre le peuple ! Vous
direz après cela que le peuple est dangereux à la Liberté !" (ibid., p. 190) ;
ibid. pp. 192–3 ; "l'intérêt du peuple est l'intérêt général, celui des riches est
l'intérêt particulier "—*Vellay*, p. 97 ; Idealization of people—*Vellay*, p.
96–98 ; Défenseur, Nr. IV, p. 173 (quotation) ; " Le peuple, cette classe
immense et laborieuse, à qui l'orgueil réserve ce nom auguste qu'il croit
avilir, le peuple n'est pas atteint par les causes de dépravation qui perdent
ce qu'on appelle les conditions supérieures. L'intérêt des faibles, c'est la
justice " (ibid.).

The silent war—Défenseur, Vol. IX, p. 488. ; *Croker*, Vol. IV, pp.
47 ff. (on Gardes Nationales as potential weapon of counter-revolution) ;
" qu'on ne me pardonne de n'avoir pu concevoir comment les moyens du
despotisme pouvaient assurer la liberté "—*Lapomaraye*, Vol. I, p. 66.
(Robespierre on Loi Martiale, 22, II, 1790) ; *Lapomaraye*, I, pp. 69 ff.—
" deux partis " ; " devons-nous déshonorer le patriotisme en l'appelant
esprit de sédition, et honorer l'esclavage par le nom d'amour de l'ordre
et de la paix ? " (p. 71).

Vellay, pp. 174 ff., 175—Constitution accepted—in spite of its faults,
at present a " point d'appui et un signal de ralliement " against counter-
revolutionary provocation ; 180 ff.—acceptance of Monarchy ; better
than rule of intrigues under guise of Republic, form immaterial ;
realities count ; Jacobins, Vol. III, pp. 12, 420.

On external war—Robespierre, *Vellay*, pp. 119, 123, 124–36 ;
Défenseur, Nr. VIII, p. 375 (" Il est deux espèces de guerre ; celle de
la liberté, celle de l'intrigue et de l'ambition ; celle du peuple ; celle
du despotisme ") ; pp. 376 ff. ; Défenseur, I, pp. 27, 32 ff ; King's
flight—*Vellay*, p. 73.

Trial of Louis XVI—Robespierre, *Vellay*, pp. 211, 212 (" Louis ne
peut être jugé ; il est déjà condamné, ou la République n'est point
absolute !") pp. 213 ff., 222, 240 ff. *Thompson* on Revolutionary justice.
Robespierre, Vol. I, pp. 94 ff. ; Saint-Just, speeches on King's trial—
Vellay, Vol. I, pp. 365 ff., 386 ff., 369 f. (reign innocently).

Distinction between offence against individuals and crimes against
nation : " Ici commence un nouvel ordre d'idées, absolument distinct
de l'ordre judiciaire . . . c'est la cause de la société contre un individu.
Quel en sera le juge ? La société elle-même. La société sera donc
juge et partie ? Oui, ainsi le veut la nature des choses . . . la raison
éternelle . . . interprète de ses jugements . . . la majorité des membres

qui composent le corps social" (Lettre à ses Commettants, Nr. V,
Ser. II, pp. 196–7) ; Saint-Just, *Vellay*, II, 228–9.
Desmoulins, Vieux Cordelier, Nr. 4, December 20th, 1793, 30 Frimaire,
an II ; "Je n'ai jamais su décomposer mon existence politique pour
trouver en moi deux qualités disparates, celle du juge et celle de l'homme
d'état. . . . Tout ce que je sais, c'est que nous sommes les représentants
du peuple envoyés pour cimenter la liberté publique par la condamnation
du tyran, et cela me suffit"—Robespierre, *Buchez et Roux*, Vol. XXIII,
p. 179.

CHAPTER III. VOLONTÉ UNE

Section (a)—Direct Democratic Action, pp. 98–107

Representative despotism—*Robespierre*, Défenseur, Nr. V, p. 217
(would not go the whole way with Rousseau) ; Défenseur, XI, pp.
525 ff., 529 ff., 543 (presqu' autant d'ennemis qu'il a nommé de mandataires), 547 ; Lettre à ses Commettants, I, Ser. 1, p. 12. ; Commettants, II,
Ser. 1, p. 30 ; Commettants, IX, Ser. 1. p. 386 ; Défenseur, V, p. 225 ;
Vellay, pp. 134, 262 ; opposition to appeal to people on Louis XVI
—*Vellay*, p. 230 f ; Lettre à ses Commettants, I, Ser. 1, pp. 5 ff. (à
Vergniaud, Gensonné etc.), as likely to cause confusion in the masses,
whereas in Défenseur, XI, p. 532, he called for summoning the Assemblées
primaires to elect a Convention, scoffing the idea of the people being
misled by aristocrats : " croire qu'une si grande multitude de sections du
peuple puisse être séduite ou corrompue ! Si quelques-unes pouvaient
être égarées, la masse serait, à coup sûr dirigée par le sentiment du bien
commun et par esprit de la liberté " ; pp. 536–8 ; Measures against
representative despotism—Défenseur, XI, pp. 536 ff ; *Vellay*, pp. 264–70 ;
Cabal Legislative—Executive engineering elections—*Vellay*, pp. 96–9,
235, 317 ; *Buchez et Roux*, XXII, p. 463 ; Défenseur, XI, p. 524 ;
IV, p. 172 ; III, p. 138 ; *L'Ancien Moniteur*, VIII, p. 90 ; IX, p. 407.
"Un peuple dont les mandataires ne doivent compte à personne
de leur gestion, n'a point de Constitution . . . trahir impunément
. . . J'avoue que j'adopte tous les anathèmes contre lui . . . par
J. J. Rousseau"—Robespierre, *Vellay*, pp. 264–5 ; "Laissez les ténèbres
et le scrutin secret aux criminels et aux esclaves. Les hommes libres
veulent avoir le peuple pour témoin de leurs pensées"—ibid., p. 270.

Majority—minority—*Vellay*, pp. 242–3 ; Défenseur, Nr. V, p. 222 f. " La vertu fut toujours en minorité sur la terre " (*Vellay*, p. 243). " Je ne connais point ici ni minorité, ni majorité. La majorité est celle des bons citoyens, la majorité n'est point permanente, parce qu'elle n'appartient à aucun parti ; elle se renouvelle à chaque délibération libre, parce qu'elle appartient à la cause publique et à l'éternelle raison " (242). *Buchez et Roux*, Vol. XXII, p. 463 (against Roland)—"Je ne connais d'autre majorité que celle qui se forme dans l'Assemblée, et non dans les conciliabules secrets et les dîners ministeriels et quand une influence ministérielle quelconque a formé les décrets d'avance, fomenté les motions, arrangé tout par l'intrigue, la majorité n'est qu'apparente et illusoire."

Direct popular action—Défenseur, Nr. XI, p. 527 f. : " L'assemblée nationale, en déclarant les dangers de la patrie, qu'elle n'a point prévenus, a déclaré sa propre impuissance. Elle a·appelé la nation elle-même à son secours. . . . La nation doit pourvoir elle-même à son salut, au défaut de ses représentants." The people of Paris as the mandatory of the people of France—*Vellay*, pp. 198–9 ; Lettre à ses Commettants, Nr. VII, p. 304 ; *Vellay*, pp. 314–15 ; Jacobins, Vol. V, p. 254.

" It is vital "—Jacobins, III, p. 673 ; Robespierre's speech, 26 Mai 1793 —*Buchez et Roux*, Vol. XXVII, p. 243 ; of May 29th, 1793—Jacobins, V, p. 213—*Buchez et Roux*, XXVII, pp. 297 ff. The minutes of the Jacobin Club do not give the full speech of 26 Mai ; the complete version is to be found in the Journal Courrier des 83 Départements. " To engage their sections "—Jacobins, IV, p. 193 ; Robespierre leading deputation —*Buchez et Roux*, XVII, pp. 79 ff.

Robespierre's rôle in 1792—*Thompson*, Vol. I, Robespierre, pp. 250– 260 ; On the technique of insurrection and the Revolutionary Commune —*Deville*, La Commune de l'an II, Paris 1946 ; *Lavisse*, Vol. I, pp. 370 ff. ; II, pp. 95 ff. ; Robespierre and demands of 1793—Jacobins, V, pp. 180, 181—" En prenant toutes ces mesures sans fournir aucun prétexte de dire que vous avez violé les lois " (8/V/1793) ; *Buchez et Roux*, Vol. XXV, p. 43 ; XXVI, p. 383 (8/V/1793) ; *Thompson*, II, pp. 12 f., 20–3 ; *Deville*, pp. 72 ff., 177 ff.

Robespierre in June 8th, 1793—*Buchez et Roux*, XXVIII, p. 169 ; Answer to Louvet—*Vellay*, pp. 197 ff. ; " Excès de ferveur patriotique ? —le patriotisme est ardent par sa nature. Qui peut aimer froidement la patrie ? " (*Vellay*, pp. 314, 315) ; *Vermorel*, p. 190. ; Défenseur, Nr. XII, p. 567 ff ; The people : The avalanche !—*Vellay*, pp. 134 f., 213 ; Lettre à ses Commettants, II, Ser. 1, p. 55 (" le peuple vaut toujours mieux

que les individus : or que sont les dépositaires de l'autorité publique ? " ;
I, p. 13 (" que le peuple est bon ") ; I, Ser. 2, p. 30 ; VI, Ser. 2, p. 285
(" Le peuple est toujours pur dans ses motifs " ; " il ne peut aimer que
le bien public, puisque le bien public n'est que l'intérêt du peuple ").
" Il n'y a rien d'aussi juste ni d'aussi bon que le peuple, toutes les
fois qu'il n'est point irrité par l'excès de l'oppression "—*Vellay*,
p. 97.

On the Constitution of 1793—*Aulard*, Histoire politique, pp. 280–314,
contains a detailed account of the debates and an analysis of the various
projects as well as of the final account ; *Alfred Stern*, Condorcet und der
Girondistische Verfassungsentwurf von 1793, Historische Zeitschrift,
CXLI, p. 3. *Albert Mathiez*, La Constitution de 1793, Annales Historiques
de la Révolution Française, Vol. V, 1928, reprinted in Girondins et
Montagnards, 1930.

Saint-Just—*Vellay*, Vol. I, pp. 426–8, 418 ff.

It is only true that Condorcet's project contained still more plebis-
citarian features, *Aulard*, loc cit., *Stern*, loc. cit. Robespierre as architect
of patriotic voting—*Thompson*, Vol. I, pp. 265 ff. ; Vote on Constitution
of 1793—*Villat*, p. 234 ; Appeal on fate of Louis XVI—Robespierre,
Vellay, p. 230 f. ; Against replacing Convention and new elections—
Buchez et Roux, Vol. XXVI, p. 47 (17 April, 1793, before the expulsion of
Girondists). After expulsion and vote on Constitution 1793, Robespierre
resisted any attempt to " substituer aux membres épurés de la Convention
actuelle les envoyés de Pitt et de Cobourg " (*Villat*, p. 242).

Sections—*Buchez et Roux*, XXII, p. 467 (opposing dissolution—
they are the people, made the Revolution alone capable of securing
order—" les, le peuple entier qui ne peut point appartenir à une faction,
quelque puissante qu'elle soit ") ; *Ancien Moniteur*, Vol. XV, p. 75 ;
Robespierre, *Vellay*, p. 264 (respectez surtout la liberté du souverain
dans les assemblées primaires . . . supprimant ce code énorme qui
entrave et qui anéantit le droit de voter, sous prétexte de le régler ").
Against permanence of Sections—June 14th, 1792, *Thompson*, Vol. II,
p. 55 (" The intriguers and the rich will spin out the meetings ; the
poor man will have to leave, to go to work "). When the Convention
decided that there shall be only two Section meetings a week, a host of
sectional popular societies sprang up at the instigation of the Hébertists
and Enragés, as there was no legal limitation on the frequency of meetings of popular societies. Robespierre vehemently attacked these
" assemblées des clubs de Section " (Jacobins, Vol. V, p. 504), and called
for strictest control over them ; Jacobins, V, p. 580 ; *Buchez et Roux*,

Vol. XXVI, p. 47 ; Catechism—*Courtois*, Papiers inédits—Robespierre, Vol. II, p. 13 f. ; *Espinas*, La philosophie Sociale, p. 148.

Section (b)—Liberty as an Objective Purpose, pp. 107–111

For state of France, see *Mathiez*, Rev. Franç., Vol. III, chs. i, iii, especially on the social problem ; *Lefebvre*, Rev. Franç., pp. 206 ff. ; *Mathiez*, La vie chère et la question sociale sous la Terreur. Saint-Just—*Vellay*, Vol. I, pp. 373 ff., 409 (" Il faut ") ; Allure commune—I, p. 374 ; République une et indivisible—I, p. 457 ; The electoral system, I, pp. 426, 432, 457 (droit de cité) ; 431 (concours simultané) ; *Hedvig Hintze*, Staatseinheit und Föderalismus im alten Frankreich und in der Revolution, Stuttgart 1928 ; *Curtis*, p. 73— Guffroy was the deputy ; Saint-Just, *Vellay*, I, pp. 354–5.

Albert Sorel, L'Europe et la Révolution Française, Paris, Vol. II, pp. 84 ff., 105 ff., 518 ff., 531 ff., ; III, pp. 111, 144, 153, 164 ff., 172, 197 ff, 250, 278 ff, 307 ff. ; *Heinrich von Sybel*, Geschichte der Revolutionszeit, Düsseldorf, 1866, Vol. I, pp. 253 ff. ; II, pp. 37 ff., 55 f., 276. *Georges Lefebvre*, Révolution Française, Cours de la Sorbonne. Convention, Vol. I, pp. 136–78. Carnot defining the natural (geographical and historical) concept of nation—*Sorel*, III, p. 310.

Section (c)—The Right of Opposition ; Outlawing of Parties, pp. 111–18

Saint-Just—*Vellay*, Vol. II, pp. 75 ff. In a way the speech could be taken as an answer to those who after the adoption of the Constitution of 1793 claimed that the Convention, having accomplished its task— created a Constitution—should dissolve and make room for a Legislative Assembly elected on the basis of the new Constitution, to rule the country in accordance with this new Constitution ; 83.

" Vous ne parlerez "—II, pp. 378, 238, 247 ; " démocratie "—II, pp. 378, 230 ff, 258 f.

Marat—" Il n'y a donc que les cultivateurs, les petits marchands, les artisans et les ouvriers, les manœuvres et les prolétaires, comme les appelle la richesse insolente, qui pourront former un peuple libre ", *Jaurès*, Vol. II, p. 228.   Saint-Just's references to democracy—*Vellay*, Vol. II, pp. 259, 265. " There is no government "—Saint-Just, *Vellay*, II, p. 375 ; Tyrants must be oppressed—76 ; the people will inherit the earth—II, pp. 247,

381 f. ; Robespierre, *Vellay*, p. 333 (There are no) ; *Buchez et Roux*, Vol. XXXI, p. 277 ; Robespierre, *Vellay*, pp. 332–3 (" domptez "). *Robespierre*, Lettre à ses Commettants, Nr. I, Ser. 2, p. 7—" Avant l'abolition de la noblesse et de la royauté, les intriguants " ; Commettants, II, Ser. 1, pp. 57–8.

Saint-Just, *Vellay*, Vol. II, pp. 268 (right to opposition), 262 ; Robespierre, *Vellay*, p. 333 ; Saint-Just—II, pp. 265, 506—" On se trompe ", 506 (force, terreur) ; II, pp. 83, 275 (" Un patriote "), 379, 238, 258 (isolationism), 382 (" Lorsque la liberté "), 230 (" l'idée particulière ").

Robespierre, *Vellay*, p. 332 (" La terreur n'est ") ; Saint-Just, Vol. II, pp. 506 (" que veulent ") ; 530 ; The counter-revolutionaries—Robespierre, *Vellay*, p. 314 ; Jacobins, V, pp. 181, 185, 350 (" journalistes odieux ").

Parties—Saint-Just, II, pp. 271–4 ; as to himself—Saint-Just, II, pp. 477 ; 237—" dictature de justice " ; pp. 386, 483 (pride), 484 (factions may fall) ; Robespierre, *Vellay*, pp. 133, 167 (" Je ne suis ni le courtisan, ni le modérateur, ni le tribun, ni le défenseur du peuple ; je suis peuple moi-même ! ") ; Défenseur, Nr. III, p. 149 (" tout parti est funeste à la chose publique ; et il est de l'intérêt de la nation de l'étouffer comme il est du devoir de chaque citoyen de le dévoiler ") ; *Robespierre*, Lettre à ses Commettants, Ser. 2, VII, p. 328 ; Jacobins, Vol. VI, p. 5 ; *Buchez et Roux*, Vol. XXV, p. 47.

Robespierre, Défenseur, Nr. IV, pp. 162 ff.—the whole struggle reduced to " premières règles de la probité, et dans les plus simples notions de la morale. Toutes nos querelles ne sont que la lutte des intérêts privés contre l'intérêt général, de la cupidité et de l'ambition contre la justice et contre l'humanité . . . adopter dans les affaires publiques les principes d'équité et d'honneur que tout homme probe suit dans les affaires privées et domestiques—véritable objet de notre révolution " (162), 164.

" Il faut une volonté une "—*Courtois*, Papiers inédits trouvés chez Robespierre, etc., Nr. XLIV, p. 15 ; *Deville*, La Commune, p. 44, suggests 16–19 Mai 1793 as the date of the note.

Robespierre, *Vellay*, p. 171 (à Brissot), " toute faction tend de sa nature à immoler l'intérêt général à l'intérêt particulier . . . sur les ruines de toutes les factions doivent s'élever la prospérité publique et la volonté nationale—voilà ma politique, voilà le seul fil qui puisse guider . . . quels que soient le nombre et les nuances des différents partis, je les vois tous ligués contre l'égalité et contre la Constitution ".

Robespierre—" Il n'y a plus que deux partis en France : le peuple et ses ennemis. . . . Celui qui n'est pour le peuple, est contre le peuple ;

celui qui a des culottes dorés, est l'ennemi né . . . que deux partis . . . corrompus . . . vertueux . . . amis de la liberté, égalité . . . défenseurs des opprimés . . . fauteurs de l'opulence (Jacobins, Vol. V, pp. 179, 180) ; Robespierre, *Vellay*, pp. 384 (" des bons et des mauvais citoyens "), 382 (" The factions are ") ; *Buchez et Roux*, Vol. XLIV, pp. 212 ff. ; Unanimity—*Buchez et Roux*, XXXII, p. 73 ; " wherever a line of demarcation "—*Buchez et Roux*, XXXIII, p. 200 (it was on June 20th, 1794, in the debate of the terrible Loi de Prairial, which set out to dispense with hearing of witnesses at the Revolutionary Tribunal, and with the prior consent of the Convention to bring before the Tribunal members of the Convention). How would democracy work ?—Saint-Just, II, *Vellay*, pp. 508–9 ; *Robespierre*—Défenseur, IV, p. 162 ; Jacobin Club —Saint-Just, *Vellay*, Vol. II, p. 536; Robespierre—*Buchez et Roux*, Vol. XXXIII, pp. 212–13 ; Défenseur, VII, p. 319 ; Correspondance, 166 bis (" Incorruptible ") ; *Thompson*, Vol. II, p. 107.

Section (d)—The Theory of Revolutionary Government, pp. 118–21

Theory of Revolutionary Government — Robespierre, *Vellay*, pp. 311 ff. ; *Buchez et Roux*, Vol. XXV, p. 43 ; 46 (barrier) ; *Ancien Moniteur*, Vol. XV, pp. 674, 688 ; " Commission épurée "—*Buchez et Roux*, XXV, p. 45. The two opposite genii—Robespierre, *Vellay*, p. 332 ; " plus son pouvoir ; mains impures "—*Vellay*, p. 315.

The impure at the top—*Buchez et Roux*, Vol. XXXII, p. 71–2 (on Danton, Petion, etc.) ; " Je n'ai pas nommé Burdon (who had interrupted him to ask to name the attacked men). Malheur à qui se nomme lui-même . . . Je les nommerai . . . " (*Buchez et Roux*, XXXIII, p. 214) ; " Je dis que quiconque tremble en ce moment est coupable ; car jamais l'innocence ne redoute la surveillance publique . . . les hommes coupables craignent toujours de voir tomber leurs semblables, n'ayant plus devant eux une barrière de coupables . . . exposés au jour de la verité " (*Buchez et Roux*, XXXII, pp. 71–2) ; Jacobins, VI, p. 214 f. " Il faut guillotiner "—*Villat*, p. 255.

Section (e)—Jacobin Dictatorship, pp. 122–31

An account of the emergence of Jacobin dictatorship and its structure —*Villat*, pp. 219 ff. ; *Mathiez*, Rev. Franç., Vol. III, chs. iv, vi, vii ;

Lavisse, Vol. II, pp. 170 ff. ; *Lefebvre*, pp. 212 ff. Robespierre—Carnet, in *Mathiez*, Robespierre Terroriste, p. 72—" d'envoyer dans toute la République un petit nombre de commissaires forts, munis de bons instructions, et surtout de bons principes, pour ramener tous les esprits à l'unité et au républicanisme . . . à découvrir et à inventarier les hommes dignes de servir la cause ".

Billaud-Varenne—" En gouvernement comme en mécanique, tout ce qui n'est point combiné avec précision, n'obtient qu'un jeu embarrassé. . . . Trois principes dans ses mouvements : la volonté pulsatrice, l'être que cette volonté vivifie, et l'action de cet individu sur les objets environnants, ainsi tout bon gouvernement doit avoir un centre de volonté, des leviers qui s'y rattachent immédiatement, et des corps secondaires sur qui agissent ces leviers afin d'étendre ces mouvements jusqu'aux dernières extrêmités " (*Lavisse*, Vol. II, p. 175) ; Danton —*Mathiez*, Rev. Franç., III, p. 76 ; *Villat*, p. 267 ; Carnot—*Villat*, p. 279 ; fall of the Hébertists—*Mathiez*, Rev. Franç., Vol. III, pp. 150 ff.

Revolutionary justice—the authorities quoted ; in addition *Arne Ording*, Le Bureau de police du Comité de Salut Public, Oslo 1930.

A. Mathiez, La terreur et la politique sociale des Robespierristes ; the same author, Les Séances des 4 et 5 Thermidor an II aux deux Comités de Salut Public et de sûreté générale, both printed in Girondins et Montagnards (important on the significance of the Lois de Ventôse).

Robespierre—*Buchez et Roux*, Vol. XXVIII, pp. 477, 202, 212. Jacobin confraternity—*Crane Brinton*, The Jacobins, passim ; *Gerard Walter*, L'Histoire des Jacobins, passim.

Robespierre on " colérer "—*Courtois*, Papiers inedits, pièce XLIV, p. 16 ; *Desmoulins* on Inquisition, Annales Révolutionnaires, Vol. I, p. 255. ; " Burning is no answer "—Jacobins, V, pp. 597-9 ; " Quand un homme se tait au moment où il faut parler, il est suspect "—Robespierre, Jacobins, VI, p. 213 ; Purging—Jacobins, V, p. 504—" Je demande que chaque société populaire s'épure avec le plus grand soin, et que les Jacobins n'accordent leur affiliation ou leur correspondance qu'à celles qui auront subi rigoureusement cette épreuve " ; " que tous les députés suppléants arrivés à Paris . . . fassent à la tribune leur profession de foi sur tous les événements de la Révolution " (p. 561).

Saint-Just's indictment speeches against Girondists—*Vellay*, Vol. II, pp. 1-31, Danton (ibid., pp. 305-32), Hérault de Séchelles (ibid., pp. 286-8).

Robespierre's ascendancy—Jacobins, Vol. VI, 155 (an obscure member Rousselin suggests civic honours to citizen Geffroy who saved Robespierre by getting the bullet which was meant for Robespierre ; the latter suspects an attempt to ridicule him and has Rousselin expelled at once) ; Jacobins, V, p. 645 ; Virtue on the agenda—" De tous les décrets qui ont sauvé la République, le plus sublime, le seul qui l'ait arrachée à la corruption et qui ait affranchi les peuples de la tyrannie, c'est celui qui met la probité et la vertu à l'ordre du jour. Si ce décret était exécuté, la liberté serait parfaitement établie "—Robespierre, Jacobins, VI, p. 210.

The Jacobin hierarchy of the elect are " le boulevard de la liberté publique. . . . Un Montagnard n'est autre chose qu'un patriote pur, raisonnable et sublime. . . . La Montagne n'est autre chose que les hauteurs du patriotisme. . . . La Convention, la Montagne, le Comité c'est la même chose," the real thing. " Every representative of the people who sincerely loves liberty ; every representative of the people who is determined to die for his country is of the Mountain." " The Jacobin Society is by its very nature incorruptible ; in it public opinion is forged, strengthened and purified." *Robespierre*, Défenseur, VIII, pp. 319 ff ; *Thompson*, II, 18, 107 ; Correspondance, 166 bis ; *Buchez et Roux*, XXVI, 47.

From the freedom of peoples to choose, to their duty to choose freedom —*Sorel*, L'Europe et la Revolut., loc. cit., especially Vol. III, pp. 162 ff., 232 ff. ; *Lefebvre*, Cours de la Sorbonne, Rev. Franç., Convention, Vol. I, pp. 229 ff. ; *Lavisse*, II, pp. 32 ff.

Cambon—" La nation française, en entrant dans un pays, poursuivant, chassant les despotes, use du pouvoir révolutionnaire. Nous ne permettons pas qu'un individu, qu'une collection d'individus usurpe cette souveraineté," *Sorel*, III, pp. 311, 12.

Brissot on pouvoir révolutionnaire—*Lefebvre*, Cours, Convention, Vol. I, 237 ; *Ed. Burke*, Letters on a Regicide Peace, London 1893, pp. 16, 121–22.

CHAPTER IV. THE ULTIMATE SCHEME

Section (a)—The Postulate of Progress and Finality, pp. 132–5

Victory—Robespierre, Jacobins, Vol. VI, p. 212.

Goodness of man—*Robespierre's* Lettre à ses Commettants, Nr. II, Ser. 1, p. 49 : " L'homme est bon, sortant des mains de la nature, Quiconque nie ce principe, ne doit point songer à instituer l'homme :

Si l'homme est corrompu, c'est donc aux vices des institutions sociales qu'il faut imputer ce désordre. . . ." ; p. 50 : " Si la nature a créé l'homme bon, c'est à la nature qu'il faut le ramener. Si les institutions sociales ont dépravé l'homme, ce sont les institutions sociales qu'il faut réformer " ; p. 51 ; Robespierre, *Vellay*, p. 255 ; " toute institution qui ne suppose pas le peuple bon et le magistrat corruptible, est vicieuse " (ibid., p. 253) ; *Saint-Just*, Vol. II, 385, 485, 503 ; Hope and anxiety—Robespierre, Commettants, II, 1, p. 50 ; " It is time "—Robespierre, *Vellay*, pp. 324, 325 ; Saint-Just, *Vellay*, Vol. II, p. 497 (difficult science ?) ; *Robespierre* —paraphrase Rousseau—*Vellay*, p. 255 ; Saint-Just, *Vellay*, I, p. 420—all arts ; Robespierre, *Vellay*, 349—" D'où vient ? "

Robespierre, *Vellay*, pp. 327, 93, 255 ff. (apocalyptic), 350 (France in advance of all), 325 (destinies of liberty), 256 : " l'anarchie a régné en France depuis Clovis jusqu'au dernier des Capets ", 349 (" tout doit changer "), 30 (freedom of press) ; Lettres à ses Commettants, VI, 2, pp. 241–8 ; *Thompson*, Vol. II, p. 1 (" great exception ") ; Robespierre, *Vellay*, pp. 349 ff. (march by détours) ; " Those who in the infancy " —Robespierre, *Vellay*, p. 351 ; Last speech of Robespierre, *Vellay*, p. 379 ff. ; Jacobins, Vol. VI, p. 210 (" very few ") ; Saint-Just, *Vellay*, II, p. 508 (" No doubt ") ; Elation and anxiety—Saint-Just, *Vellay*, II, p. 485 ; I, p. 419 ; II, pp. 183, 385, 476, 491 ; Robespierre, *Vellay*, p. 277 ; *Défenseur*, III, pp. 113 ff. ; Jacobins, V, p. 27 ; Robespierre, *Buchez et Roux*, XXXII, p. 45 ; " Doux et tendre espoir de l'humanité, postérité naissante, tu ne nous est point étrangère ; c'est pour toi que nous affrontons tous les coups de la tyrannie ; c'est ton bonheur qui est le prix de nos pénibles combats ; découragés souvent par les objets qui nous environnent, nous sentons le besoin de nous élancer dans ton sein ; c'est à toi que nous confions le soin d'achever notre ouvrage, et la destinée de toutes les générations d'hommes qui doivent sortir du néant ! Postérité naissante, hâte-toi de croître et d'amener les jours de l'égalité, de la justice et du bonheur ! "—Robespierre, *Vellay*, p. 155 ; *Becker*, Heavenly City, chose this passage to illustrate the eighteenth-century religion. Posterity takes place of eternal bliss.

Section (b)—The Doctrinaire Mentality, pp. 135–8

Robespierre, Jacobins, Vol. VI, pp. 214, 212 (" The Revolution ", " institutions sages ") ; *Vellay*, pp. 327 ff.—democracy ; Lepeletier's scheme—*Villat*, p. 240. *Michael Oakshott*, Rationalism in Politics (Cambridge Journal, 1947, Vol. I, Nos. 2, 3).

Section (c)—The Reign of Virtue, pp. 139–43

On Power—Saint-Just, *Vellay*, Vol. II, pp. 386 (" power is "), 507 (" one wants ") ; I, p. 422 (" gentle tyrant ") ; I, p. 421 (not force) ; I, p. 419 (" Every people for virtue ") ; II, p. 507 (the harmonious natural pattern, and freedom) ; II, p. 386 (force for " state of simplicity ") ; Compare Robespierre, *Vellay*, pp. 257, 253 ; *Ancien Moniteur*, VI, p. 631 (" fuyez la manie ancienne des gouvernements de vouloir trop gouverner, laissez aux individus . . . familles ") ; *Vellay*, p. 263.

Robespierre on the revolutionary order—*Vellay*, pp. 327 ff., 351 (two sorts of egoism), 329, 330, 352 (" le but ", " à quoi se réduit ? "), 350 (" passage du règne des crimes à celui de la justice ") ; Saint-Just, *Vellay*, Vol. II, p. 501 (education) ; II, pp. 330, 331 (the virtuous people) ; 328, 329 ; The aim—Robespierre, *Vellay*, pp. 325 f., 348 (Sparta).

Section (d)—Saint-Just's Institutions Républicaines, pp. 143–6

Saint-Just on Institutions Républicaines, *Vellay*, II, pp. 230 (" Un état "), 385 (" C'est par là "), 477, 485, 491 (Thermidorian speech), 487. The Scheme of Institutions—ibid., pp. 495–507 ; " We have to substitute "—ibid., pp. 495, 506, 507 (Dans le premier), 230, 502 (single official) ; Où est la cité ?—ibid., pp. 264, 270 ff., 503 (lâche plaisir) ; Religion—ibid., pp. 524 ; 508 (Révolution glacée).

The expression Institutions Républicaines is to be found already in Rousseau and Mably.

Saint-Just proposing dictatorship—*Barère*, Memoirs (Engl. transl.) ; Vol II, pp. 174–5 ; *Mathiez*, Girondins et Montagnards, pp. 160, 163 ; *Guerin*, Vol. II, pp. 273–6.

Section (e)—The Civil Religion and Condemnation
of Intellectuals, pp. 146–8

Robespierre, *Vellay*, p. 366—attack on intellectuals ; a rapid instinct —ibid., p. 361 f. ; Attack on the Encyclopædists for persecuting Rousseau—Défenseur, Nr. II, p. 97 ; à la honte—*Vellay*, p. 365 f. ; Helvetius' bust—Jacobins, IV, p. 550 ; " What silences "—Robespierre, *Vellay*, p. 361 ; On religion—*Vellay*, pp. 359–69 ; Lettre à ses Commettants, VIII, 2, 337–49 ; *Buchez et Roux*, Vol. XXX, pp. 278, 287, 322 ; XIII,

445 ; XXV, p. 5 ; Vermorel, pp. 337 ff. ; Saint-Just, *Vellay*, Vol. II,
p. 524.
   Mathiez, Rev. Franç., Vol. III, p. 177, takes a rather crude view of the
issue ; *Thompson*, Robespierre, I, p. 216, recognizes the ancient Jewish
character of Robespierre's belief in Providence ; *D. Guerin*, La Lutte de
Classes, Vol. I, ch. ix, pp. 405 ff. ; vii, pp. 425 ff. "Les charlatans toujours
nécessaires ", the heading is enough to give an idea of Guerin's approach :
" L'attitude déiste des déchristianiseurs découlait d'ailleurs de cette
carence fondamentale ; ils n'osèrent s'attaquer à l'idée de Dieu parce
qu'ils ne voulurent et ne purent toucher à l'ordre social qui entretenait
le besoin de Dieu."

CHAPTER V. THE SOCIAL PROBLEM

Section (a)—The Inconsistencies, pp. 149–52

   On the social and economic problems of the Revolution—*Albert
Mathiez*, La vie chère et le mouvement social sous la Terreur, Paris
1927 ; *Georges Lefebvre*, Les paysans du Nord pendant la Révolution
française, Paris 1924, a work of stupendous erudition and research ;
Jean Jaurès, Histoire Socialiste . . ., devotes maximum attention to the
economic realities and social and economic thought in the Revolution.
His quotations, as usual, are most illuminating ; *Georges Lefebvre*, La
Révolution et les paysans, Europe 1939, 378–90 ; *Edouard Dolléans*,
La Révolution et le Monde Ouvrier, ibid., 390–407 ; *Daniel Guerin*,
Espinas, *Laski*, The Socialist Tradition, *Maxime Leroy*, have already
been referred to. ᷐ Their works are devoted to the growth of socialist
thought, as is of course *A. Lichtenberger*, Le Socialisme et la Révolution.
   A special Economic History of the French Revolution remains to be
written, and it is to be hoped that M. Labrousse will continue his great
work, to cover the whole period of the Revolution in all its social and
economic aspects.
   On the Enragés see *Mathiez*, Vie chère, pp. 121 ff., 135 ff., 224 ff. ;
Guerin, Vol. I, ch. i, pp. 71 ff., ch. ii, 118 ff., ch. iv. v.
   On Dolivier—*Jaurès*, Hist. Socialiste, Vol. VIII, pp. 211 ff. ;
III, p. 392 ; on Momoro—*Jaurès*, IV, p. 327 ; *Lichtenberger*, Le Socialisme,
p. 94 ; on Lange—*Jaurès*, VI, pp. 128–51. There is nevertheless a definite
Rousseauist feature in Varlet's thought. He speaks of the " constant

will " of the majority of the nation—the poor—to live and not to be oppressed and exploited. " Dans tous les États, les indigents forment la majorité ! . . .", *Jaurès*, VII, p. 36 f.

A special study on the influence of ancient social conflicts and ancient social radicalism upon eighteenth-century and Revolutionary thought is called for.

To quote only two utterances made as early as 1790 ; on the growing social rift : Petion on scission—" Le Tiers État est divisé ; la bourgeoisie, cette classe nombreuse et aisée, fait scission avec le peuple. . . . La bourgeoisie et le peuple réunis ont fait la Révolution ; leur réunion seul peut la conserver . . ." (*Jaurès*, Vol. III, p. 333 f.) ; Mallet du Pan—" Le jour est arrivé où les propriétaires de toutes classes doivent sentir enfin qu'ils vont tomber à leur tour sous la faux de l'anarchie. . . . héritage sera la proie du plus fort. Plus de loi, plus de gouvernement, plus d'autorité qui puissent disputer leur patrimoine aux indigents hardis et armés qui, en front de bandière, se préparent à un sac universel " (*Jaurès*, III, p. 388).

Saint-Just and laissez-faire—*Vellay*, Vol. I, pp. 373, 375, 385 ; the unforeseen results—II, pp. 238 ff. ; " renverser l'empire de la richesse "— *Villat*, p. 286.

The Enragés were incensed by Saint-Just's earlier speech, and decried him in a poster as one of those who " dine well every evening ". " Levez haut le masque odieux ", *Mathiez*, Vie chère, pp. 140 ff. ; *Jaurès*, Vol. VII, p. 31.

Section (b)—Class Policy, pp. 152–4

Fatal contradiction—St. Just, *Vellay*, Vol. II, pp. 238 ff.

Robespierre's catechism—what is our aim ?—internal danger from bourgeoisie—*Courtois*, Papiers inédits, Vol. II, pp. 13–15.

Growth of economic dictatorship—*Mathiez*, Vie chère, Pt. II, chs. iii, iv, vii, ix ; Pt. III, chs. i–iii, ix ; *Villat*, pp. 225 f., 251 f.

Billaud-Varenne, Éléments de Républicanisme, *Lichtenberger*, pp. 121–2 ; *Chaumette*—Mathiez, Rev. Franç., Vol. III, p. 74 ; *Jaurès*, Vol. VIII, p. 271 f. ; *Guerin*, Lutte, Vol. I, pp. 168 ff.

Saint-Just as economic dictator, when representative of the people —Orders of 3 Nivôse, an II, 28 January 1793, at Strassbourg, *Vellay*, Vol. II, p. 160 ; 9 Pluviôse, an II, 28 January 1793, at Lille, *Vellay*, II, p. 186 ; 15, 17, 24 Brumaire at Strassbourg, *Vellay*, II, pp. 132, 138, 143–6.

Section (c)—Fundamental Questions, pp. 154–60

Robespierre's speeches on Supplies—Lettres à ses Commettants, IX, 2, pp. 391 ff. ; Declaration of Rights, *Vellay*, pp. 245–254 ; the old ways—*Robespierre*, Commettants, Nr. IX, pp. 392–5 ; principes du droit de propriété—Robespierre, *Vellay*, p. 247 ; "véritable principe" —Robespierre—*Buchez et Roux*, Vol. XXII, p. 177 ; "vous commencez une nouvelle carrière où personne ne vous a devancés", ibid., p. 176.

Saint-Just—"quelques coups", *Vellay*, Vol. II, p. 238 ; Institut. Republic., II, pp. 511, 514 ("doctrine which puts these principles"); "pour réformer mœurs"—p. 513 ; *Robespierre*—wealth national, surplus —individual—Lettres à ses Commettants, Nr. IX, pp. 396 ff. ; moral principle of property—*Vellay*, pp. 247 ff. (Declaration of Rights) ; *Vermorel*, pp. 183, 192–3 (inequality ; right of bequest).

Saint-Just, *Vellay*, Vol. II, p. 79 ("the bread") ; II, p. 238 ("Les malheureux") ; p. 241 (Revolution not fully accomplished) ; p. 248 ("que l'Europe") ; p. 238 (right of property and political loyalty) ; pp. 242, 248 (Ventôse laws).

Lois de Ventôse—*Mathiez*, La Terreur et la politique sociale des Robespierristes ; Les séances des 4 et 5 Thermidor an II.

On the reception given by the people to the Laws of Ventôse— *Lichtenberger*, p. 171 : Latour-Lamontagne reports : " dans tous les groupes, dans tous les cafés . . . joie universelle . . . c'est à présent, disait on, que la République repose sur des bases inébranlables ; aucun ennemi de la Révolution ne sera propriétaire, aucun patriote ne sera sans propriété . . . Comme colons Romains. . . ."

The radical utterances of Robespierre as political opportunism— *Aulard*, Hist. Polit., p. 291 ; *Guerin*, Lutte de Classes, pp. 233 ff. ; Robespierre—if people hungry . . .—Jacobins, Vol. V, p. 44 ; *Buchez et Roux*, Vol. XXVIII, pp. 410–11 ; Vol. XXIX, 25 ; yet condemnation of Enragés—Jacobins, Vol. V, pp. 330, 336 (scélérats, déguisés sous l'habit respectable de la pauvreté).

Saint-Just : follow father's business and do not make politics— *Vellay*, Vol. II, p. 267 ; S.-J.—"il faut calmer" : II, p. 369 ; not class consciousness, but against wealth that is evil—Défenseur, Nr. XII, p. 591— " Combien le peuple fut grand dans toutes ses démarches . . . Riches, égoistes, stupides vampires, engraissés de sang et de rapines, osez donc encore donner au peuple le nom de brigand ; osez affecter encore des craintes insolentes pour vos biens méprisables, achetés par des bassesses ;

osez remonter à la source de vos richesses, à celle de la misère de vos
semblables ; voyez, d'un côté, leur désintéressement et leur honorable
pauvreté ; de l'autre, vos vices et votre opulence, et dites quels sont les
brigands et les scélérats. Misérables hypocrites, gardez vos richesses
qui vous tiennent lieu d'âme et de vertu ; mais laissez aux autres la
liberté et l'honneur " ; Jacobins, Vol. V, p. 44—" le peuple souffre, il n'a
pas recueilli le fruit de ses travaux ; il est encore pérsecuté par les riches " ;
Robespierre's embarrassment—*Vellay*, pp. 246 ff. : âmes de boue ;
opposition to—Jacobins, VI, p. 43 ; Aristide, Crassus—Défenseur, IV,
p. 176 ; " Chétive marchandise "—Jacobins, V, p. 44 ; Wealth is its
own punishment—Jacobins, V, p. 179 ; " L'opulence est une infamie "—
Saint-Just, *Vellay*, II, p. 514 ; " La République ne convient "—*Buchez
et Roux*, XXV, p. 337 ; the Girondist endeavour to frighten the " haves ",
ibid. The bogy of communism and loi agraire—" Ne les a-t-on pas vus,
dès le commencement de cette révolution, chercher à effrayer tous les
riches, par l'idée d'une loi agraire, absurde épouvantail, présenté à des
hommes stupides, par des hommes pervers ? Plus l'expérience a démenti
cette extravagante imposture, plus ils se sont obstinés à le reproduire,
comme si les défenseurs de la liberté étaient des insensés capables de
concevoir un projet également dangereux, injuste et impraticable ; comme
s'ils ignoraient que l'égalité des biens est essentiellement impossible dans
la société civile ; qu'elle suppose nécessairement la communauté qui est
encore plus visiblement chimérique parmi nous ; comme s'il était un
seul homme doué de quelque industrie dont l'intérêt personnel ne fut
pas contrarié par ce projet extravagant. Nous voulons l'égalité des
droits, parce que sans elle, il n'est ni liberté, ni bonheur social : quant
à la fortune, dès qu'une fois la société a rempli l'obligation d'assurer à
ses membres le nécessaire et la subsistance par le travail. . . . Les richesses
qui conduisent à tant de corruption sont plus nuisibles à ceux qui les
possèdent que à ceux qui en sont privés " (Défenseur, Nr. IV, p. 175) . . .
" l'égalité des biens est une chimère " (Robespierre—Declr., *Vellay*,
p. 246) ". . . moins nécessaire encore au bonheur privé qu'à la félicité
publique. Il s'agit bien plus de rendre la pauvreté honorable que de
proscrire l'opulence " (ibid.) ; *Vermorel*, pp. 185 ff., 189.

Section (d)—Economic Restrictionism and Individualism, pp. 160–4

Saint-Just, *Vellay*, Vol. II, p. 509—on the social aspect of virtue ;
Robespierre—on Communism, see Section (c).

Saint-Just on social security—*Vellay*, II, pp. 506, 508 ; 516, 522, 528, 533-5.

Happiness of Persepolis, and bliss of Sparta—Saint-Just, *Vellay*, II, 267 ; in the Institutions (*Vellay*, II, p. 513) saddles the counter-revolutionary adventurer Baron Batz with responsibility for having been the first to throw out the idea of maximum.

It has been pointed out by Jaurès that in one sense the opponents of the Jacobins were more progressive than Robespierre, Saint-Just and their followers. Whereas the latter, adhering to social and ethical asceticism, had no insight into the forces and significance of the gathering Industrial Revolution, no understanding for economic expansion, diversification of human needs, and the growth of production and consumption as an expression of a higher civilization, men like Sieyès and Vergniaud (*Jaurès*, Vol. VIII, p. 123) displayed a much more modern attitude. Sieyès thus wrote (*Jaurès*, II, p. 10) : " Les peuples Européens modernes ressemblent bien peu aux peuples anciens. Il ne s'agit parmi nous que de commerce, d'agriculture, de fabriques etc. Le désir des richesses semble ne faire de tous les États de l'Europe qu'un vaste atelier ; on y songe bien plus à la production et à la consommation qu'au bonheur. Aussi les systèmes politiques aujourd'hui sont exclusivement fondés sur le travail ; à peine sait-on mettre à profit les facultés morales qui pourraient cependant devenir la source la plus féconde des véritables jouissances. Nous sommes donc forcés de ne voir dans la plupart des hommes que des machines de travail." This status would have appeared in the eyes of a Robespierre or a Saint-Just as the worst possible degradation of man and citizen, which no gains of mass production and industrial organization could offset.

" Ne pas admettre "—Saint-Just, *Vellay*, Vol. II, p. 537 (Fragments) ; Marat—*Jaurès*, II, p. 248.

Jaurès (VI, pp. 118 ff.) quotes an astonishing petition of November 19th, 1792, by the Gobelins Sections containing, besides demands for the " taxing " of grains, a maximum price for commodities of first necessity, enforced sales, a central provisions bureau conducted by elected officials, a " loi agraire des fermages " as distinct from a " loi agraire des propriétés ", to promote agricultural production, and lower agricultural prices. Nobody was to have at his disposal more than 120 arpents. Similar demands are to be found in peasant cahiers on the eve of the Revolution (*Jaurès*, III, p. 392). The demand for limiting the size of holdings on the land had its counterpart in demands to prohibit the ownership of more than one shop or workshop.

Although Marat could on more than one occasion incite the poor to pillage shops and stores, in a true Enragé fashion (*Jaurès*, VII, p. 41 f.), his condemnation of the Enragés at other times was couched in terms that any Girondist and bourgeois would have approved. He described their demands as "mesures . . . si excessives, si étranges, si subversives de tout bon ordre, . . . tendent . . . à détruire la libre circulation des grains et à exciter des troubles". "Si l'utopie de Saint-Just est encore la dernière contrefaçon de Sparte, celle de Babeuf est la première cité collectiviste"—has been well said by *Lichtenberger*, Socialisme, p. 6.

PART III. THE BABOUVIST CRYSTALLIZATION

CHAPTER I. THE LESSONS OF THE REVOLUTION AND OF THERMIDOR

Section (a)—The Messianic Climate, pp. 167-70

A full bibliography on Babeuf is given in *Maurice Dommanget*, Pages Choisies de Babeuf, Paris 1935, a wholly admirable collection of texts. The relevant primary sources used in this work are (works by Babeuf) : Correspondance de François Noël Babeuf avec Dubois de Fosseux . . . de 1785 à 1788, which forms part II of Vol. II, of *Victor Advielle*, Histoire de Gracchus Babeuf et du Babouvisme, d'après de nombreux documents inédits, Paris 1884, in itself more a source-book than a history ; Cadastre Perpétuel ou Démonstration . . . pour assurer les principes de l'Assiette et de la Répartition . . . d'une Contribution unique ; co-author Audiffred, Paris 1789 ; Du Système de dépopulation, ou la vie et les crimes de Carrier, Paris, an III, 1795 ; Opinion d'un citoyen des tribunes du club ci-devant électoral sur la nécessité et les moyens d'organiser une véritable société populaire, published by G. *Lecocq*, Un Manifeste de Gracchus Babeuf, Paris 1885 ; Défense Générale de Gracchus Babeuf devant la Haute-Cour de Vendôme, in *Advielle*, Vol. II, Pt. I ; and minor writings and manuscript material to be found in *Dommanget*, Pages Choisies, and in *Albert Thomas*, La Doctrine des Égaux. Extraits des œuvres complètes, Paris 1906 ; G. *Deville*, Notes inédites de Babeuf sur lui-même, La Revol. Franç., Vol. XLIX, 1905.

Journals : Journal de la Liberté de la Presse ; Le Tribun du peuple ou le Défenseur des Droits de l'Homme par Gracchus Babeuf ; L'Éclaireur du peuple, ou le Défenseur de 24 millions d'opprimés.

Primary sources for the Conspiracy ; *Philippe Buonarroti*, Conspiration pour l'égalité dite de Babeuf, suivie du procès auquel elle donna lieu, et les pièces justificatives, Bruxelles 1828 ; The English translation by *Bronterre O'Brien* (the famous Chartist), History of Babeuf's Conspiracy for Equality, London 1836, has been very helpful. The documents published by the Directoire : Copie des Pièces saisies dans le local que Babeuf

occupait lors de son arrestation—Haute Cour de Justice ; Suite de la Copie des pièces ; Débats du procès instruit par la Haute Cour de Justice contre Drouet, Babeuf et autres, Vols. I, II, III, IV ; Extrait du procès-verbal des séances du Conseil des Cinq-Cents 23 Floréal, an IV ; Exposé fait par les Accusateurs Nationaux près la Haute Cour de Justice-Vieillart —6 Ventôse, an V ; added to it Pièces lues . . . par l'Accusateur ; Résumé du Président de la Haute-Cour de Justice, 2, 3, 4 Prairial.

Modern Works : *Alfred Espinas*, La philosophie sociale, etc. ; *M. Dommanget*, Babeuf et la Conjuration des Égaux, Paris 1922 ; *E. B. Bax*, The Last Episode of the French Revolution, London 1911 ; *David Thompson*, The Babeuf Plot, London 1947 ; *Albert Mathiez*, Le Directoire ; *Albert Thomas*, La pensée socialiste de Babeuf avant la conspiration des Égaux, La Revue Socialiste, 1904, Vol. XL ; 1905, Vol. XLI ; *Gerard Walter*, Babeuf 1760–97 et la Conjuration des Égaux, Paris 1937 ; *Georges Lefebvre*, Rapport-Temps Modernes, IX Congrès International des Sciences Historiques, Paris 1950, pp. 561–71 ; the same, Où il est la question de Babeuf, Annales d'Histoire Sociale, Tome VII, 1945, Hommages à Marc Bloch ; *A. Galante Garrone*, Buonarroti e Babeuf, Torino 1948.

Special aspects : *G. Thibout*, La Doctrine Babouviste, Paris 1903 ; *M. Dommanget*, La structure et les méthodes de la conjuration des Égaux, Annales Révolutionnaires, XIV, 1922 ; the same author, L'Hébertisme et la Conjuration des Égaux, An. Rev., XV, 1923 ; *Abel Patoux*, Le faux de Gracchus Babeuf, Saint-Quentin, 1913 ; *Paul Robiquet*, L'Arrestation de Babeuf, La Revol. Franç., Vol. XXVIII, 1895 ; the same author, Babeuf et Barras, Revue de Paris, 1896.

On *Buonarroti* : *Paul Robiquet*, Buonarroti et la Secte des Égaux, Paris 1910 ; *Georges Weill*, Philippe Buonarroti. Les papiers de Buonarroti, Revue Historique, 1901, 1905 ; *W. Hænisch*, La vie et les lettres de Philippe Buonarroti, Paris 1938 ; *Samuel Bernstein*, Buonarroti, Paris 1950.

On *Babouvism* of later days : *G. Sencier*, Le Babouvisme après Babeuf. Sociétés Secrètes et Conspirations Communistes—(1830–1848), Paris 1912 ; *G. Weill*, Le Parti républicain en France, 1814–70, Paris 1900 ; *I. A. Tchernoff*, Le Parti républicain sous la Monarchie de Juillet, Paris 1905.

" Forerunner "—*Advielle*, Vol. II, Correspondance 32 ; *Dommanget*, Pages, p. 49 ; " That modern philosophy "—*Advielle*, II, Corresp. 38, 47–8 ; " Morale demontrée "—ibid., 189 ; Babeuf's letter, March

21st, 1787—*Advielle*, II, Corresp. 117 ; Dubois's reply—ibid., 129 ; a
joke ?—ibid., 181 ; the arrangements in Utopia—*Advielle*, II, Corresp.,
120, 129, 169, 173, 175, 180 ; " Electrified " ; " Leur âme "—Pièces
saisies, Vol. I, p. 147 ; Similarly *Buonarroti*—Conspiration, Vol. I, p. 117 ;
Polemic with Antonelle—Tribun, XXXVII, 132, 136–7 ; Suite des pièces,
pp. 9–24 ; *Dommanget*, Pages, pp. 268 ff. ; " Avant la Révolution "—
Dommanget, Pages, p. 45, n. 1 ; *Deville*, Notes inédites ; " spoiled him "
—first letter to Coupé, *Dommanget*, Pages, pp. 110 ff. ; défaut inhérent—
Dommanget, p. 103 ; *Dommanget*, Pages, pp. 104–5 f. (Vanity ?) ; 240–1 ;
Tribun, XXXIV, 51–2 ; Tribun, Prospectus—5, 6 ; *Dommanget*, Pages,
pp. 230–1 ; suffering for Revolution—letter to Coupé, *Dommanget*,
p. 105 ; " publicisme—unique vocation "—ibid., p. 110. The names
Camille and Gracchus—Tribun, XXIII, 5 ; *Albert Thomas*, La Revue
Socialiste, 1905, Vol. XLI, p. 73. ; *Advielle*, Vol. I. p. 67.

Section (b)—The Lessons, pp. 170–2

On the Thermidorian and Directoire régimes *Albert Mathiez*, Le
Directoire ; *Georges Lefebvre*, Les Thermidoriens, Paris 1937 ; *Raymond
Guyot*, La Révolution Française, Livre III, 1795–1799 (Peuples et Civiliza-
tions), Paris 1930 ; *L. Villat*, La Revol. et l'Empire, Vol. I, Clio VIII,
1, Paris 1936. Also *Lavisse*, op. cit., II ; *D. Guerin*, op. cit. ; *A. Aulard*,
Hist. Polit.

Babeuf's early criticism of the régime, before he returned to the fold
of pure Robespierrism to become the preacher of Communist egalitarianism, is characteristic, and at times acute. It is to be found in his
Journal de la Liberté de la Presse, Nr. XVIII, 3, 4 ; XIX, 3 ; XX, 3 ;
XXI, 5 ; Tribun du Peuple, XXIX, 265–70; *Dommanget*, Pages, pp.
194–6 ; Tribun, XXVIII, 237–8, 240, 244 ; Tribun, XXIX, 265–8,
275–6 ; *Dommanget*, Pages, pp. 193–9 (contains an analysis of the failure
of the Left, with an assurance that it is destined to win) ; Tribun, XXX,
290–1; *Dommanget*, Pages, pp. 200–1 ; Tribun, XXXIV, 6–9 ; *Dommanget*,
Pages, pp. 233–36 ; *Advielle*, Vol. I, pp. 145–7 ; 168–9.

The Constitution of 1795, and Boissy d'Anglas—*Lavisse*, Vol. II,
pp. 274–5, 283 ; the adjective " Revolutionary " as title was banned—
ibid., p. 257.

Section (c)—Babeuf, pp. 172–5

"Je suis désespéré, ma bonne amie, de voir la détresse où je te laisse"—letter to his wife, Paris 16/VIII/1789—*Advielle*, Vol. I, pp. 57, 61.

Self-dramatization—for instance, Péroraison de la défense générale devant la Haute Cour (62 Séance, 28 Floréal, an V)—*Dommanget, Pages*, pp. 306 ff. ; *Espinas*, p. 390 ; *Advielle*, Vol. I, p. 314 ; " Moi déplacé "—first letter to Coupé, *Dommanget, Pages*, p. 103 ; " Atlas "— Prospectus of Tribun, 5–6 ; *Dommanget, Pages*, pp. 230–2 ; Tribun, XXXIV, 5 ; *Advielle*, I, p. 220 (letter to the Directory after his arrest) —megalomania. His failing at decisive moments—*Advielle*, Vol. I, p. 330 (a characteristic appreciation of Babeuf's appearance at the Court by the accuser), Vol. II, p. 302 ; Débats Haute Cour, Vol. II, p. 86.

About Babeuf's early years—*Advielle*, Vol. I, first part. Babeuf claimed to have been born on Christmas night, December 25th, 1760 . . . " dans une cabane . . . que le Rédempteur ", and to have therefore been christened Noël. In fact he was born on November 23rd, 1760. Of a similar trustworthiness is the story of his father having been a tutor to the former Emperor Joseph II of Austria, *Advielle*, Vol. I, p. 5. He was in fact a deserter from the French Army—*ibid*., p. 7. Fraud of all property claims—Tribun XXIX, 284–5. About the traditions of Picardy see *Lefebvre's* Introduction to *Dommanget's Pages*, p. 3, and G. *Lefebvre's* two articles just cited, Où il est la question de Babeuf, and his *Rapport*, IX Congrès International des Sciences Historiques. Humiliation by aristocracy—*Advielle*, Vol. I, pp. 43–5, 48 : invited by a Marquis in a flattering letter, he was asked to lunch with the servants.

Babeuf's enthusiasm at outbreak of Revolution—*Advielle*, Vol. I, p. 53 —contains an interesting instance of the way in which the " aristocratic plot " (*Lefebvre*, Quatre-vingt neuf), was reflected in the popular mind ; his reaction to the early atrocities (murder of Foulon, who was allegedly to replace Necker, and Bertier de Sauvigny, the Intendant of Paris), *ibid*., p. 55 : " Oh ! que cette joie me faisait mal ! J'étais tout à la fois satisfait et mécontent ; je disais tant mieux et tant pis. Je comprends que le peuple se fasse justice, j'approuve cette justice lorsqu'elle est satisfaite par l'anéantissement des coupables, mais pourrait-elle, aujourd'hui n'être pas cruelle ? Les supplices de tous genres, l'écartellement, la torture, la roue, les bûchers, le fouet, les gibets, les bourreaux multipliés partout, nous ont fait de si mauvaises mœurs ! Les maîtres, au lieu de nous policer, nous ont rendus barbares, parce qu'ils le sont eux-mêmes.

Ils récoltent et récolteront ce qu'ils ont semé, car tout cela, ma pauvre femme, aura à ce qu'il paraît, des suites terribles ; nous ne sommes qu'au début."

Babeuf's activities in his province—letter to Sylvain Maréchal, *Advielle*, Vol. I, pp. 105-9 ; *Espinas*, pp. 210 ff. (recounts all the prison sentences) ; *Dommanget*, Pages, pp. 91-7 ; 131 ff. ; " des frères souffrants et laborieux ne virent en moi qu'un ami compatissant et un protecteur, pour les riches égoistes je ne fus qu'un dangereux apôtre des lois agraires " (*Advielle*, I, p. 107). *Advielle*, I, pp. 93 ff.

The forger—Lettre à Menessier, 2 Frimaire, an II, *Dommanget*, Pages, pp. 147 ff. ; *Abel Patoux*, Le faux de Gracchus Babeuf ; *D. Thompson*, p. 15 ; *Espinas*, p. 217 f.

Extreme misery in Paris, invocation to Rousseau—*Advielle*, Vol. I, pp. 105 ff., 108 ; like Rousseau—*Dommanget*, Pages, p. 155 ; " Meurs si c'est ton plaisir "—*Advielle*, I, p. 221. Babeuf's last letters—*Dommanget*, Pages, pp. 309-19 ; *Advielle*, Vol. I, pp. 222-7, 337-41.

Section (d)—Buonarroti, pp. 175-8

The Histoire de la Conspiration appeared for the first time in 1828. *Lefebvre*, Rapports, IX Congrès, 1950, p. 561, quotes *Galante Garonne*, Buonarroti e Babeuf, Torino 1948, on the influence of the agricultural system of Corsica on Buonarroti's Communist ideas. *Buonarroti*, Observations sur Max. Robespierre, ed. Ch. Vellay, Chalons sur Saône 1912. *Carnot* in the Mémoires, written by his son—" le parti babouviste comptait des cœurs généreux comme Buonarroti " ; *Advielle*, Vol. I, p. 292 —tribute paid by accusateur Bailly to Buonarroti ; *Alexandre Andryane*, Souvenirs de Genève, Paris 1839, pp. 136-9, 154, contains glowing descriptions of Buonarroti of the first quarter of the nineteenth century ; *Robiquet*, Buonarroti, pp. 154-5 ; *A. Ranc's* Preface to his edition of *Buonarroti's* Gracchus Babeuf et la Conjuration, Paris 1869. *Buonarroti* said about himself : " Dès mon adolescence, un institueur, ami de Jean Jacques et d'Helvétius, m'inspira l'amour des hommes et de la liberté. J'agis, je parlai, j'écrivis conformément à ces préceptes et j'en reçus la récompense. Les grands me décrièrent comme scélérat ; les imbeciles metraitèrent de fou." " I am going "—*Robiquet*, Buonarroti, p. 243 ; The peoples advancing—*Ranc*, Introduct. to Conspiration, XI. ; *G. Weill*, Buonarroti, Revue Histor., 1905, Vol. LXXXVIII, p. 322 f.

CHAPTER II. BABOUVIST SOCIAL PHILOSOPHY

Section (a)—Equality and the Social Contract, pp. 179–81

Equality—*Buonarroti*, Vol. I, pp. 9 ff. (trans. Bronterre O'Brien, 11 n.) ; " to restrain ",—" The want of food "—ibid., 10 n., 11 n. *Babeuf* on equality in the Social Contract—Tribun, XXXIV, 12 ; *Dommanget*, Pages, p. 237 ; Tribun, XXXV, 102 ; (elixir) *Dommanget*, Pages, p. 255 ; Tribun, XXXV, 92 ; *Dommanget*, Pages, p. 255 ; *Advielle*, Vol. I, p. 393 (" aucun n'ait trop ") ; Babeuf refers to Diderot (meaning Morelly), Robespierre, Saint-Just, Raynal, Harmand de la Meuse, Antonelle ; *Advielle*, II, p. 34 ; Tribun, XXXV, 93–9 ; *Dommanget*, p. 256 ; *Buonarroti* : to Rousseau and Mably—in the first place, p. 9 ; *Advielle*, II, Défense 34 ; " stifling passions "—*Buonarroti*, 10 n. ; " This social order "—*Buonarroti*, p. 8 ; Réponse à M.V. (appearing as a reply from Babeuf, actually written by Buonarroti), *Buonarroti*, II, Pièces justificat, pp. 217 ff. ; Individualism—Pièces saisies, 182, 61 pièce, 7 liasse (Création d'un Directoire Insurrecteur, pp. 169–182) ; " Enchained fate " —Tribun, XXXV, 105 ; *Dommanget*, Pages, p. 261 ; *Advielle*, Vol. I, p. 395 (wrongly quotes Barère instead of Saint-Just as author of the slogan " puissances de la terre ") ; Letter to Germain, *Dommanget*, Pages, p. 207 ff.

Advielle, Vol. II, Défense, 34–5—Babeuf : " J'ait dit qu le code social qui a établi dans sa première ligne que le bonheur était le seul but de la société, a consacré dans cette ligne le type inattaquable de toute vérité et de toute justice. C'est là en entier la loi et les prophètes."

Section (b)—Vision of History as Vision of Class Struggle, pp. 181–4

Violation of Social Contract—Tribun, XXXIV, 13 ; *Dommanget*, Pages, p. 238 ; ." the most foolish "—*Buonarroti*, 12 n. ; Cadastre perpetuel, XXVI, XXVIII, XL ; different professions—Tribun, XXXV, 103 ; *Dommanget*, Pages, p. 259 ; *Advielle*, Vol. II, Défense 39 (a worker outdistancing others should be treated as a pest) ; Cadastre, XXX–XXXI ; feudalism—*Advielle*, II, Corresp. 190 ; *Dommanget*, Pages, p. 68 ; " good luck "—Cadastre, XXXIII ; superstructure—*Dommanget*, p. 259 ; Tribun, XXXV, 103 ; Commerce—Letter to Germain, *Dommanget* pp. 207 ff. ; Bizarre codes—*Advielle*, II, Corresp. 190–5 ; false teachings

320 NOTES

superstitions—Cadastre, XXXV ; *Dommanget, Pages,* p. 90—" peu de
nations se sont pénétrées de cette vérité, cependant infiniment simple à
saisir : que la principale puissance réside indubitablement du côté où le
nombre des bras est le plus considerable . . . que vingt cinq pouvaient
avoir une valeur plus qu'égale à un ". " Ces lois sont homicides : elles
sont destructives du contrat social primitif qui a nécessairement garanti
le maintien, perpétuellement inaltérable, de la suffisance des besoins "—
Tribun, XXXIV, 13-14 ; *Dommanget,* pp. 238-9 ; Tribun, XXXIV, 13 ;
Dommanget, p. 238—" voilà la déclaration solennelle des plébéiens aux
patriciens, et le prologue sérieux de l'insurrection et de la révolution.
Cette guerre des plébéiens et des patriciens, ou des pauvres et des riches,
n'existe pas seulement du moment où elle est declarée. Elle est perpétuelle,
elle commence dès que les institutions tendent à ce que les uns prennent
tout et à ce qu'il ne reste rien aux autres. Il semble aux riches, qu'en
feignant la sécurité, en s'efforçant de faire croire aux pauvres que leur
état est inévitablement dans la nature, c'est là la meilleure barrière contre
les entreprises des derniers ; mais quand le déclaratoire insurrectionnel est
proclamé, alors la lutte s'engage vivement, et chacun des deux partis
emploie tous ses moyens pour faire triompher le sien " ; " Le plèbe met en
réquisition toutes les vertus, la justice, la philantropie, le désintéressement.
La patriciat appelle à son secours tous les crimes, l'astuce, la duplicité,
la perfidie, la cupidité, l'orgueil, l'ambition."

" La société est une caverne "—Tribun, XXXIV ; Permanent civil
war—Tribun, XXXV, 76-7 ; *Dommanget, Pages,* p. 251 f. ; Tribun,
XXXIV, 11-14 ; *Dommanget,* pp. 236-8 ; Cadastre perpetuel, XXIX ;
Dommanget, 90 ; " No rights, no duties "—*Dommanget,* p. 102, Correspondant Picard, November 1790—" nous nous dispenserions encore
de faire servir nos bras ". The actual expression " bras croisés " comes
from Marat, " Ami du peuple ", 30 / VI / 1790, as Dommanget points
out. " Such moments "—*Advielle,* Vol. II, p. 30 ; Tribun, XXXVII,
136 ; *Dommanget,* pp. 271- ; Manifeste des Égaux, *Buonarroti,* II, Pièces
justific., pp. 130 ff. ; " extrêmes se touchent "—second letter to Coupé,
Dommanget, pp. 122, 126 ff.

Section (c)—The Interpretation of the French Revolution, pp. 184-7

Analysis of French Revolution—" C'est là où se repose "—letter
to Coupé, *Dommanget, Pages,* p. 122 ; " alone offers "—*Buonarroti,* II,
p. 214. Story of Revolution—*Buonarroti,* the first part of his History ;

Babeuf—Pièces saisies, 139–148, pièce 44, liasse 7 : " plusieurs révolution, depuis 1789 " ; *Dommanget*, Pages, pp. 284 ff. ; Babeuf's letter to Bodson, in Suite des Pièces, pp. 52–4, 9 Ventôse, an IV ; National grandeur as motive in 1789—Pièces saisies, 142 ff. ; Vicious majority, virtuous minority—Pièces, 143, 4, 5 ; "L'un qui veut le bien"—Tribun, XXIX, 264 ; The two Republics—Tribun, XXIX, 263 ff. ; *Dommanget*, pp. 192–3 ; Robespierre alone—Pièces saisies, 147–8 ; potential adherent of loi agraire—*Advielle*, Vol. I, p. 392 ; *Dommanget*, pp. 129, 130 ; Pièces saisies, 104, pièce 25, liasse 7 (Saint-Just's Institutions) ; lip service to liberty—Tribun, XXXIV, 8–9 ; *Dommanget*, pp. 235–6 ; System of egoism, system of equality—*Buonarroti*, I, pp. 6–10 ; Babeuf as second Gracchus, and follower of Robespierre—Suite des Pièces, p. 54, pièce 48, liasse 15 ; " des résultats ", " de marquer "—Pièces saisies, 139, 140 ; Égalité chimérique—Tribun, XXXIV, 8–9 ; *Dommanget*, pp. 235–6. Greatest happiness " with certainty "—Suite de Pièces, 326 ; Pièces saisies, 59, pièce 10, liasse 7 ; Suite des Pièces 59–62 (letter of Germain to Babeuf) ; " elle ébranle déjà l'Europe, elle affranchira l'univers ", Pièces saisies, p. 66 ; The Manifesto of Equals—*Buonarroti*, II, pp. 130 ff., *Bronterre's* translation, pp. 314–17.

Section (d)—The Evolution Towards Communism, pp. 187–95

Babeuf's early ideas—*Advielle*, Vol. II, pp. 31, 33 ; II, Correspondance 190, " Code universel procurât à tous les individus indistinctement, dans tous les biens et les avantages dont on peut jouir en ce bas monde, une position absolument égale " ; ibid., 193–4 (Jean Jacques and the woods) ; " honnête médiocrité "—Cadastre XXXII.

Babeuf, July 8th, 1787, to Dubois—*Advielle*, II, p. 192 (Corresp.) : " Il faudrait probablement pour tout cela que les rois déposassent leur couronnes, et toutes les personnes titrées et qualifiées, leurs dignités, leurs emplois, leurs charges."

Loi agraire, 66,000,000 arpents—Cadastre XXXII—" la terre, mère commune, eût pu n'être partagée qu'à vie, et chaque part rendue inaliénable ; de sorte que le patrimoine de chaque citoyen eût toujours été assuré " ; *Dommanget*, Pages, p. 107 f. : " Le Créateur a voulu que chaque être possédât le rayon de circonférence, nécessaire pour produire sa subsistance", ibid., p. 122 (second letter to Coupé) ; " la réclamation"; "le pain de l'esprit", ibid., pp. 126, 107 ; " stipulation . . . immédiatement",

ibid., p. 107 ; "industry to remain as at present", 125. *Albert Thomas,*
Revue Socialiste, Vol XL, p. 705. *Dommanget, Pages,* p. 96.
    Context of natural rights—Cadastre XXXV—" quel titre ? Mais,
Messieurs, par leur qualité d'hommes, par le droit qu'a tout pupille
devenu majeur de revendiquer des dépouilles qu'un tuteur infidèle a eu
la lâcheté de lui ravir ".
    The Terror as weapon of social policies—*Advielle,* Vol. I, pp. 113–14 ;
Du Système de dépopulation, pp. 25 ff. ; *Dommanget,* p. 178 ; political
rights meaningless, without social security—" et que servent donc toutes
vos lois lorsqu'en dernier résultat elles n'aboutissent point à tirer de
la profonde détresse cette masse énorme d'indigents ? "—*Dommanget,*
p. 128 (second letter to Coupé) ; Government is a charity Committee,
ibid. ; in sympathy with Robespierre's programme—Du système de
dépopulation, pp. 32–4 ; " Le sol d'un état doit assurer l'existence à
tous les membres de cet État ; je dis que, quand dans un état la minorité
des sociétaires est parvenue à accaparer de ses mains des richesses foncières
et industrielles, et qu'à ce moyen elle tient sous sa verge, et use du
pouvoir qu'elle a de faire languir dans le besoin, la majorité, on doit
reconnaître que cet envahissement n'a pu se faire qu'à l'abri des mauvaises
institutions du gouvernement ; et alors, ce que l'administration ancienne
n'a pas fait dans le temps pour prévenir l'abus ou pour réprimer à sa
naissance, l'administration actuelle doit le faire pour rétablir l'équilibre
qui n'eût jamais dû se perdre ; et l'autorité des lois doit opérer un
revirement, qui tourne vers la dernière raison du gouvernement per-
fectionné du Contrat Social : que tous aient assez et qu'aucun n'ait trop.
Si c'est là ce que Robespierre a vu, il a vu (à) cet égard en législateur.
Tous ceux-là ne le seront pas qui ne tendront point par des institutions
qu'il soit impossible d'enfreindre, à poser des bornes sûres à la cupidité et à
l'ambition, à affecter tous les bras au travail, mais à garantir, moyennant
ce travail, le nécessaire à tous, l'éducation égale et l'indépendance de
tout citoyen d'un autre ; à garantir de même le nécessaire sans travail à
l'enfance, à la faiblesse, à l'infirmité et à la vieillesse. Sans cette certitude
du nécessaire, sans cette éducation, sans cette indépendance réciproque,
jamais vous ne parviendrez à rendre la liberté aimable, jamais vous ne
ferez de vrais républicains. Et jamais vous n'aurez la tranquillité intérieure,
jamais vous ne gouvernez paisiblement, jamais la poignée de riches ne
jouira avec sécurité d'un regorgement scandaleux, à côté de la masse
affamée. Que les premiers soient justes et ouvrent les yeux à la vérité, à
leurs propres intérêts : ils s'exécuteront eux-mêmes ; autrement la nature
(elle fut toujours juste), quand la mesure est comblée, quand l'essaim

du peuple à qui tout garde-manger est fermé, est devenu dévorant, force toutes les digues ; alors cette guerre intestine, qui subsiste toujours entre les affameurs et les affamés, éclate."

Famine—" Il faut qu'elles soient "—Tribun, XXXV, 77 ; *Dommanget*, p. 145 ; Lettre à Chaumette, 7 Mai, an II, *Dommanget*, pp. 142-3, vehemently protesting against the proposed article for the 1793 Declaration of Rights on the sanctity of property—violation of the natural, inalienable rights of man : " combinaisons meurtrières . . . calculs assassins . . . " In praise of Robespierre's definition of property in his draft of a Declaration—" digne mandataire . . . notre Lycurgue ". This main preoccupation of Babeuf brings him near to the Enragés— " le peuple voulait que l'aliment nécessaire à tous fût borné à un prix auquel tous pussent atteindre ", ibid., p. 145.

The State to take over whole organization—Lettre à Germain, *Dommanget*, Pages, pp. 207 (10 Thermidor, an III), 210 ff. (after a violent attack on commerce and trade and their practices) ; " à l'abri de vicissitudes ", ibid., p. 214.

Against loi agraire—Tribun, XXXV, 92 ; *Dommanget*, Pages, p. 255 ; Manifesto of the Equals, *Buonarroti*, II, Pièces justif. ; Débats du procès de Vendôme, tome II, 88 ; Pièces Saisies, 271, pièce 20, liasse ; Army mobilization—Tribun, XXXV, 105 ; *Dommanget*, p. 262 ; *Buonarroti's* Account—Conspiration, I, p. 84 ; *Mathiez*, Directoire, p. 161 ; " Organisation savamment combinée "—first letter to Coupé, *Dommanget*, p. 107 ; Total equality, no distinctions of worth—*Advielle*, Vol. II, pp. 36-42 ; Tribun, XXXV, 104; *Dommanget*, p. 260 ; " assurer à chacun et à sa postérité, telle nombreuse qu'elle soit, la suffisance, mais rien que la suffisance "—Tribun, XXXV, 105 ; *Dommanget*, p. 261 ; " magasin commun " (ibid.) ; absolutely equal and universal education—ibid ; " que les productions de l'industrie et du génie deviennent aussi la propriété de tous " (*Dommanget*, p. 260) ; " la folie meurtrière "—ibid.

Reformism—Tribun, XXXVII, 132-6 ; *Dommanget*, Pages, pp. 268 ff; " la caste "—XXXVII, 136 ; " qu'au contraire "—*Dommanget*, 272 ; Suite des Pièces, 9-24, pièces 5-13, liasse 15 ; " sociabilité prête à se dissoudre "—comes from Morelly ; " happy catastrophe "—Pièces Saisies, 182, pièce 61, liasse 7 ; Bodson—Suite des Pièces, p. 57 ; Germain— *Espinas*, p. 238 ; *Advielle*, II, pp. 93 ff. ; *Buonarroti*, I, 88, 114.

" Where is the man ? "—Lettre à Germain, *Dommanget*, Pages, p. 214 ; " Let that Government "—Tribun, XXXV, 105-6 ; *Dommanget*, pp. 229, 262 ; *Advielle*, Vol. II, p. 42. " Once private property removed " —Lettre à Germain, *Dommanget*, pp. 210 ff.

CHAPTER III. THE STORY OF THE PLOT OF BABEUF

Section (a)—The Prehistory of the Conspiracy, pp. 196-7

The dilemma of the Left after Vendémiaire—*Mathiez*, Directoire, p. 130 f. ; *Buonarroti*, I, p. 64 ff. ; *G. Walter*, Babeuf, pp. 91 ff. Attempts at organization, Panthéon—*Buonarroti*, I, pp. 52 f., 69 f., 77 ff., 95 ff. *Advielle*, I, pp. 195 ff. ; *Mathiez*, Directoire, p. 141 f. ; *Bax*, The Last Episode, p. 91 f.

Section (b)—The Story of the Plot, pp. 197-200

Organizing the plot—the Brumaire attempt—*Buonarroti*, I, p. 81 ; A Central Committee formed and dissolved, ibid., p. 94. Babeuf's arrest after the appearance of Tribun Nr. 35, and escape—*Advielle*, Vol. I, p. 181 ; Mme Babeuf, " cette grande conspiratrice, qui ne sait ni lire, ni écrire "—arrested in February, 1796 (Pluviôse), ibid., p. 185 ; *Buonarroti*, I, p. 81.

The Secret Directory—*Buonarroti*, I, p. 114 ; *Bax*, p. 105 f. ; on Sylvain Maréchal—*Dommanget*, Sylvain Maréchal, Revue Internationale, 1946. He was a minor Atheist poet, already an active propagandist before the Revolution. It has never been explained why he was never prosecuted for his part in the plot. He was the author of the inflammable Manifesto of the Equals, which Marx and Engels regarded as the fore-runner of the Communist Manifesto.

On the other members—see *Espinas*, p. 264 ; *Advielle*, Vol. II, p. 254 f.

The Grenelle Legion—*Buonarroti*, I, p. 158 f. ; *Mathiez*, Directoire, p. 231 f. ; Royalists and Montagnards—*Buonarroti*, I, 163 ; *Espinas*, 291 ; Pièces saisies, pp. 83 f. ; Babeuf's postscriptum to the chief Agents—Pièces, ibid ; On Grisel and Barras—*Robiquet*, Babeuf et Barras, Rev. de Paris, 1896, pp. 204 ff ; the same author, L'Arrestation de Babeuf, Rev. Franç., 1895, Vol. XXVIII, pp. 300 ff.

The last meetings—*Buonarroti*, I, pp. 179 f., 184 f. ; II, 1 f. ; *Bax*, 16 f. Significance—*Walter Gerard*, Babeuf, pooh-poohs the whole thing from every point of view ; *Mathiez*, Directoire, p. 214 f. ; *Guerin*, II, 360.

Carnot's statement in the Mémoires of his son—Revue de Paris, 1896, Vol. III, p. 304—Directoire " eût infailliblement succombé, sans l'arresta-tion de Babeuf et ses complices, que la chose publique courut alors le danger que peu de personnes ont apprécié ". The Government was menaced on both flanks, by Royalists and Jacobins, and from within by Barras.

CHAPTER IV. DEMOCRACY AND DICTATORSHIP

Section (a)—The Definition of Democracy, pp. 201–3

First letter to Coupé—*Dommanget*, Pages, p. 107 ; " On ne doit pas plus pouvoir équivoquer en matière d'égalité qu'en matière de chiffres " (108). *Buonarroti* on term democracy—Débats du procès, Vol. II, p. 275 ; Conspiration, Vol. I, p. 23 (" that public. order ") ; C'est l'obligation—Tribun, XXXV, 100–1 ; *Dommanget*, p. 256, 7 ; Formal freedom . . . " how would "—*Buonarroti*, p. 34, n. 1. ; " Charity Committee "—*Dommanget*, p. 128.

Tribun, XXXV, 83 ; *Dommanget*, p. 250 : " Il est temps de parler de la démocratie elle-même ; de définir ce que nous entendons par elle, et ce que nous voulons qu'elle nous procure ; de concerter enfin, avec tout le peuple, les moyens de la fonder et de la maintenir."

" Ils se trompent, ceux-là qui croient que je ne m'agite que dans la vue de faire substituer une constitution à une autre. Nous avons bien plus besoin d'institutions que de constitution. La constitution de 93 n'avait mérité les applaudissements de tous les gens de bien, que parce qu'elle préparait les voies à des institutions. Si par elle ce but n'avait pu être atteint, j'eusse cessé de l'admirer. Toute constitution qui laissera subsister les anciennes institutions humanicides et abusives, cessera d'exciter mon enthousiasme ; tout homme appelé à régénérer ses semblables, qui se traînera péniblement dans la vieille routine des législations précédentes, dont la barbarie consacre des heureux et des malheureux, ne sera point à mes yeux un législateur, il n'inspirera point mes respects. Travaillons à fonder d'abord de bonnes institutions, des institutions plébéiennes, et nous serons toujours sûrs qu'une bonne constitution viendra après. Des institutions plébéiennes doivent assurer le bonheur commun, l'aisance égale de tous les co-associés."

The insistence on Institutions is, of course, an echo of Saint-Just's *Institutions Républicaines*. " Salut en démocratie "—Pièces Saisies, I, 256, X^e pièce, liasse 9 ; beyond mere republicanism—*Advielle*, Vol. II, p. 107 ; " Des hommes "—Débats du procès, Vol. I, p. 284 ; purification

—Tribun, XXIII, 4-5 ; " la dernière "—*Buonarroti*, Encyclopédie Nouvelle, 1840, 325 ; *Advielle*, I, p. 301—" bonheur commun—n'était autre
chose que la vraie Démocratie, but de la Révolution et but de toute
association civile " . . . " Tel fut le contrat primitif " ; Suite des Pièces, 9
—" à ce démocratisme parfait qui ne se contente pas du passable, mais
qui veut le mieux en matière d'organisation sociale ".

Pièces Saisies, 271, pièce 20, liasse 9 (peculiar spelling)—" ce que c'est
que démocratie, que c'est absolument le bonheur commun legalité réele
et non chimérique et illusoire " ; *Dommanget*, pp. 247-8.

Section (b)—Anti-parliamentary, Plebiscitary Ideas, pp. 203-7

The social potentialities of political democracy—two letters to Coupé,
Dommanget, Pages, pp. 103-21 (Aug. 20th, 1791), 121-30 (September
10th, 1791, printed also in *Espinas*, pp. 404-10). La plénitude des droits—
ibid., p. 127 ; Est ce but—corrollaire—122-3 ; Robespierre, Petion
—pp. 106, 129-130.

Form solid heads—106 ; party procedure, " as to the principal
speaker "—110 ; " Ne seront discutées "—p. 117 (" aucune modification,
dans le sens restrictif de la liberté et de l'égalité, ne pourra être apportée
à la présente Constitution ") ; Every Assembly a Constituante—p. 111 ;
Albert Thomas, Revue Social., Vol. LV, p. 708, rightly remarks that the
obvious contradiction between the principle that every Assembly is a Constituante, and the principle of one track freedom to legislate, is explicable
only by Babeuf's wish to prevent the freezing of the social system by a
Constitutional law. 110-11 : " Établir que la seconde législature est
tout aussi constituante que la première, en vertu de ce principe . . . de
maintenir intacte dans son ensemble . . . toutes ses parties la constitution
telle qu'elle a été décrétée, que s'il convient à une génération de se rendre
esclave, cela n'altère en rien le droit de la génération suivante à être
libre " ; Popular control over parliament—pp. 111 ff. ; deputies' reports,
Curators—pp. 118 ff. ; Qui s'absorbe—p. 113 ; publicity—p. 116
(" point de demi-publicité ") ;· petitions—ibid., p. 117.

Section (c)—Can the People be Trusted ?, pp. 207-8

" Manie de pluralité des voix " ; " La majorité " . . . " Ceux
qui . . . "—*Advielle*, Vol. I, pp. 41, 42 ; Babeuf's disappointment—

Tribun, XXIX, 265 ; *Dommanget*, pp. 193-4 ; Tribun, XXIX, 197 ; Tribun, XXXI, 313 ; *Advielle*, i, p. 302 ; II, Défense, 52, 42—" mais je ne me faisais pas la trop illusoire présomption de les y résoudre . . . les chances contre la possibilité de l'établissement d'un tel projet sont dans la proportion de plus de cent contre un " (but then this was said in the Defence before Court) ; *Buonarroti*—" The philosophers ", Conspiration, Vol. I, p. 89 ; As dogma of natural religion—ibid., pp. 104-5 ; " Such morals "—ibid., p. 89 n.

Section (d)—The Idea of the Enlightened Vanguard, pp. 209-14

Reference to will of people—Tribun, XXIII, 7 ; Tribun, prospectus, 3-4, 5-6 ; *Dommanget*, pp. 229-31 ; Pièces Saisies, 25—The banners of the insurgents were to bear the inscriptions : " Quand le gouvernement viole le droit du peuple, l'insurrection est pour le peuple et pour une portion du peuple, le plus sacré et le plus indispensable des devoirs ", " Ceux qui usurpent la souveraineté doivent être mis à mort par les hommes libres."

Albert Thomas, Revue Social., 1904, p. 699 ; Correspondant Picard No. 2 ; *Advielle*, Vol. I, p. 80—" Une loi d'Athènes, la plus admirable peut-être de toutes . . . tout citoyen est autorisé à se pourvoir contre un jugement de la nation entière, lorsqu'il est en état de justifier qu'il est en contradiction avec les lois établies pour assurer la liberté et les droits sociaux de la majorité du peuple."

" C'est aux vertus "—Pièces Saisies, 170, pièce 61, liasse 7 ; Tribun, XXXI, 316 ; The optimistic reply—Tribun, XXXI, 317 ; *Advielle*, II, Défense, p. 30 ; Authorization to revolution—Tribun, XXXVI, 115-16 ; *Advielle*, II, Défense, p. 30—" Ou bien . . . crime "—ibid.; pp. 24 ff., people accepting wrong Constitution.

Dommanget, Pages, pp. 265 ff. : " Révolutionner . . . c'est conspirer contre un état de choses qui ne convient pas ; c'est tendre à le désorganiser et à mettre en place quelque chose qui vaille mieux. Or, tant que tout ce qui ne vaut rien n'est pas renversé et que ce qui serait bon n'est pas stabilisé, je ne reconnais point qu'on ait assez révolutionné pour le peuple . . . que cette dernière révolution s'appelle incontestablement la contre-révolution . . ., il s'ensuit que la révolution est à refaire, de l'aveu même des contre-révolutionnaires." " They " call us anarchists, desorganisateurs, us who want really to organize society and bonheur commun. . . . " They " are the real anarchists and oppressors, désorganisateurs, having created this wicked and absurd régime. The latter way appeared too long—Babeuf's letter to Charles Germain, 10 Thermidor, an III, *Dommanget*, Pages, pp. 217 ff. ; " delirious " —ibid., p. 218 ; Vendée plébéienne—ibid., pp. 220, 257 (Manifeste des Plébéiens) ; Buonarroti on Babeuf and Owen—*Robiquet*, Buonarroti, p. 273 ; Homage to popular sovereignty—*Buonarroti*, I, p. 137–8 ; " as conformable "—ibid.

The existing régime illegal—*Advielle*, Vol. II, Défense, pp. 27 ff. ; Prosecution—Exposé de l'accusateur Vieillart. Débats à Haute Cour, Vol. I, p. 74 ; Séance, 6 Ventôse, p. 8. ; Boissy d'Anglas—" lorsque l'insurrection est générale, elle n'a pas besoin d'apologie, et lorsqu'elle est partielle elle est toujours coupable "—*Lavisse*, Vol. II, p. 278 ; Compare Robespierre's reply to Louvet.

Robespierre as Legislator—Tribun, XL, 258 ; 5 Ventôse, an IV, 24/11/1796 ; *Mathiez*, Fall of Robespierre, pp. 236–7 ; the people to be activized—Babeuf, Prospectus to Tribun, *Dommanget*, pp. 228–9 ; " I shall make you brave "—Tribun, XXXV, *Espinas*, pp. 254–5 ; " L'indignité "—*Advielle*, Vol. I, p. 151 ; " The union of authority "— *Buonarroti*, I, p. 116 f. ; " Criminal conspirators "—ibid., p. 118 ; " the whole truth "—Prospectus, Tribun, *Buonarroti*, p. 120—progress of public reason ; " bon esprit public "—Pièces saisies 197, pièce 84, liasse 7. *Espinas*, p. 280, is very insistent on the contradiction between the desire for publicity and conspiratorial design. No isolation of leaders—Tribun, XXXVII, 137–8 ; Prospectus de Tribun, *Dommanget*, p. 231—" Loin des défenseurs du Peuple, loin du Peuple lui-même, cette diplomatie, cette prétendue prudence Machiavélique, cette politique hypocrite qui n'est bonne qu'aux tyrans. . . . Expérience . . . dans un état populaire, la vérité doit toujours paraître claire et nue. On doit toujours la dire, la rendre publique, mettre le Peuple entier dans la confidence de tout ce qui concerne ses grands intérêts. Les ménagements, les dissimulations . . . parte . . . des coteries d'hommes exclusifs et de soi-disant régulateurs, ne servent qu'à tuer l'énergie, à rendre l'opinion erronnée, flottante, incertaine, et, de là, insouciante et servile, et à donner des facilités à tyrannie pour s'organiser sans obstacles. Éternellement persuadé qu'on ne peut rien faire de grand qu'avec tout le peuple, . . . il faut . . . lui tout dire, lui montrer sans cesse ce qu'il faut faire, et moins craindre les inconvénients de la publicité dont la politique profite, que compter sur les avantages de la force . . . Il faut calculer tout ce qu'on perd de forces en laissant l'opinion dans l'apathie . . . tout ce qu'on gagne en l'activant . . . "

Yet Babeuf much admired Machiavelli and sought guidance from him, Pièces saisies, 70.

Section (e)—The Theory of Revolutionary Dictatorship, pp. 214–21

Buonarroti on interim period—Conspiration, I, p. 134 n. ; " This difficult task "—ibid ; " dictature de l'insurrection "—Pièces saisies, 173, pièce 61, liasse 7 : Première instruction aux agents principaux ; also *Buonarroti*, II, Pièces justificatives, p. 114 ; " To what "—*Buonarroti*, I, p. 139 n. ; " Invest a man "—*Buonarroti*, Conspiration, pp. 139–40 ; Robespierre, pp. 11–12.

Robiquet, Buonarroti, p. 281, curiously misunderstood the relationship between popular sovereignty and the general will in Babouvist thinking : While on the one hand Buonarroti maintains—he argued—that the people is incapable of regenerating itself and even of choosing the leaders of such a regeneration, he claims at the same time " que la liberté consiste dans la soumission de tous à la volonté générale ! "

" And though the Secret Directory "—*Buonarroti*, Vol. I, pp. 132–3 ; " Autorité révolutionnaire et provisoire—for ever from influence " —ibid. ; " proposing to the people "—ibid., pp. 138–9 (Bodson and Darthé's plan of personal dictatorship) ; " extraordinary and necessary " —*Buonarroti*, I, p. 42 ; Première instruction du Directoire Secret— Pièces, 172, pièce 61, liasse 7 ; Pièces saisies 169, pièce 61 ; *Buonarroti*, II, Pièces justificatives, Nr. 6.

" Alors il y a justice, il y a nécessité que les intrépides, les plus capables de se dévouer, ceux qui se croient pourvus au premier degré d'énergie, de chaleur et de force, de ces vertus généreuses sous la garde desquelles a été remis le dépôt d'une constitution populaire que tous les Français vraiment libres n'ont jamais oubliée ; il y a alors justice et nécessité que ceux-là convaincus d'ailleurs que l'inspiration de leur propre coeur, ou celle de la liberté elle-même, qui leur fait entendre plus fortement, plus particulièrement sa voix, les autorise suffisamment à tout entreprendre ; il y a justice et nécessité que d'eux-mêmes ils s'investissent de la dictature de l'insurrection, qu'ils en prennent l'initiative, qu'ils revêtent le glorieux titre de conjurés pour la liberté, qu'ils s'érigent en magistrats—sauveurs de leurs concitoyens "—*Buonarroti*, II, 114. To re-establish Constitution of 1793—*Buonarroti*, I, pp. 48, 119, 132.

Amar—*Buonarroti*, I, pp. 143, 145 (Montagnards form a Committee) ; 155, (the measures proposed by Secret Directory—Acte Insurrecteur,

Buonarroti, II, Pièces justificatives, 244 ff.), 166 ff. ; 168—Bodson's bitter attack on the Montagnards for having politically and morally failed to defend the Revolution, with him is Germain ; Rossignol and Fillon, old Hébertist generals, and Drouet, the postman who recognized Louis XVI at Varennes, were for fusion ; 171 ff.—the conditions of the Secret Directory ; 173—rejection by Montagnards.—Pièces saisies, 82–5 ; The objections to personal dictatorship—Pièces, 130–1 ; . . . "la dictature de l'autorité, et non la dictature de l'homme . . . serait d'exciter la méfiance . . . ressemble trop à monarchie. . . . Et s'il n'est point capable (2 words missing), vous le déposerez pour le remplacer, vous avilissez votre mesure ; et s'il est mal intentionné, et plus fort que vous ? . . . D'ailleurs je ne connais personne parmi vous . . . Dictature à chaque circonstance, route ouverte à tous les ambitieux, effaroucherait le peuple," *Advielle*, Vol. II, p. 121.

Babeuf disclaimed before Court all dictatorial designs " . . . que le parti des démocrates ne doit point avoir de chefs "—*Advielle*, Vol. II, pp. 95 ff. ; II, pp. 120 ff ; *Guerin*, La Lutte, Vol. II, pp. 350 ff.

Germain, pressing Babeuf to assume personal leadership : " Tu t'es déclaré le Tribun du peuple ; certes, ce titre, cette qualité dont jusqu'à ce jour tu t'est montré si méritant, t'impose l'obligation de tracer au peuple . . . le plan, le projet d'attaque, je dis plus tu ne dois t'en reposer sur cela qu'à toi. . . ." Follows condemnation of divisions of opinions and deviations . . . " Oui, tu es le chef actuel des démocrates qui veulent à ta voix fonder l'égalité ; tu es le chef reconnu par eux : c'est donc toi qui dois, qui peut seul leur indiquer la voie ou leur désigner celui qui la leur indiquera " (Suite des Pièces, 62). Germain was only twenty-two at the time, an officer in the Hussars.

Darthé (former public accusateur at the Revolutionary Tribunal at Arras), " est tellement convaincu que la dictature c'est le seul moyen de faire le bien, qu'il n'y aura que la raison politique qui l'en fera départir : ainsi c'est sous ce rapport qu'il faut le combattre ", Pièces Saisies, 130 f. ; *Advielle*, Vol. II, pp. 120 ff.

Bodson, the old Hébertist, in a letter containing acute analysis of the psychological factor—Suite des Pièces, 55 ff., pièce 49, liasse 1—calls upon Babeuf to take the lead, not as a successor to somebody else, but as an original leader : " Je pense et je suis convaincu que, suivant l'impulsion de ton coeur, la véhémence de tes sentiments, tu y réussiras plus facilement que de suivre les traces d'hommes, que tu dois avoir le noble orgueil (quels que soient les services qu'ils ont pu rendre à la patrie) de dépasser ; ne regarde point en arrière, ne vois que le bonheur et la

reconnaissance de la postérité " (57) . . . " Crois que l'autorité de
Lycurgue, Rousseau, Mably vaut bien celle de nos légistes modernes."
The attempt to link up with the Revolutionary Government was
calculated to alienate many people. Men were tired of the Revolution
and wished for stability. Furthermore, the disciple and colleague
of Marat and Hébert could not free himself of resentment against
Robespierre and his friends, *Dommanget*, Pages, p. 286, n. 1.

Babeuf's *apologia* for Robespierre—Suite des Pièces, 52–5 ; *Dommanget*, pp. 284–6 ; Tribun, XL ; *Buonarroti*, Conspiration, p. 138 ;
Buonarroti, Robespierre, p. 12 : Saint-Just was right to propose Robespierre as dictator ; " to speak to people ", Legislative initiative, " to impart
to the laws "—*Buonarroti*, pp. 200 ff. ; " The annihilation ", " neither
mercy "—*Buonarroti*, p. 50 ; " To pretend . . . Why did "—ibid. ;
" manifestly outside pale "—ibid., p. 51 ; " Every advance "—ibid.,
pp. 226–7 ; Babeuf : " I liberated "—*Advielle*, Vol. II, pp. 78–9 ;
Dommanget, Pages, p. 284, n. 1. Suite des Pièces, 52–4 ; Rossignol—
Robiquet, L'arrestation de Babeuf, Rev. Franc., Vol. XXVIII, p. 296.

CHAPTER V.   THE STRUCTURE OF THE CONSPIRACY

Section (a)—Organization and Propaganda, pp. 222–6

M. Dommanget, Structure, Annales Révolutionnaires, Vol. XIV,
1922, pp. 177–96, 281–97 ; *Mathiez*, Directoire, pp. 185 f. ; Seminary—
Buonarroti, p. 83 ; *Guerin*, II, 359 f. ; *G. Walter*, Babeuf, pp. 124 ff.
Pièces saisies, 170, pièce 61 to liasse 7, 171–9 ; Suite des Pièces, 320–5.
Buonarroti, Vol. I, pp. 114 ff. (" la résolution "), 70 ; II, Pièces justificatives, 108, 111 ff., 113 ff ; *Dommanget*, Structure, p. 181 ; Secrecy and
loyalty—Discours des accusateurs, faisant suite, Vol. IV, pp. 29–30 ;
Dommanget, Structure, p. 182 f. ; Pièces saisies, 179, pièce 61, liasse 7
(" invisible ") ; Suite des pièces, II, p. 163—Journals—*Buonarroti*, Pièces
justificatives, II, p. 126.

Who is who among the Agents ?—Débats et jugements de la Haute
Cour, III, pp. 290 ff., 328, 341—Joseph Bodson was one of them (Discours
des accusateurs . . . suite aux débats du procès Babeuf, Vol. IV, p. 153).
Most had been minor officials in the Revolutionary administration and
judiciary, and Thermidorian prisoners. The only worker was Moroy
(Débats et jugements, III, p. 292) ; *Dommanget*, Structure, p. 182.

Methods—Pièces saisies, 285–97 (reports of Agents on the popular mood) ; Suite des Pièces, 103–9 ; 187 ; Pièces saisies, 197 (petits réunions, coteries) ; 249 (lists of counter-revolutionaries) ; 201–4 (warnings against the Government's attempts to cajole the Left ; and the misleading rôle of the Montagnards) ; Dommanget, Structure, 194 (women). Samples of Agents' Reports— Pièces saisies, 283, 284, 285 ; Pièces—283 : "L'esprit public du 12-me arrondissement est dans un état satisfaisant ; tous les jours les républicains font des prosélytes ; les murmures du peuple ont été hier des plus véhéments. Le gouvernement y a été maudit avec les plus grandes imprécations ; et chacun manifestait le plus grand désir de secouer le joug de la tyrannie directoriale. . . . Cet arrondissement n'est composé que de la classe ouvrière, la plus précieuse de la société, ce qui donne un champ libre aux ennemis de la patrie d'en égarer la majeure partie, mais non sans ressource. . . . L'ouvrier commence à sortir avec plaisir de cet engourdissement, où il avait été retenu par les tanneurs, mégissiers, couverturiers, et autres fabricants dont cette classe dépend pour le travail" (285) ; Mécontente-ment contre gouvernement . . ., 1793 Constitution . . . nombre des prosélytes s'augmente. . . ."

Mathiez, Directoire, pp. 191 ff., as well as Dommanget, Structure, pp. 185–6, points out that the readers of the Tribun du Peuple were mostly old terrorists, people of the middle and professional classes, and former civil servants, of Robespierrist leanings, who were glad to support a journal which engaged in violent attacks on the Directory. The Tribun was too expensive for poor workers altogether, and the subscribers seldom exceeded the number of 2,000. L'Éclaireur was cheaper and had a wider circulation. Mathiez gives lists of subscribers of the Tribun.

Propaganda among troops—Pièces saisies, 193 ff. ; Suite des Pièces, 330 : "vous pouvez même les assurer que dès le jour même où ils auront aidé le peuple à ressaisir sa puissance, rien ne leur manquera plus : . . . pour toute la vie à tous les soldats. Ce ne seront plus des promesses éloignées et faciles à éluder que nous donnerons ; ce sera la réalité simultanée et immédiate" ; Drink—Dommanget, Structure, p. 196 ; Grisel's report—Pièces saisies, 42–8 ; Suite des Pièces, 128, 130, 174 (Conspiratorial spies in the police) ; Financial difficulties, Buonarroti, Vol. I, p. 165 f. ; "cette Révolution"—Suite des Pièces, 100 ; Débats, Vol. II, p. 96 ; Pièces saisies, 109 f.

"It would be folly"—"Un mot pressant", Buonarroti, Pièces justifi-catives, Vol. II, p. 241 ; "I oppose"—ibid. Buonarroti's account of resources—Conspiration, Vol. I, p. 188 f. The weary mood, Espinas,

p. 293, *Mathiez*, Directoire, p. 146 (unemployed workers go to Panthéon meetings, employed ones stay away), *Dommanget*, Pages, pp. 291-7.

Hesitations—Circular of the Secret Directory to Agents 18, Floréal, *Buonarroti*, Pièces justificatives, Vol. II, (XIX), p. 270—the Directory wishes to calm the impatience of the people ; *Buonarroti*, I, p. 151 f.

Section (b)—The Plan of the Insurrection, pp. 226-31

Plan of insurrection—*Buonarroti*, Vol. I, pp. 154 ff., 157, 192 ff., 196 ff. ; Suite des Pièces, 245, 247-52 ; Pièces saisies, 55-9, contain instructions amounting to a real pattern of a coup d'état. Exemplary justice—*Buonarroti*, p. 153 ; dissolution of authorities—Pièces saisies, 240 ; Suite des Pièces, 87 ; " It is infinitely essential "—Pièces saisies, 240 ; Terrorist measures—" Tuer les cinq "—*Advielle*, Vol. II, Défense, 270 ; Pièces saisies, 238-42, pièces 34-5, liasse 8—" tuer . . . faire main basse " (in Darthé's handwriting) ; " toutes autres exterminations "—Pièces saisies, 25-6. Loophole left for members of Government who have rendered services to the cause—*Buonarroti*, Vol. I, p. 196 ; II, Pièces justif., p. 286, was meant to give a chance to Barras ; " women inciting and offering civic crowns "—*Buonarroti*, I, p. 194.

Measures of instant distribution—Pièces saisies, 148-51, 86-8 ; Buonarroti's explanation, Vol. I, pp. 155, 196, 203 ; II, Pièces justif., p. 265 ; the people exercising sovereign rights—*Buonarroti*, I, pp. 156 f., 199 ; the compromise between legal positions—*Buonarroti*, I, pp. 171 ff., 182 (union with Montagnards) ; restoration and amelioration of pre-Thermidorian system by popular approval—ibid., pp. 156 f., 199 ff., 297 f. ; Commissars—ibid. (pp. 205-6, 304 f.) ; *Buonarroti*, II, Pièces justif., Nr. XXV, Vol. II, p. 292 (" drawn up ").

Special Seminar—*Buonarroti*, Vol. I, p. 305 ; dismissals, reappointments, disarmament, release and imprisonment—ibid., pp. 301-5 ; concentration camps—*Buonarroti*, II, Pièces justif., p. 304 (Nr. XXVIII, " Fragment d'un projet de décret de police ") ; *Buonarroti*, I, p. 306 (" terrify . . . only means of safety ") ; Theatrical display—*Buonarroti*, II, Pièces justif. (pièce XVII), p. 256 ; Tribun, XXIX, 266 ; *Dommanget*, Structure, p. 194.

Mathiez, Directoire, p. 212 ; *Lefebvre*, in preface to *Dommanget*, Pages, p. viii ; *Guerin*, Lutte, Vol. II. p. 377 ; G. *Walter*, Babeuf, pp. 256 f.

CHAPTER VI. THE ULTIMATE SCHEME

Sections (*a*), (*b*), (*c*), *pp.* 232–47

The main, and almost sole, source material for this chapter is the second part of *Buonarroti's* Conspiration, which offers an account of the ultimate aims of the plot. Another important authority is the Réponse à une lettre signée V. M., publiée et adressée à Gracchus Babeuf, Tribun de peuple (expressing doubts on the viability of the Communist system), which together with the Letter forms Pièce XIII of the Pièces justificatives, in Vol. II of *Buonarroti's* Conspiration (pp. 213–29), and was written by Buonarroti himself. It contains a succinct exposé of the Babouvist scheme for the future and an answer to various criticisms.

The marks of true democracy—*Buonarroti*, Vol. I, p. 231 ; multiplicity and opposition of interests, ibid., pp. 233, 294–5 ; 313 (Upon the consolidation . . . until then) ; Gradual procedure—towards popular sovereignty ; At beginning the Administration composed—only of faithful French citizens, only those in National Community—I, 277–8 ; Citizenship rights acquired—I, pp. 232 ff.

Babouvist democracy—Vol. I, pp. 230, 239 ; 250–3, 259–77 ; The Grand National Economy—I, pp. 206–18 ; Community of sentiment —I, pp. 210 ; 228–9 ; 238, 255–8 ; 278–94 ; Shall the human " mind " ? —I, p. 285 ; press—I, p. 291, *Buonarroti*, Encyclopédie Nouvelle, 1840— " Babeuf " ; Arts and sciences—*Buonarroti*, I, pp. 285 f, 292–4 ; Encycl. Nouv.—" Babeuf " ; Conspir., I, pp. 223 ff. ; Tribun, XXVIII. Babeuf in 1792—*Dommanget*, Pages, pp. 134 ff.

Anti-intellectualism and restriction on press—Encycl, p. 327, " Les seules connaissances nécessaires aux citoyens étaient celles qui devaient les mettre en état de servir et de défendre la patrie. Point de corps privilégié par ses lumières ; point de prééminences intellectuelles ou morales ; point de droits ; même au génie, contre la stricte égalité de tous les hommes. Lire et écrire, compter, raisonner avec justesse, connaître l'histoire et les lois de la République avoir une idée de sa topographie, de sa statistique et de ses productions naturelles, tel était le programme de l'education commune à tout le monde. Cette prudente limitation des connaissances humaines était aux yeux du Comité la plus solide garantie d'égalité sociale. S'appuyant sur l'autorité de Rousseau, qui affirme que jamais les mœurs et la liberté n'ont été réunies à l'éclat des arts et sciences, il avait même été jusqu'à refuser de se prononcer sur l'utilité des perfectionnements ultérieurs des arts et des sciences par les citoyens plus versés que les autres dans ces matières. Du reste, la presse devait être sévèrement renfermée dans le cercle des principes proclamés par la société " (*Buonarroti*, Encycl. Nouv., Babeuf) ; Back to the land—Vol. I, pp. 220 ff. ; National isolation—I, pp. 261 ff. ; Religion—I, p. 254 ; Education—I, pp. 229, 254, 278-84 ; Nationalization of leisure—I, pp. 254, 258.   *Bronterre*'s translation, Babeuf, was used.

INDEX

346 INDEX

Eighteenth-century philosophy (*contd.*)
idea of man 25-7, 28-34, 50, 132-3,
249-51, 254
inconsistencies in economics, individualism, and restrictionism 5-6,
25-7, 35, 50-2, 58-64, 149
influence on Babeuf 167-8
influence on Buonarroti 175
liberty and the rights of man 4, 26-7,
35-6
natural order 17-27
origins of political Messianism 3-6,
17-65
origins of totalitarian democracy
34-7, 38-49, 249
paradox of freedom 34-7, 62-4
premises of Robespierre and Saint-
Just 132-3, 139-43, 147
property 5-6, 50-65
rationalism 4, 28-31, 147
realize promises of—aim of Robespierre 20, 80
Rousseau and 19, 43-4
schism into two types of democracy
1, 5-6, 20-1, 70
secular religion 21-4
self-interest, utilitarianism 31-4, 56
single principle of social existence
17-21
social harmony and virtue 32-4, 49,
62
social philosophy 5-6, 50-62, 149-50
socialism 50-2
source of liberal democracy 1-3, 35-6
summed up by Condorcet 18-19
summed up by Sieyès 69
See Condorcet, Diderot, Helvetius, Holbach, Mably, Morelly,
Rousseau
"Elect" 232
Elected assembly, distrust
Babouvists 203-7, 218, 229, 235
Robespierre 98-100
Rousseau 46, 48, 49
Elections 92, 105, 122-3, 215, 217, 229
Electoral lists, scrutiny 105
Electorate, control by 98-100, 171,
203-7, 235-6

Eligibility, ineligibility, political
grounds 73, 87, 98, 105, 206, 214-
15, 235-6
Élite 211
Émigrés 124, 159, 199, 228
Emile, by Rousseau 39, 246
Empiricism 25, 28-9, 250
friend of freedom 4
liberal 1-3, 20, 26
in politics 4, 25, 47, 70, 71, 253-5, 258
and rationalism in eighteenth century
28-9, 261-2
See Apriorism, Doctrinaire
Encyclopedia 40, 147
England 44, 59
English economists 186
Enragés 79, 150, 153, 162, 174, 196, 309
Robespierre and 158
Equality
absolute of rewards—Babeuf 181-2,
193, 238
Babouvist idea 179-81, 184, 195, 219,
229, 232, 235-6
Babouvist ultimate scheme 232-3,
237-8
basis of Babouvist confraternity of
spirit 240-7
common ownership its condition
55-6, 190, 191-2
condition of "real" democracy
202-3, 215-16, 232-3
distribution—"portion égale" 187,
193, 238
eighteenth-century natural order 29,
50, 54-8, 60, 149, 250-3
formal, illusory 185, 202
inherent in natural rights 50, 179-80,
183
inherent in social contract 179-80,
182-4
liberty 62-4, 202, 249-51
loi agraire 188, 190
Mably and Morelly 53, 54-8, 276
popular sovereignty 202-3
religious dogma 208, 246
Robespierre 91, 94, 142, 156, 159,
184-5
Saint-Just 88-9, 161-4

Equality (*continued*)
Sieyès 75-7
Equals, Égaux, Babouvists 106, 251
arts and sciences 241-2
and Montagnard deputies 198-9, 209,
216-8
story of conspiracy of 196-200
structure of conspiracy of 222-31
See Babeuf, Babouvists, Buonarroti,
Conspiracy of the Equals
Equilibrium of social forces 45, 88, 91, 95
See Balance
Eschatology 10
Esprit de corps 74, 94
Esprit révolutionnaire 19, 49, 261-2
Estate, Fourth 6
Estates General 64, 70 73, 74
Étatism 62, 160
" Eternal justice ", " principles " 80,
142, 159
Ethics, morality
capable of scientific proof 18, 21-2,
29-31, 34, 167
class struggle 156, 181-2, 184-6
corroded by class domination 182,
184, 195
enforced 33, 37, 54, 57-8, 62, 140-2,
180, 232, 240-1
politics 4, 30, 37, 39-41, 132, 140-2,
148, 180, 208, 232, 240-1
religion 21-2, 57-8, 62, 140-2, 148
See Virtue
Europe, old 130-1
unity of 110
Exclusiveness 1-3, 10, 135-8, 250-5
of creed, doctrine, principle, social
pattern
Babouvist 167-8, 169-70, 178, 180,
192, 195, 201, 232-47
eighteenth-century 17-21, 30,
35-7, 40, 45, 50, 53-4
Jacobin 78-80, 83-4, 104-7,
107-10, 115, 119-22, 128, 132-48
Sieyès 70-3
and freedom 1-3, 12, 135-8, 253-4
Babouvism 240-5, 253-4
eighteenth-century 5, 20, 30, 35-7,
40-2, 53-4

Jacobin 83-4, 107-8, 111-18, 128-9,
131-3, 137-8, 140, 143, 147
and opposition 111-18, 135-8, 232-3
and parties 44, 115-18, 232-3
and popular sovereignty 2-3, 249-53
Babeuf, Buonarroti 180-1, 201,
203-7, 211-18, 232-6
Jacobins 84-6, 104-7, 113-18,
127-9, 131
Rousseau 43-9
Sieyès 70-5
and vanguard 48-9, 209-18
at war 119-22, 131, 136-8, 253-4
Executive 64, 92, 104
Babouvist ultimate scheme 236
Council 103-4, 123, 217, 236
and Legislative 88, 91-3, 99, 103, 104,
236
in provisional Babouvist authority
216-18, 229
in Revolutionary Government 119
1793 Constitution projects 103

" Factions " 115, 117, 186
See Party
Factory, industry 61, 154
Family 246
Farmer 62, 164
Faubourg St. Antoine 199
Federalism, *fédérés* 101, 107, 114, 123,
128, 241
" Fermage " 163
Festival, patriotic 23, 146, 247
Feudal system 19, 50, 110, 130, 151, 181,
182
" caste " 182
dues 79, 173
monarchy 87
privilege 75, 94
property 130, 173
" Feudiste " 167, 173
Feuillants 105
Finality postulate of a denouement 12,
36, 80, 132, 135, 186-7, 195, 238,
249, 253-4
See Exclusiveness, Messianism
Finances 108, 155
spirit of condemned—Holbach 60

Le Chapelier, Loi 94
Lefebvre, Georges, Professor 230
Legal competence proof 97
Legal evidence 126
Legal safeguards 126
Legion of the Police 188, 225
Legislation
" easy science " 133
object of 45, 232, 236
restrain passions 57, 141, 180
restrict size of property 59
weapon of class exploitation 51, 91,
181–2
Legislative Assembly, the 79,98,100,171
Legislative initiative 206, 218
Legislator, the ; legislators 60, 71, 89,
91, 102, 176, 186, 208
all-powerful to shape social order and
hearts 30–1, 33, 42, 63
Babeuf on Robespierre as 211
Diderot 40, 51
Educator 31, 42, 49
individual, natural order 34–7
Revolutionary vanguard 48–9
Robespierre 91, 102
Rousseau 42, 49, 176
to know to put the right question 46,
117–18
Legislature 88, 92, 104, 171
absolute supremacy 64
Babouvist scheme 214–16, 235–6
Condorcet 103–4, 109
Revolutionary Government 119
Robespierre 92, 99, 119
Saint-Just on 88, 103–4
Legitimacy principle, in politics 19, 40,
49
Legitimate Government — Babouvist
210
Legitimate majority—Robespierre 109
Legitimate revolution 102, 210
Leibniz 28
Leisure 247
Lepeletier, de Saint-Fargeau, Félix,
member of Secret Directory 190,
198, 199
Lepeletier, Scheme of Education (de
Saint-Fargeau, Louis-Michel) 137

Lèse nation 97
Letronne 44
Levelling incomes 190
Levies on rich 152, 153, 190
Liberal democracy 1–3, 70, 249
See Democracy
Liberalism, liberals
economic 45
reaction to totalitarian Messianism
5–6, 20–21, 254–5, 258
Robespierre, Saint-Just 134, 139–43
Sieyès 75, 76
Liberation of man, from personal
dependence 91
Liberation of peoples 130
costs of 130
Liberty :
absence of constraint 2, 107, 111
absolute collective purpose 2, 8, 107,
108
agriculture and 58
aim of Revolution—Robespierre
102, 142
ancient, modern 11, 47, 89–90, 112
antithesis reached 36–7, 58, 62, 137–8,
143–6, 147, 240, 249, 253–7
associationist philosophy, malleability
of man and 30–1, 32–4
Buonarroti : power of State 180, 250
clash with Revolutionary purpose
78–80, 108, 132
commercial expansion, danger to 59
dangers from exalting politics 47, 102
" destinies of . . . " 134
" despotism of " 113
dictatorship to save 145, 215
direct democratic sovereignty of
people 100–2, 103–5
the doctrinaire enemy of 4, 35, 71, 75,
108, 114, 253–4
eighteenth-century 4, 35–6
empiricism, ally of 4,20,47,71,253–4
equality 3, 62, 142, 185, 205, 257
exclusive harmonious form of social
existence 2–3, 12, 38–9, 58, 84, 87,
107–8, 143–7, 240–1
freedom of choosing and obligation
to choose 40, 131

Party, parties (*continued*)
system in Britain 44–6
vanguard of single-party dictatorship
6, 48, 122–9, 211–13
See Jacobins
Passions 55–7, 142, 180
Patricians 170
Patriot, patriotic 103, 114, 128, 138, 171,
280–1
conduct 125
conscience 97, 125, 126
reputations (deputations ?) — Saint-
Just 145
rites 127
Peace 129
People, popular
agent in politics 92–3, 98–102, 104–5,
107, 209–14
anti-popular interest 83, 84, 98,
184–5, 219, 233
democracy 253
disappointment at 105–7, 137, 145,
207–8
embodied in Jacobins 116, 128
embodied in Robespierre 184–6,
220–1
general will 43–9, 84
government not of—Robespierre 92
of old, " conspiracy against " 91–3,
133–4, 139, 181–3
triumph of liberty 112–14, 228,
233–7
idealization of 90–5, 102, 105, 134,
139–40, 232
immature, young 48, 105, 106–7,
207–8, 209–16, 219, 232–3
the nation 93–4
parties, enemies of 114–16
power, of controlling veto and direct
action 46, 48–9, 98–102, 104, 203,
205, 235–6
representative despotism 98–102
right to resist oppression, insurrection
48, 100–2, 104, 209, 210, 219, 226
Robespierre 90–5, 96
social category 93, 96
suppression of enemies, no oppression
112–14

vanguard, leadership 46, 48–9, 105,
107, 209–14
virtue 105, 139, 158
war of 96
will, choice, election 90–1, 92, 95,
112–13, 209
See Popular sovereignty
Permanence of sections 124
Persepolis 161
Petion 206, 309
Petition 46, 92, 94, 104, 206
Philipeaux 126
Philosophes 21, 27, 28, 132, 134, 141,
261
Philosophy. *See* Eighteenth-century
philosophy
Physiocrats 30, 44–6, 188, 282
laissez-faire, economic liberalism 5,
45, 150
monarchic absolutism 45
natural order 5, 36, 276, 282
Picardy 173
Pitt 106
Planning, social 149, 154–5, 239, 240
Plato 8, 28, 32, 41, 186
Plebeians 170
Plebiscitary democracy 88, 93, 250–1
Babeuf 203–7
and dictatorship 46–8, 104–5, 203–7,
235–6
Saint-Just 117
See Democracy, Dictatorship, People,
Popular sovereignty
Plot of Babeuf 80, 197
See Conspiracy of the Equals, Babeuf,
Babouvists
Polis 246
Political
consciousness 47, 92, 169, 194, 207–8
equality, rights—formal 89, 91,
185–6, 189, 202
loyalty, condition of property
ownership 151
Messianism 1–13
morality 134
non-political level 2, 47
" ordre véritable "—Sieyès 70–2, 78
organization—Babouvist 232–6

A

b

366 INDEX

Unity
of Republic 103, 109
of will, purpose 116, 216, 233, 240–1
Universal happiness 210
Universal liberation, people's 111
Universal pattern of moral behaviour
29, 30, 114, 167, 179
Universal social order 28, 148
Universalism of Left totalitarianism
6–7, 136, 167
Universe 32, 148
Unofficial organization, French de-
mocracy 127, 171
Utilitarianism 18, 31–4, 52, 148
Utility 3–4, 32, 54
Utopian pattern 53, 138, 146, 232–47

Values, universal, human 7
Vanguard 48–9, 106, 218, 209–14, 280–1
See Enlightened Revolutionary party
Varlet 150
Vassals 182
Vendée plébéienne 213
Vendée revolt 107, 109
Vendôme Trial 20, 200, 210
Ventôse laws 126, 157, 159, 162, 171,
228, 237
Vergniaud 125, 147, 291
Veto, power of 78, 171, 206
Vieux Cordelier 128
Vincennes Regiment 225
Vincent 126
Violence 53, 57, 102, 104
See Coercion, Terror
Virtue, vertu 49, 146–7, 232
on the agenda 129
disposition, test 141, 159, 186
egalitarian 138, 184–6
eighteenth-century 4, 5, 11, 31–5, 49,
51, 56, 57
leadership 138, 184–6

liberty equation 120
love of 247
people 92, 102, 139
poor 25, 115, 142
rationalist pattern 4, 5, 143
reign 62–5, 80, 139–43, 155, 249
of Republic 25, 115, 142
Robespierre—representative of 184–6
Saint-Just 84, 91, 143–4
terror 114, 115
Voltaire, Voltairian 22, 148, 173
"Vote par appel nominal" 105
Voting, open 105
Voyer d'Argenson 177

Wage earners 153
Wages 182
War 130
Declaration France renounces 129
pay for itself 129
state of 119
theory people's—Robespierre 95
Wealth
immoral 129, 151, 159, 181, 184
increase 59, 61, 156
Welfare State 257
Weltanschauung 181
Western European consciousness 70
Western tradition 3, 249, 252–3
Will
of man, people, actual, real, ultimate
3, 40–2, 48, 84, 209–12, 254
single imposed 104, 207
See General will
Witnesses, dispensed 126
Word of God 9, 10
Work, obligation to 2, 38, 180, 229,
238
right to 156, 188
Worker 48, 59–62, 192, 238, 239
Workers' State 253